The Internet, the Web, and eBusiness

Formalizing Applications for the Real World

Kai A. Olsen

The Scarecrow Press, Inc.
Lanham, Maryland • Toronto • Oxford
2005

SCARECROW PRESS, INC.

Published in the United States of America
by Scarecrow Press, Inc.
A wholly owned subsidary of
The Rowman & Littlefield Publishing Group, Inc.
4501 Forbes Boulevard, Suite 200, Lanham, Maryland 20706
www.scarecrowpress.com

PO Box 317
Oxford
OX2 9RU, UK

British Library Cataloguing in Publication Information Available

Library of Congress Cataloging-in-Publication Data
Olsen, Kai A.
  The Internet, the Web, and eBusiness : formalizing applications for the real
world / Kai A. Olsen.
      p. cm.
  Includes bibliographical references and index.
  ISBN 0-8108-5167-9 (pbk. : alk. paper)
  1. Internet. 2. World Wide Web. 3. Electronic commerce. I. Title.
  TK5105.875.I57O485 2005
  004.67'8—dc22

                                                    2004024293

⊖™ The paper used in this publication meets the minimum requirements of
American National Standard for Information Sciences—Permanence of
Paper for Printed Library Materials, ANSI/NISO Z39.48-1992.
Manufactured in the United States of America.

*To the Internet and the Web for
making this book possible*

Contents

Preface

Late in 1990 Tim Berners-Lee got the very first Web page up on his display. Today there are countless numbers of Web pages, and more than five hundred million people all over the world are connected to the Internet. With the amazing advances in technology and the rapid dissemination of services, it is easy to forget that the Internet and the Web, like any other technology, have to interface with the real world. Even with the short history of the Web, many have already learned the hard way that success does not come easy, that there is "no silver bullet" even if one is creative in the use of the latest technology.

There exists an abundance of books on the Internet and the Web. Most predict that these technologies will have a profound impact on everything from business to entertainment. They tell you to jump on the train now, to avoid being left in the technological backwoods. This book is somewhat different. We try to view the Internet and Web technologies without the "hype." Focusing on the interface between the technologies and the real world, we shall see not only where these technologies have their advantages but also where the limitations become apparent. That is, the future is in the technical possibilities filtered through the real world constraints.

> The **future** is in the technical possibilities filtered through the real world constraints.

The perspective of this book allows us to focus on the difficulties of introducing a new technology to the real world. The book has the practical goal of letting the readers use these new technologies to their full advantage. While we cannot give a formula for evaluating Internet and Web applications, we introduce a way of thinking that can be of help in order to find the areas where the probability of success is greatest. This will give readers an understanding of where we are today, and where we will be tomorrow.

> To use the computer, the application area must be **formalized** i.e., described in a formal and unambiguous manner.

Formalization is the basis for all computer applications. That is, in order to use the computer, the application area has to be described in a formal and unambiguous manner. This is the fundament for all computer systems, as well as for the new applications that are offered via the Internet and the Web. In the real world we find areas that have been formalized centuries before the first computer was developed, such as banking, and areas that seem to be impossible to formalize, such as natural language. Most systems fall in between; they consist of both open and closed parts, parts that can be formalized and handled by a computer and parts that have to be handled by human beings. As we shall see, this perspective is of invaluable help when evaluating computer systems, to see where the new technology can be applied successfully, to weed out the overoptimistic applications, to know where the going is straightforward and where we will meet difficulties. We can use this perspective on a macro scale to predict the future of the Internet, Web, Web services, eBusiness applications, or a new standard, such as XML. We can also use it on a micro perspective to identify the functions in a system that will be most difficult to implement.

The real world does not consist of physical objects only. The electronic bits representing the balance of a bank account are as real as the paper bills. The institutions that work with *symbols*, such as banks and insurance companies, are as real as any farm or manufacturing plant. While Internet technologies can support physically oriented businesses, they can often do the whole job when the raw materials are bits and bytes, as we see with Internet banks and the distribution of music.

The **symbolic** part of the world is as important as the physical part.

In a world where technological development goes at a record-breaking pace, it is easy to overlook the fact that the technology needed for many applications may be many years away. We do not have the large, high resolution and lightweight display needed to eliminate paper; neither do we have the everlasting battery needed for true mobile computing. In addition, there may be *cultural and social constraints* that act as boundaries as to how far we can go in applying new technology. While the video telephone (i.e., a phone that conveys both picture and sound) can be offered at a reasonable price using existing technology, it seems that this is a product that consumers do not want. That is, the limitation of the ordinary telephone is perhaps a virtue.

As we see, the new technologies come with promises of new and interesting applications. However, these theoretical possibilities must be filtered through a set of real-life constraints before the really successful applications emerge. This is our setting.

This book has six parts. In part 1, we build a foundation for understanding computer applications. We draw the distinction between formalized and unformalized processes and then discuss how the formalization level of data and processes determines the functionality of applications. This background is needed in order to evaluate the potential of the new

B2C (business-to-consumer) has a human being at one (final) end of the communication line.

B2B (business-to-business) describes services performed by computers without involving human beings.

technologies. Part 2 introduces the basic Internet and Web standards, and gives a discussion of its potential. Part 3 provides an overview of the formalization of eBusiness applications within the B2C (business-to-consumer) category—what we really should have defined as computer-to-person applications (i.e., where we have a human being at one end of the communication line, whether this is a private citizen or a company employee). We shall present numerous examples and analyze these using the basic ideas introduced in the first part of the book. In part 4 we look at the formalization of B2B (business-to-business) applications, or what we more precisely should have specified as computer-to-computer applications. Here we introduce the standards that are needed to transmit data with a high level of formalization (e.g., to transmit an invoice between two computers). In part 5 we take a look into the future, before we sum up and conclude in part 6.

This book will be useful for students taking an introductory course in computing, for social science students who want to know more about Internet and Web technology, for managers and designers of Web projects, and for those who are interested in seeing how the new technology will affect their lives or their jobs. It does not require any background in computing science, but experience in using PCs and the Internet will be an advantage.

Ways to Use This Book for Teaching

For use as a text for introductory courses, the main goal of this book is to give students a broad selection of topics from computing in general and of the Internet and Web technologies in particular. For all of the topics presented, it is important that students are given the opportunity to form their own arguments and opinions. The discussion part after each chapter provides ideas for exercises and discussion topics that may help accomplish this.

The book contains a great many topics and an instructor may not be able to cover all of them in a single semester. It is recommended to allocate readings depending on the backgrounds of students and their disciplines. Part 1 may be a good starting point for all types of students. The remainder of the book may be used selectively, with instructors chosing to emphasize different parts and chapters depending on the prerequisites of their students and their disciplines.

Students with a good background in IT can skim through part 2, but some of the chapters (e.g., chapter 10, Searching, or chapter 12, Web Presence), may be suitable for case studies. Students without an IT background will need most of part 2 to get a basic understanding of the technologies but may choose to skip the more technically oriented chapters (e.g., chapter 15, Dynamic Web Pages, and chapter 16, Embedded Scripts).

Part 3 gives an overview over all B2C applications. An instructor may choose to cover the whole or to give exercises and tasks where students selectively read these chapters to get background material. It is, however, important that students learn the difference between services that are entirely symbolic and services that also have a physical part.

In part 4, B2B Technology, less technically oriented students can skim through chapter 27, XML, concentrating on the other chapters of this section. Part 5 offers a set of cases that are suitable for class discussions independent of discipline.

Acknowledgments

This book is about the Internet, Web, and eBusiness and is dedicated to these services. I could have said that this book could never have been written without the aid and support given by these technologies, but that seems ludicrous. Instead, I shall express my deepest appreciation for the contribution of all the content providers on the Web, both within the public domain and subscription services that make it possible to get updated news and information at any place in the world, at any time.

With email I can maintain an important global network, to colleagues and students in many countries, independent of difficulties posed by time zones and distances. In working with this book I have had invaluable help from colleagues, students, consultants, and friends all over the world. My deepest appreciation goes to Erik Aandahl, Andreas Berre, Jo Berre, Judy Molka-Danielsen, Bjørn Guvåg, Rune Haagensen, René Nesbakk, Veronica Phillips, Børre Sandvik, Per Sætre, Mike B. Spring, Anne Karin Wallace, Trond Wefring, and Jim Williams. In addition, Martin Dillon at Scarecrow has offered valuable comments and suggestions. Susan Higgins has very professionally (and patiently) corrected my spelling and moved all my commas to the right places.

Finally, I would like to give my sincere thanks to the Norwegian Professional Writers Association (NFF). Without their support this book would not have been written.

Trademark Notice

The following are trademarks or registered trademarks of their respective companies:

ActiveX, Microsoft, Visual Basic, Visual C#, and Windows are trademarks of Microsoft Corporation; Apple MacIntosh is a trademark of Apple Computer, Inc.; Netscape is a trademark of Netscape Communications Corporation; Java is a trademark of Sun Microsystems, Inc.; AltaVista is a trademark of Digital Equipment Corporation; Yahoo! is a trademark of Yahoo!, Inc.; Google is a trademark of Google Corporation; eBay is a trademark of eBay, Inc.; Maple is a trademark of Maplesoft; Mathlab is a trademark of Mathworks, Inc.

Introduction

Moore's law, a doubling every year or second year of the number of transistors per integrated circuit.

The dot-com failures show us that there is no general application of Moore's law for the Internet, a doubling in capacity every year or second year is restricted to hardware—it does not hold for market shares, nor for revenue. The dot-com failures do not imply that there is something wrong with the Internet or the Web, just that the limitations of these new technologies were not understood in a stock market situation that Alan Greenspan called "irrational exuberance."

One reason for the euphoria may be the black box nature of the computer. It may be easier to dazzle venture capitalists and others with fascinating computer applications than to sell a technology where the basic principles are more apparent to the layman. However, if we go back to the nineteenth century, we see that railway technology had a similar market impact. The technology itself was viewed as so promising that there was an abundance of capital, and in a few years, around 1870, hundreds of companies were engaged in laying new tracks. The lack of valid business models for many railroads soon became apparent, and in a few years nearly half of the railroad bonds were invalid. This did not imply that railways did not have a future, as we know they nearly monopolized land-based travel for a century, had a deep impact on society, and made some of the pioneers immensely rich.

The Internet and Web technology will have a similar impact. It will affect us, as employees, managers, business owners, students, professors, venture capitalists, or private citizens. These technologies will be a threat to some, opportunities for others. This book tries to give a balanced view of the possibilities offered by the Internet and the Web. Through examples, and through an analysis of the pros and cons of these technologies, we shall see how the new economy will affect our society and business life—today and in the future. Most important, we will show how we can take advantage of the opportunities that the Internet offers.

From the physical side, the Internet is a network of networks spanning the world. That is, millions of computers connected by high-speed optical fiber cables down to ordinary telephone lines. The computers may be ordinary PCs, specialized computers called routers that are able to read a message of one network and transmit it onto another or huge servers that can store a nearly unlimited number of Web pages and that perform all the processing needed to administer these pages. While the hardware and software is important, it is the underlying *standards* that have opened the world for the Internet and the Web.

These include: a network protocol (TCP[1]), an international address scheme that defines a unique address (IP[2]), a globally unique address (URL[3]) for each computer file, standards for encoding email (SMTP[4], MIME[5]), for describing the layout of Web pages (HTML[6]) and for transmitting these pages (HTTP[7]). New standards for describing document content (XML[8]) for business-to-business communication are on their way. Using these standards, telecommunication companies can take advantage of the rapid improvement in computer and network technology to offer affordable Internet connections and services. These services are the foundations for building the eBusiness applications that may change our society, as the railways did more than a hundred years ago.

The basic functionality of the Internet is to provide *fast and cheap transfer of bits* (binary digits) from any computer in the world to any other (i.e., to transfer digitized text, data, images, video, and sound). Thus, what we have is a way of transmitting any type of symbolic data that can be coded as binary digits.

Symbolic is a key word in this book. Are you a symbolic worker (i.e., do you use a major part of your work time entering, editing, transferring, and storing symbols)? For most of us the answer is yes. And a yes implies that Internet technology will be a challenge. Our business may be education, administration, economy, science, production....We may work with text, pictures, music, money, drawings, or any other type of data, but all of these are symbolic by nature. These symbols may be represented as bits (i.e., binary digits in a computer). Letters may be simply translated to binary form using a code lookup table; pictures can be represented as a collection of pixels (picture elements), each giving the color and brightness values of this point in the picture. Music may be represented as grooves on an LP record, but can as easily be coded as a digital value. Money can be represented as bills and coins, but may exist also as numbers in a virtual form. An insurance policy may be printed on paper with all the correct signatures, but it may just as well reside in a computer system, verified by digital signatures. Thus, a new technology that offers the opportunity to transmit

Standards are as important as the basic technology. Tim Berners-Lee did not invent a new technology, but he defined the standards that were needed for implementing the Web.

Symbols, as distinguished from physical objects, can be represented as bits, stored in a computer and transmitted over the Internet.

data inexpensively from anywhere to everywhere will affect the way we do business.

Are you selling groceries, clothes, or working as a mechanic? Clearly a part of your job is to work with *non-symbolic items, items that have weight* (sometime defined as atoms, in contrast to bits). We cannot transport apples or clothes via the Internet; neither can we use this technology to repair a car (although some manufacturers have Internet-based systems for diagnosis of engine malfunction). While the Internet cannot handle the main part of these jobs, it offers opportunities to change the way we are performing the symbolic or the administrative part. The Internet offers a new channel to consumers that may be used by a technology-optimistic grocer to let customers order their groceries directly from home, or, for a more mundane application such as marketing. The mechanic may use the Internet to get part numbers or repair procedures or he may allow customers to book appointments for inspections, oil changes, and so forth, directly via the Internet.

Formalization is another important concept in understanding computer applications. If an application is formalized (i.e., with well-defined procedures and data), then, and only then, can it be handled by a computer. Only formalized or closed applications can be described as a computer program, the part that is needed to turn a general computer into an "application machine," whether it is a word processor, a banking system, or the system for an online store. Tasks that are *unformalized*, open tasks, cannot be processed by a computer. The advantage of describing an application as a program is, of course, that the tasks and processes can be automated. When tax regulations and tax data, for example, are described as a program, this one program can calculate taxes for all citizens, running repeatedly with a different data set each time.

We find few of these formalized, fully automated programs on our personal machines and the Web. Here the tasks are solved through *interaction* with the user, that is, where the user activates the next process by clicking a command button or providing input from the keyboard. This human-computer interaction allows us to use the computer to support processes that have both open and closed parts. Word processing is a typical example. The computer handles the formatting part while the human being takes care of the writing. If the process of writing a document is categorized as occurring on three different levels, lexical (characters, words), syntactic (grammar),

Atoms, physical items (that have weight) cannot be handled directly by computer systems and can only be transmitted or distributed using traditional channels.

Closed tasks can be formalized and handled by a computer.
Open tasks cannot be described in a formalized manner; these must be handled by humans. Most services will consist of both open and closed parts.

With the Internet and the Web the **terminal**, the access point to the bank, booking system, or company database can be the PC in the customer's home.

and semantic (meaning), we see that the computer takes care of the lexical part, while the human is in charge of the semantics, the meaning of what is written. We may, however, get some computer support on the syntactic level, for example, through grammar checking programs.

For the last fifty years we have seen that many fully "formalized" jobs have disappeared, while others have changed profoundly. We still have accountants, but a computer does the practical part of keeping the books. Telephone companies still have operators, but computers now handle most of their services. Air traffic controllers rely on computers to do their work, but may soon be replaced by computers. There is a similar development in the cockpits where the role of the pilots can be more that of supervision than of actually flying the plane. In the manufacturing industry robots and other computer-controlled machinery have been replacing workers for the last forty years, increasing the effectiveness of those that are left.

Intermediates may no longer be needed when we find terminals in every home and office. Or, more correct, since they are no longer the only ones with a key to the vault, they have to prove their value through the quality of the services they offer.

If one or more of the tasks that you perform can be described by a well-defined procedure, it is probable that computers already have had an effect on your life. Some formalized jobs have, up to now, been protected from a computer takeover by limited data access. Banking provides a good example. Banking is, and has to be, a formalized process. Functions for deposits and withdrawals have followed clear and well-defined processes for many hundreds of years. A travel agency may be another example. However, even if these functions are formalized, traditionally only banks and travel agencies have had access to the software and data needed to perform processes such as bill payment or airline booking. Today, with the Internet, we do not need these intermediaries to perform these functions. With improved software, better user interfaces, and the Internet and the Web, the "terminals" are moved from the bank or travel agency to the consumer's PC. We get direct access to our bank accounts and can book our own tickets. The Internet has removed the data access barrier, and is—as we shall see in this book—in many ways revolutionizing the end user markets, for banking and other formalized applications.

While the *non-formalized jobs* are better protected from a computer takeover, the Internet will change the way these jobs are performed. In the medical fields, for example, general practitioners perform tasks that are still unformalized. That is, even if they follow procedures while treating patients these are not so well defined that they can be described as computer programs.

In most cases human beings are needed to diagnose and treat patients, but the computer is an important tool for many supporting tasks, for example, for storing, retrieving, presenting, and editing medical records. The Internet and Web will have a profound influence here as well, and are already used for transferring medical records, accessing medical literature, transferring prescriptions to pharmacies, and so forth. Some doctors will give patients limited access to records over the Web and let them make appointments by Internet. Test results may be communicated to patients by email. It may even be possible for the doctor to perform a checkup for follow-up patients via the Internet, where the patient has a video camera and other special equipment in his home.

The Internet will change the way we regard *ownership* of data. While medical records were on paper, the only practical solution was to store these where they were used, in doctors' offices and in hospitals. Computerized records and the Internet open the way for other solutions. Perhaps the patients should take control of these records and let doctors access the record using the Web. Then all our doctors will have access to the same data, and all the data will be stored in this one record. If we are hospitalized during a vacation in Italy, the hospital there could be allowed both to retrieve the records and to enter information on the new case.

While the basic technology behind the Internet may be complicated, it is offered to us in such a way that it can be used by *everybody* and can be afforded by almost everybody (at least in the industrial countries). School kids have their own Web pages, use email for communication, and even the owner of a small garage may see the benefits of setting up a system that allows customers to make appointments directly. Thus the Internet can "replace" the office staff that they never could afford.

The Web is a *democratic* technology, clearly a medium for the people. This is, of course, also one of its strengths. Many of the applications presented in this book require a large part of the population to have access to the Internet to get the full benefit of the technology. In contrast to newspapers, radio, and TV, the Web can be used for both input and output. That is, one can take an active participating and creative role, along with the more passive consumer role on the Web. When everybody is an information provider the Web becomes *anarchistic.* There is data on everything, written by professionals or amateurs, gov-

Ownership of data may change in a Web-centered world. Who has the rights to your medical record—you or your doctor? While handwritten notes stored in a drawer in the doctor's office may be viewed as the property of the doctor, a formalized computer-based record may be more accessible for others, and the question of ownership is actualized.

Democratic, the Web enables users to be both information consumers and producers.

ernments as well as crackpots, superficial or in-depth, left or right, right or wrong.

A new technology is often viewed from two opposite viewpoints, and the Internet is certainly no exception. A few commentators used the initial, limited prototypes of the new technology or its first failures to view this as a flop — interesting gadgets of no use to serious business. We heard these arguments while trying to introduce the first PC, back in 1975. At the time it was certainly no match for the mainframes and minicomputers. However, only seven years later IBM went into this market, and started the PC revolution that had such force that it closed down most of the incumbents, the mainframe and minicomputer manufacturers and also destroyed IBM's near monopoly on the computer market. Some commentators had a focus on technology and tried to describe the revolutionary aspects and the dramatic influence it would have on society. These futuristic views may be given based on the merits of the technology only, as if it existed separately from the rest of the world. While such a technological view may be reasonable when discussing prices, memory capacity, or Internet bandwidth, it is certainly too limited when discussing applications of the technology.

Power structure on the Internet and Web seems to mirror the real world.

For example, many propose the Internet and the Web as a tool for democracy, enabling all to be both information-providers as well as consumers. From a technological point of view this is certainly correct. The Internet/Web offers possibilities of easy access to information, and many of us have at least a home page. The question is, will the technology be used in this way when it meets the real world? Alas, on the Web, as everywhere else, we find that power is difficult to dislodge. The traffic goes to Yahoo! or MSN, not to our home pages.

The large and powerful *organizations* from the physical world are also starting to dominate the virtual world. They provide organization to this anarchy, more complete coverage, more professional presentation, and so forth. They can use their position in other areas, TV, newspapers, in industry or business to promote their websites. However, there are exceptions. On the net we may find other persons with similar interests to our own, create interest groups on a global basis, participate in chat groups, comment on newspaper articles, or offer our personal book review. But still, the majority of transactions go to a very limited number of sites.

In-depth information may be provided by the Web. However, it is not clear if this is what users want.

Many applications require **social change**, and will thus take time to implement.

What about the possibilities of using the Web to get in-depth information on political disputes, news, and so forth? Theoretically, this is certainly the case. Modern high-capacity disks can store millions of Web pages, with hypertext to link from one page to the other. Documents can be disseminated over the Internet to be presented in a multimedia format in a browser. That is, all the technical limitations of earlier media have been removed. Still, it must have disappointed many that most hits are on headline news and entertainment.

Perhaps the future lies somewhere between the conservative and radical viewpoints. The Internet and the Web introduce new ways of doing business, of organizing our society, but it will be an evolutionary more than a revolutionary change. While the short history of the Web may be called revolutionary, even explosive, we should note that the first Internet activities started thirty years ago, and that the Web has been here for more than a decade. While the progress in technological development in the last twenty-five years has been amazing, we should not forget that most new applications require social change.

The XML standard, for example, enables computer-to-computer communication on a high formalization level, but requires acceptance of strict *document standards* by everyone involved. This was not the case for HTML, which only views documents on a layout level. The exponential growth rate of HTML was based on this low formalization level. HTML is as easy to use as a sheet of white paper. Its weakness is that formalization on a layout level does not allow for high-level functions, such as accurate searching. But this is also its strength. XML is more like a form. We have to develop a "form" for each application area and test to see if this handles all possible exceptions. This is not easy since a form that is to be handled by a computer cannot have an open "comment" part, everything has to be described within the more closed fields of the form. Then we have to endeavor to get everybody to accept our standard. Clearly, this is much more of a social than a technical process. The proposed standards are only a small part of the work, to get acceptance meetings and diplomatic negotiations are required.

While the reward for formalizing a process will be great (automation), the formalization process itself may be both difficult and time-consuming. We shall explore these issues in the following chapters.

Notes

1. Transmission Control Protocol
2. Internet Protocol
3. Universal Resource Locator
4. Simple Mail Transfer Protocol
5. Multipurpose Internet Mail Extension
6. HyperText Markup language
7. HyperText Transfer Protocol
8. eXtensible Markup Language

PART 1
Fundamentals

Discussions on computers are very often concentrated on hardware, software, and applications. One seldom takes the time to study the fundamentals of computing, even if this part can help us to understand the possibilities and limitations of computer technology.

These basics will be covered here. The importance of formalization is covered in chapter 1. We shall see that any task has to be described completely and unambiguously before the computer can do the job. We shall also discuss the concept of machine intelligence, showing that this can also be a question of formalization.

Chapter 2 presents the types of data that can be represented in symbolic form (e.g., as bit codes in a computer). We shall also see that the symbolic parts of our society are replacing physical parts as the most important and that the computer thrives on this development.

Less fundamental, but just as important, are the technical and cultural constraints. These are covered in chapters 3 and 4, respectively. Some technical limitations may disappear with new versions of equipment and software, while others seem to be more difficult to overcome. Cultural constraints, from copyright to privacy issues, are also restricting the possible applications for a computer.

1 Formalization

For many, the computer is a black box. This makes it difficult to see the inherent **limitations**.

For many people computer technology, and the Internet, is a black box. In contrast to bicycles, cars, and excavators it is difficult to understand how computers work and to see the possibilities and the limitations. This problem is augmented by all the novel applications that are presented in the media, intelligent computers, speech recognition, language translation, and so forth, to the extent that the idea of computers replacing human beings for all tasks is seriously discussed. Many find proof of the everything-is-possible idea in the revolutionary developments within hardware. We have all heard how a multimillion dollar, room-sized mainframe of the 1960s is exceeded in functionality by a thousand-dollar laptop of today. Since the advent of LSI (Large-Scale Integration) technology Moore's law[1] has predicted that integrated circuit complexity would double every year and then every second year as the technology evolved to VLSI (Very Large-Scale Integration). A doubling every eighteen months on the average, or the corollary that the price of chips decreases by 50 percent in this time span, is a remarkable achievement. Today, even an inexpensive PC offers more disk space, memory capacity, and processor speed than most users need.

The **intelligent computer** is still far off, even if we have seen prototypes of "intelligent" applications for nearly fifty years.

In spite of the advances of computer hardware many of the visions from the 1960s and 1970s have not come true. We are still far from the intelligent computer; important tasks such as natural language translation are still not realized. In the fifty years of computer history, we have heard from all kinds of professionals that these radical computer applications are just around the corner. It has been prophesied that in ten, twenty, or fifty years, computers will handle most of the tasks that are performed by human beings, from decision making to language translation. Today, prophets have learned from the overoptimistic statements of their predecessors (we can test the twenty-five years prognostics given in 1975) and are now talking in the much safer hundred or two hundred years perspective.

Regrettably these prophesies are often given uncritical media coverage. It seems that the black box nature of the computer is a barrier against the skeptical questions that may follow presentation of other futuristic technological visions. When we give a press conference to introduce our inexpensive people's helicopter we are met with skepticism, especially if the prototype only runs on the ground. However, the same journalists may accept our natural language speech-to-speech translation or other intelligent computer systems without a critical question. A more recent example is that of a video system that is supposed to detect criminals as they enter a ball game, or the cell phone where we can talk one language and let the listener hear another.

Even more mundane applications that use existing technology can be troublesome. It has been estimated that about one-third of all failed or abandoned software projects cost the United States alone billions of dollars every year.[2] Many of these failures have been large corporate and government systems. Medical systems and systems for handling social security have had especially high failure rates. These systems seldom fail due to the computer hardware; the problems are usually in the software. This does not imply that hardware engineers are smarter than their colleagues in software. Instead it is an indication that software developers have the toughest part of the job.

While hardware is mass produced and sold as general machines, it is the task of the software developer to bridge the gap between this general machine and the actual application. It is the software engineer that has to build a system that conforms to the requirements of the real world. In the simplest case this may be a translation of real world concepts into computer programs and databases. In practice, however, the software engineer will find that the real world data and its tasks are too *open* to be described directly as database structures and computer programs. That is, in the real world we utilize the flexibility of human beings to interpret data, to apply the right procedure, to make low-level decisions based on an overall strategy or a higher goal. For a computer application these data and processes must be *closed*, that is, they must be described in a formalized manner. As we shall see this formalization process is not an easy task.

We may experience some of the pain that faces software developers when we fill out a structured questionnaire. Give us your views on the president, the economy, the Saturday night show—by inserting a number between one (excellent) and five (poor) in the appropriate box. If you are a conservative or a liberal, check here. What we are doing with forms is translating views from an open to a closed world. We may be able to

---

While hardware is mass produced at low cost, it is up to the **software** developers to bridge the gap between the formalized hardware and the real world applications.

Technology moves forward at a rapid stage, but this is seldom true for the applications. Modern computers are affordable and powerful, but often used for applications that were available many years ago. The Internet and the Web are an important exception.

present our opinions on the president in several pages but here we have to compress our point of view into one digit.

Many of the successful computer applications that we have today were available many decades ago. In the 1970s we had word processors, spreadsheet programs, and database systems. NASA used digital photos already in the sixties, and the first digital camera came on the market as early as 1981.[3] The first versions of Enterprise Resource Planning (ERP) systems, which integrate functions such as manufacturing, distribution, financials, and human resources, emerged in the early seventies. In many ways I use my PC today for the same functions as in my first job, in 1975. While the basic word processing functions, that of dynamic, editable text were available on my 1975 PC (at that time called a microcomputer), the one font, limited capacity, no graphics version has been replaced by a word-processing system that offers full layout control, a variety of fonts, graphics, tables, spellchecker, grammar control, and much more. Still, the greatest advantages of using a word processing system could be realized thirty years ago, but at a $20,000 price tag (with inflation, about a hundred times the price of a modern PC). The greatest advance of the last twenty-five years is perhaps that the computer has become more affordable. The combination of increased power and smaller size has created the potential for widespread use.

Henry Ford produced the first affordable car in 1914.[4] Although a modern car has a large set of new features, improved engine, transmission, and steering, the greatest advantage of having a car, personal transportation, was there already in the twenties. It may be a sacrilege to compare computer technology, the brainchild of our modern society, with the more mundane automobile industry, but there is perhaps a stronger similarity than we want to admit.

Evolution is more common than revolution, also within the computer field.

In the early days of PCs we had a fairly optimistic view of the possibilities that lay ahead. Moore's law was already in effect. We could develop applications, knowing that the next version of the hardware would have increased capacity. In 1979, three years before IBM entered the PC market, we connected a twenty megabyte (MB) disc to a PC, creating a database machine, a computer with software and disk drives that could execute high-level commands for storing and retrieving medical records. It was a big deal, also physically, as four men were needed to move the disk drive. We used the machine in a system for primary health care, where a number of doctors, each with an NPC (a network, diskless PC), were connected to this common archive for medical records. It did not take much fantasy to be able to envision the continuing hardware development. Of course, just as a modern car would have impressed the Model T-Ford owner, we are really impressed by the functionality, small size, and affordability of the modern PC.

However, the ability to connect to every other computer in the world would have been even more impressive. While the T-Ford owner would marvel at modern highways, we would have been daunted with the Internet and the Web. Yes, there were roads in the twenties and computer networks in the 1970s. But, few of us could have envisioned a future with a road to every place, with an Internet connection in every home. In practice, the Internet is like any other transportation net, with local roads, hubs, and highways, but from most users' perspective it looks as if every computer is directly connected to every other computer, in many ways as we envisage the telephone network.

Similarly it would have been difficult to predict the advances of digital music and digital cameras. While the basic principles behind these devices are fairly simple, what astonishes is that it has been possible to develop cameras with millions of reliable and fast sensors and music players with enormous memory capacity at prices that can compete with the analog devices.

This book, however, is not about the past. We will be looking into the future, the next, not the last, twenty-five years. In order to do this with some sense of realism, we need to open the black box of computing. We need to understand the fundamentals, the limitations, and the possibilities for these new technologies. This does not imply that we shall study the inner works of a computer. An in-depth focus will not give us the overview that we need. Instead, we shall concentrate our discussion on *formalization*. An understanding of this concept will give us the background needed to see into the future, and to perform an analysis of new computer and Internet applications.

> If we are going to use the word **revolution**, it should be used for:
>
> - The affordability and power of the PC.
> - The Internet and the Web.
> - Digitalizing data.

1.1 Formalization

> **Formalization**, the process of giving an exact and unambiguous specification of data, tasks, and processes.

A computer requires that both data and tasks be formalized. For data we require an unambiguous representation, for example, representing numbers with binary digits, letters using standard code tables (e.g., the ASCII[5] or Unicode character sets). Similarly, tasks must be described by well-defined, unambiguous procedures. These procedures can then be represented in computer programs, for example, in programming languages such as Visual Basic, Java or C#. Eventually, special systems (compilers or interpreters) will transform these programs into binary digits, so that they can be executed on a computer.

In many areas the computer came to a preset table, as both data and routines were already formalized. Banking is a good example. Banks were among the first institutions to use computers extensively. Why? Because they had the capital needed to buy the expensive mainframes? That may be part of the answer, but the real reason why banks were pioneers in using computers is that the groundwork had already been laid. Banks started their process toward automatic computing several hundred years ago, by formalizing processes. A deposit, or a withdrawal, had to be carefully entered in the books, under the appropriate account. Customers had to sign withdrawals and got receipts for deposits. Ledgers and cash were balanced at the end of the day. These strict procedures were needed in order to keep track of a large set of transactions, to safeguard the customers, and to avoid embezzlement. Formalized procedures simplified training, and had the advantage that all employees worked in the same way. When the first computers arrived, the software developers could simply rewrite these formalizations in a programming language, transferring data to structured files or later, to database systems. The advantage was *automation* of procedures, as these could then be executed repeatedly on a computer with new data sets.

We see that the introduction of computers in many ways resembled what happened during the Industrial Revolution. Here physical processes, such as spinning and weaving, were given an exact description as a sequence of simple mechanical operations, and this "formalization" made it possible to construct machines that automated these processes. The same happens today, but more in a symbolic than a physical world.

Not all processes in banks are formalized. Credit and loan approval may be based on a careful study of the customer's financial history, and perhaps also on what kind of personal impression she makes. However, in order to automate some of these processes, banks are developing formalized procedures for loan approval, for example, for loans below a certain threshold to private citizens. There may be weak points in such a formal evaluation that may be exploited by some customers,

Formalization has been an ongoing effort for hundreds of years.

When formalizing an application there may be "**leftovers**," subtasks that cannot be formalized.

New technology often requires a **formalized environment**. Just as cars require roads with even surfaces, computer applications demand environments where every piece of data has a clear and unambiguous definition.

but the advantages of introducing a cheap and fast automatic process will often surpass the drawbacks.

When formalizing a process one can try to implement the earlier manual processes. For the bank loan approval procedure this may imply accessing several electronic records, the customer's financial history with the bank, collecting credit data from other sources, and perhaps also data from a questionnaire or an interview. Often, however, formalization can take a new approach, independent of manual methods. The Vikings read environmental indicators to navigate. They used the position of the sun, moon, planets, and stars. The flight direction of a seagull could give important information, as well as the freshness of drifting seaweed, picked up by the waves from a nearby coastline. But modern navigational systems do not have video cameras that try to detect the polar star or seagulls. Instead, they rely on a satellite network, such as the GPS (Global Positioning System[6]). GPS consists of "formalized stars" in fixed orbits that send coded beacons that make it possible to compute one's position with great accuracy nearly anywhere on the planet by use of small and cheap handheld devices. Cash registers in supermarkets do not use video cameras to identify each item, replicating the human cashier. Instead, the recognition-environment is formalized by giving each item a bar code, a set of vertical bars that can be read by a simple laser scanner. This UPC code (Universal Product Code) uniquely defines any product.

Horses and wagons opened the U.S. continent. The pioneers found the way by careful evaluation of the terrain, avoiding steep cliffs, fast running rivers, marshland, and thick forests. Today, a network of roads simplifies transportation. A freeway offers expectations of a (relatively) smooth surface, a wide road, divided traffic, entrance and exit ramps, no crossing traffic, and signs that give us the necessary directions. These expectations allow us to drive in a relaxed state at high speeds, even at night on roads that we never have been on before. While it is possible to create a car that steers itself on such good roads (several prototypes have been made) it does not seem to be a practical solution. The degree of road formalization is not high enough to defining *driving* as a formalized process. Still, a well-functioning automatic pilot for the car would seem to be an interesting product, since so much of our time is (wasted) on driving. In order to develop this automatic pilot we can go in two different directions, either mimic human drivers by making

A first approach to formalization may be to try to **mimic the human being**, that is, to develop programs that work as a human. However, simpler and more reliable methods may include a formalization of the environment.

When formalizing a task one focuses on the result, not on the way the manual processes were performed. This often leads to **radical new ways** of performing the task.

smart devices or formalize the environment to a higher level, allowing for new ways to solve the driving task.

The first approach would include video cameras, radar devices, and other gadgets to sense the environment. These data would then have to be entered as input to a program that controls the wheel, gas pedal, and brake. Even with the great advantages in sensory equipment this will not be an easy program to make. While driving can be very relaxing at times, allowing us to listen to music, look at the countryside, and have a conversation, there are situations when we use all the sensory organs and all our brain capacity to make the right decisions. We may unexpectedly see something in the road ahead. Do we have to brake, veer, or can we just go straight ahead? If an automatic pilot has to take these decisions the tasks must be formalized. The decision program will have to distinguish between a rock (brake or veer), a small snowdrift (go ahead), an empty cardboard box (go ahead?) or a full box (brake or veer). It must be able to interpret the intentions of fellow drivers (is he really going to turn, why is she slowing down, does he want me to pass?). Humans have a better ability than computer programs to make decisions in these unexpected cases, and we have the context knowledge that is needed to do the right thing. Of course, this does not imply that we always make the right decision. There are unaccountable accidents that occurred because the driver made a reflex action, for example, throwing his car out of the way of a cat; saving the cat but ending up with a serious accident.

Clearly, the other alternative—to formalize the road to a higher level, seems to be more promising. This can be done by putting "virtual rails" in the road, cables that gadgets in the cars can follow. Timers and sensors can be used to control the distance to nearby cars. Such a system may reduce the driver's workload, but exceptions would still be a problem for a completely automatic system. To get automation we may have to go all the way, as with the automatic trains that run in controlled environments on elevated rails or in tunnels. Doors on the platforms, which do not open before the train arrives, restrict access to rails. Sensors are used to check if all doors are closed before the train leaves, and doors will reopen if they are blocked, perhaps with a prerecorded message that asks passengers to keep away from the doors. In such an environment the actual programming of the automatic pilot will be a simple task.

For example, even this simple code can take the train out of the station:

```
Close doors (command to all doors)
Repeat
        Read status (from sensors in the doors)
Until status = all closed

Send ready signal to central computer
Wait for go-ahead signal from central computer
Start train (a signal is sent to the engine)
```

This program will close the doors, go in the repeat-until loop until the "all closed" status is received, and then wait until the train is permitted by the central scheduling computer to leave the station. The automatic pilot can then accelerate the train until the right speed is attained, running the train at this speed until a sensor indicates that the train is approaching the next station, reducing speed gradually and stopping at just the right place at the next station (indicated by other sensors) and then opens the doors. It will wait the required time and then repeat the program shown above. Such trains are already in use in cities and airports, and will become a standard for most modern metro lines.

If you are a metro train driver, your job may be in line for a computer takeover. But note that even a metro train needs some additional formalization before we allow the computer to take over. While a human driver can at least make an effort to stop if someone has fallen onto the track, this will be very difficult to achieve with a computer-controlled train. Perhaps one could install devices to sense if there are any obstructions, but it is far easier and more reliable to formalize the environment to such an extent that passengers do not have access to the rails, as described above. This tells us that the effort to formalize old metro networks will be a major task, and that a full automation of road traffic may be impossible, even with "virtual rails." However, intermediate systems may be used to improve the efficiency of the driver. As an example, systems have been proposed where one driver can control a "train" of virtually connected trucks.

It is interesting that the job of an airline pilot is viewed by most as a far more complicated job than driving a bus (and with much better pay), but from the view of a computer it is much simpler. We already have an environment of satellites and radio beacons that is used for automatic flight control. With modern

We formalize our **physical environment** by roads, train tracks, beacons, GPS systems, flight patterns, and so forth. Where formalization goes all the way, a computer may replace human beings, for example, for driving a train or piloting a plane.

navigational systems planes may be controlled by automatic pilots onboard and automatic flight controllers on the ground. As
passengers we may demand to have at least one pilot up front,
but a computer may perform the actual steering of the plane.
We already have completely automated systems that can handle
everything from takeoff to touchdown. These systems will
make it possible to pack aircraft closer in the air, to reduce con-
gestion, and to prevent delays. So while we all agree that the pilot does a more complicated job than the bus driver since the
pilot has more data to consider, more instruments to read, more
controls to set, less time to make decisions, a lower margin for
error, and more catastrophic consequences of an error, the pilot's job is much easier to formalize. The decisions that have to
be made are to a large extent based on formalized data such as
course, altitude, speed, radio signals, engine data, and so forth,
and the decisions themselves can be calculated based on these
data. The computer works faster than the human pilot and the
human flight controller can work with greater accuracy and will
be more reliable. While the bus driver's job seems so much
simpler with only a few instruments and controls, the open nature of the decisions that have to be made make a computer
takeover highly improbable. This has, of course, nothing to do
with the bus itself, but is a consequence of the environment, determined by the unformalized nature of roads, traffic, and passengers.

Symbolic or virtual environments may be formalized by cre-ating fixed proce-dures, requiring un-ambiguous data, by passing laws and regulations, and so forth.

While computers have been successful in banks and planes
it has been much more difficult to develop social security and
medical information systems. The difference is in the formalization level of the institutions. As we have seen, banks have
had formalized routines for hundreds of years. Within social
security the rules and regulations offer possibilities of interpretation. This is not a fault of the regulations, but more a consequence of systems that handle data about people. Since the
needs for social security come in all forms, the regulations need
to be flexible. If a computer is to be used to determine support,
the rules and regulations have to be formalized to a higher degree, as well as the related data. Twenty years ago Norwegian
regulators changed the system for giving social support for
housing expenses. With the new rules taxable income, rent, and
the type of house determined the support level, criteria that enabled the computer to calculate the correct amount for each client. Of course, such a system may give support where it
shouldn't (rich ship owners with good tax lawyers got support)

and some clients (perhaps with a dramatically poorer situation today compared to last year when the data was collected) would not get the support they needed. However, the advantage was automation of a manual system that was expensive and time-consuming to administer.

It is interesting to note that the formalization process for these types of systems has often been carried out as a part of the software development process. In many cases the results of the formalization, the interpretations chosen for each case, have been described only in the computer programs; the actual background regulations may not have been changed. This is one reason why many organizations are still running very old systems, and find it difficult to update to more modern hardware and software. The old computer program has become a de facto standard for the interpretation of the regulations, not only an implementation. The ghost is in the machine. A reengineering effort will therefore have to extract specifications from the old system.

Similar problems have been encountered within medical information systems. Parts of these applications, for example, the "hotel" part of a hospital or an inventory system, are formalized and are open for a computer takeover. Other parts, such as interpreting test results, are more difficult to handle. While early developers saw medical systems as just another computer application, it became clear that there were problems with the level of formalization. Different doctors used different names for the same diagnosis, medication, and so forth. However, as with social security the advantage of using computer systems has promoted efforts to raise the formalization level, for example, by introducing more unique identifiers for diagnosis. Even then, medical systems have proven to be more difficult to implement than other systems. While it is natural to register every transaction in a bank and while it is possible to stress the need to follow inventory routines in a manufacturing industry, it is perhaps not so easy to get doctors and nurses to follow such routines in an emergency situation in a hospital. The whole hospital environment, treating patients, working toward a diagnosis, selecting a treatment, naturally sets the focus on the open, unformalized parts. This is not an easy setting for imposing standardized and strict regulations. It is interesting to see that one of the most successful implementations of medical information systems have been in a privately owned Japanese hospi-

*Formalization may change the **nature** of the task, giving somewhat different results from the previous open implementation.*

tal.[7] Here the culture may be right for establishing rigid rules that are to be followed at all times.

Medical systems need a formalized environment to function, where someone can set the standards and require that these be followed. Other hospitals have given up on the formalization, and have instead chosen to implement image and text-based systems. With document image systems the old records are stored as images, formalized to the level of pixels, a pixel representing a point in the image. With such systems doctors get fast access to records, but there is no possibility of using the data for higher-level functions, for example, for statistics or medication control.

1.2 Machine intelligence—is it possible?

Machine intelligence—is it just a question of formalizing the tasks that we consider intelligent?

From the very first computer sixty years ago, computers have taken over more and more tasks that were previously performed by human beings: calculations, word processing, planning, control systems, archiving, communication, etc. Many of these tasks were tedious routine tasks that required very little intelligence from the human operators. However, other tasks have been of a form that certainly required intelligence on the part of the human being. But our most advanced computer systems, for planning, air traffic control, routing, information storage and retrieval do not require intelligence. While many of these programs are complex, and certainly have required intelligence from their developers, the programs themselves can be compared to calculators.

The best **chess programs** use brute force (i.e., calculating every possible move several steps ahead), instead of trying to mimic the human player.

New application areas are not captured by the intelligent computer, but by formalizing tasks. Even the success of chess programs, often presented as an example of the intelligent computer, is based on formalization. Chess, with its eight by eight board, thirty-two pieces, each governed by exact rules and the unambiguous goal of setting the opponent checkmate is clearly a formalized system and thus a candidate for a computer application. The problem of chess is the very high number of possible games—calculated to ten in the power of 120! For human beings, intelligence, experience, and a good strategy are needed to master this game, to overcome the impossibly high number of combinations.

While humans can operate in **open environments** (e.g., performing according to overall goals), a computer needs a **closed environment**, where it is possible to give unambiguous instructions.

The first chess programs tried to mimic human beings. They were developed by chess experts and had a lot of general chess knowledge. Today, the programs that beat the best human players are based on a very different strategy. Instead of using chess knowledge to foresee the next steps, special processors have been developed that can evaluate every possibility many moves ahead, even within the limited time constraints. The computer has mastered chess by brute force, not by intelligence. In this respect, mastering chess does not convey more intelligence on the part of the computer than the fact that it can do bookkeeping more accurately and faster than a human being.

Can machine intelligence be decided by the Turing test? The idea of the test is to sit at a terminal and decide if there is a human being or a computer at the other end.[8] Should we try to ask questions that require intelligence, for example, questions from an IQ test? The problem is that we may get a similar answer from both the human being and the computer. Further, we do not have any guarantee that the human being at the other end is especially intelligent. He may fail to answer our question, while the computer finds a premade answer in its database.

Instead, we need questions that go to the heart of the difference between human beings and computers—questions that address the open areas where computers cannot perform. As an example we will enter the following three stories on the terminal (the last sentence of B and C has been changed slightly from A):

A.   In the middle of a forest, there was a hunter who was suddenly confronted with a huge, mean bear. Full of fear, his attempt to shoot the bear was unsuccessful. He turned away and started to run as fast as he could. Finally, he ended up at the edge of a very steep cliff. His hopes were dim. But, he got on his knees, opened his arms and said, "My God! Please give this bear some religion!" Then, there was a lightning bolt in the air and the bear stopped a few feet short of the hunter. The bear had a puzzled look for a moment, and then looked up into the sky and said, "My God! Thank you for what I am about to receive. . . ."

B.   In the middle of a forest. . . . The bear had a puzzled look for a moment, and then looked up into the sky and said, "My God! Thank you."

C.   In the middle of a forest. . . . The bear had a puzzled look for a moment, and then looked at the hunter that begged, "My God! Do not let him eat me"—to no avail!

The task (for the human being or the computer) will now be to classify these stories as, *humorous*, *sad*, and *incomprehensible*. We may have to repeat this test several times to get a good confidence level, but we will find that human beings nearly always manage this task, while the computer will have to resort to random guesses. Terms such as humorous, sad, and incomprehensible seem impossible to formalize, and as we see from the above example small changes in the story make a huge impact. In these open areas human beings rely on our real-world understanding. This cannot be represented in a computer, not because of the vastness of data but because we cannot find the representations that are to be used as a basis for formal reasoning. Simple formalizations, such as looking for keywords or special combinations, will not work in this case. Even a semantic analysis, impossible with the methods that we have today, will fall short—we need more than just the meaning. One has to be a human being and have the experience and feelings of a human being, to solve this task.

Figure 1.1 Which letters are shown here?

Many open tasks performed by **humans** seem to be impossible to formalize, and can therefore never be taken over by a computer.

In some applications it is important to determine if there is a human or a computer at the other end. The reason is often to avoid automatic programs that try to retrieve proprietary information. The common way to perform this "Turing test" is to employ our excellent abilities for pattern recognition. A set of letters, such as in the example in figure 1.1, is then displayed on the screen and the user is asked to type the sequence in an input field. If the answer is "ABC" it is highly probable that there is a human at the other end.

We find open situations in most tasks, not only in storytelling and pattern recognition. Laws are not formalized and must be interpreted by human beings (i.e., lawyers, juries and judges). This is not a weakness, but the strength of a system that can be adapted to every new situation. In contrast to the computer, human beings do not need advanced programming to handle exceptions, but can make a decision based on an overall view of the problem area. We can make these decisions even with insufficient data, by using experience or context knowledge to fill in the gaps.

In the 1970s and 1980s much effort by major research institutions went into the development of expert systems. The idea was to capture these "human" abilities, making systems that could mimic tasks. The early results were promising. In medicine, for example, prototype systems could give a medical diagnosis as well as the human experts, as proved by several tests.[9] In these tests both human experts and the expert system were given medical data (laboratory results, etc.) in a *formalized* form on a set of patients, and the expert system came out as the winner, especially for diseases that occur infrequently. Does this imply that machines will replace medical doctors?

These tests were performed more than twenty years ago, and in spite of the good test results expert systems never got a strong foothold in medicine.[10] What we learn is that human practitioners do not rely on formalized data only, that they often can make a diagnosis or at least put forward a hypothesis just by looking at a patient. In this way human beings are more effective than a computer, as fewer tests have to be taken and treatment can start earlier. So why did the computer do so well in the tests? The answer is that the tests were performed on formalized data only. The human doctors were not able to see the patients; they got the same data as the computer. So what this test proves is that the computer may perform as good as or even better than humans in a formalized playing field. A great achievement for these diagnosis programs, but this is not the real world.

Figure 1.2 Formalizing a task, something is left out (left), a close match (middle), and over-formalization (right).

Figure 1.2 illustrates the problem we face when we try to formalize a task. In the figure to the left the formalization (the rectangle) only captures a part of the task (the irregular area). In the middle example we find a closer match, while the example to the right represents an over-formalization. The discrepancy between the task and the formalization will depend on task domain. Within the field of medical diagnosis the situation may be more of what we have to the left of figure 1.2, where a formal system only manages to capture a part of the task area. In banking, for example, we may have a situation as illustrated in the figure in the middle, a close match between the task area and the formalization. Even if we have a close match there are parts of the task, exceptions, special functions, and so forth, that are not covered by the formalization. We also see that the formalization may extend beyond the borders of the original task. An example may be formalized loan acceptance procedures, where some persons may qualify based on formalized data only, but perhaps not qualify if parts of the process had been performed manually, for example, by a personal interview. If we go to more detailed tasks, for example, payroll processing, we may find a complete match between the task domain and a formalized system. Over-formalization, illustrated in the figure to the right, may be a part of bureaucratic systems where data are collected and processes introduced for every possible contingency, representing overkill for the normal case indicated in the figure.

1.3 Levels of formalization

Data and processes can be **formalized on many levels**. The formalization level determines the functionality of the formalization.

With **coding**, any type of symbolic information may be represented in a computer (e.g., coding letters as numbers).

We have seen that a formalized application area is a requirement for using the computer. On the most basic level the computer can only handle bits, data stored as zeroes and ones. This representation has been chosen because to achieve it, only two different coding levels need to be represented electronically, using one voltage for a one, another for a zero. Then simple transistors can be used to store these numbers physically in the machine. A drawback of this coding scheme is that more digits are needed to represent a number, for example, we need four binary digits to represent the number eight (binary 1000), while the largest number that we can store in a byte (8 digits) is 255 (binary 11111111). However, in electronics it is far easier to represent *many* of something simple than *few* of something complicated. This is especially true for the large-scale integration techniques used today for producing computer processors and memory. In fact, the cost of repetition of a simple electrical circuit, such as a transistor, is so low that the cost per memory bit is approximately $0.00000001.

Symbol	Value
,	44
-	45
.	46
/	47

Symbol	Value
A	65
B	66
C	67
D	68

Symbol	Value
a	97
b	98
c	99
d	100

Table 1.1 ASCII Table (examples)

While numbers can be stored directly in binary form, other types of symbolic data can be represented using simple coding schemes, for example, the ASCII table for representing symbols as numbers. Some examples are shown in table 1.1. As seen, an A is coded as the number 65, B as 66, etc. With this simple table we can convert all letters to numbers, and thus they can be represented in the computer. This coding can be performed already by the keyboard. When we type an A number 65 is transmitted to the computer. Of course, if the A is to be displayed on a computer screen the opposite conversion will be performed, from numbers to the figure that represents an A on the screen.

Images are, on the lowest level, represented as sets of *pixels*, where each pixel represents a point in the image. On the display screen, as on a TV, each pixel is represented by a red, blue, and green dot. A picture on a 1000 by 1200 screen will consist of 1.2 million pixels (1000*1200). On a good color screen, three bytes (byte = 8 bits), each capable of representing a number between 0 and 255, are used to set the color and brightness of each pixel. For example the value 255 will indicate maximum red, blue, or green, while 0 will indicate that the pixel should not light up. If we do the multiplications we see that we need 3.6 million bytes (MB) to represent the picture.

The level of formalization determines the functions that can be performed on the data. An image, for example, may be represented as a low-level collection of pixels, or at a higher level as geometrical objects, with lines, rectangles, circles, and so forth. *Paint* programs use image (pixel) representations, and allow for detailed editing (i.e., to control the color and brightness of each pixel). To make the user interface more effective the

Low-level formalization offers flexibility, but does not often provide as effective operations as higher level formalizations (e.g., the low-level formalization of documents as characters is convenient, but limits the operations that can be performed on the documents).

programs use metaphors such as brushes, spray cans, and geometrical objects, but we can also zoom in and set individual pixels if we want. If we draw a line in the paint program, it will be converted and represented as a sequence of pixels. Thus, any line, straight lines to freehand, can be painted on the image. If we want to change the display, for example, by moving the line, we will in principle have to delete the pixels and try again. The program does not have an internal representation of a "line," this concept is just a part of the interface, similar to the brushes and spray cans.

In contrast, *drawing* programs use a geometrical representation of each object. A line will be represented by its two endpoints, a circle by its origin and radius, a rectangle by the coordinates of the opposite corners, etc. These are given with attributers for color, thickness, fill options, and so forth. Each object on the display is represented in this form within the program, in an internal data structure. What we see on the display is a generated picture. A rendering algorithm will loop through the picture's data structure and create the pixels that are needed to represent the drawing on the display. The line object, for example, is given as an input parameter to a routine that generates the pixels needed to draw the line. It will start at one endpoint and calculate the x,y-positions along the line one pixel at a time.

The user can select an object by clicking on or close to the object on the display. The drawing program will compare the click-position to the geometrical attributes of each object to identify one of these. If the user hits the delete button, this object will be removed from the data structure, and the display is redrawn without this object. The user can choose to modify objects in many ways, for example, by moving one of the endpoints of a line, increasing the radius of a circle, or changing the color of a rectangle. Both the paint- and the draw-representations have their advantages and disadvantages, which is the reason why we have both types of programs, the low-level paint and the higher-level draw.

As we have seen, characters are represented by numbers using the ASCII table or any other character-to-number conversion table. On the next level we may represent text as sequences of characters, what we call strings. A basic string-representation may be sufficient for a simple editor such as Notepad, for storing the text in a file or for transferring the text via the Internet. However, only basic string operations such as deleting and inserting characters will be available. In order to handle words, paragraphs, spelling, and grammar higher-level formalizations are needed.

In some of the first bibliographic retrieval systems documents were represented as plain text. This has the advantage of simplicity, but does not allow higher-level functions. For example, a search for the author "Addison Wesley" will return books published by "Addison Wesley" or even books where these words are part of the title. In order to distinguish between title, author, and publisher these concepts must be added to the text, for example, by using tags. This is illustrated in the example below, a record from a bibliographic system using XML markup, a topic which we will consider in more detail in chapter 27.

```
<title>A Doll House</title>
<author>Henrik Ibsen</author>
<publisher>Oxford Press</publisher>
<location>Oxford</location>
<price>$10</price>

<original title>Et dukkehjem</original
title>
<original publisher>Gyldendal
    </original publisher>
<original location>Copenhagen
    </original location>
<first published>1879</first published>
```

Higher-level formalizations offer improved functionality, but need structured data.

This example shows that we may add an abundance of tags in order to identify all attributes of a data record. Using such a simple scheme we can now limit a search to the author-field, print all titles, find the lowest price, etc.—but only for documents that follow our scheme and use our vocabulary. While standards like XML offer a basis for structuring documents, defining vocabularies, and identifying fields within the document, this is only the first and simplest step in formalizing data to a higher level. The big problem will be to identify and standardize vocabularies, and to have everyone following these standards.[11] Even a markup-language, such as the one in the above example, can only be used in the more "administrative" part of a document, title, author, publication, publisher, date of publication, page numbers, sections, paragraphs, etc. The textual part of a paper or a book, the content part, must probably still be an open text, only formalized at a character level.

Note that this is very different from a record-based database system, where every field is specified. However, markup languages allow us to define something in-between, semi-formalized records that can be used for everything from questionnaires to maintenance forms.

Level	Formalization	Coding (example)	Functionality (examples)
1	Character	ASCII or similar character-to-number coding.	String editing, inserting and deleting characters.
2	Character sequence, sentence, and paragraph.	Rules to identify words (enclosed by spaces or punctuation) and paragraphs.	Insert and delete a word, avoiding breaking a word at line ends, inserting space between paragraphs.
3	Lexical	Dictionary	Spell checking.
4	Syntactical	Word classification, grammatical rules.	Grammar checker.
5	Semantic	Representing the meaning of words and expressions.	Logical searches, translation, computation.
6	Pragmatic	Representing the "meaning of meaning" or meaning in context.	Full text analysis.

Table 1.2 Formalization of natural language text on different levels

Table 1.2 presents different formalization levels of natural language text, from a low character to a high semantic representation. The higher the level the more functions can be performed. A simple editor works on the character level, while a word-processing system may work from a lexical to a syntactical level. Using Microsoft Word as an example, we see that in addition to basic editing functions the system can provide simple spell and grammar checking. For spell checking MS Word cannot tell if a word is used and spelled correctly, the function is limited to checking if a word is in the dictionary or not. It does not replace a human proofreader, but can be of great help in finding and correcting certain kinds of simple typos (those that lead to spellings that are not found in the dictionary). The grammar checker is even more restricted. It can only analyze

Most **word processors** work on the lowest formalization levels, leaving the higher level parts to the user.

the simplest of sentences, and its suggestions for improvement may often be wrong or meaningless. It requires the user to know the language in order to accept or reject the suggestions. Still it is a very useful feature, especially when writing in a foreign language. Then we can easily make the silliest mistakes, some of which the grammar checker will find with ease.

The formalization level of a modern word processor can be determined to be between a lexical and a syntactical level, perhaps getting a score of 3.5 on the scale used in table 1.2. For full proofreading features the system will have to work on a semantic level (i.e., the system would then have to represent the meaning of the text). On this level, other functions, such as language translation would be possible. However, formalization of natural language has proven to be very difficult to achieve. Natural languages are a product of human communication. They are highly dynamic: new words, expressions, and styles of writing are introduced every day. In contrast to programming languages, such as Java, C#, or Visual Basic, natural languages are not designed. Dictionaries and grammar rules are not defined up front, but are mere attempts to keep up with language development in retrospect.

In some respects the **ambiguousness of natural language** may be a disadvantage, but in most cases it helps us to deal efficiently with a dynamic and complicated world.

Natural languages are not formalized, and this is perhaps their great strength. In contrast to a formalized programming language, a natural language allows us to introduce and talk about concepts and processes that we cannot define, perhaps that we do not fully understand. Further, natural languages are very effective. By relying heavily on context, we do not have to say everything. "I'll see you at noon" is enough. It is not necessary to give the place and the date, "Have you called Bob?" may be perfectly clear, even if there are many "Bobs."

Natural language formalization has been an area for intensive research, as the reward of success will be enormous. In our economy, language is one big barrier to effective international cooperation. The European Union may have programs to support language skills and for internationalization, but even at academic conferences the deficiency of foreign language skills is an impediment to effective communication.[12]

In the 1960s the U.S. navy presented the first primitive versions of an English-Russian translation system. Today, we find translators on the Web that try to handle English, Spanish, French, German, and other languages. An example is shown in figure 1.3 where we have used Google's translator tool on this paragraph, translating into Spanish and then back to English. As seen, the results are reasonably good.

En los años 60 la marina de los E.E.U.U. presentó las primeras versiones primitivas de un sistema inglés-ruso de la traducción. Hoy, encontramos los traductores en la tela que intentan dirigir inglés, español, francés, alemán y otras idiomas. Un ejemplo se demuestra en el cuadro 3 donde hemos utilizado la herramienta del traductor de Google?s de este párrafo, traduciendo a español y entonces de nuevo a inglés. Según lo considerado, los resultados son buenos razonable.

In 60 years the navy of the E.E.U.U. presented/displayed the first primitive versions of a system English-Russian of the translation. Today, we found the translators in the fabric who try to direct English, Spanish, French, German and other languages. An example is demonstrated in picture 3 where we have used the tool of the translator of Google?s in the first part of this paragraph, translating to Spanish and then again to English. According to the considered thing, the results are good reasonable.

Figure 1.3 Example of natural language translation using Google's translator.

Natural language is in the open realm, and is impossible to formalize in the general case.

The problem remains to develop systems that can give a correct translation. Today, the level of these translation systems is at the point where they can give a reasonably good idea of the contents of a text, for example, to determine if a full manual translation is of interest. Some approaches try to use a combination of automatic and manual translation, where a human translator modifies the computer output. In many cases this results in a strange sentence structure. My students often complain that the help text provided with U.S. software, translated to Norwegian, is unreadable, and that the only way to understand the text is to translate literally back into English. That is, the words are Norwegian, but the sentence structure is English.

In the general case **machine translation** is impossible. However, these applications may work within closed worlds.

There are exceptions. Machine translation has been very useful within closed worlds, such as translation of weather forecasts. With some discipline when creating the original text, a limited vocabulary may allow for a high-level formalization that can facilitate automatic translation. One may argue that these limited successes with the translators already in place is just a starting point, and that it is just a matter of continuous improvement before natural language translation will be solved. The problem with such an argument is that while it is quite easy to design a prototype translation system, one may need quite different methods to design a full functional system.

Figure 1.4 Norwegian-English dictionary

As an example we shall design a Norwegian-English translating system. This will be based on an electronic two-way dictionary, stored in the database table presented in figure 1.4. With the following program we have a simple translator that translates from Norwegian to English:

```
Private Sub translate_Click()
   Dim stdset As Recordset
   Dim query As String

   query="SELECT English FROM dictionary
      WHERE Norwegian ='" & inputWord & "'"
   Set stdset=CurrentDb.OpenRecordset(query)
   outputWord=stdset!English
   print outputWord
End Sub
```

This simple seven-sentence program (written in Visual Basic) reads a word ("inputWord") in Norwegian, makes a query to the dictionary database table, selects the English translation for this word, and outputs the result, translating one word at a time. With a few more program sentences, a continuous two-way translation can be achieved. In testing the program we find that the Norwegian sentence "Her er jeg" is translated to "Here am I," which is understandable but not quite correct. Are such minor details just a matter of more effort and more capital? We will soon find that synonymy (many words, one meaning), polysemy (one word, many meanings), and the dynamic effects of language complicate our efforts, that there are words that cannot be translated easily, expressions and metaphors have different interpretation in the two languages, and that the structure of the two languages is quite different. The correct translation of a word will not always lie in the word itself, but we may have to look at the sentence, the paragraph or, in the worst case, need information of what kind of document this is. Take the word "web" as an example. It has many meanings. Note also that it was translated into "fabric" in the example shown in figure 1.3. We see that we have to work on a semantic level to be able to perform the correct translation. We also have to consider style, a personal letter requires a different selection of words than a formal document, as well as a letter from a teenager compared to an elderly person, and certain professions may also have their own way of using terminology.

Computers can be applied when an area is formalized, but are of little help in the **process** of formalizing.

It seems highly improbable that we shall be able to represent this form of context information in a computer, or that we shall be able to develop the methods that are needed for the utilization of this knowledge. While existing translators (such as the one offered through Google) are far more advanced than this simple example, our case illustrates the problem. To develop full language translators we need a full formalization of natural language, as these programs must work on a semantic level in order to give a correct translation. This is a task for linguists more than programmers, and advances in computer technology will be of little help here. Thus, the fact that we can present a prototype is no guarantee that the final problem will be solved.[13] Language translation may, however, have a future in areas where it is possible to close the application, for example, by restricting the freedom of words and constructs in the original text. Perhaps we can use such semi-formal languages in writing specifications, for accounting, and for other applications, trading flexibility for the possibility of automatic translation.

Formalizing data to high levels is a complicated task that is often performed by specialists, by data base administrators.

While natural language is an especially difficult area to formalize, the formalization task is not simple even in domains that are more closed. In banking, for example, much effort goes into deciding which data to store on each account, and how this data is to be represented. In such a process many questions will arise. For example, can a customer have more than one checking account? Can an account be owned by more than one customer? Should state and zip code be stored in two or in one field? What about foreign addresses—how shall a name be stored? Most businesses have database administrators that handle this work, but as many of the questions will affect or be affected by business policies the answers have to be provided on a top-management level.

In fact, a major part of the work involved in making software systems goes into answering these questions, as shown by the following example. In a system recently developed for a local firm that just celebrated its seventy-fifth anniversary, the concept of a delayed order came up. A formalized description was needed since the system was going to report total delays in each monthly period. "A delay," said the production manager "is calculated as the days between the promised due date and the delivery date. If a delivery was promised Monday, but performed on Wednesday we have a two day delay." Reasonable enough, but he was not so sure when the system counted three days between Friday and Monday, or twenty-four days when the company was not able to deliver on the last day before the summer holiday. This only shows that formalizing is a complicated task, and that ambiguousness that has thrived under a manual system becomes very apparent when a computer system is installed.

Other examples of formalization are social security numbers, other ID numbers, product code identifiers, license numbers, bank routing numbers, etc. These are all there to make it easier for a computer system to identify persons and objects. Since a clear and unambiguous identification is so important, we are given these codes to remember.

1.4   Cost-benefit of formalization

*Formalizing may offer great **advantages**, but comes at a price.*

To avoid theft we need to limit access to our property, so that only authorized persons can get into our house. A few may implement this function by hiring a butler or a doorman, but most of us have to rely on locks. A lock offers access to anyone with a key. This is a simple and cheap way of formalizing the concept of access. But, while a doorman can use his intelligence to handle special cases, the lock opens only for those with the right key. There is no way of handling exceptions. We feel foolish when we have locked the keys in the car, and we are worried when the keys are lost since they may get into the hands of the wrong persons.

*"**Intelligence**" in computer systems can break down where the formalizations are too simple.*

With the high cost of heating, many of us install control systems that automatically lower room temperature at night. Clearly this is a convenient way of saving money and protecting the environment, until Saturday night when the late guests start freezing. The problem is that our formalization of "night" as being between 11 p.m. and 6 a.m. is too simple; the control unit only has the major rules, not the exceptions.

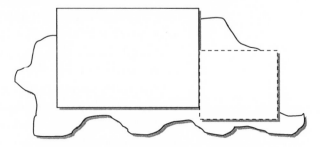

Figure 1.5 Expanding the formalized system.

It is difficult to achieve a one-to-one **correspondence** between an open task and its formalization, represented by the closed part.

If we return to our illustration of the formalization problem (figure 1.5) we find that the formalization, for example, night temperature setting (illustrated as a rectangle), does not cover all parts (Saturday night). We can expand the formalization by extending the functionality of the timer (the dotted rectangle), to let it use a different setting for Saturdays, for example, from 2 a.m. to 8 a.m. The cost is that of a more complicated device and the need for more data. It may be more in conformance with our needs, but may still not handle all exceptions, for example, letting us freeze if we stay up late on a Friday or keeping the room unnecessary warm when we go to bed early on a Saturday. These situations can also be handled by an extension to the program, but require even more data to function. However, there is always the possibility of a smart engineer finding a shortcut, instead of just adding input complexity. In this case, a simple solution may be to add a motion detector to a simple energy-savings system, keeping the heat on at night as long as there is someone in the room (but this system may again keep the room warm for the cat the whole night). As we see, the problem may be formalized, but it may be a major effort to enter all the data needed to get a close match between the formalization and our needs.

A refrigerator that orders food automatically via the Internet has been proposed as one possible futuristic net-application.[14] Very convenient—we will never be out of milk or any other item. But we have to remember to tell the fridge that we will be away this weekend; that we no longer can stand chocolate milk; that we are trying to stay away from high-fat cheeses; that we are expecting a lot of guests this weekend; that we have been recommended to eat more vegetables; that the cheese we bought was an unsuccessful experiment, etc. An alternative solution offering less autonomy to the refrigerator will be to let us call it up on the cell phone on our way to the grocer, letting it describe what it contains. Still, this will need complicated technical implementations (how much milk is left in the carton, are the tomatoes still good?). So while this is a possible product, we again see that the task of administering such a fridge may be extensive, perhaps just the type of work that we wanted to avoid in the first place?

In our homes, and in many smaller institutions, we enjoy the flexibility offered by open functions. We buy when we like, what we like, and at the last moment we may decide to go to a restaurant instead of eating at home. A "smart refrigerator" that does its own ordering will violate this flexibility. Alternatively, we will have to give it all the data needed so that the system can keep track of our decisions (i.e., to "follow" the irregular border of the open function). So when we decide to eat at a restaurant instead of going home, we have to call our intelligent fridge. It may even protest if it already has bought the ingredients for tonight's dinner! Some users may get a kick out of having these dialogues with their refrigerators, but most of us would feel very silly.

In computer systems, "intelligence" is used in an effort to simplify the user's tasks, for example, Microsoft Word can give us an automatic bulleted list. This is triggered when we write a bullet symbol, such as a minus sign, at the beginning of a line. The word processor assumes that we've started a bulleted list, and will automatically insert this symbol in front of successive lines. This is often a useful feature, but was irritating the day I tried to make a simple budget, with both minus and plus items. MS Word assumed that the minus sign was the start of a bulleted list, and started all successive lines with this symbol.[15] In Norway many typists have the problem that the preposition "i" (meaning in) is changed to a capital I automatically. This autocorrect feature is user controlled, but many users do not know which feature is causing the problem, nor how it can be eliminated. Microsoft Excel's way of saving me unnecessary typing is as irritating and even more dangerous. When typing

Formalization and automation often run counter to **flexibility**. In our homes we may prefer flexibility, while a business may put a priority on efficiency.

grades, A, A-, C+,..., I suddenly found that all subsequent C grades became C+ grades, that is, whenever I typed a C (after giving the grade C+ to another student) Excel would suggest C+. Since the enter key is used both to leave the field and to confirm this suggestion all my C students got C+ grades. This feature can, of course, be turned off but this requires that the user notice the problem, that he understands that this is a feature and not an error, and that he knows how to turn if off. The program is designed to assume what the user wants to do and act on this before it has the complete picture—just like any other dumb assistant. Today, when I get a new version of any piece of software the first thing I do is to turn off most of this "intelligence."

This must not be seen as an argument against automation. Automation makes our life simpler in many cases. Lights that go on when it is dark (controlled by a light sensor), when someone passes by (infrared sensors), sprinkler systems that water the lawn when necessary, and the automatic choke system on modern car engines that regulates the air/gas mixture are all useful. These systems work because there is a good fit between our needs (the open part) and the formalization (the closed part). Sure, there may be situations where these devices do not perform ideally, for example, putting on the lights for a passing cat, sprinkling the lawn before a downpour, but these exceptions come at a minor cost and do not affect the overall goal of the system.

For most applications the formalized functions will be more rigid than the open, manual functions. Whereas a human being can use her intelligence to handle exceptions, the computer needs to be preprogrammed for each special case, and will also need data that enables it to distinguish between the cases. With regard to formalization the cost is in the lack of flexibility, the advantage is the possibility of automating the formalized tasks. However, large organizations or organizations that handle many transactions have already accepted many of the formalization costs, as more formal systems were needed just to keep track of all the data and to provide efficient processes. Here the number of transactions itself is a barrier against flexibility, and the extra formalization needed for using a computer is often negligible. Thus we often find the lowest formalization cost where the advantages of automation are the greatest. This is why a computerized inventory and ordering system may function very well at a grocery store, but not at our home. The gro-

Open functions are **flexible**, while closed (formalized) functions often are more rigid.

Open systems are more common in our private lives than in a business environment. In the latter case high transaction volumes often require closed systems.

cer will have many thousands of different articles, and may have a large quantity of each in the shelves. Then a formalized system for identifying each item, for ordering, inventory, and for cash registers is required for efficient handling. This system will be needed independently of the use of computers. That is, the cost of formalization, rigid routines, and a loss of flexibility has already been paid. The grocer cannot make a last minute decision to close the store and take a walk in the park instead.

1.5   Interactive computing

If tasks have both **open and closed parts**, the ideal systems seem to be that of a human working in close cooperation with a computer.

In the early days of computing, programs were run without human intervention. Batches were set up with a set of programs and all the data, represented on punched cards. The stack of cards was read into the computer and the programs were executed one after the other, giving output to a line printer. Today, most programs are interactive, communicating with the user during processing. This is true even for many programs that run in devices. For example, a car computer takes input from the driver through the accelerator and may provide output through the instrument panel.

Interaction provides for greater flexibility, as the user can react on the basis of previous output from the machine. We go from a predefined command system, "do this job, here are all the data and instructions," to more of a dialogue with the computer. For example, we can ask an airline booking system to present available bargain tickets and then choose which of the offers that we want. Instead of one program doing all the processing on pre-made input data, the program is split into smaller functions that we invoke from the user interface. Data are entered one field at a time, which provides for continuous error control. Input may be simplified if the program can offer default values, and errors can be avoided by letting the program control input and giving a message wherever there is a problem. The system is, of course, still formalized but the involvement of the user in the process allows for greater flexibility.

Interactive systems can give us the best of both worlds, human handling of open tasks, while the computer handles the closed parts.

The principle of interactivity is manifested in modern user interfaces, which are designed along a "control panel" metaphor. The user is in control. The machine is the assistant that executes the tasks according to the user's instructions, when the user decides. The human being is the expert, not the system. The computer performs the tasks for which it is best suited:

computation, archiving, transmission, and presentation of data. The human being makes the decisions and controls the high-level aspects of the tasks, following overall strategies and goals.

Interactive systems offer the best of both worlds, utilizing the ability of human beings to do the overall planning and decision making, while the computer is in charge of storing, retrieving, presenting, and transmitting data, as well as the computations.

Most interactive systems offer user control over data, and which processes to invoke. Some systems allow even greater flexibility by letting the user write program functions. This can be done with high-level functions within special domains, such as the "programming" of formulas in a spreadsheet system or by mathematical programs such as Maple and Matlab. "Application generators," such as Microsoft Access, offer simple application design, allowing forms, data tables, and database queries to be described visually, adding programming code where needed. Full flexibility is achieved within programming languages, such as Visual Basic, C#, and Java, which allow for detailed descriptions of what we want the computer to do.

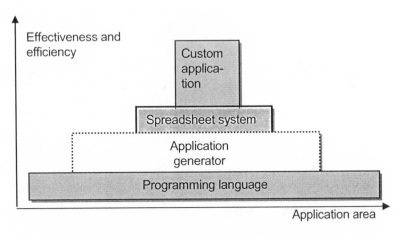

Figure 1.6 Balance between application area and efficiency.

Flexibility can be obtained at the cost of efficiency; it is difficult to get both at the same time.

The flexibility offered by interactive systems and programming languages does come at a cost in that the higher-level functions that make a program simple to use also narrow the application area. This contrast between simplicity and applicability is illustrated in figure 1.6. The systems that are most efficient in use and that require the least input from the user have the most limited application area. Some devices, such as an electronic clock, would have been displayed as a vertical line in this figure; they are very efficient since they require very little input, but can only perform one task. Programming languages such as Java can be used for all applications, while custom-designed programs will have a narrower application area, however with higher-level functions that make these programs more efficient within their specialization area. Spreadsheet systems and application generators are somewhere in the middle of the range.

To make this point clear we can compare a pencil and a word processing system. The pencil has very few limitations; we may use it for all fonts and symbols, but these have to be drawn by hand. The word processing systems may have a limited font set and drawing capabilities, but are much more efficient to use.

The flexibility offered by programs such as word processors, spreadsheet systems, and Web page editors are achieved by the fact that these systems are only assistants. They only do part of the job, editing and formatting text, handling numerical data and formulas, and creating Web pages, respectively. Their effectiveness comes from the fact that they are each dedicated to an important application area, and that they can offer all the functionality needed within this area. However, all higher-level tasks are left to the user.

This is just another part of the picture that we discussed earlier with regard to formalization, such as the example regarding natural language translation. Formalization to a high level may be achieved within limited domains (e.g., translating weather forecasts, ledgers), but not for general applications. The narrower the application area the higher the level of formalization that can be achieved.

Exercises and Discussion

1.   Instructions to a driver may be as follows: "If you see children next to the street, drive carefully past," to a airplane pilot: "When you pass reference point 2A, change course to 234 degrees, climb to 9000 ft and set speed to 423 mph, maintain speed and course for 3 minutes, before taking a 90 degree turn to the right, increasing speed to 500 mph." Which of these instructions are the

easiest to give to a computer program? Discuss the formalization aspects involved.

2. Discuss the following two statements: (a) "She is very intelligent, she can do complicated math without pen and paper" (b) "This computer is very intelligent, it can calculate the right answer in a millisecond."

3. We have a large warehouse, with millions of different items. Your task is to describe a system that makes it easy to find the location of every item, that is, when the user provides the identifier of the item your system should tell where it can be located. How would you solve this task? We are especially interested in how you will formalize locations.

4. The warehouse described above has a large outdoor area, where huge items can be stored. Can you formalize locations here as well?

5. "See you at noon," "give my regards to Mary," "do you want another cup" are common utterances, but try to look at these sentences as a computer program would do. Are they as clear as they seem?

Notes

1. Gordon E. Moore, a co-founder of Intel, recognized the trend that became known as Moore's Law, one of the driving principles of the semiconductor industry.

2. Ewusi-Mensah, Kweku. 2003. *Software Development Failures*, MIT Press.

3. The Sony Mavica, that captured video frames on to a minidisk. True digital cameras, that used image sensors to convert light to digital data came some years later.

4. See for example the home page of the Model T Ford Club of America, http://www.mtfca.com.

5. ASCII (American Standard Code for Information Interchange) offers a table for digitizing characters as bytes. With ASCII coding each of the 128 characters in the table is given an 7 bit code.

6. For information on GPS, see for example: http://www.aero.org/publications/GPSPRIMER/.

7. http://www.kameda.com.

8. Alan Turing, the British mathematician, proposed this test in his 1950 paper "Computing Machinery and Intelligence," *Mind*, 59, 433-560. He predicted that it would be possible to solve the test within fifty years. The time is up and we are as yet not significantly closer to the answer.

9. Shortcliffe, E.H. 1976. *Computer-based Medical Consultations: MYCIN*, American Elsevier, 1976.

10. In situations where there are no human experts available e.g., in a submarine, expert systems may provide help in setting a diagnosis. But telemedicine, where experts are available over data networks are a more realistic alternative when experts and patients are physically separated.

11. We shall return to these issues later in our discussion of XML in part 4 and the semantic Web in part 5.

12. In one conference I attended the Finnish speaker could not understand the question posed by an Italian. An American saved the day by translating the question from Italian-English to English, and the answer from Finnish-English to English that the Italian could understand. While citizens of smaller countries are forced to have foreign language skills, citizens of the larger European countries can manage with their own language only (i.e., until the day they participate in international work). One can understand why language skills and student exchange are prioritized areas for the European Union.

13. We explored these thoughts in the book *Jervell & Olsen: Hva datamaskiner ikke kan* (What computers cannot do), Universitetsforlaget (1982, 1985) and Brøgger (1985)—Norwegian and Danish editions only.

14. The first (prototype) products are already on the market.

15. In the XP version one can use the backspace key to undo the automatic bulleting.

2 Symbolic Data

Over the last ten thousand years we have migrated to a world where the **symbolic processes** often seem more important than the physical.

Perhaps a Stone Age man could have used a computer to draw sketches of his rock carvings. Apart from this early art, his world was one of physical objects where computers would not have been of much help. The first letters or symbols emerged five thousand years ago, where inhabitants in Babylon found it convenient to represent oxen, barrels of grain, and baskets of fruit as symbols on small pieces of clay. A Roman calculator, a keeper of accounts, would certainly have found a computer useful. Later on monks and priests would probably have welcomed word processing systems. From the seventeenth century, London-based import companies, such as the East India Company, could have utilized a modern inventory system, so much more convenient than using books.

What we see in these ten thousand years is that more and more symbolic tasks are introduced. "Symbolic" jobs are created where one works with symbols instead of physical objects. We get whole institutions that are "symbolic" (e.g., banks and insurance companies). Even in companies that produce physical objects, manufacturing plants, the symbolic parts often become more important than the physical. The competitive advantage of car manufacturers, shipyards, computer manufacturers, and others lies more in handling design, logistics, marketing and finance than in the basic physical processes, such as assembly or welding.

For most employees, the ability to read, write and organize becomes more important than physical skills. This development from the physical to the symbolic workplace has been accelerating over the last fifty years. In modern industrial plants workers become symbolic operators, for example, instead of handling a tool directly the operations are performed through an advanced computer-programmed machine. In an aircraft, more automation and control mechanisms such as automatic pilots are removing the physical parts of flying. Working with data from manifests, instruments, and guidance systems the modern pilot is to a large extent a symbolic worker. The pilot follows most others in our western societies. Not only are more and more jobs symbolic, but the symbolic institutions are becoming the most important, among these banks, insurance companies, and entertainment organizations.

Symbolic objects may have physical **representations**, such as paper bills and coins, tickets, videotapes, and books.

Many of our everyday objects are symbolic. The paper value of a hundred dollar bill is marginal. However, it is a *symbol* of a value and since this symbol is globally recognized, it can be changed into goods or services. The paper bill is just one out of many *representations* for the symbol "value." A book is a physical object. It has weight. So does the VHS tape. The book and the videotape are representations for the text and the movie, respectively. In some cases we are interested in the representation itself, the first edition of an old book, a book printed on exquisite paper or bound in leather. In most cases it is the content that is of interest (i.e., the symbolic weightless book). Characters on paper are just one out of many possible representations. The airline ticket is a document that allows us to board a certain flight on a certain date. This "right to board" is a symbol that can be represented using other media than paper, for example, using a frequent flier or credit card, or perhaps just by offering a code at the gate.

The physical representation can easily be replaced by **digital** numbers, for example, representing money as bits in a computer.

An alternative and convenient form for representing these symbols is as bits, as binary digits in a computer. That is, instead of representing the $100 value as a paper bill, we store this number in a computer. Here it may represent the balance of a bank account, the amount of a transaction, interest calculated, etc. We get a compact representation, independent of wear and tear, but most important, we get a representation that is open for automatic handling: storing, calculating, or transmitting. A computer program can automatically calculate interest on this amount, or use it as a basis for computing an account balance. Electronic amounts can be stored efficiently on computer disks, or transmitted at high speed over global networks. The advantages of an electronic representation are so clear that today only a small fraction of monetary value is represented in its original form, as bills or coins. We get many of the same advantages in using bit representation for other types of data as well, whether they are text, music, video, pictures, tickets, or any other type of symbolic data.

A drawback of using a different internal representation from the external is that we need to convert data from the outside to the inside form, and vice versa. That is, from digital numbers, letters, pictures, and sound to bits during the input process, and from bits to other symbolic forms during the output part. This mapping is performed through peripherals, which convert binary digits to characters, graphics, or physical operations (or vice versa).

Device	Function
Keyboard	Character input
Mouse	Input of (relative) position
Printer	Character and graphical output
Display	Character and graphical output
Video recorder	Continuous graphical input
Loudspeakers	Sound output
TV	Graphical output (video)
Scanner	Graphical input (pixels)
NMC[1] machine	Physical output (e.g., positions, speed of tool)
Robot	Output of physical operations

Table 2.1 Peripheral devices

Table 2.1 lists some of the most common peripheral devices. Since all of these are bit driven, we get the benefits of both worlds; an internal representation that is easy to represent electronically and various representations suitable for the real world.

2.1 Symbolic structures

Programming languages offer the possibility of entering unambiguous statements, where the meaning of every statement is absolutely clear.

While the internal low-level representation in a computer is in the form of bits, programmers and system designers are free to use any form of higher-level symbolic structures to represent data and processes. We have programming languages that can represent data as integers, floating point numbers, as text strings and operations through statements for formulas, selection, iteration and all the other basic operations that a computer can perform. These languages have unambiguous syntax and semantics. While natural language, such as English, allows us great freedom in how we construct sentences, programming languages have a fixed command vocabulary and a strict grammar. We can introduce new identifiers for variables and processes, but there are clear methods as to how this can be done. In this way the meaning of every statement, the semantics, is under control. There is nothing unclear and ambiguous about a computer program, there is only one way to interpret it correctly, just as with mathematical formulas.

As tasks and programs get bigger the emphasis is toward constructs that allow us to use even higher-level concepts, to organize the millions of code lines into symbolic structures that can be developed and maintained in an orderly manner. We found such constructs even in the very first programming languages. Here higher-level operations could be described in the form of procedures (subroutines, methods) and data could be structured in the form of records. The idea is to make new, custom operations out of simpler basic operations. For example, we may need the ability to sort a sequence many places in a program. Instead of adding the code wherever needed, we instead define a procedure *sort* that does the job. In order to make *sort* applicable to different types of data we will define *sort* so that it can work on abstract data, to be replaced by actual data whenever we need sorting. In this way we can build a hierarchy of higher-level operations. Similar constructs exist for creating structured data, for example, we can define a record *employee* that contains all the attributes that define a hired person (name, social security number, salary, etc.).

Object-orientation, a way of modeling the world through objects that consist of data and methods (processes).

The first programming languages only had these two constructs, procedures and records, for building the program structure. Later on, one found that additional constructs were needed, for example, a *modular* structure that could contain both procedures and record descriptions. Today, *object-orientation* is a common technique for organizing operations and data in a computer program. Here data and the procedures (methods) that work on these data are described as a *class* structure. A basic idea is the principle of *encapsulation*. The class presents itself to the outside through the methods it can perform, the detailed implementation of these methods are "hidden" within the class. For example, a class may offer a method for sorting a file. To use this method we need a description of this method, for example, that it requires the name of the file with the data, but we do not need to know how the sorting is performed.

With an object-oriented approach we try to develop a set of building blocks that can be reused many times. For example, in a college archive system, there may be a class describing *students* and another for *employees*. While the first may have a method for registering an exam, course code, year, and grade the second may have methods for calculating salary and tax. However, since both students and employees are persons, we may find many common features in the two classes, both data and methods. For example, each class may have attributes for name, address, social security number, etc., and perhaps methods for presenting and changing the address. To avoid duplication of code these common attributes may be described in a third class, a class *person*. We can then declare that both the student and employee classes should *inherit* the properties or attributes from the class person, such as name, address, and a method for checking social security number.

Classes describe a mold or template for making objects. Whenever we have a new student we create a student-object based on the generic class. Now we can enter the attributes that describe the individual. In this way we build an organized structure in the computer that can perform all the operations that the user needs.

The **building blocks** of software may be low-level program statements, or high-level components. Ideally we want to develop a new application just by combining a set of these high-level parts.

In designing these program-structures care must be taken to make them both efficient and flexible. This is easiest when we control the application area, for example, when we design software for virtual worlds, such as software tools for user interface development, graphical systems, mathematical packages, and so forth. Here we are in full control. In real-world applications, however, we may find that the foundations on which we built our class- and object-structure are not as solid as we expected, and that changes in the environment or organization may force a complete restructuring of the program. In some cases we may even find that a less structured program will be the most flexible.

System development and programming is expensive. The idea is to bridge the gap between the needs and requirements of the real world on one side and a generalized machine on the other. That is, our task is to convert a general machine into something that can solve our problems, into a word processing system, a manufacturing planning and control system, a flight guidance system, etc. Even if all of these applications are different, there will be common parts, and one way to reduce development costs is to explore commonality, to reuse software components. Object-oriented techniques are interesting here. Classes can be reused at a programming level, for example, the general Java classes developed for application A can be used also for application B. Or we can use object-orientation at a tool level. Visual Basic, for example, offers system designers components for Internet access, for presenting a video clip, or components used to design an input form, such as text boxes, radio buttons, menus, etc. That is, if one needs to provide the ability to play movie clips to a program this can be done simply by adding a standard component to the user interface of the program.

If we are in the process of constructing a website, for example, an online bank, we will find that several of the things we need are available as premade components. There will be components for checking a credit card and for transferring funds. These components are offered in precompiled form, ready to be run on any computer where they are registered. For example, the component to check a credit card can be executed on a machine run by the credit card company. In practice, we will only have to design a small part of the system ourselves, such as the user interface and special functions. Components and other forms of basic software help us to narrow the gap between the general computer and the application.

While we are free to choose the internal symbolic representation of our system there are two requirements. It must be possible to translate the structure into bits, so that it can be run on a computer. This task is performed by language translators or compilers, converting the class structures from a high-level programming language, such as C# or Java, into binary code that the computer can execute. At the other end, the internal structure must be presented in a form that is suitable for the user, for example, to a graphical user interface with menus, command buttons, and forms. What we get is a formalized "pipeline" of data and commands all the way from the user interface to the low-level bit representation inside the computer, moving through different symbolic structures.

2.2 Transmitting symbols

Some organizations try to cope with a paper-based world by scanning all incoming mail, storing letters in **image form**. However, the low formalization level, that of pixels, limits the operations that can be performed on the documents.

While it is difficult to transmit the value of $100 as a paper bill, this is no problem with a bit representation, for example, withdrawing this amount from one account and depositing it into another. Then the data can be sent directly over a communication network, at great speeds, without any costly change of the underlying representation. Compare this to the cumbersome operations needed to do the same task with real money.

With the Internet a business letter can be transmitted as an email, or as an attachment to an email. On the receiving end the electronic letter can be forwarded automatically, stored on a disk, made searchable based on contents, and edited if necessary. Compare this to sending the same letter through the mail, which requires a translation of the bit representation used within the word processor to paper, to a form that requires physical handling of letter and envelope. At the receiving end the envelope has to be sorted and physically transported to the addressee. All further handling of the letter, copying, archiving, etc., has to be done manually. It may also be necessary to enter data from the letter, for example, date, sender, receiver, title, and more into information systems. Some institutions have chosen to avoid manual handling by scanning all documents when they are received, storing these as page images (as pictures). From now on, the letters can be transmitted, stored, and forwarded in electronic form. The formalization level, however, is that of pixels and the document data cannot directly be subjected to searching or editing.

Another disadvantage is that the image files tend to get very big, even if packing methods can reduce file sizes. However, with the disk and bandwidth capacity we have today companies with a modern IT infrastructure can handle images without problems.

The image version of the document can be enhanced by using OCR (Optical Character Recognition) techniques.[2] OCR programs can recognize characters with high accuracy and will translate these from image form to character codes. That is, at best these programs can translate the document back into its original electronic form.

The advantage with image scanning and OCR for a business is that they offer the advantages of electronic document handling, without forcing any standard on their customers. For example, the image scanning systems are solely based on the paper format, and can handle documents independently whether they are produced through handwriting, typewriters, or modern word processing systems. While OCR systems will have problems with handwriting, they can handle any form of typed document as long as the typing quality is reasonable.

Image scanning, OCR, and fax machines, along with other systems that rely on paper, should be viewed as temporary systems that help us transform from a paper to an electronic world. In the long run we should expect that the majority of documents that are received by a business will be electronic, sent as emails, attachments to emails, or as highly structured XML documents. The advantage with the latter is that they can be handled with higher-level functions. These functions can retrieve fields such as item number, quantity, and customer number from purchase orders and can insert these in an order file, available for other functions higher up in the value chain. To get to this "nirvana" of computing we need standards, from the network level and up to document levels, from the way we send bits on communication networks to the way we structure an order form.

OCR (Optical Character Recognition) is used to transform a document from an image representation to a higher-level character representation.

Symbols represented as bits can be **transmitted** over data networks at high speed.

Data communication networks have been available for decades. Businesses have used this technology to transmit data between branch offices and the head office computing center using call-up or fixed telephone lines. What is new with the Internet is standardization, price, and availability. Proprietary protocols, as defined by the different computer manufacturers, have been replaced by an open standard—TCP/IP. The IP, Internet Protocol, offers means of accessing every server on a global basis, using a unique IP address. The TCP (Transmission Control Protocol) allows the computers to exchange data in a standardized manner.

While standardization provides for widespread communication, this is made physically available by breakthroughs in technology, where optical fibers, wireless technology, and faster processors have made data transmission inexpensive. The telecommunication companies have made huge investments in digging ditches and laying down new cables, setting up communication towers all over the world or putting new communication satellites into space. Smart solutions have been found for the utilization of existing installations. Power companies, for example, use their power lines as a skeleton for a communication network by spinning optical fiber around the lines. With audio modems, digital to audio converters, data traffic can be transmitted over ordinary telephone lines. With new technology, these twisted pair lines can be used for moderately high bandwidths, offering the possibility of having several telephone "lines" and a fast data "line" all on the old telephone line, avoiding laying a new cable into every office and home.

When Bill, Joe, and Susan get data communication from their home, this is a revolution, offering possibilities for new ways of symbolic communicating, for new ways of doing business. While TCP/IP defines the underlying standard for transmission, standard formats for messages and contents are as important. For messaging the global standards are SMTP (Simple Mail Transfer Protocol) and MIME (Multipurpose Internet Mail Extension), for contents HTML with the accompanying HTTP standard for transmitting the HTML pages. On the next level, XML seems to be the promising tool.

Exercises and Discussion

1. Let us say that you could bring a portable (with ever-lasting batteries!) with you in a time machine back into history. Choose a time period you know before year 1900 and discuss to what applications the portable could be used.

2. Think about the people you know and their work. Would you characterize them as mainly symbolic or physical workers? How many do you find in each group?

3. A waiter performs both physical and symbolic tasks. What are the symbolic?

4. Money can exist in paper form or as bits in a computer. Discuss advantages with the later form.

5. Name different representations for music.

Notes

1. Numerical Control Machines, such as computer-controlled lathes, drill presses, and milling machines.
2. See for example Bunke, H. and Wang, P.S.P. (eds.). *Handbook of Character Recognition and Document Image Analysis*. World Scientific Pub Co. (May 1997).

3   Constraints on Technology

In the previous chapters we have discussed fundamental issues, such as symbolic processes and formalization. While these issues set limits for what we can achieve with computers there are also practical considerations that can set barriers against implementing all the theoretically possible applications for a computer. In this chapter we shall consider some of the practical limitations we face when using technology.

3.1   Hardware development, standards, and integration

In the last decades **hardware development** has given us more and more powerful computers, to the extent that most users have a machine that has more resources than they ever will be able to use.

In 1975 my University received one of the first PCs, or microcomputers as they were called at that time. This had an Intel 8080 processor, 32 KB[1] RAM memory, no hard disk drive, but had two 8" diskette stations, each with a capacity of 128 KB. The price tag was about $20,000—in 1975! Today, we can get a thousand times more powerful computer at a fraction of the cost.

Perhaps the *cost* factor has been the most important. Our early PC was used for word processing, spreadsheets, and for storing and processing data records, not very different from the use of a modern PC. But while the 1975 version was only affordable for the few, a PC is today affordable for nearly anyone—at least in the industrial countries.

Increased computer power has been used to improve the **quality** of applications, better word processors, higher quality video and music, etc.

The rapid increase in computer *power* and the functionality of peripheral devices has made it possible to increase the quality and functionality of these applications. While the 1975 version of word processing was character based, the modern versions offer graphics, a choice of many font types, spelling and grammar checking, etc. But we do not need a 1000 MHz processor for this type of functionality. Most users had their needs satisfied with the processor capacity that was offered years ago (i.e., for traditional computer applications).

However, many new applications need these processor speeds. Today we can play interactive games with amazing graphics or use the PC to play DVDs. High speed servers can let us search huge databases in a split second, and offer interesting possibilities for developing and executing complex mathematical models, for example, in order to improve the accuracy of weather forecasts.

These technological advances can also be seen in the form of *smaller* components, for example, components that can be used to create laptops, PDAs (Personal Digital Assistants), also called palmtops, and other mobile equipment. Along with advances in wireless technology, we can in principle be connected at all times. This is clearly an advantage for some, but perhaps not for all.[2]

If there have been tremendous technological breakthroughs within certain technology areas, we cannot expect important advances in all areas. Batteries, for example, still have very limited capacity, are heavy, and not too good for the environment. Even if the incentive to develop something new and better is enormous, in this and in many other areas we only see a slow evolution of existing technology, far apart from the "Moore's law" development for chip integration. Display technology is another area where developments have come more slowly. We still use the CRT (Cathode Ray Tube) technology, developed in the 1930s, even if this has disadvantages in the form of power consumption, size, and weight. New LCD (Liquid Crystal Displays) are starting to compete with CRTs on office computers, but this technology has other drawbacks. The large resolution, lightweight, and inexpensive displays needed for so many applications are still far in the future.

While trying to look into the future we should not forget that novel technology often has to compete with established technology and that new standards have to compete with the existing ones. While the latest flat display TV technology can rely on the NTSC[3] and PAL[4] standards already in place, they are also restricted by the limited resolution of these standards. To really get the benefit out of larger TV screens we need a higher bandwidth signal, as in the digital HDTV (High Definition TV) standard, which offers theater-like TV performance in our homes. But here we face the problem of moving from one standard to the next, a step that requires large investments from all parties involved.

These collective switching costs were accepted when moving from black and white to color TV, since the advantages of getting color were clearly a good enough incentive. Color technology was also made *compatible* with the previous technology (i.e., color signals could be received as black and white on old sets). Viewers could take this step at their leisure, for example, waiting until the old TV set had to be replaced anyway. The current incentives for the next step, to HDTV, may not be so

---

While we have seen tremendous **technological breakthroughs** in some areas, development goes much more slowly in others. Research and development does not always give us the products that we need.

After making investments in building **infrastructure** for one technology, we need very good arguments to replace all this equipment with another.

strong. The improved resolution may be of interest for sport and nature programs, but will be less important for other types of TV programs. As with the change to color TV the new technology requires high investments both on the producer and consumer side, and no one seems to be willing to take the first step. An additional problem today is that a new standard not only affects the TV itself, but also the equipment that consumers use along with the TV, such as a VCR, cable box, DVD, and video game console. That is, the infrastructure we build to support one technology makes it more difficult to introduce another, noncompatible, technology.

Integration, using one technology for many applications, often seems both a simple and flexible solution. In practice, however, we find that different functions may have very different technological requirements.

With everything digitized, TV, telephone, data transmission, etc., an integration of the different media becomes possible, thus offering the possibilities of new applications and new services. The first implementations of two-way interactive TV are already here, thereby making it possible for viewers to send response to programs or advertisements from the remote control. Interactive TV can offer users control over what to see. For example, we can choose to follow our favorite athlete in a broadcast from an Olympics marathon, or order the pizza shown in the advertisement just by pressing a button. The backward channel can be established by using the TV cable, an Internet or telephone connection or by using a cell phone network.

However, integration of services may cause problems. An example could be the integration of telephone and data services. Here we will find that there is a difference in priorities. Telephone companies work to reduce delays and to keep the line open as long as possible, accepting some loss of information. This is seldom a problem as human beings correct minor missing parts in a conversation automatically. Data network providers tolerate delays and that information must be retransmitted, but cannot accept loss of information. Redundancy through fault tolerant coding may correct a few missing bits, but if more information is lost data networks are programmed to send the lost packages once more.

Integrating these two different strategies on one network will be difficult, but clearly possible with the advantages we see in today's network technology. TV and video signals may be transmitted on the same network, but since these media require much higher bandwidth there may still be practical and economical reasons for keeping TV on separate networks.

3.2 Software

Software has always been the problem area of computer-based applications. While hardware engineers can give us reliable, fast, and cheap equipment, software is often unreliable, expensive, and time-consuming to build. Software development is a shaky business. As we have seen, hardware development takes place in a formalized manner, defined by the specifications for the new equipment. That is, a computer resides within its own specifications. This is not the case for application software that has to adjust to an eternally changing world. In short, hardware designers can create a computer according to their own specifications, while it is the job of the software developers to increase the functionality of the machine so that it can be useful for a real-world application.

On a superficial level a computer program can be seen as something very flexible. With an editor the program can be changed in minutes, new functions can be added and existing functions modified. In practice, large programs may be more resistant to change than buildings made in concrete. Computer programs may have been developed over a long period of time and may have reached a stage where they are no longer just a representation of an application or a set of specifications, the program *is* the application and the specification. That is, there may not be any manual way of performing the tasks, and the task may not have a complete specification outside the program. The program has made itself invaluable, just like an employee that refuses to document what he does or to teach others the tricks of the trade.

A computer program may be flexible and easy to **modify**. However, large programs, especially programs that have been developed and maintained over many years by many different programmers, have a complexity that makes them extremely difficult to change.

This situation became almost too apparent when we moved into the new millennium. Companies had to rehire retired Cobol[5] programmers and others with a competence in yesterday's tools in order to modify the programs so that they could handle dates into the new millennium. Systems that had an expected lifetime of five to ten years were still in use twenty to thirty years later. The cost of replacing these systems is enormous, and since they can be used yet another day—why not?

While most bugs may have been removed from these legacy systems, we can in no way expect that modern software will be bug free. This is partly due to the fact that software is *complex*, and minor errors may have large effects. A house will not fall down if the carpenter did not put in a nail correctly or if the concrete for the foundation did not have the optimal amount

Digital technology offers extreme flexibility, but also the opportunity of introducing bugs into software.

of water. But even small errors in a software product may result in a collapse of the whole system. That is, the physical world is *analog*, continuous in a way where everything is fine as long as we are on the right side of the line. A house will have a much stronger foundation than it needs, and the carpenter may put in many more nails than the theoretical minimum. But every line of program code is of importance in a software system. An error in one of the million lines of a big system may not only have an effect on the actual function, but may bring the whole system crashing down.

Another problem is the race to get on the market with new systems. That is, the first versions of a new software product are often released before they are completely tested and may therefore have serious flaws. Smart users acknowledge the problem and avoid installing the very first versions of a software product, at least for systems that are used for important tasks. Within the world of software it is very often smart not to be number one. The positions somewhat farther behind in the implementation queue are safer.

"Writing great software is hard under the best of circumstances, and the Web is among the worst of circumstances."

(*Commerce Solutions, Web Technology*, Microsoft Press, 1999)

Developing software for Web applications is especially hard. On the Web we do not have the same control as in stand-alone or client-server[6] systems, in terms of the number of users or the available resources. Our portal may break down when it becomes too popular, and the streaming video application may not work if the backbone Internet or the ISP (Internet Service Provider) does not manage the load. Instead of having a set of friendly users, we may be faced with inexperienced users, users with very different backgrounds, and even hostile users that try to break the system. However, in later years we have seen the advance of a set of tools for developing Web applications. These tools handle at least some of the problems that we face on the Web, and some of these are so easy to use that we can set up a full online store in a couple of days. While this provides efficient solutions, to a large extent we have to rely on the toolmaker for the quality of the solutions, for example, to ensure that the system does not have any security loopholes.

3.3 Usability

Due to the technological breakthroughs of size, power, and price the electronics market is flooded with computer gadgets of all types. Some may be really useful, but often there is a tendency to make what is possible, instead of using the technology to support the customer. This technology-centered view is to some extent supported by a market where it is "cool" to have and use the latest of the latest.

We also see these tendencies in products that fill traditional roles. Digital watches show the time, but will also offer an abundance of functions that are easy to implement, but which may only have an interest to a minority of users. Modern telephones come crammed with functions, and often become so complicated to use that most users only master the most basic functions of calling out and receiving calls. It seems that a more productive approach would be user centered, where the focus is on the users and the functionality that they need. Fewer, generic functions that are easy to use are perhaps better on these devices than an abundance of specific functions hidden within complicated menu structures.

With graphical displays, desktop systems, menus, and help facilities the systems themselves can help us explore new functions. Modern systems present what they can do through the interface, making commands and data visible.[7] For example, when we choose the "print" command in MS Word, a form is displayed showing all the different options—the form shows us what the system can do. Menu- and form-based systems invite exploration. If we make an error or are not satisfied with the results we can backtrack with the "undo" command, perhaps the single most important command in modern software systems. In addition, most of these systems come with large help facilities. These may be helpful for the novice, explaining the functionality of the system and "how to do" setups. However, they are often not as helpful when it comes to giving advice for solving specific problems. There are so many different problems than can occur for different configurations of equipment and operating systems, for users with different backgrounds and competence, for different types of data, that it is impossible for a help system to cover all situations.

Most users find a "level of convenience" in a system, which may be as low as using an advanced word processing system as if it were a typewriter. This is illustrated in figure 3.1. Most users would be more efficient if they spent some time to learn more advanced functions, moving to higher proficiency levels (as illustrated by the dotted lines). Handbooks, courses, and training sessions may be used to elevate the users to these higher levels. The system itself can also participate, offering

Interface usability can be supported by menus, forms, and help systems, but requires reasonable screen real estate to function well.

Modern user interfaces are based on high-resolution displays of reasonable size. It therefore becomes a great challenge to maintain **usability on smaller devices**.

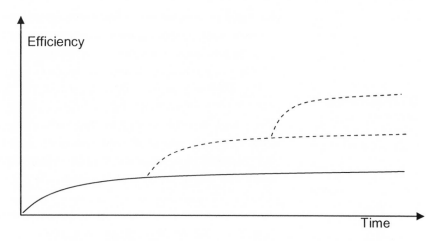

Figure 3.1 Most users find a too low "convenience" level in using a system

"tip of the day" and help agents that can offer context-dependent advice.

This is much more problematic with PDAs, mobile phones, and other gadgets, where functions may be hidden behind number codes, cryptic commands, or in deep menu hierarchies. My office telephone, for example, looks like and is a small computer. It has an LCD display and a full but primitive keyboard, and offers numerous functions. I never use it for anything other than the most basic functions, and this is true for 95 percent of our faculty. While many of the functions offered would be useful, they are hidden within a too primitive user interface. None of us seems willing to study the manual to attain higher user levels, even if this could be more efficient in the long run. However, next to my telephone I have this wonderful PC, with its full-size keyboard and excellent 21-inch display. That is, a new technology, the PC, comes in *addition* to phones, but as both technologies become commodities integration may be required. Instead of putting a primitive PC in the telephone we need an integration of the devices, putting the telephone into the PC. Then we can use the large display on the PC to make functions visible, to select from the address book by a mouse click, to set up forward and reply functions by filling out forms, etc.

On the Web we have the advantage of being able to make functions and data visible, at least where the browser runs on a standard PC with a full display. With scripts,[8] small pieces of code that are embedded in the HTML pages, we can offer error

Good **user interfaces** can limit the frequency and consequences of errors, but not always.

checking and advanced help facilities on the client system. Without scripts all communication has to go via the servers (i.e., the user provides input, the page is sent to the server and a response page is then returned to the user).

Web technology is still not mature. Web user interfaces come in all forms and are often difficult to understand and use. There may be no clear distinction between required and optional data, commands and links may be labeled inappropriately and inconsistently, the user may be asked to provide data that the system already knows, the system may require special formats for date, names, addresses, etc. Today, we can go into a brick and mortar shop, find the things we want to buy, pay, and then leave. On the Web many online stores require us to register and provide a lot of personal information. This may be useful if we are to become regular customers, but way off the mark if this is the one time we want to get something from this store. This should also be a concern for the companies themselves. Tests have shown that a large fraction of potential customers turn away when the user interfaces become too complicated, when they are asked to provide too much data, or when the whole process becomes too cumbersome.

It is interesting to observe that many companies apparently look at the Web interface as a technical issue, leaving the job to the technical experts while the interface really should be discussed in board meetings. This is the place where the customers meet the company, a place to set standards for service, and to present the company profile just as in physical locations, brochures, or other advertisements. The Web, and any other computer system, should in principle give the same high level of service as we previously had with more manual communication. For example, we would not accept that the bank returned our letter because we had used a date format with dots between the numbers instead of slashes, but many Web pages do. Neither would we accept that the travel agent answered "no flights available" to a question, we would expect that she offered alternatives, however on the Web the "not available" answer is often used. As we have seen, we cannot expect the same flexibility from a computer system than what we would get from a human. However, it is not difficult to build in at least some basic flexibility, for example, in decoding different date formats, offering different flight as alternatives, and so forth.

However, as with PCs we should expect to see an evolution toward more standardization, to a de facto "look and feel" of

On the open Web **user diversity** can complicate interface design. We can view the interface as a filter. Only the users that master the interface are allowed to pass into the Web application.

Digital technology can offer extensive functionality. Often carried on to an extent where it becomes **counter-productive** (i.e., making the devices more complicated to use than their analog predecessors).

these systems. There are already very good systems on the Web,[9] and soon these will form "standards" that others will follow. Users will become more knowledgeable, will master more complex interfaces but will also learn to require quality, turning away from the worst examples. A disadvantage for user interface designers on the open Web is that users may come from many cultures, use different languages and terminology, and have different background, experience, and knowledge. In more closed cases, as within a company, the situation is much simpler. Here we know more about the users, and variation in knowledge can be leveled out by training. This is not possible in the open Web.

3.4 Errors

Errors in hardware, software, or in use are, alas, an inherent part of using technology.

A laptop can be carried everywhere, and it is quite convenient to be able to take along important documents and databases on a business trip. But a laptop can also be lost, destroyed, or stolen. Do you have a complete, updated backup of all documents and data? What are the risks to your privacy or company security if the laptop data falls into other people's hands?

In the long run we do not need criminals to lose information. Even if modern technology is reliable, disks will crash some day, batteries will stop working, and processors and computer memory may become unreliable. Without good backup routines for the portable equipment, data may be lost. Or you may find yourself in front of a large gathering with PowerPoint slides that will not come up on the big screen.

A **modern disk** can hold gigabytes of data that can be stolen, lost, or destroyed.

Errors can occur in networks, in software, as well as in hardware. Errors performed by users can be reduced by good user interfaces, especially by "undo" commands that help us avoid the consequences of unwanted actions. But there are always possibilities for making creative errors.[10] In computer systems the fear is of losing data, in other systems the consequences may be even more serious. For example, the $1 billion accident at the Pennsylvania, USA, Three Mile Island nuclear power plant in 1979, occurred when the operators were misled by a status light. They thought that the light indicated that an important valve was closed, while the light only indicated that the close button had been pushed.[11] There are numerous other examples where "human error" is really a fault of the user interface.

In 1996 the European Space Agency lost its $7 billion Adriane rocket forty seconds after takeoff, due to a programming error. An automatic guidance system determined to shut itself down after failing to store a 64-bit number into a 16-bit space. The error checking code that is often used to detect such errors and to perform a graceful recovery had been determined unnecessary in this case. There are numerous other examples of similar programming errors, many of which have led to huge monetary losses and some that have resulted in loss of life.

Automation simplifies, but makes systems vulnerable. When the automation breaks down there is often little we can do.

Automation is necessary in rockets, but automation is also used in many other cases to improve efficiency, that is, letting the system handle the process without, or with a minimum, of intervention from the user. The first cars had to be started through a process of pumping gas, opening switches, and turning a handle. Today, this is automatic. We turn the ignition key and an electric starter turns the engine. An automatic process has replaced a manual one, simplifying the everyday use of a car. The cost is that we become more dependent on the technology. Today, few car owners have the mechanical knowledge to perform anything but the simplest error checking when the car will not start.

Modern stores rely on point-of-sale (POS) terminals. The cashier's task is limited to scanning the tags. All other functions, such as finding the right price, adding, checking a credit card, performing the payment transaction, withdrawing items from inventory, and printing a sales slip are performed by the POS terminal. If the terminals do not work the store must close. There is no way that these functions can be handled manually. Many cashiers would even have problems adding up the items as the ability to add numbers is not important in a computerized world.

Fifty years ago office workers could light a candle during a power failure and continue working. Today, we might just as well go home in such a situation. To some extent our reliance on technology may be seen as a danger. However, the fact that we allow technology to have such an influence on our everyday life and our organizations may be a demonstration of the fact that we trust the systems to work correctly, at least most of the time. In life-critical situations the probability of a hardware breakdown can be reduced by using redundant systems, perhaps using as many as three computers so that we will know which machine to ignore when the results differ.

Centralization of processing offers effective solutions, but may have dramatic consequences in error situations.

Errors are a part of using technology, and will be reflected in lost time, service costs, and in lost efficiency when we are not able to work as planned. In error situations the capacity of modern technology is a two-edged sword. In Norway centralized banking transaction systems offer an efficient infrastructure, but a large number of customers were affected for a whole week during the summer of 2001 when the system was down due to human errors after installing new disk units. In 1990, a programming error caused a major service outage on the AT&T U.S. National Telephone Network. This was probably the outage that affected most customers since the invention of the telephone. We see that modern technology may make the systems efficient, but the consequences of serious errors are much greater than in the simpler, distributed systems that they replaced.[12]

Errors in Web systems are frequent. For example, few systems check that all parts are up and running before presenting the input forms to the user. Often we find that only the input part is functional, allowing us to enter all data before we get an error message that tells us that our transaction cannot be stored due to an unavailable database. Most users would never have accepted a similar lack of service in the physical world or on the telephone, but we seem to blame ourselves when companies offer us error-prone Web systems.

3.5 Malicious attacks

Earlier, in the childhood of computing, unreliable hardware was a serious problem. However, at that time nobody even had the intention of performing malicious attacks on computer systems. Today the latter is a serious problem. While these attacks may come in many forms the most serious for ordinary PC users are the viruses. A virus is a computer program that may be stored, or store itself on your computer. When started it may do everything from giving you a "have a happy day" screen message to destroying everything on your hard disk. It is called a virus since it may be spread from computer to computer on the Internet, in much the same way a virus is spread from crop to crop, or from human to human.

Viruses exploit unprepared users or loopholes in mail systems, browsers, or operating systems. The virus may be activated by a user that clicks on the wrong attachment or visits the wrong Web page. However, it is quite a dangerous situation when a virus attack is only a click away. Open the wrong attachment and your hard disks may be destroyed, your mail system may be clogged down and personal files may be sent to others. In other situations the virus may use flaws in the underlying software to be able to infect your machine with malicious programs. In many ways viruses exploit the formalism and standardization that exist today. For example, when nearly everybody uses Microsoft Outlook as an email program, we get a common infrastructure that can be exploited, very similar to the real world where bugs exploit large fields with the same crop.

The functionality offered by modern operating systems is a part of the problem. Not only do they allow programs to set system parameters but they have also opened themselves to the Internet. In most cases this is to the benefit of the user, making it easier to install new programs or new components. But, this also offers a way for a virus to infect and damage a machine.

Simple means of protection are to keep operating systems updated at all times, something which in practice demand a good Internet connection, which also increases the probability of being attacked. Antivirus programs that scan all incoming data to see if they contain the code patterns of known viruses are a must if your computer is on the net. However, these need continuous updates to work effectively. To avoid being affected through the browser we can set this to the highest security level, restricting the functionality to a minimum, but will then probably not be able to use a large set of services that requires some control over our system in order to work properly. That is, if we bolt the door we can keep thieves away, but may also restrict access for others. We can further protect transmissions by cryptography and certificates that tell who we are and that give us control, as to who we have at the other end. Such systems are used today for most critical applications, for example, for monetary transactions.

Not everyone has installed virus protection programs, or has not updated these or the operating system code frequently enough. When nonprotected computers are connected to the Internet, they will assist in propagating viruses, just as people without the necessary vaccines in the real world. Perhaps we need a system of "health certificates," where one needs a clear bill before a computer can be connected to the local ISP, where the ISP needs a clear bill before the servers can be connected, etc.

Hacking and virus may be used as a **weapon** against cultures, countries, or organizations.

Attacks on our systems, whether they are physical or virtual, make us move toward a more **closed society**, with locks, limited access, control points, etc.

The seriousness of virus attacks has not been foreseen. System development has been focused on positive and open functionality, making efficient systems where everything is possible. For example, a philosophy for the last versions of operating systems has been to move the desktop toward the world, to integrate network functionality to the point where there is no distinction between a file stored locally or on the network, if a computer is connected by wire or over a wireless system, and so forth. Perhaps we will see a step back in future versions, where there is a more clear distinction between the secure local world and the dangerous world beyond. As with crime in the physical world the greatest harm to mankind may be the indirect consequences that we have to leave the open systems and exchange these with more closed and proprietary systems.[13]

3.6   Maintenance

Technology, both hardware and software, needs **maintenance** that may be expensive both in time lost and in direct costs.

While it is easy to focus on functions and be amazed by the specifications when buying a new electronic device, we should note that technology comes at a price that is much higher than what we pay in the store. Maintenance of a simple home computer can be both expensive and time-consuming. Portable equipment needs recharging or new batteries. Displays, disks, mice, and keyboards do not last forever. Many users are astonished the day the disk drive makes funny noises, and crestfallen when they find that data is no longer accessible, even if it is just a question of *when* this will happen, not *if*.

Software also needs to be maintained. There are few PCs where everything is working as it should. While the installment process of new products and versions has become simpler with modern operating systems, we often experience unwanted results. The new program may not work on our system, it may need a newer version of the operating system, and if it works, we may experience that it is no longer possible to start other programs. The reason may be that the new program comes with common software components that other applications do not accept.

The problem of software incompatibility will increase as we use more devices, laptops, PDAs, etc., that need to communicate, for example, to synchronize data. The problem may be solved if we are willing to replace all our devices at the same time, for example, by having the same version of the operating system on both the office computer and the laptop, and get a

PDA that can interface to this system. However, this may be expensive and we may end up with incompatible systems that are no longer able to communicate with each other. The more devices the more administrative work to keep them all up and running.

Many technical problems arise from **incompatibility**, between different versions of a system or between systems.

While operating systems may present a version problem, we have a format problem with data. This is seldom a big problem when we go from one version to the next, as new programs usually have the ability to read and convert older formats. However, for most users the data stored on 8" and 5" diskettes are no longer accessible. Document formats only from a few years back may be impossible to import to the current version of the system. Today, we have a myriad of storage devices, zip drives, jax drives, USB keys,[14] CDs, DVDs, videodisks, and many different kinds of solid state memory. The Beta format of videocassettes is forgotten, the VHS tape standard (with different formats, NTSC, PAL, etc.) may be replaced by DVDs, which may be replaced by high-definition DVDs, and so forth. While I can go through the paper pictures taken by my great-grandfather a hundred years ago, probably no one will be able to see my videos or digital pictures in a hundred years, perhaps not even in ten. That will occur if one does not take the time to convert into the new media before the old disappears. A printout on a typical ink jet printer will be to no avail, as the ink will fade in only a few years' time.[15]

3.7 Scalability

Scalability, offering service to everyone independent of the number of users, is a problem on the Web where the whole world is full of potential users.

Client-server systems allow us to compute fairly accurately the resources needed for a system to give adequate response times, by taking into account the number of users and the resources they will need from the server. This is very difficult on the Web, where there are an unlimited number of potential users. In peak situations, during ordinary office hours, or for example in the pre-Christmas period for an online store, we may experience service deterioration, where the numbers of requests are more than servers and networks can handle.[16] Some systems manage this situation by limiting access, at least letting some users get their request through, like having a queue of customers outside the store, while other systems admit everyone with the consequence of lowering throughput as most system resources are consumed in handling the queues. A sluggish Web system is often worse than no system, as so many

Web processes demand good response times to function. This is the case for browsing, searching or for all processes that have to be performed in many steps, such as booking an airline ticket.

While some argue that the Internet is too slow for eBusiness, we may hope that new technology can keep abreast of the bandwidth needs. Fiber optic technology will offer increased bandwidth and faster routers (net switching devices), developments in software and hardware support scalability of sites, making it easier to adjust demand and resources.[17] Servers may be geographically distributed, allowing for splitting up the workload, and offering systems that are robust with regard to failure in parts of the network. Rush hour traffic will come at different hours around the world and may differ from company to company. Some may even have a slack around Christmas time, and free server capacity may be sold or lent to others. Users may learn to do their heavier Web work outside rush hours, and will be able to do their transactions faster and more accurately as user interfaces get better and as they get more experience.

*New technology gives us more powerful servers and faster networks. This may give us **faster access**, if the additional resources are not consumed by new and resource-intensive functions.*

The danger is that content providers may offer data in new and more demanding formats, such as high quality sound and video, thus offsetting any capacity improvements that can be made. We may end up with a situation similar to the one we have on many roads, where the demand-capacity equation is balanced by the time we are willing to spend waiting.

3.8 Display quality

Display quality is improving, but can still not offer us the contrast, light weight, and flexibility of paper.

The quality of displays is an important factor for the success of many Internet applications. A computer display has inferior contrast and resolution to that of paper. Take a modern high quality display out in the sun and see the text disappear. Even in favorable conditions and with a good display, one will find that it is more tiring to read from the screen than from paper. A newspaper lets us see two big pages at a time, and we can spread the pages of a report over a desk, enabling us to see many pages simultaneously. Paper is lightweight compared to displays, and does not need batteries or a power connection, nor an expensive viewer.

Even if direct manipulation interfaces with scrollbars and previous/next buttons enable the user to flip to new pages with a button click, it is still not as easy as flipping through paper.

LCD displays have offered us portable viewers, with fairly low weight and reasonable resolution. But we are still far off from making displays or viewers that can compete with paper in resolution, size, weight, or contrast. The first versions of "electronic paper" that are coming out may have paper-like letter quality, but do not resemble paper in any other ways as they need a display device.

While we wait for the ideal viewer that manages to combine the advantages of both paper and electronic systems, the choice of medium will be based on cost-benefit functions. Today, creation of documents is performed on computers. The flexibility offered by word processing systems overcomes any disadvantage of the quality of displays. The direct and mechanical key to paper connection of the typewriter has been replaced by a flexible digital system. The binary digits produced by the keystrokes, a code for each character, can be stored temporarily in computer memory, permanently on disks, and viewed on a screen where the opposite conversion, binary digits to graphical symbols, is performed. The flexibility of displays retains the flexibility of bits in the computer, allowing easy editing and WYSIWYG[18] updates on the screen. The functionality of modern word processing systems allows us to go beyond characters, creating multimedia documents that include hypertext links, graphics, images, video, and sound as part of a document.

Until recently the end result from the word processor has often been a printout of the document, needed since dissemination was based on letters and fax. Today we see a change. Many of the documents that we produce are not converted to paper form; instead they are mailed as attachments to email messages or stored on the Web. In the end they may be printed on paper before they are read. However, dynamic documents can only exist in their full version online. In the paper version we find no hypertext links, no video or sound. Even for more traditional documents the electronic versions have advantages over their paper counterparts. Electronic documents can be edited, forwarded to others, stored on a disk, or subjected to automatic searching. The paper version does not offer the same flexibility. In some cases, however, this may be an advantage, such as for copyright protection or a signature.

Computer programmers were always heavy paper users. We used to joke about the prophecies of the "paperless society," among the piles of program printouts in our offices. Even

*The promised **paperless society** is still far off, but displays are competing with paper in areas where the electronic medium offers other advantages.*

*The Internet makes **electronic distribution** of documents easy.*

*If we can avoid the paper printout and read the document on the **screen**, we can utilize all the dynamic features, such as searching, hypertext, and animation.*

if the final program had to be represented as bits, we used paper and pencil to sketch, to write code, and for proofreading, and we printed a new clean paper copy of the program after every change. Today, programming is performed directly on the computer. The program editors are better, displays are larger and have increased resolution. Also we use tools, such as form layout programs and wizards that are only available online. The printouts no longer clutter a programmer's office.

Function	Paper representation	Bit representation
Reading	High quality.	Acceptable quality.
Presentation	Book, binder, sheets.	Computer display, projector.
Continuous update	Not easy.	Easy.
Links	Manual.	Automatic (hypertext).
Searching/retrieval	Manual, limited.	Automatic, on all attributes.
Storing	Manual, difficult for big collections.	Automatic, in practice, unlimited storage.
Copying	Semiautomatic, moderate costs.	Automatic, inexpensive down to zero costs.
Dissemination	Printing and mailing.	Over Internet or on CDs or other media.
Annotations by reader	Pencil, limited.	Typing, extensive.
Multimedia	No.	Yes.
Simulations, demos	No.	Yes.
Conversion to other media	No.	Yes (e.g., to print, graphics or sound).
Equipment needed	None.	Computer, display, power...
Competence needed	Basic reading skills.	Basic reading skills and computer proficiency.

Table 3.1 Advantages of paper versus bit representation.

Table 3.1 shows the advantages and disadvantages of paper and bit representation. Since the electronic medium has both pros and cons, we should expect that the effects are different for different types of documents. Today, we have seen that programming and typing are performed on the computer. Manuals are often disseminated and presented in a bit-format as all the bit-advantages favor online manuals. Online we can exploit multimedia presentation forms, easy updates, searching, hypertext links, dynamic examples, etc. For software manuals the disadvantage of using a computer is converted to an advantage. The user is already on the computer when help is needed—no additional equipment is required. For other manuals the unlimited storage capacity, the possibilities of simple updates, and excellent online search possibilities often make electronic dissemination the only choice.

3.9   Cost-benefit

Since technology comes at a cost we need **clear advantages** before going for a technical solution. These advantages are often found within a critical mass of data, computation or frequency of use.

As we can see, technology comes at a price that includes the initial cost of buying the equipment and training as well as recurring costs for maintenance, upgrades, and error handling. These costs vary with the complexity and the robustness of the technology, but as all computer users have experienced, nothing ever works smoothly. To compensate for these costs we need a real advantage in using the technology. For computer systems, the efficiency of automation and the improvement in quality are the important advantages. This is clearly linked to the frequency of use. All of us experience a beginner's problems when using a program or navigating a website. For a one-time user it may be a tedious process to book airline tickets online, while a frequent user will give the right commands immediately, having stored all profile data in the system, keeping abreast with updates and changes, and so forth.

For most applications we therefore have a *critical mass* of usage, before the cost-benefit equation balances. Most of us prefer a word processing system to pen and paper, a spreadsheet system to using a calculator (for complex calculations), and perhaps email to letters. Within business environments the data volumes are so huge that these critical masses can be obtained for most functions, and for some functions there are really no alternatives since only a computer can handle the huge transaction loads.

For private use the need for using an application may not be as strong. It is therefore a challenge to keep the cost side to a minimum. We need robust hardware that runs with a minimum of maintenance. We need operating systems that simplify installation of new software and that protect inexperienced users against making errors. We need systems that can reinstall themselves when errors occur. We need automatic backup systems so that we do not lose all documents, software, photos, etc., the day when the disk drive will not work. Most important, infrequent users need intuitive user interfaces.

In many areas a new application may fulfill a need. Word processing systems, spreadsheets, copiers, cell phones, and fax machines where embraced rapidly by businesses, even if they demanded new equipment and in some cases, also extensive training. However, in other cases the advantage of the new technology may not be so apparent. Ordinary TV to HDTV is an example that we have discussed earlier. Here many customers may find that the benefits are not great enough to defend the high costs of a replacement. We face a similar situation with cell phones, where most customers seems to be satisfied with the bandwidth that is offered with current digital systems, at least to the extent that most are not willing to pay the high costs of getting a faster service. So, functionality has to be improved if costs must be reduced. However, often the only way to reduce costs is to get many customers, thus this is really a question of finding the killer application.

SMS (Short Message Service) was an application that found itself. It uses existing and simple technology, but still creates important revenue for European telecommunication firms.

Finding killer applications is not easy. However, sometimes an application just emerges out of nothing. The SMS (Short Message Service), the ability to send short text messages between cell phones, has become enormously popular in Europe, and provides an important revenue base for the cell phone companies. This was the killer application that found itself, as nobody thought that customers would be willing to type these messages on numeric keypads.

In the simple case, a new technology has clear **advantages** for customers, for example, that it removes well-known drawbacks of existing technology. In other cases, the new technology offers functionality that has as yet not been experienced by customers.

To find the killer application for the promised broadband services we need to find something more sophisticated, probably something oriented toward multimedia. The telecom companies are already selling phones with cameras, and are trying to teach the customers to send picture messages as an enhancement of the simple SMS. With the resolution one has today these pictures can be sent without broadband. However, if customers embrace this technology the next step, toward high quality pictures and video clips, will be a natural one. The problem is that we now run into areas where few users have any expertise. How do we apply pictures in a useful way in everyday communication? In order to introduce the technology we will have to teach users how they can apply the new media (i.e., the companies have to create a *need*). This is time-consuming, expensive, and very risky. Further, the companies that create this new market have no guarantee that they are the ones that will reap the greatest benefits.

Since the first computers, the Colossus[19] and the Eniac,[20] we have seen enormous breakthroughs in technology. This has given us computers that are extremely powerful, fast, reliable, and so small that they can be made portable. Advances in network technology, routers, optical fibers, etc., make it possible to connect these computers, and let them work together in global networks. Still, in the quest for *killer applications*, we have a tendency to look toward futuristic technology, such as high bandwidth wireless networks or even further into the future, quantum computers—significantly more powerful than what we have today.

But the PC you can get from your local computer store for $1000 is already significantly more powerful than the million-dollar computers from the 1950s. That is, the technology for the killer applications should already be here. As we see, when the applications meet the real world, technology is only a small part of the success equation.

Waiting for the **next generation** of technology to get a killer application seems to be a bad excuse, what we have today is yesterday's next generation.

Exercises and Discussion

1. There is a common belief that everything can be invented, it is just a matter of the right economic incentives. Can you find a counter example of a product that would have been welcome, but that is not available today? As a starting point you may investigate the gadgets that you use, laptop, cell phones, etc. Is something missing?

2. Usability is an important issue, especially when more and more people are using computers. Can you find examples from the system you use, for example, Web systems, where it is difficult to find information, easy to make mistakes, or systems that demand excessive data?

3. Determine your "level of competency" in word processing from the table below, by finding the highest level that conform to the functionality that you have used.

Level	Competence	Examples
1	Typewriter	Type, error correction through backspace key.
2	Text editing	Type, select, cut, paste.
3	Simple layout	Page setup, portrait, landscape, adjust margins.
4	Checking	Use grammar and spell checker.
5	Tables and drawings	Can insert tables, make drawings.
6	Styles	Headers defined as header styles.
7	Advanced layout	Two-column format, text boxes.
8	Cross references	Dynamic references to figures, tables, sections.
9	Track changes	Track changes in a document.
10	Merging	Merging database and document.

Discuss how you can increase your level of competence. What do you think that the benefits may be? As an example consider the user that employs styles for headers instead of just increasing font size. Then the system will automatically create a table of contents, avoid putting a header at the bottom of the page, and guarantee that all headers follow the style chosen.

4. The following is an input field for a date in a Web user interface:

   Date: [＿＿＿＿＿＿] [mmddyy]

   This field requires a date in the specified format. Discuss the possibilities for errors. How can this interface be improved in order to reduce the possibility of an error?

5. The following is a part of a header from a flight booking system:

Departure from PIT to NYC (all airports) on Dec 12.

   How can this interface be improved?

Notes

1. KB, kilo byte, 1000 bytes, where a byte is eight binary digits, sufficient to hold an ASCII character.

2. We shall discuss wireless technology in more detail in chapter 13.

3. National Television System Committee (NTSC), a television standard first developed in the early fifties. Is today used in the United States, Canada, Japan and in many South American countries.

4. Phase Alternation by Line (PAL), adopted in 1967 and used mainly in Europe.

5. COBOL, formerly the most used programming language, has today been replaced by more modern, often object-oriented, languages.

6. A client-server system consist of a server, usually a powerful computer with large disks, and a set of connected clients (ordinary PCs). This gives us the advantages from both worlds, the flexibility and rapid response time from a local PC, and data and software sharing through the central server.

7. For a more detailed discussion of these issues see for example Dix, Finlay, Abowd, Beale (2003). *Human-Computer Interaction*, third edition, Prentice Hall Europe.

8. Scripts are discussed in detail in chapter 16.

9. Amazon (www.amazon.com) has, for example, excellent Web pages.

10. Using Microsoft Word, I inadvertently gave the "close" command instead of "print," and subsequently answered "no" to the "Do you want to save the changes you made to X" question (I did not want to save, I wanted to print), losing the last updates to my document. This standard question broke down in this context.

11. President's Commission. 1979. *Report of the President's Commission on the Accident at Three Mile Island.* New York: Pergamon Press.

12. On the other hand modern technology allows us to keep numerous copies of data at different locations, all updated to the last second. A disaster at one location may affect performance but may not result in loss of data.

13. The problem will then be to protect the systems from physical attacks, especially the high bandwidth systems that rely on cables. A cut with an axe in the right place may be enough to take out major communication channels, a bomb within a central telephone office could interrupt service for millions of lines.

14. The USB Key uses flash memory to replace floppy drives or CDs as temporary storage media. It can be inserted into the USB (Universal Serial Bus) slot of a computer, will come up as a disk, and can store from 16 to 1000 Mb. The device is so small that it can be connected to a key ring.

15. Use of special photo paper will prolong the lifetime of printouts.

16. In this infancy of online shopping an overloaded Web system may even be considered an advantage as it restricts the number of orders that can be received. As we have experienced, many online shops do not have the logistics system in place for filling even the orders that get through.

17. CNN had obviously a good plan for handling a crisis. On September 11, 2001, after the World Trade Center terrorist attack they managed to service all requests by removing all graphics from their sites, using all available servers to provide simple text-based news.

18. What You See Is What You Get (WYSIWYG).

19. A machine made by the Government Code and Cipher School, Bletchley Park, Bletchley, England during World War II, perhaps the world's first computer.

20. Developed by University of Pennsylvania, Philadelphia, under a secret project for the U.S. Army's Ballistics Research, often recognized as the world's first computer.

4 Cultural Constraints

Even if an application is within the constraints mentioned earlier, from formalism to technical consideration, there may be reasons why the application is not accepted in the marketplace. These may be based on:

- *Legal issues*, for example, that copyrights may belong to companies that use existing technologies.

- The problem of *critical mass*, the difficulty of moving everyone to a new technology. Some services require that all—or close to all—have access to the technology.

- *Social issues*, the new technology may be effective within some areas, but may have negative side effects, for example, that they reduce social interaction.

- New technology may force a change to existing *power structures.*

- *Knowledge and experience*, new technology may require new skills.

- *Conservatism*, users may be happy with the situation as it is and are often not willing to invest time and money in unknown technologies.

- *Threat to privacy*, the risk of losing data or that unauthorized persons can access personal data.

Each of these constraints is discussed in detail below. Some of these constraints are closely connected to the technological issues discussed in the previous chapter. For example, the skill requirement will very much depend on the user interface, but it is still valuable to look at these areas from a cultural and social point of view.

4.1 Copyright

Is it possible to maintain **copyright** in a digital world, where everybody has access to the dissemination technologies?

We have had recording devices for many years, tape machines, cassette recorders, and VCRs. Copying, however, was limited by getting access to the source material. The possibilities were either to copy from a broadcast signal, radio or TV, or to borrow the source from a friend. Analog medium also had the disadvantage that quality deteriorated for each new copy. This situation has changed in two respects. The Web now acts as a source for all types of material. Here one can find an abundance of music files, but also books and whole movies. Secondly, what we get from the Web is in digitized formats, where the copying process can be performed without quality reduction. That is, the sound quality of a piece of music retrieved from the Web can be as good as on the CD that we bought in the store for $15.

The copyright owners see copying from the Web as an infringement on their rights and are fighting numerous battles in the courts. To date they have won several, but they may be losing the war. This is like a Norwegian *Troll*. If one managed to cut off its head, three more would grow out. Today, the big battle is about music; tomorrow it may be about movies or textbooks.

The record industry, the publishers, and movie distributors have built their business models and attained market shares based on their ownership of the technology. When the technology becomes available to all it is difficult to see how they can retain their central position of control. Of course, record companies and publishing houses offer more than just the printing press, they select products to publish, give advice, perform marketing, pay contributors, etc. However, in order to perform these tasks they need revenue from the products that is significantly higher than the price of making and distributing a new copy, thus offering the incentive for pirate copies. We shall present case studies related to these issues in chapter 22.

4.2 Critical mass problem

Many applications do not become efficient before they have reached a **critical mass**, while others demand that nearly all have installed the technology.

The owner of the very first telephone had no one to call. The telephone, like email and many other communication technologies, needs a critical mass of users before becoming efficient.[1] Email has a history of thirty years, and has become the main communication channel for many groups. IT-related academia and industry have been the pioneers. In these fields everyone has had a PC, a network connection, and the skills needed for decades. They use their computer on a daily basis and we can expect that they look into their email account at least once a day. To use myself as an example, I sent my first email in the late 1970s. Today, Internet is my one important communication channel, phone and letters are of secondary value.

Other areas of business are advancing into email as well. Today, we expect that airlines, travel agencies, and newspapers can be contacted using email, but cannot be sure that the plumber, electrician, local garage, even our insurance company or bank, will have an email account and read their mail regularly. Many firms still use telephone and fax where it would be far more efficient to use email. But each of these faces the same problem. Email first becomes efficient when all or at least a large part of their suppliers and customers use this medium. Until then many seem to view email communication as an add-on, and do not establish good routines for handling this form of communication. We face the same problem for private communication. Should we call, send a letter, or write an email? A letter can reach everybody, but an email will only reach those who have an email account and who look into this account regularly.

The applications of the future are here **now**!

An electronic bank may solve this problem by only offering service to customers that have an email account and who are willing to communicate electronically. This is more difficult for public organizations that are there to serve the whole population. Email can be offered as an alternative input/output channel, but a public organization cannot require that everybody use the electronic media. For this reason we may never see Web-based elections for state officials. Even if alternatives were provided for those without an Internet connection, it could be seen as undemocratic that parts of the population had easier access to the voting system than others. In addition, there is the problem of maintaining security, avoiding hackers, and denial-of-access.

In his 1999 book, *Business @ the Speed of Thought*,[2] Bill Gates tells us how we can succeed in the digital economy. Yes, he talks about new and interesting applications, but one of his points is that we should try to utilize email, this more than thirty-year-old application. Bill Gates is correct; email is an important tool for many businesses. It is important as an inter-business tool, but has interesting applications in contact with ordinary customers. Here it is already replacing other media such as telephone, fax, and paper-based mail. As we shall see in chapter 7, email has tremendous advantages in many areas. Even then, it shows how difficult it is to get a new technology accepted and used by a majority.

4.3 Social factors

Media may also be characterized by an open-closed taxonomy.

Humans are social animals. We work and live in close contact with others. While virtual contacts can replace some parts of face-to-face meeting, they clearly cannot replace all.

If we sort different communication methods along a continuum from closed to open, we will find forms (e.g., on the Web) at one end and personal contact at the other, with email, telephone, and videoconferencing in between. While email is an efficient medium, it is not open for socializing in the same way as a telephone. That is, if we rely only on email for contact with customers we may lose the personal strings that may be important in many contexts. In some situations this may be an advantage (i.e., where efficiency is of primary importance). In other situations it may be a disadvantage since close relations with customers may be needed to convey trust, to handle exceptions and complicated situations, and so forth. We acknowledge the merit of different media when we use a Web form to order a movie ticket, use email to send a complaint to a company, send a birthday card through the post, the telephone to discuss which restaurant to go to, and meet personally for a job interview.

Can a **videoconference** replace physical meetings?

Even a videoconference, where sound, images, and documents can be conveyed over the channel, is far from a face-to-face meeting. To some extent this is due to limitations in the technology. In most videoconferences we can see and hear the person talking, but we do not see what effect the words have on all the other participants. Are they shaking their head, nodding, are they bored or enthusiastic? This may change with more bandwidth, more cameras and larger displays. Still, a videoconference may not provide the options to talk off the record and socialize that we have at physical meetings.

The limitation of virtual media, compared to face-to-face meetings, may not always be a constraint. In some situations we can utilize these constraints for our own purposes. For example, in the virtual world users can choose their own personality and acquire skills that would have been impossible to get in the physical world. In the virtual world we can start again, without all our handicaps. We can be stronger, smarter, prettier, younger, and swifter in the virtual world. Today, we see that these possibilities are exploited by providers of sex telephones, as well as by developers of Internet games.

4.4 Power structures

The incumbent record industry was not the pioneer in using the Web for distributing music, neither were the existing bookstores, banks, or travel agencies the first with Web solutions. The reason was, of course, that they were happy with the situation as it was. The "Player Piano" environment described by Kurt Vonnegut,[3] where everybody was eager to invent new technologies that made them jobless, is science fiction. In the real world many of us are not very willing to adopt technologies that turn our world upside down. But there are always techno-pioneers that invent and utilize new technology and sometimes we are forced to accept change.

New technology offers an **opportunity** for start-ups.

The turbulence in the computer industry, with newcomers driving away strong incumbents, shows that it is not so easy to control these new technologies. IBM, once in control both of computer hardware and software, has been forced to give the leader's jersey to others. In opposition to many industries that rely on land, natural resources, or large plants, a symbolic industry, such as the computer software industry or even parts of the hardware industry, can start in a garage. On the other hand the possibility to retain power within these industries is less than in many others. The music industry may try to resist customers using the Web as a source of material, but this is a technology change that they do not control. Moving from CDs to the Web is not comparable to moving from LPs to CDs. CDs (or DVDs) represent a technological change that is clearly within the business and market models of the record industry. The Web, however, is what is called a *disruptive* technology, a technology change that cannot easily be absorbed within the existing structure of a business. Business may resist such changes, but will in the end often be forced to accept the new technology. We shall return to these issues in part 5.

The global economy is an accelerator for these changes. If unions are reluctant to accept new technology and layoffs that may come as a result, there is always the argument that the competitors will do it, perhaps in another country. The shop owner that earlier enjoyed a monopoly in his hometown, now faces competition from Internet stores. The European Union has simplified customs between their member countries. Together with the Euro, the common European currency, this increases competition over national boundaries in Europe. If one wants to be in control, global control is often the only answer.

4.5 Conservatism

There are **eager beavers** that will try any new gadgets, as well as **technically adverse** that will never move to the new technology.

Acquiring and using new gadgets is a way of expressing that we are "in" and trendy. We will therefore always have a group that gets the latest designer cell phone, PDA, or any other device. However, at the other end we find a group of more conservative users that are satisfied with things as they are and are not willing to use time and money to get something new, even when the new technology proves itself superior to the old. For service providers, this implies that it is difficult to phase out older technology and ways of doing business based on this technology. Analog telephone will be here for many years to come, as will music cassettes. Years will go by before the last check is written, and even then many people will never come online. So while new technology and new services are introduced at a record-breaking pace, the older technology will take much longer to disappear. Some services and devices will not go before their users go. In the computer industry, magnetic tape was supposed to meet its demise twenty years ago but it is still a prime backup and data transmission media.

Conservatism in technology may be based on sound principles. "If it ain't broke don't fix it" tells us that the value of something that works reliably is very high. The new technology may be better, but has not proven itself over years of usage. There may be unknown problems that occur when we try to implement the new systems, connect them to other systems, or when some users complain that they don't get the functionality that they were used to. We shall return to some of these problems in later chapters.

4.6 Privacy and security

In chapter 3 we discussed exception situations due to faults with hardware, software, or the way systems were used. As long as systems were stand-alone or connected over private networks this discussion of exceptions was complete. However, with the open Internet a new kind of situation has arrived; that of malicious attacks on the integrity of computer systems—designed to destroy data, to steal computer power, or to take down networks or other systems by overloading channels.

Hacking relies on the openness of the Internet and the Web, but forces the systems in the opposite direction, toward more closed environments.

Some attacks may be performed by technically oriented hackers to show what they are able to do, and have often very limited consequences. Still, in many ways these hackers harass the very openness of the Internet and the software platforms that they so heavily rely on. Well-known institutions, such as the FBI and Microsoft, are prime targets. Hacking these sites not only guarantees publicity, but also proves hacking proficiency, thus creating an interesting loop of negative feedback, the more security the higher the gains of breaking into the site.[4] Since negative publicity is expensive, these institutions need a secure system that does not allow anybody to tamper with their site, or the sites of their employees. For institutions such as banks or hospitals, the consequences of unauthorized persons getting access to data are so serious that security is a primary concern, in the virtual world just as in the physical. To establish trust, these security concerns go well beyond protecting confidential data since even the hacking of rather harmless Web pages can reduce customer confidence.

As in the physical world, mono-cultures open for **virus** attacks. The standardization we have for operating systems, Web browsers, and mail programs makes it easier for computer viruses to multiply and spread.

We have seen that viruses, often transmitted as attachments to email messages, are a serious problem. Even when no data is lost, it is quite embarrassing, also a violation of privacy, when all our contacts understand that we opened the "I love you" attachment immediately as it was received. A virus may also install software on your system that monitors all activities. In the worst case such programs may discover user names and passwords; in other cases it is to report statistics to their mother site that can be used for marketing.

Just as with hacking some may send innocent *viruses* for "fun," but other may have a clearer political agenda (e.g., to attack a company, the western world, or the U.S. economy) or economic agenda, for example, to exploit the victim's computer resources in order to send spam messages.[5] To a certain degree this form of symbolic warfare was possible even with the older technology, by use of telephone, fax, or letter. However, these action forms had a democratic nature, as one needed many collaborators to block the switchboard of a company or state agency or to overwhelm a senator with mail. Today, only one person armed with a computer and the right software can do this. More dangerously, it is now possible to attack internal systems without using physical force, from a secure position far from the point of attack. This form of warfare is undemocratic in yet another respect. That is, major companies and institutions often have the know-how available to set up adequate protection against virus attacks. Small companies and inexperienced users are therefore often hit harder by the viruses that are globally disseminated.

"**Big-brother**" may be implemented without technology (Gestapo, Sadam's Iraq).

Crime would be much more difficult to perform in a **cash-free** society.

Not much can be learnt from automatic **supervision** of email messages and other transmission channels, there is a large discrepancy between words and their meaning and intention.

From the very first advent of computers there have been warnings that these can be used to control ordinary citizens. With many types of data in electronic form and powerful processors it becomes practically possible for governments to scrutinize email, follow electronic funds, keep registers, etc. While this is absolutely true we should remember that the German secret police, the Gestapo, was able to control both their citizens and those of occupied countries during World War II, without computers. That is, the threat of misuse of power is independent of technology.

Tracing electronic money can be very useful in the fight against crime and tax evasion, especially as we move toward less use of cash. In not so many years, with POS (Point of Sale) terminals in every store and when most of us use plastic cards for payment, there is the possibility of a society without cash. For practical purposes we may keep the small change for buying a candy bar or newspaper or for a tip, but all larger amounts may be paid electronically. Governments can enforce this by putting a fee on cash transactions, or requiring that all large cash deposits or withdrawals be reported to tax agencies. While this will not give full control over the black part of the economy, one can make it very difficult to use money earned here. Such a system will clearly reduce financial crime and tax evasion, but will at the same time reduce some of the freedom we have to use money without being traced. However, as with all other security measures we have to find a balance between control and privacy. For ordinary law-abiding citizens who have their tax deducted directly from their income, a cash-less society may have only advantages.

Electronic supervision may also be used to find criminals and terrorists. However, the belief in automatic supervision methods of email and telephone seems pretty naive. As we shall see in chapter 10 (Searching the Web), an automatic program cannot grasp the meaning of a text. Instead, one has to rely on the occurrence of words. But ordinary citizens may use words such as "murder," "attack," and "bomb" in their messages, and smart criminals can so easily use code, for example, by replacing dangerous words by the more innocent. An action plan can then be covered as a discussion of football results, a cryptographic message can be hidden within an innocent budget, etc. The law enforcing agencies may get a lot of data by studying who's calling who, data that can be collected by automatic methods. However, the new technologies have also offered new possibilities for the criminals. Messages can be hidden within spam mail. It can be distributed to millions as an advertisement, even if it is only meant for a few—the persons that have the ability to decode the message.

4.7 Conclusion

We have discussed some of the cultural constraints that slow down the advance of new technological applications. The idea here has been that the introduction of new technology into the real world is more than just a question of technical possibilities and functionality.

Exercises and Discussion

1. Discuss why record companies are working so hard to protect their copyright today. What has changed in the last twenty years?

2. In addition to face-to-face communication, what other forms of communication are you using? Think about the last communication you initiated, what media were used? Were there other options, and if so, why did you choose this particular method?

3. Discuss what kind of data is stored about an average citizen in different computer systems. In what respects can these data be considered harmful? How can we protect ourselves?

4. Discuss the idea of a cash-less society, a society where all monetary transaction go electronic by the use of Internet and bank cards. What will happen to crime? Are there transactions that will be awkward without cash, or are there technological solutions for these as well? What will the advantages and disadvantages be for the average citizen?

Notes

1. The usefulness of a communication device is often calculated as the square of the number of users in the network.

2. Bill Gates with Colin Hemingway. 1999. *Business @ the Speed of Thought, succeeding in the digital economy*, Warner Books.

3. Kurt Vonnegut. 1952. *Player Piano*, MacMillan.

4. There exists "brag-walls" on the Web where hackers can post screen shots of their successes.

5. The word "spam" comes from a canned meat product, and was perhaps given its new meaning when a Usenet-reader reacted negatively to a commercial launched on all Usenet services in 1994 by asking everybody to "send coconuts and cans of Spam" to the company involved. The word was also used in a Monthy Python sketch where a group of Vikings interrupted the story by singing "spam, spam, spam, spam, spam, spam, lovely spam!"

PART 2
Internet and
WWW

While we discussed fundamentals in the previous part we shall here discuss the underlying technology for the Internet and the Web. Internet protocols, the standards that are used to let computers communicate over the Internet, are discussed in chapter 5. In chapter 6 we present the basic Web standards, HTML for describing a layout of a Web page, and HTTP for transmitting these pages between computers. While these chapters are somewhat technical, an understanding of the basic concepts is needed: in order to see the possibilities, the limitations and, as important, to avoid being overrun by experts and their jargon.

We shall then present a set of interesting applications, and study what ramifications these will have; email in chapter 7, Web browsers in chapter 8, and the World Wide Web itself in chapter 9. We continue with a presentation of Web searching in chapter 10, where we introduce important concepts such as precision and recall, and discuss problems of information overload and filtering.

In chapter 11 we discuss portals, or how we can develop an index for the Web that can be of aid in helping us to satisfy an information need. This problem is discussed from the opposite side in chapter 12 (i.e., how we can be visible on the Web, promoting a Web site). The ideal of a democratic Web where everyone can be a publisher is not so easy to implement in practice, as it is not easy to be "seen" among billons of other Web pages, some of which are heavily marketed through other media.

Will the world of computing change when we go wireless, with mobile computing? We discuss these issues in chapter 13, along with a presentation of these new technologies. Will the problem of usability go away if we implement automated solutions where Web pages push information to the user? We discuss this technology in chapter 14. In chapter 15 and 16 we go into details on more advanced topics such as dynamic Web pages and embedded scripts. These chapters are also somewhat technical, but they explain how the more advanced Web pages are developed (e.g., pages that allow for user input through fill-in forms).

We end this part by giving an introduction to peer-to-peer computing in chapter 17. This technique exploits the unstructured Internet, and creates networks where all participants are equal. Peer-to-peer computing opens for new and interesting applications, for example, file sharing.

5 Internet Protocols

A **protocol** is used to administer communication processes.

Communication is controlled by protocols. On a simple radio system this may be performed by simple keywords such as "Roger," "Over," "Out," etc. Computer transmissions need more elaborate systems, but the idea is the same. Machine A tells B that it wants to send a message. After the initial "handshake" process where contact is established, the message may be sent, most often divided into convenient packets. Packets have a header that includes address, number of bytes, and additional data that B can use to determine if the package was successfully received.[1] If there are errors B can ask A to retransmit the package, or A will do this automatically if it does not get confirmation from B that the message was received.

Divide-and-conquer, on the Internet messages are split into small and simple packets that are sent individually through the network.

The Internet is a packet-switched network (really a *collection* of networks with a set of protocol standards). Messages are converted into a number of fixed-size packages that can be transmitted over the network. This strategy is typical within all computing applications; complex objects are divided into smaller and handier objects. For example, if we get a transmission error within a packet, only this packet must be retransmitted, not the complete file. The drawback is that the system must be able to handle a large number of objects (i.e., many packages instead of a few files), but high volumes of simple objects do not constitute a problem for modern communication technology.

The important part of the Internet is the open, **standardized protocols**.

The Internet uses an addressing protocol called IP, Internet Protocol. This protocol is used to provide the routing function for the package transmitted across the networks. This implies that the IP protocol not only has to be part of the end systems, but also of the intermediate *routers*. A router is a computer that connects two networks, receiving packets from the one and transmitting them on to the other.

The IP header has a 32-bit source and destination address, in addition to other parameters. That is, the Internet address is defined in a number that can hold 32 binary digits. In theory this can be used to identify more than four billion Internet addresses. At the time the protocol was designed, this was thought to be more than enough, however, due to the explosive growth of the Internet 32 bits is becoming insufficient to address all machines in the network. A new standard, known as IP6, has therefore been developed, offering 128 bits for both the source and destination addresses.

The 32-bit IP address is usually presented in a format called dotted decimal notation, for example, as 158.38.10.00. This address identifies the networks and the hosts, in a hierarchical addressing scheme. Numeric IP addresses are acceptable for computers, but not for human beings. A textual address was therefore introduced, and a name server (a table of network servers) is then used to translate this name into the numeric IP address. Names are organized into domains indicated by a suffix, for example:

With a 32-bit number the **IP addressing** scheme uniquely addresses any computer on the net.

- *com*, for commercial organizations
- *edu*, domain name for U.S educational institutions
- *no*, the Norwegian domain
- *org*, domain name for nonprofit organizations

Name servers map the numeric and computer-oriented IP address into a format that is better suited for humans, and vice versa.

Domains[2] are organized hierarchically. On the next level *pitt.edu* is the domain name for University of Pittsburgh, *uib.no* for University of Bergen (Norway) and *ibm.com* for IBM. On the bottom level of this naming tree, individual hosts are assigned Internet addresses. A "table," called a DNS—domain name server, will perform the name to IP address translation. This DNS is distributed via the Internet.

When an email is sent the local host will query the local domain name server for the IP address corresponding to the name, the email address. If the name is known at this level the IP address is returned, otherwise the name server queries other available name servers, until the address is found.

| Application layer |
| Transport layer |
| Internet layer |
| Network access protocol |
| Physical layer |

Figure 5.1 The TCP/IP layered architecture.

Layered architectures are used to simplify the complexity of the communication protocols.

The communication task is organized into a layered architecture, as shown in figure 5.1. On the bottom layer we find the physical connection, the twisted pair (telephone), coax, optical, or wireless communication lines. The network access protocol, the next layer, handles the connection between the computer and the network.[3] The transport layer, here consisting of the TCP (Transmission Control Protocol), built on top of the Internet layer with its IP addressing scheme, will split messages into packets and offer reliable interchange of data between hosts, including error checking and retransmitting of lost packets.

If this sounds complex you are right. It is! On the top level we want to send email and access Web pages. On the bottom level we may have a simple twisted pair wire, for example, a telephone line. The gap is too wide. So, in order to simplify we define these layers, where every layer performs part of the job. As ordinary users, however, we seldom have to think about the lower levels.

While the Internet and Web technologies introduce their own standards they rely on **accepted standards** for the underlying levels, such as TCP.

While there are many protocols for data transmission the great advantage of TCP is that it has been generally *accepted*. Virtually all operating systems can read and create TCP packages. This standard is one of the foundations of the global acceptance and use of the Internet. With TCP data is put into packages, each of which is assigned a TCP header. The header gives the address of the source and destination, the sequence number of the packet, a checksum, and several other bits of control information. The sequence number is used by the receiver, to acknowledge the receipt of the package and to check that all packages are received. Note that TCP does not guarantee that packets are received in sequence. Packets may take different routes through the network, and may appear out of order. This is fixed by the destination machine that organizes packages in accordance with the sequence number before these are presented to the user application (e.g., a browser or an email system).

Finally, we have the application layer that provides support for the various user applications. Several applications have been standardized to work on top of TCP/IP, among them:

New standards can easily be built on top of TCP/IP, allowing us to send email with or without attachments, retrieve Web pages, etc.

- Simple Mail Transfer Protocol (SMTP)
- File Transfer Protocol (FTP)
- Internet Message Access Protocol (IMAP)
- Multipurpose Internet Mail Extensions (MIME)
- Hypertext Transfer Protocol (HTTP)

SMTP provides a basic protocol for the exchange of email messages, FTP is directed toward file transfer between machines (using commands such as GET <file> or POST <file>), IMAP allows a client to access and manipulate electronic mail messages on a server and MIME allows for "complex message bodies," enclosing files, graphics, audio clips, etc.[4] HTTP is the protocol for transmitting Web pages (to be discussed in the next chapter). As seen each of these application protocols serves a special purpose, as mail or file transfer, but they all use TCP/IP as the foundation for carrying out their task.

Such layered architectures are used in all areas of computing. The idea is to capture and isolate the characteristics of each level. For example, there are many different types of networks and different types of low-level protocols. Since this information is isolated within the network layer, the transportation layer can work independently of this lower layer, if the interface between these two layers is standardized. The transportation layer will then build a package, including header information, and ask the network layer to do the transmission job. On top of the transportation layer we find the application layer that consists of email systems, Web browsers, etc. These applications will use the transport layer to transmit messages, using higher-level protocols that include the requirements of the application program.

Another way to view the layered protocol architecture is to see it as different levels of formalization. The physical layer operates with electromagnetic signals, the network layer understands terms such as packets and machine addresses, the transport layer understands terms such as *file*, and the email program understands concepts such as email addresses, messages, and attachments. The word *understands* is used on purpose since the protocols really have a conceptual understanding of these concepts that allows them to handle the objects in very different ways. For example a good email system can filter messages, send automatic replies, handle attachments or archive messages manually or automatically, and perform actions such as forward and reply.

A layered architecture implies the idea of formalization on **different levels**, from physical signals to email messages.

The email system will define a message as a document, for example, a sequence of characters, with a header. The header includes the address of the receiver, of the sender, a subject field, and other information. Some of this information is provided by the user, as shown in the example in figure 5.2, other data is collected by the email system from information given at setup time.

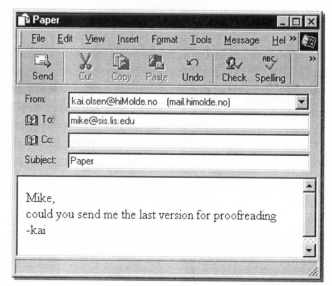

Figure 5.2 An email message (example) as shown in Microsoft Outlook.

The email system will pack the header and content information into a package defined by the SMTP protocol. The sender will then open a TCP connection to the receiving machine, expecting an acknowledgement that the receiver is ready. The message itself is sent using a MAIL command to identify the originator of the message, one or more RCPT-commands that identify the receivers and a DATA-command to transmit the actual message text. The destination address includes the textual IP address of the receiving mail server. This keeps track of all accounts at (@) the server. For example, the mail server identified by *mail.himolde.no* recognizes the account *kai.olsen*.

On top of all the layers we find the **user layer**, where concepts and protocols are defined socially.

Note that the conceptual understanding of a message by the email system does not include the content of the message. If we replaced the text in figure 5.2 above with "tjbjhj hnjhn" it would still be a message for the email system (if the email system has a spelling checker, this would state that the words are not in the dictionary). The writing and reading of messages is therefore performed on a higher layer, a *top layer* or *user layer*. This layer also has its protocols, but these are not formalized to the same extent as on the other layers. I may sign my messages as above, but it will be no problem if I forget, since the email system will include my email address in the information sent to the receiver. I can include a title, leave it out or, if I reply to an incoming message I can let the system retain the title text. In a long conversation, the original title will often still be used, even if the conversation has moved to new topics. Not really a problem, since human beings rely on context information to understand a message. Out of context, however, many email messages may be incomprehensible.

Modern email systems rely on the MIME protocol. The purpose of MIME is to address limitations in SMTP. Most important, MIME enables the user to attach files of different types to email messages, for example, text-, image-, audio-, and video-files. For communication MIME has been a very important step forward, as we shall see in chapter 7.

A drawback of the current mail protocols is that they do not give adequate protection. It is, for example, quite easy to forge the senders address. We see examples of this in many spam messages.

Exercises and Discussion

1. As an exercise get your own IP address at http://www.lawrencegoetz.com/programs/ipinfo/.

2. Protocols also exist in everyday life. Try to set down a simple description of the protocol that we use when having a telephone conversation. It will be less formal than computer protocols, but it is still important to follow the "rules." Discuss.

3. For very many years it has been possible to buy a stamp anywhere in the world, put it on a letter and mail it to any place. Go to the Internet and see if you can find any historical data on the work that lay behind this universal postal standard for international mail.

4. Discuss the importance of international standards for communication.

Notes

1. A simple mechanism is to add up all the data in the packet, using the underlying data codes as numbers, and store this "checksum" in the packet. The receiver can then perform the same calculation and compare results to the checksum. If the two are identical there is a high probability that the received packet is correct.

2. IP address space allocation, protocol parameter assignment, domain name system management, and root server system management functions are today handled by the non-profit corporation ICANN (The Internet Corporation for Assigned Names and Numbers).

3. This may be implemented with protocol standards such as X.25 (packet switching) or Ethernet (for local area networks).

4. For a more detailed review, see Connected: An Internet Encyclopedia, http://www.freesoft.org/CIE/

6 Development of Web Protocols

On the Web everybody was intended to be an **information-provider** as well as consumer.

Tim Berners-Lee first developed the World Wide Web as an Intranet for CERN, the European Center for Particle Physics.[1] His idea was to implement a system which allowed researchers at CERN to exchange scientific documents, allowing everybody to publish as well as to retrieve documents from the Web. He developed the Hypertext Markup Language (HTML) to capture the layout of documents in a standardized format, independent of the word processors or editors that were used to create the document. HTML is based on the Standard Generalized Markup Language (SGML).[2]

Berners-Lee based his development of these standards and the first software on a set of basic ideas:

- *Simplicity*. It should be easy to create Web pages, and to implement the browsers needed for retrieving, presenting, and creating pages.

- *Hypertext*. The page structure and connections should be based on links embedded in the text, where the user could go to another page just by clicking on this hypertext link.

- *Everybody* should be able to create Web pages (i.e., very different from other media such as TV or newspapers where the creative part is for the few).

- *Universal*. The Web should be a universal system, open for everybody everywhere.

- *Distributed*. There should only be a limited need for centralization.

The most important feature of HTML is its **simplicity**.

He worked hard to propagate these ideas, especially to have the developers of browsers include editing functions. Hypertext was the important foundation for his ideas about the Web. Initially, Berners-Lee distinguished between internal and external links. Later, he saw that this was more a technical than a fundamental distinction, and a general link scheme was adopted. Today, we see that Microsoft follows the same path in new releases of their operating systems, where the distinction between data stored locally, on the server, or globally on the net is removed.

The URL offers a **unique identifier** for every page on the Web.

Since the Web soon was envisioned as something more than an Intranet for CERN, it was natural to build the transmission protocol for HTML pages, the Hypertext Transfer Protocol (HTTP), on top of TCP/IP. HTTP defines a set of commands that are used by the browser to request HTML pages, one of these being the GET-command. The GET-command requests a specific file from a particular server that resides on the Internet. The server and file are identified by a Uniform Resource Locator, a URL. A URL consists of the IP address of the server, and information to identify the Web page within the server. For example, the URL

`http://www.ii.uib.no/persons/index.html`

identifies a page *index.html* within the folder *persons*, on the server identified by *ii.uib.no* (a name server will replace this name by the numeric IP address). It also indicates that the HTTP protocol is being used. When the browser sends a GET-command, the HTTP server on that host will retrieve the Web page and return it to the browser. HTTP is a stateless protocol, that is, after the transfer has been made the server can forget everything about it. In principle there is no recollection of the transfer and no data is stored.

The Web protocols are **stateless** (i.e., it does not remember that you have been here before). Every access is the first.

A stateless protocol simplifies the administration of tasks, as each transaction is performed as an atomic (self-contained) unit, making it easy for a server to handle a large number of requests and avoiding the problem of non-terminated sessions (where a user gives up in the middle of a process). But what if we need more than one request to do the job, for example, to successively select the next page of results returned by a query? Such a session can be simulated by including the historical data needed in each step. Thus what is a logical transaction, as seen from the user's point of view, may have to take place through a series of atomic transactions, where each transaction has to offer the complete transaction history up to the present. For example, when you request the second page (or twentieth page) of search results, all data from the initial search is sent to the server with the additional information that the second page (or twentieth page) of results are wanted. The server may now perform a completely new search, disregard the first page of results, and return the second page.

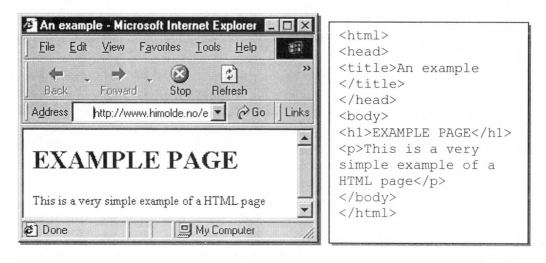

Figure 6.1 HTML page example (browser presentation and source)

Tags are used to add layout information, and, in some cases, structural information.

The role of HTML in this process is to describe the layout of a Web page. A simple example is presented in figure 6.1, showing how we use this markup language to describe fields and effects. For example, by enclosing the page title in <title> and </title> tags it can be identified by the browser. Similarly a major header is enclosed by <h1> and </h1>, a paragraph by <p> and </p> and bold text by <b> and </b>. A markup language has the advantages that the end result is a standard text without any special characters. It can therefore be stored as a text file and edited by a text editor.

Markup languages are, in principle, easily extendable. New tags can be added at any time. Of course, these additional tags will not take effect before new versions of the browser can be programmed to handle these tags. HTML browsers are usually programmed to ignore any tag that they cannot recognize. This has the disadvantage that tag errors may not be found (a tag such as <tittle> will just be ignored), but has the tremendous advantage that old browsers can display pages that include new tags. However, since these new tags are ignored, users with old versions of the browser may see a different page from those that have a new version. Thus page designers must be careful when new constructs are employed.

The **href** tag allows us to embed one-way links in a Web page.

One of the most important HTML constructs is the *a-href* tag which enables us to create a hypertext link to any other Web page. This tag defines an anchor and the *href* attribute defines the URL to the linked-to Web page. For example,

```
<a href="http://www.uib.no/index.html">
     University of Bergen</a>
```

will create a link to the page defined by this URL. The actual link will be hidden by the browser, which will display the text "University of Bergen," usually presented with an underline and/or a special color so that it can easily be identified as a link to the user. When the user clicks on this link the browser will create a GET-command for the page, retrieve it from the HTTP server, and present it on the display.

It is to Tim Berners-Lee's credit that he managed to keep HTML simple. It must have been very difficult to avoid designing a more complex link system. For example, the one-way HTML links have the disadvantage that all of us experience, in that they may refer to a page that has been removed, deleted, or perhaps, has never existed. These situations could have been handled by a two-way link system, and/or by linking through a central register. More advanced links, however, would demand a much more elaborate system, and would generate a huge administrative load—perhaps making the explosive growth of the Web impossible. With the Berners-Lee design we can link to any page, without asking permission or changing the destination page. Since the link is only represented in the from-page, there is no limit to the number of links that a system can handle. Other KISS (Keep it Simple Stupid) effects are the fact that HTML files are also text files, and that browsers ignore tags they cannot recognize.

Tim Berners-Lee never intended HTML to be a language used by human beings. His idea was that the editing functions of the browsers would insert the necessary HTML tags, in the same way as a word processing system inserts format instruction in the text. When we select a sentence in MS Word, for example, and click the "italics" button, MS Word will automatically include the necessary tags in the underlying representations that users never see. However, the HTML tags were so simple that many users created HTML pages directly, using Notepad or a similar text-editing tool. This process was simplified by the "View Source" command of a browser, where the underlying HTML representation of a Web page could be viewed, studied, and copied. In the pioneer days of the Web people were even hired based on their ability to write basic HTML.

The author of a Web page is completely in control of the links. She can choose freely **where to link** and how to present the link on her page.

HTML pages were intended to be produced by programs, not humans.

It is quite possible that if the HTTP protocol and the HTML language had been designed by a committee instead of by Tim Berners-Lee, we would have received a much more complex and elaborate system that would have hampered the explosive growth that we see today. His great achievement was not to develop new advanced technology, but to offer a simple system that made it easy to create Web pages and to implement browsers. HTML is based on SGML, but while SGML offers the possibility of defining very elaborate markup languages HTML is extremely simple. At the same time it offers satisfactory functionality. Of course, the HTML of today is much more than the initial standard, but the major KISS functionality has been retained.

XML (Extensible Markup Language) is another important offspring from the initial SGML. Its idea is to offer what HTML lacks, such as functions for structuring document content. We shall return to XML in chapter 27.

Exercises and Discussion

1. HTML is a based on SGML, utilizing just a fraction of the SGML functionality. However, while HTML was an instant success SGML was not. Discuss the importance of simplicity. Can you find any other success examples of simplistic technologies?

2. All browsers will accept erroneous HTML pages and try to present these as best as they can. Are there any disadvantages with this approach?

3. Try to develop a simple page in HTML. You can design the page using any editor (e.g., Notepad). If you give the file an ".htm" extension, you can open it in the browser by clicking on the file icon. Did the browser display the page? (If you want to put the page on the Web you need to move it to a Web server.)

Notes

1. See his interesting book, *Weaving the Web* (with Mark Fichetti), HarperSanFransisco. 1999.

2. The idea behind SGML was to develop a generalized language for creating and describing documents, with a clear separation between content and layout. The first working draft of the SGML standard was published as early as 1980, and the standard was accepted by various bodies about five years later. Early applications were within the publishing industry for book and article creation, and for manuscript interchange between authors and their publishers.

7 Email

The most important aspect of email is its **asynchronous** nature.

In principle, email is asynchronous; that is A can send a message when it suits her, B can read it when it suits him. This is similar to ordinary mail and fax, but very different from telephone or video conferencing. You can send an email to a busy person, perhaps a person working in a different time zone, without interfering in this person's schedule. This is the basis for an efficient communication system. Each of us follows our own schedule, at the same time as we collaborate with others over a fast and efficient medium. Email gives us the best of both worlds. While standard email is asynchronous, it can be used for more synchronous two-way communication, utilizing the fact that email transfer is fast. Chat or instant messaging programs can set up such a direct link between the parties.

Email is text-based.[1] Text is standardized, can be presented on any type of display and printed on any printer, does not require much screen space, and can be created, edited, and represented efficiently in any computer. Text does not require high bandwidth, and email can therefore be used efficiently with any type of equipment or connection. In an age when we marvel about novel technologies such as powerful processors, high-definition TV, interactive video, and visualization it is easy to forget the flexibility, expressiveness, and compactness of text.

Basic email is **simple** and works on all platforms.

A global communication system cannot expect that everyone will be equipped with the latest models. But the simple text-based world of email can be handled by any computer, any operating system, and transmitted fast over any type of network, even on the simplest dial-up connections. That is, email works on all platforms. The strength of this medium is manifested today, as we utilize new technological advances in mobility and miniaturization, such as the mobile telephone, instead of just going for power and capacity. While most email messages are in plain text, some email systems also allow different fonts and images. However, the receiver needs the same system, or a system that accepts the same protocol, in order to be able to see more than the plain text.

SMS (Short Message service) are simple and work on most cell phones.

We have seen that telecommunications companies in Europe have been surprised by the enormous popularity of the short text-based SMS messages. The answer to this development is in the message itself—the convenience of being in contact all the time, is more important than the layout. SMS has the advantage that it can be created and read by most cell phones. The simplicity of the technology and the limited bandwidth needed makes it an inexpensive way of communicating. If we are critical, we may argue that these one-sentence messages are a symptom of a lack of literate skills in the younger population, but it can just as well be explained by the fact that the numeric keyboard does not allow for heavy prose. And perhaps SMS is just what we need in order to make those sharp and witty statements that we hear actors utter in the movies. We have no script with SMS, but the asynchronous nature of the dialog gives us time to find the right words. We may say that the need to be in continuous contact with friends shows a lack of planning and organizing skills, but this need may also be viewed as a way of socializing. SMS shows clearly that the cell phone companies have an important market in the younger population, as much for entertainment as for anything else. But other groups are coming along. For example, SMS is also a simple way for businesses to keep their customers informed: "your order has arrived," "flight is thirty minutes delayed," "$1000 has been inserted in your account."

The low **formalization level** of SMS, email, and HTML offers flexibility.

SMS messages and email retain the low formalization level of a blank sheet of paper. The only structured information is in the address fields (the phone number), the note itself can be composed as one likes. While the early email protocols were based on 7-bit ASCII characters, newer protocols use more bits to represent characters, which opens the way for special letters and national language characters.

Email is based on the IP, Internet Protocol. An email address identifies a person (a person's email account) uniquely in the world, it is simple and often easy to remember, especially where a syntax of <first name> . <last name> @ <institution> . <country or type of institution code> are used (e.g., kai.olsen@himolde.no).

Email offers data in electronic, computer readable format (i.e., the data received is in electronic form). This enables the receiver to store messages on disk, to edit messages, to copy content into other applications. Messages can be forwarded to others, and replies can be sent just by a button click. Email messages can be printed, but the system itself is paper free.

Email may be handled by **automatic procedures** that perform actions based on the formalized part of messages.

Many email systems offer automatic procedures for handling incoming email. We can, for example, specify that messages from a given address should be transferred directly to a folder, or that messages with a given word in the heading should be forwarded to another mail address. It is possible to specify a message that will be returned automatically, as a response to all messages ("I am on vacation…") or to messages from a given address ("Bill, you can call me at …"). Or, perhaps more importantly, we can ask the system to block messages from a list of sites, "spam" mail that we do not want to see.

The MIME protocol opens for **attachments** to email. With this we can exploit the de facto format standards of documents, spreadsheets, and other applications.

Email systems using the MIME protocol can attach files to the messages. These files can be of any type: computer programs, data files, databases, text files, images, word processing documents, spreadsheets, etc. This is a simple to use, extremely useful function that to a large extent replaces the more cumbersome FTP (file transfer protocols). What makes MIME so important is that it allows us to utilize the de facto standards that have emerged over the last ten years, Microsoft Word for word processing, Excel for spreadsheets, and Adobe's PDF format for printable documents. Whether I work with colleagues in Pittsburgh or Rome, papers are exchanged as MS Word documents. In industry, data can be exchanged in a formalized manner using Excel spreadsheets, using the spreadsheet as a standard vehicle for the data transfer, utilizing the tabular structure, named fields, etc. At the receiving end, programs can then retrieve the data directly from the spreadsheet system. PDF is today the (de facto) standard for distributing documents in a read-only form. Word and other document files can easily be converted to PDF. The PDF files can be stored on a Web page or distributed to readers as attachments. The PDF file can then be read using a simple viewer program that can be downloaded for free.

The **sender** of an email can be a computer program, sometimes also the receiver.

A sender of an email message can be a computer program. An event can activate the program that creates an email message based on data retrieved from a database, for example, offering bargains three days ahead of a flight of leftover seats or notifying the customer that the book he wanted can be picked up at the library. Not all computer-generated emails are as useful as these. As many users with public email addresses have experienced, spam or unsolicited mail is becoming a major problem. Most of these unwanted messages can be deleted just by looking at the header or sender, but some come so well disguised (e.g., faking a sender's address, perhaps an address from your own organization, using a general header) that we may be far into the message before we know its purpose. The costs of handling spam can be enormous. If we use thirty seconds to identify and delete a spam message, a message sent to a million people will take one man-year just to have it removed from all the inboxes.

Spam, unsolicited email is becoming a major problem. It can be handled by legalization (best) or by software filters.

Of course, unsolicited mail is not only a problem in the electronic world, but emails are so inexpensive to send that it may be worth the effort if only one out of a million accepts an offer. Many institutions try to remove spam at an early stage, for example, by letting the mail server filter out messages from suspected sources, where there is an incompatibility between name and IP address or messages that can be identified as spam by their vocabulary.[2] The latter case is potentially dangerous, as genuine messages may be removed along with the garbage. Perhaps a better method is to have a personal and a public mail box, setting up message rules that split the incoming flow of messages to these two boxes. The private inbox can then be used only for senders that already are in your address book. You will have to look at both inboxes, but while the private will have mostly messages of interest we will have to look at only selected messages in the other. A problem here is that messages with a faked sender's name may go into the wrong inbox. Alternatively, we can operate with two email addresses, one that we keep protected and the other a public address.

While the EU and some U.S. states have passed laws to ban unsolicited email, that is, enforcing the same rules for email as for fax,[3] others are moving toward a system where one can ask to be removed from distribution lists.[4] The latter solution is not so good. Not only do we collectively waste years in sending removal messages, but we have no guarantee that these will have any effect. Probably the unsubscribe mail is just a confirmation that we have a working email address, that can be used for further spam messages. Even if we are removed from the email distribution lists of the first company, we can now legally be spammed by all others.

In some cases, the receiver of an email may be a computer. We may, for example, send a message asking that we be included, or excluded, from a mailing list. Some of these messages have the disadvantage that they require a strict format, which to some degree violates the openness of email messages. In most cases it will therefore be simpler to provide this type of formalized information using a Web form.

	Email	SMS	Mail	Telephone (voice)	Fax	Video conf.
Asynchronous	Yes	Yes	Yes	No	Yes	No
Synchronous	(Yes)	Yes	No	Yes	No	Yes
Computer readable text	Yes	Yes	No	No	No	No
Images	Yes	Limited	Yes	No	Yes	Yes
Data files	Yes	No	Yes	No	No	(No)
Fast	Yes	Yes	No	Yes	Yes	Yes
One to many	Yes	Limited	Yes	Limited	Yes	Limited
Costs	Low	Low	Medium	Low- high	Medium	High
Forward	Yes	Limited	Limited	Limited	Limited	-
Automatic handling	Yes	Limited	No	Limited	No	-
Automatic generation	Yes	Yes	Yes	Limited	Yes	-

Table 7.1 Comparison of different communication media.

A comparison of different communication media is given in table 7.1. As seen in the table, email has advantages in many areas. It is already a strong competitor to the telephone, fax, and ordinary mail and within organizations that are ahead in computer utilization, such as universities and research centers, it is clearly the dominant communication medium. Today, we see that email replaces other forms of communication within the business community, and as Internet communication becomes more common in homes, it will also be a strong competitor here.

The asynchronous nature of email and its other advantages make it a formidable tool for creating more efficient businesses. Email discussions, where each member of a group can send his thoughts to all the others may not replace the need for meetings, but can make meetings much more efficient. Through the email discussion ideas can be presented and their merits discussed by all, before a meeting is called to make the final decision. In most situations email is more efficient than the telephone, not only because of its asynchronous nature, but because it leaves a text copy, which can be used as a reminder, forwarded to others, or stored in an archive. Using distribution lists a manager can send her thoughts to *all* her employees, a professor a message to *all* his students, a company a message to *all* customers, as simply as sending a person-to-person message. Just as important, since an email does not interfere with the receiver's schedule and can be answered very efficiently, an employee should be able to email a comment to the boss, a student her professor, and companies should encourage feedback from customers.

The send-to-all feature may have drawbacks. Often we see that messages are forwarded or sent to all employees, instead of distributing to a more limited list. This just-in-case philosophy leaves us with what we can call "internal spam" in our inboxes.

There are, however, requirements for efficient use of email that should not be forgotten. Users need a computer, which may be everything from a cell phone to a desktop machine, an Internet connection, and an address. They need typing and writing skills, although we do not require messages to be literary works of high quality, the medium requires the abilities to put thoughts into writing in a clear and efficient manner. There are several examples where the ease of the email system, sending fast reply not only to the sender but also to all recipients, has resulted in a misunderstanding, the dissemination of private or confidential information or angered recipients (colleagues, customers, or managers). While an ordinary letter gives us some time to think before it is mailed and while a telephone allows us to make amends and a statement in a personal conversation can be given with a smile, the email, in its fast and short messages, may be efficiently brutal. Some of the advantages of email may become a disadvantage in these situations. The angry message we send a colleague or an employee can be forwarded to others and may be read out of context, leaving the recipients with a written statement that we cannot easily explain away.

However, any medium, whether it is a letter, telephone, or email, requires a set of user-level protocols to work, such as "Dear Mr. ...," "We refer to your letter of ...," "Sincerely...," "This is Pat, can I talk to ...." These protocols may not always be known, but they are important in person-to-person communication. Next time you call a friend say "Hello" when *she* answers the telephone, and study the consequences of violating the protocol. Email is not different, even if we leave out many of these phrases. By including the receiving message, your answer is set in a context. Keep in mind that even if the message may be received by the recipient's server almost immediately, it may not be read for many days. Keep the text simple, clear, and to the point. Remember that the medium may also be used in a conversational manner; you do not have to say everything in one message. Understatements and hidden jokes may not be understood, especially if your messages are sent to persons in different countries, with different cultures. Harsh words and strong criticism may have a stronger effect than intended, and should be avoided. While most persons would be very careful when wording or proofreading a mass-distributed letter before it goes to the publishers, we often do not take the same considerations before sending an email.

Compared to a letter, email does not offer the same chances of second thought; the message may be sent immediately. Therefore, before hitting the "send" button, go through this checklist:

We can develop **human protocols** for communication on top of the technical protocols.

- Do I want to send this?
- In this form?
- To all these recipients?
- Will it be forwarded, to whom?
- What will the effect be?

However, as one gets used to the medium, email will go as smoothly as the telephone conversation. After more than twenty years with email, the greatest problem with this technology seems to be its *advantages*. Email is so efficient that it has become the number one communication channel for very many people. Individually addressed letters or nonprivate telephone calls are often exceptions for heavy email users. While we still use the telephone or personal visits to handle complicated cases, many of the tasks that were previously organized using personal visits or telephone as a routine, are now handled over email. Then the disadvantage may become apparent— communication becomes impersonal. While a telephone call and a personal visit open the way for talking more than just shop, an email message is often short and down to basics. The asynchronous nature of email does not provide for a conversation in the same way as a telephone, where we inspire each other and where the conversation may flow freely from one topic to the other. That is, with email we find that the focus is on the closed parts, the more open parts are left out. At the same time the need to meet with others in person is reduced, as all routine tasks are handled over email. When this drawback of email is recognized it can also be compensated, for example, by setting up personal meetings with customers, colleagues, or employees regularly.

Can email be **too efficient**?

There is not much glamor to email. Compared with 3D Virtual Realities the text-based nature of email messages seems something out of the past. This may be one reason why many institutions have still not utilized the advantages of this application. However, while practical virtual reality may still be decades away, email is here today to make communication more effective. That is, if we can handle the problem of spam and viruses within email attachments (chapter 3.5).

Exercises and Discussion

1. While email and SMS are asynchronous, telephone is synchronous. How would you characterize *chat*?

2. What is the difference between getting a Microsoft Word document in PDF- and in DOC-format?

3. Discuss the problems that are incurred by spam. What are the remedies for reducing or removing this problem?

4. A problem related to spam is that too many email messages are relayed internally in an organization. Investigations show that many employees use hours a day to get through their email. Discuss the background for this problem, and what one can do to reduce the number of emails in everybody's inbox.

Notes

1. Most email programs can also create and render messages in HTML format.

2. One of my employers decided to do something about the spam messages that cluttered the mail system, and a novice was set to define the keywords that were used to identify spam. Encouraged by early successes, more and more words were added to the "bad word" list. After "sex," "spicy," and "credit card" were included, nearly all spam disappeared. However, so did many other email messages. For example a colleague did not receive an email from his travel agency because he had ordered a "spicy Asian" in-flight meal.

3. This is the "opt-in" option, where we explicitly have to express our wish to be on a mailing list.

4. This is the "opt-out" alternative, where we explicitly have to be asked to be removed from a mailing list.

8 Browsers

The **img-tag**, making it possible to embed images in HTML opened a new world of Web applications.

As we know a browser is a program for displaying Web pages. Most browsers also have a system for creating and modifying pages. The first browser was a simple line-based, text-only program that was developed by Berners-Lee. It was available on the CERN server from 1991. However, the Web did not really take off until the National Center for Supercomputing Applications (NCSA) at the University of Illinois at Urbana-Champaign offered the more advanced Mosaic browser in 1993. Marc Andreessen and the rest of the design team worked hard to incorporate requests from early Web users in Mosaic, which was both a browser and an editor. The most important new feature was the img-tag, making it possible for the first time to have images as a part of a Web page. This opened a whole new world of layout and applications. Later on the Mosaic team founded Netscape, while Microsoft bought the company that licensed Mosaic.

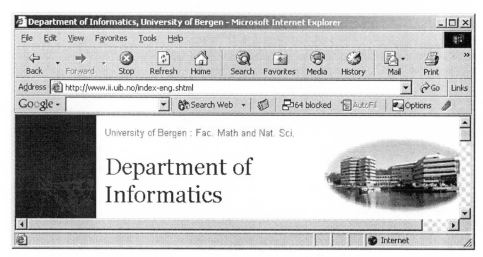

Figure 8.1 Browser window (Internet Explorer)

The main job of a browser, such as Netscape or Internet Explorer, is to retrieve and display HTML pages. As we have seen in chapter 6, a page is retrieved based on the URL. URLs can be entered by users directly in the address field, as shown in figure 8.1, retrieved from a bookmark or "favorite" archive or extracted from a link. To simplify navigation, the browser offers forward and back buttons, as well as a list of previously visited sites. The browser uses the HTTP protocol to request and retrieve pages, for example, by using the GET-command within this protocol. HTTP works on top of an Internet protocol, and defines an envelope for the transmission of Web pages, with fields for source and destination URLs, size of the page, the HTML version that is used, etc. The browser strips off this header information before the page is displayed.

For the user the browser is the window to the world. By navigating among URLs the user can point his window in any direction, at any source. Behind the scenes the browser will issue the GET-commands, retrieve the HTML pages, and display them. Ideally, we want immediate feedback. This is especially the case when we are "surfing the Web," moving from page to page in our quest for interesting data. We do not know exactly what we want, and may only spend a few seconds on each page before we follow another link, replacing the contents of the browser window. In many ways Web browsing resembles scanning more than reading. This should be acknowledged when we design Web pages. Ideally they should be efficient to download, and the main contents of the page (title, abstract, important hypertext links, etc.) should be presented in the browser window, without the need for scrolling.

The display of the page is, as we have seen, controlled by HTML. HTML has changed dramatically over the last ten years. Not only do we have an image tag in the standard, but modern HTML also recognizes a larger variety of layout commands, offers image-maps where input can be given by clicking on a map or image, defines simple animations, and so forth. An important feature is the form-tag, allowing the user to enter input data that can be sent to a Web server for processing.[1] Thus the original concept of using the Web to retrieve information has been replaced by two-way functionality where the browser can get data from the user, and send this off to the source. In fact, HTML is moving toward a full user interface language, with not only passive layout functions, but with all the features that we expect: text boxes, radio buttons, command buttons, etc.

The newer versions of HTML describe dynamic pages where it is possible to embed *scripts* in the page source. The script, a small program, is recognized by the browser and can be executed directly or based on an event such as a button click. In this respect a browser can be viewed as a virtual computer. This computer exists on top of the physical computer and its

---

The browser is our **window on the world**.

Web **surfing** works best when response times are small.

With **forms**, the browser can be used as a terminal to specialized applications. HTML is moving toward a full **user interface** language.

A browser is a **virtual computer** that can run simple programs (scripts).

operating system. For reasons of security, the virtual computer may have limited access to local resources, for example, not being able to read and write to local disks. The advantage of this approach is a high degree of portability. A script or an applet (a small application program, usually written in Java) can be downloaded from the source and run within the browser, independently of the computer and operating system used. The disadvantage of this approach is that processing may be slow; running a program in a virtual computer on top of a physical computer is not efficient. In addition, all resources that the program may need (such as mathematical functions, fonts, images) must be downloaded from the source, even if similar resources exist locally. Data can only be temporarily stored by the browser, and any permanent storage must be on the server. We shall cover these issues in more detail in later chapters (chapters 15 and 16).

With **plug-ins** we can give our browser new functionality.

As an alternative to running scripts or applets on the browser, its functionality can be extended by *plug-ins*. A plug-in is a program module that can be downloaded, embedded in the browser, and executed on the local physical machine (i.e., not in the virtual machine as an applet), in the same way as the browser is executed. Plug-ins offer a flexible way to extend browser functionality. For example, we can download plug-ins for playing music or video, for giving 3D capabilities to the browser, and so forth. New versions of plug-ins can be obtained without having to get new versions of the browsers, and users with limited resources can stick to the original browser, avoiding allocating extra space for resources that they do not need.

The transfer protocol for HTML pages, HTTP, is **stateless**. It has no memory of earlier transactions.

As we have seen, HTTP is a stateless protocol, meaning that each request is treated as a single discrete entity, not as a part of a longer sequence. The browser requests a page from a server by issuing a GET-command, and the server can forget about the transaction when the page has been returned. There is therefore no need for login and logoff functionality, and for administering requests and users. The drawback is that it becomes difficult to implement services which are performed as a sequence of commands. However, as we have seen state information can be provided to the server as additional information in the next request (chapter 6). Another option is that a server can assign the browser to store a "cookie," a small text file, on the browser's local system. A cookie usually includes an identifier that the browser will return to the Web server on its next visit. In this way the server can recognize you and connect requests. For example, if you provided name and address in the first visit to the site, this information can be retrieved from server disks based on information from the cookie at subsequent visits.

The extended functionality has made browsers more vulnerable to attack and can violate your privacy. Cookies can give away information that you considered private; an applet should not be able to access permanent storage on your computer, but due to the complexity of the software, loopholes in the security system could allow applets to delete or create files. One mechanism for avoiding these problems is to provide systems where the user can select the level of security wanted, or the level of service.

Cookies will aid the server in identifying the user.

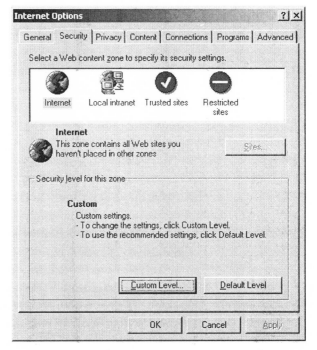

Figure 8.2. Setting security levels in Internet Explorer.

An example is shown in figure 8.2, which allows websites to be cataloged into different zones, each with their own security level. For example, we may accept a lower security setting on our local Intranet and on trusted sites than on the open Internet.

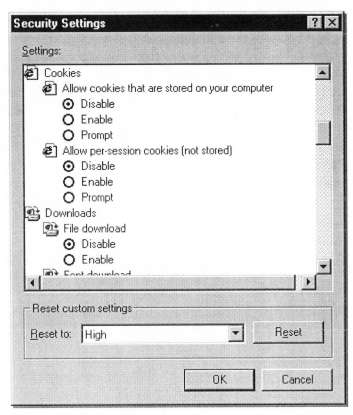

Figure 8.3 Setting restrictions (Internet Explorer)

We can now specify restrictions that should apply on each level, as seen in figure 8.3. For example, we can tell the browser not to accept applets, plug-ins, or cookies, or, to give warnings in given situations. The disadvantage of a high security level is of course that the functionality of our Web browsers will be reduced and that some sites become unavailable—or that we will have a high administrative overhead by cataloging sites and setting security parameters. Thus, most users run their browsers with a low or medium security level, choosing functionality over security or, as is perhaps more common, never thinking about the security risks at all.

For a secure transaction, for example, with an online bank, it is important that:

1. The browser can determine that the bank site is secure and genuine.

2. The bank server can determine that the customer is genuine, and that he is who he says he is.

3. The data communicated cannot be read or changed by unauthorized persons.

These secure transactions can be handled by the HTTPS protocol. Here *certificates* are used to ensure the identity of the communicating partners, and transmissions are coded using a secure cryptography system. A certificate acts as a signature for the site or the client. It is implemented as a complex digital code, with a public and private part. I give the public key to the bank that uses this key to encrypt messages they send to me. The coding system is so clever that only I can decrypt these messages, using my private key.[2] Thus, if the message is intercepted on its way from source to destination, it cannot be read without the private key. If it is tampered with, this will immediately be detected at the receiving end. This may seem complicated, but the browser takes care of everything: storing the certificates, offering public keys to the parties that we are communicating with, coding and decoding messages, etc. In fact, the only way we may notice that the transaction is secure is that the URL starts with "HTTPS," indicating a secure http, instead of the common HTTP. In addition, we may get a dialog box for selecting the certificate to be used. Alternatives to HTTPS are the somewhat similar: S-HTTP (secure HTTP) and the more advanced SET (Secure Electronic Transaction) protocol.

Online shopping requires the user to enter personal information, such as name and address, and credit card information. To simplify these transactions, the browser can offer to save this information in a *wallet*. A site can then retrieve this information directly from the wallet, and we avoid reentering these data. The wallet is protected by passwords.

In the discussion of transaction security on the Internet and the Web, we often forget that security is a relative issue. We can put two locks on every door in our house, but the burglar can enter through a window. We can put alarm systems on all windows, but to no avail if we forget to activate the system when we leave the house. By using the security mechanisms that are implemented in the browser, we can decrease the probability of fraud, making it more difficult for a hacker to break in, but as in the physical world, we can never get a completely secure system. The highest risk is not in the hardware or the software, but in the users themselves. The passwords we use

HTTPS is used for reducing the probability that others can read or change transmissions.

Security on the Internet, as elsewhere, is a **relative** issue.

may be too simple or not changed often enough; we may leave a password on a piece of paper or simply forget to log off.

The advantage of a computer system in such cases is that if fraud occurs, it may leave a digital track to the criminals. The only thing a hacker can do if he gets access to a bank account is to move money to another account. From here he may get access to the money, but a trail is left behind that increases his risk of being caught. The bottom line, however, is that security is expensive, and that a complicated access system may scare customers away. Most banks and credit card companies are therefore willing to take the risks, online as well as offline.

Crime on the net may be detected and investigated following **electronic tracks**.

As seen, the browser is our window to the outside world. It gives us the possibility of accessing information and services from a myriad of sites, but is also a way in for those with malicious intents. As in other parts of life we have to find the right balance between openness, functionality, and efficiency on one hand and the need to protect our assets and privacy on the other.

Exercises and Discussion

1. For any Web page go to the "View" menu in your browser and select "Source". This will show you the underlying HTML code for the page, a complete formal description of the page. Compare this code to the formatted page. It is the job of the browser to format the page according to the HTML description. Based on these data, discuss what the browser does.

2. To make communication more effective and to simplify the input required from the user the browser can keep records of sites visited, of items and pages downloaded from these sites, of search items entered, cookies, etc. Discuss the privacy issues that are involved here if another person gets access to your PC.

3. On the server side one may store information on accesses to a site, IP addresses, or user names where a login is required. Discuss the privacy issues involved here.

Notes

1. We will return to these issues in more detail in chapter 15.
2. Private-public key system utilizes the fact that it is difficult to factorize (e.g., 8 into 2*2*2) huge numbers. The public key defines the creation of these huge numbers, and the private part shows how they can be factorized (i.e., decrypted).

9 World Wide Web

The Internet has had an **explosive** growth, but so have many other communication technologies.

It has been argued that the adoption rate of the Internet has exceeded that of earlier mass communication technology by several orders of magnitude, but few real data have been presented to prove this claim. In their early days radio and television also had fast adoption rates, and we must not forget that the Internet has been here for more than thirty years. But, if we view the Web as a separate technology it has had a tremendous impact in just a few years. Tim Berners-Lee tells us that the initial Web opened with an almost blank page, today there are several billion Web pages.

We find all kinds of contents on the Web, from amateurish pages with the simplest of layout to pages made by graphic designers and Web journalists. It has become a medium for non-profit organizations and for global industries. Most sites are open and free, others are hidden behind passwords, certificates, and cryptography. We find answers to primary school exercises, official reports, and scientific papers. Some sites are an explosion of multimedia techniques; others look as if they have been printed on an old-fashioned typewriter. Pages may not have been changed since the day they were created; some are updated every few seconds.

The Web is like a combination of white and yellow pages, where each and every one can have a virtual presence. A home page with pictures of friends and family, professional interests, or our hobbies; a place to present our views, the organization, or political party; a place for marketing and selling; to disseminate documentation or to meet with others in the virtual room.

In 1962, Marshall McLuhan noted that, "The new electronic interdependence recreates the world in the image of a *global village*."[1] Since then, many have reused the term to describe the way we use the Internet and the Web to make the world smaller, or to create virtual or electronic communities. While the government and other large organizations can use the Internet as a tool for more efficient communication, the new medium offers unprecedented possibilities for very small organizations or groups. Since these may be spread over wide areas with only a few persons at each location, contact between group members has been difficult to implement. Suddenly, with the Internet and the Web, one gets unprecedented ability to keep in contact with very limited costs. Email, distribution lists, newsgroups, chat rooms, and websites have in many ways removed the physical distances between group members.

On the positive side this has made it possible to create virtual networks of people sharing a very special disease, a special job, interest, or hobby. Immigrants can keep in touch with their own culture, read the local paper from their home town, keep updated on minor and major events, even participate in local discussions, and so forth. On the negative side we see that subgroups such as Nazis, terrorist organizations, child pornographers, and criminals use the Internet to organize their activities. Electronic communication provides the means of keeping transmissions secret, for example, by using cryptography to hinder insight into email messages. In this respect, the Internet and the Web provide an additional advantage for such groups, so instead of supporting cross-nation and cross-cultural exchange we see that the Internet can support polarization and fragmentation.[2]

One clear "global village" effect has been that information is now instantly available all over the world. Earlier marketers could launch a product in the United States one year, in Europe the second, in Asia the third… etc., keeping up production over many years. Today this is impossible. We see that this fact is acknowledged. Movies, books, CDs, toys, etc., are launched all over the world on the same day. So, when we in Norway earlier had to wait months and perhaps also years to get a new movie, we now can see it in our home town theater before it is launched in LA (the 9-hour time difference works in our favor here).

The **low formalization** level of HTML (layout) lies behind the high degree of flexibility offered.

We have seen that the simplicity of creating HTML pages was behind the explosion of content on the Web, but this explosion would not have been possible without the low formalization level of HTML, its "blank sheet of paper." HTML is only a layout language, and can therefore be used for any type of text. The structure requirements are extremely simple, and most browsers will display pages even when we do not follow the rules, for example, by inserting missing tags, ignoring tags that cannot be recognized, etc. Just as we can use a word processor for any type of document, all types of information can be saved in HTML. HTML sets no requirements to the contents or structure of a page. This is both strength and a weakness. It's like the boomtowns of the West in the nineteenth century. Anybody could set up a building since there were no regulations, no cen-

The low formalization level is also a **weakness**, as the Web is created without any formal overall structure.

tral plan, no permissions to obtain, no bureaucracy, and whole towns could emerge in a few weeks.

Today, most HTML pages are created by Web design systems or other computer programs. For more structured information, static Web pages are replaced by dynamic pages, pages that are created by programs on the fly. Dynamic pages have the advantage that they can extract information from underlying databases. For example, instead of having a static HTML-based telephone list that must be updated separately from all other archives, the telephone list can be created when needed based on a human resources database. We shall return to dynamic Web pages in chapter 15.

Hypertext is the ideal tool for the Web, enabling us to link to the source instead of copying or rewriting information. That is, we can create the context for a Web page just by linking.

With the URL each page has a unique identifier; the HTTP protocol ensures that it can be transmitted via the Internet and HTML that it can be presented on a screen. While the hypertext idea has had limited success (except for manuals and help systems), the Web has really become *the* hypertext application. Of course, hypertext is an ideal technique for the Web. For example, when we create a "home page," describing persons, institutions, or special interest groups these "objects" do not exist in a vacuum, but are highly connected to other objects. Our personal Web pages can link to the Web pages of friends and families, to the company where we work, to our alma mater, to the portal of the city where we live, etc. The advantage is that we can provide complete information, where we only have to enter and maintain a fraction of the data ourselves.

The simple **link system** of HTML cannot guarantee that a link goes to a live destination.

The drawback of the simple, unidirectional links is that links may go nowhere or page contents can be changed in a way that violates the semantics of a hypertext link. In practice, however, these problems can be reduced by careful consideration of which links to include. For example, a link to another institution should go to the relevant home page. This page may be changed repeatedly, but the "idea" of the page, to act as a port to the institution, should remain stable. We should also expect that the URLs themselves will stabilize, as the expense of changing a well-known URL will be as high as changing the name of a company. Even where the URL is changed, most institutions will leave a link at the old address, redirecting users to the new site.

The Web is easy to adopt. It is also easy to be an **information-provider**. But most of the traffic goes to a very limited number of sites.

The Web has a similarity to radio, TV, and newspapers in that it is easy to adopt. As we have seen, it distinguishes itself from other media by the fact that on the Web everybody can be information-providers as well as consumers. In this way the basic structure of the Web can be called democratic. However, the frequency of hits on a page is, to a large extent, determined by the influence of the organization behind the website. Today, most of the traffic goes to a very limited number of sites, sites that are created and maintained by professional organizations. So, on one hand we talk about Web diversity and the billions of pages and on the other hand we talk about Internet usage— knowing that the traffic is not as diverse as the pages.

On the Web, a user has a higher possibility of selecting the information she wants, by using portals, search engines, or going to certain sites. Concerns have been raised that if every individual targets the information they want, we will no longer share a common ground and that the Web in this respect poses a threat to democracy. For example, with the Web a person can decide to only look at sport sites, not getting any other news. This point of view may be attacked from several directions. Information selection is not connected only to the Web. We have TV channels, newspapers, and journals with a very limited scope. People may live in a place or a culture with little or no contact with outsiders. Further, the most successful websites are often general sites, like those of newspapers, TV stations, and portals that provide headlines and news over a large set of topics, just as in the physical world. However, perhaps democracy is more threatened when everybody gets the same information, than when each and every one of us makes an individual choice.

When the Web emerged, it promised empowerment of its users. No longer would we be in the hands of the TV or newspaper editors. On the Web we could go directly to the sources to get in-depth information on the candidates, the economy, the environment…. A nice thought, but not very realistic. TV has established its role as the main communication channel in competition with other media that also offered possibilities of in-depth information, such as newspapers, books, and libraries. We find a good example in elections. Here citizens have an abundance of in-depth information on the candidates, from newspaper articles, books, political programs, reports, etc., but many seem to form their opinion based on political ads or superficial TV debates. While the Web may offer more convenient access to the information sources, it does not provide the user with the time, skills, and motivation for utilizing these sources. Probably TV news presents what viewers seem to

We can use the Web to broaden, narrow, or deepen our horizons. We can get in-depth information, but most of us end up by getting just the **headlines**.

want, a superficial selection of the most interesting stories, compacted to a few minutes.

When we access the site of an Internet bank or an online travel agency the Web is used only as a standard interface. Within the site we are really navigating a database structure, the bank accounts, the flight information, or the hotel database. These data are formalized at a high level, as a record structure with well-defined fields. The tools that we use within the site, for example, a search tool, are designed to work on this database structure and in this way are very different from the tools that work on HTML formatted pages. In these sites, hidden from the rest of the Web, most of the HTML pages will be generated on the fly, based on input from the user and on the results from the database queries. In this way one combines the advantages of two worlds, the Internet standards and availability of browsers can give everyone access to specialized and closed databases, with a high formalization level.

The disadvantage of the "boom town" creation of the Web is that the billions of Web pages that exist today are highly unstructured, with exception of the closed databases. This is only a small problem when a page is to be studied by a human being. Our capabilities of pattern recognition and understanding text based on context are so flexible that we can get information out of nearly any page. And, as we have seen, the Web standards can be used to access closed databases where we can work on more structured data.

Ideally we would like to be able to access many of these closed systems at a time. For example, to have a search tool, or an "agent" that looks for a cheap hotel, a best bargain on a book, and so forth. Then a higher degree of formalization and page structure would be welcome. We shall discuss these issues in more detail in the next chapter, and also return to the same ideas in part 4.

> Is the **medium** the message or do we retain usage patterns independently of the media?

> When accessing a bank or a travel agency system we are within a **closed domain**, separated from the open Web.

Exercises and Discussion

1. Try to find out, by interviewing or searching the Web, how many of your friends and colleagues have a personal Web page (a home page). What kind of information do they offer? Is the page updated?

2. Design you own home page. Think about what kind of information you will provide. Is the target group friends, colleagues, or others? Make a sketch of the

page, and implement a simple version using HTML or a Web design tool. Some word processors let you save a document by "save as Web page/HTML," which allows you to make your home page using this tool.

3. In some cases the target groups of your home page will be very different (e.g., friends and future employers). Discuss how this problem can be handled.

4. Links to other pages will be an important part of a home page. Originally, a basic principle of hypertext was the ability to embed links within the text (e.g., that words and terms can also act as links). Today, however, we often see that links are grouped together in a frame to the left (as a menu) or under the text. Discuss why so many seem to depart from the original hypertext idea.

Notes

1. McLuhan, Marshall. 1962. *The Gutenberg Galaxy.* London: Routledge & Kegan Paul.
2. See Cass R. Sunstein. 2001. R*epublic.com*, Princeton Univ. Press.

10 Searching the Web

One of the great advantages of having data in electronic form is that it can be subjected to automatic searching. This is of special interest on the Web, due to the sheer volume of data. However, as we shall see, Web searching is not always easy.

10.1 Precision and recall

When a bank clerk needs a list of accounts with a negative balance she will expect a 100 percent correct answer—if the computer does not include all the customers with a negative balance, and only these, there must be an error either in the programs or in the data. Do we get a 100 percent correct answer when we search the Web? No, very often we get many nonrelevant references returned from the search engines, and we have no guarantee that the most interesting documents are included in the list. Sometimes, we have to give up, without a relevant answer to our query.

Precision =

$$\frac{\text{\# relevant returned}}{\text{\# returned}}$$

Recall =

$$\frac{\text{\# relevant returned}}{\text{\# relevant in total}}$$

Within information retrieval the terms *precision* and *recall* are used to describe the quality of a document retrieval result.[1] Precision is a ratio of the number of relevant documents (references) in the result set over the total number of documents returned. For example, if five out of every ten returned documents (references) are relevant, the precision will be 0.5 or 50 percent. In the bank example precision will always be 100 percent, as only accounts with a negative balance are returned. On the Web precision may be much lower, as the results are often "polluted" by nonrelevant references.

Recall is defined as the number of relevant documents returned, compared to the number of relevant documents in the database. That is, if the search engine returns two hundred relevant documents out of a potential of a thousand, recall will be 0.2 or 20 percent. While the bank clerk will expect a recall of 100 percent (i.e., all the accounts with a negative balance will be returned), recall on the Internet will be very low. In fact, for most search engines recall will be small independent of the query, since the engines only index a fraction of all Web pages.

For many users, however, recall is of no importance. As long as our information need is satisfied, it does not matter if other pages could give us the same or similar information. We may go to the Web to get information on a country or a city, and will usually be satisfied when we find a site, perhaps of the local tourist bureau, that provides what we want. Of course, we know that there may be other pages with this information, even better pages, but since we have satisfactory results there is no need for further probing. When we try to find the *cheapest* hotel in Rome, the *best offer* for a weekend in New York or data on *all* airplane accidents, recall will be more important. Since the search engines cannot offer any reasonable values for recall, the only way to satisfy these types of questions will be to try to find pages that give an overview (e.g., to start with a travel information site that lists hotels in Rome).

Why can we expect 100 percent correct precision and recall using the banking system, and not when using a search engine on the Web? We know that both the data and the functions of the bank and Web applications are formalized; otherwise we could not apply the computer. However, the key to the discrepancy in the reliability of the results from these two applications lies in the fact that the data are formalized on different levels.[2]

100 percent recall and precision require that the data have been **formalized** to the level of the queries.

In the bank we will find a database with account records. Each record has a unique account number, a reference to the account owner and a number giving the balance. This structure has been determined by the bank's database administrators, who have specified the attributes (fields) of an account, the length and format of each field, and so forth. This has been done keeping in mind the functionality needed from the banking system. What they have done is to define the term *account* in a formalized manner. When the clerk enters her query the computer will retrieve all records where the number in the balance field is less than zero. We get 100 percent results as the query and the data are formalized on the same level (i.e., the computer or database system knows the terms used, balance, account number, name, address, etc). This shows us that the database administrators did a good job; they defined the terms needed for the type of queries that are presented to the database system.

However, if the bank clerk tried a different type of query, for example, to find all customers with red hair, the database would not be able to give an answer, since hair color is usually not an attribute of a customer that is stored within the system. If the clerk wants a list of all *good* customers, this may not be easy to provide, even if the basic data may be available. She could try to formalize the term "good customer" as customers with more than $10,000 in their account. But this simplification may miss customers that have spread their money over several accounts, customers that by chance have a low balance at the moment, reliable customers that pay high interest on their bank loans, etc. On the other hand, a customer that only uses the bank to cash checks, moving the money to another bank later on, may be included in the "good customers" list. The clerk can try to elaborate the specification to handle some of these flaws and create more complex queries. In the end she would always have to expect a recall and precision below the 100 percent level, as there is no direct way of formulating her high-level query.

A remedy will be to explicitly define the term "good customer" using only formalized terms (e.g., in the way some airlines give you a frequent flyer update to silver or gold cards based on the mileage points you have collected). Then the database system will give a 100 percent answer, determining accurately which customer should have which type of card. Of course, we see that this is only a way of moving the problem one step up, since we now may have a discrepancy between the common understanding of "good customer" and the mileage point definition. However, this formalized definition has the advantage that the discrepancy to the real-world term of a good customer will be open and known by the whole organization, and not hidden within lower precision and recall.

10.2 Search engines

As we have seen, HTML documents are formalized on a layout level, as characters and words. A page may have a few meta fields, such as title and keywords, but these are not required. In practice, the search engines rely on the low-level data, expressions and words that can be retrieved from each page during an indexing phase. But these will, in an isolated form, not be a good representation of the author's communicative intentions. But there is no other remedy for the search engines. These indexing programs store the URL for each significant word in the text, making it possible to find the page based on one or more words. The engines use spiders, programs that traverse the Web to find relevant pages, or a Web master can explicitly submit a page for indexing, if she does not want to wait for the spider to come along. While the numbers of pages that are indexed are impressive, it is still only a fraction of the total number of pages on the Web. The Web grows too fast, even for the most efficient spiders.

It is also a problem that data may be hidden from the spiders. Data may be stored in databases, and will require logins, passwords, or other user input to be retrieved, and thus for all practical purposes be hidden. Data may also be stored in other formats than HTML, such as MS Word or PDF files—an "invisible" Web that is not covered by all search engines.[3] Updates create another problem. Many Web pages are highly dynamic, and some need to be reindexed every day. In practice, even if most engines try to reindex the most popular pages quite often, it can still be weeks between each update. If the page has changed in the meantime, the last indexing may no longer be valid.

Spiders are used to find and index Web pages described in HTML, XML, and perhaps also PDF format.

10.3 Discrepancy between user's information need and the query

The concept of **"information need"** may be described as a collection of terms—the query.

The search engines operate on a string or word level. There is no understanding of higher-level terms such as address, account number, balance, flight number, etc. There is no date of publication, nor a formalized field for "author." Even where a title and keywords are provided there is no common ground for understanding these words, since the Web covers so many languages and topics, and since authors come from all professions and categories.

The problem we face is to map our *information need* into one or more keywords, perhaps using the Boolean operators, such as **not**, **and**, **or**, to better express our need. The success of this mapping, and retrieval results, will depend on:

1. The formalization level of the query
2. The connection between the higher-level concepts and the query terms
3. The specificity of the terms

Let us start this discussion by looking at the simplest queries, for example, finding the home page of School of Information Sciences, University of Pittsburgh. In this case we have a high degree of formalization. The task is to find a given home page and the "concepts" are simplified by the use of names. While there may be many "Schools of Information Sciences," there is only one in Pittsburgh. Similarly you should be able to find my home page directly or indirectly by providing "Kai Olsen" to a search engine. In other cases, polysemy, the fact that a word has many meanings, may cause problems. Golf is a sport, but also the name of a car and the communications code word for the letter *G*. However, often these cases may be made more specific by adding additional terms, for example, "Volkswagen Golf." But then, we will not find the American version of this car, which goes under the name of Volkswagen Rabbit.

Web searching is complicated by the fact that the Web itself is a very inhomogeneous collection of documents.

The diversity of the Web does not only encompass topics, but also the nature of the documents. While a bibliographic database normally consists of only one type of documents (e.g., scientific papers), we will have all categories of documents on the Web. If we formalize our need for a description of the Rabbit car by a "Volkswagen Rabbit" query, we will get an abundance of cars for sale advertisements, names of dealers, and, if we are lucky, also one or more pages giving specifications of this model. The search engine may help us, however, by using a scheme to identify the most important pages. Google, for example, will put a priority to pages that are linked to by many other pages, in fact, using the Web to index the Web. Thus, the official Volkswagen pages may come up first in the result set. This works fine in most cases, but tend to make the practical Web more static and less dynamic, maintaining the existing structure. When there are competing pages it may be different for a new page to be seen among the incumbents. Since there initially will be few links to the new page the search engine will list the other pages first. So, if you are to promote the Web site of a new business or just your home pages, make sure that the site is recognized by many others (i.e., asking them to create links to your site).

While names are a great help in searching, helping us to identify persons, places, brands, and products, some names are more specific than others. It is easier to use the Web to get an overview of hotels in Nome, Alaska than in Los Angeles, where there is an abundance of hotels. Similar, it is easier to find a person with a special name than one with a common name. However, if we know where the person lives, it will be a great help if the latter lives in Nome where there are 3,505 inhabitants, and not in Los Angeles with close to ten million inhabitants.

10.4 Natural language

Where names are not available we have to rely on natural language, coping with synonymy, polysemy, and the precision of

The open nature of **natural language** reduces search effectiveness.

terms. Due to synonymy we may miss some interesting institutions in our search for "computing science" education, since these may use the synonym "informatics." Perhaps institutions within "information science" would be of interest, but these home pages may not use our keywords. While these problems occur in all bibliographic systems, they are worse on the Web due to the non-homogeneous nature of the documents. For example, the word "plasma" has one meaning for a medical database, another for a database consisting of documents in the field of physics. That is, when we search a medical database we may utilize the sublanguage of medicine to formalize queries, using terms for diagnosis, treatments, medicines, etc., expecting that we share a common vocabulary with the authors of these documents. Further, the nature of the data may provide additional search clues. In a database of scientific papers we will have the option of limiting a query to words in the title, the keyword part, or the abstract. Perhaps we can ask the system to give added weight to documents where keywords are found within headers. Here we profit by our common understanding of the form of such papers.

Sublanguages can aid searching in homogenous databases.

On the open Web there is no such common understanding. The pages will have authors from all professions, amateur as well as professional. Here "plasma" may have all the four meanings offered by an English dictionary (blood, protoplasm, a green translucent variety of quartz, and an ionized gas), and perhaps also others if we go beyond English. The documents may be in any form: notes, memorandums, reports, letters, minutes of meetings, product description, brochures, scientific papers, etc.—in any conceivable form. On the open Web we will therefore have all the disadvantages of natural language searching, with few possibilities of enhancing queries by using context information.

Are the words **precise** enough?

However, we may encounter problems even before we submit keywords to a search engine. Often it may be problematic just to find the words that describe our "information need." For example, we may want to buy a new, inexpensive car. Our information needs can then be to get a list of the various models available. While this is fairly clear to a human being, it is not so easy to pose such a question to a search engine. We may try "inexpensive cars," or perhaps "car **and** (inexpensive **or** cheap)." The problems we face are that inexpensive and cheap are relative terms, and often used as a default in marketing. The search will include pages that describe cars for sale, rentals, maintenance, etc., and may exclude pages where cars are listed with their price. In such cases an experienced searcher may try a different approach, for example, to find an auto magazine on the Web, and then try to get an overview of inexpensive cars here, since the direct approach is so difficult.

An alternative would be to include more terms in the query, perhaps using the keyword **not** to exclude pages. In practice, this is not always easy. More specific terms may improve precision, but will reduce recall. In addition, many ordinary users have problems using Boolean operator terms correctly, especially when **or-** and **not-** operators are included. This is caused by the rather informal way these terms are used in natural language. The waiter may give you a choice of "Italian, French, and blue cheese dressing with baked or boiled potatoes," where a mathematician would use parentheses and different operators.

We get a more common understanding of Boolean queries if we only use the **and**-operator, asking the search engine to include only pages that contain all the query terms. Most search engines assume that we imply an **and** when we give more than one keyword, but this is really not a Boolean **and**, since the engine will also list references (farther down in the result set) where only one of the keywords occurs.

Boolean operators are not always intuitive.

10.5 Information overload

We can use Boolean **and**-operators to limit the size of the result set, reducing the problem of information overload. Information overload occurs when we get too many documents back, where irrelevant documents make it difficult to find what we want. The basic problem is, of course, that while computer technology has given us efficient ways for creating, storing, and disseminating information, our ability to read documents is as slow as ever. While a search engine may return thousands of references, we may only have the time to examine a few, perhaps not more than twenty or forty references for an average query.

Table 10.1 illustrates the problem. It shows the number of references returned by the AltaVista[4] search engine in a test performed some years ago on the topic that we are discussing here.[5] Most of these queries, even the quite specific queries numbers four and seven, resulted in information overload—an unwieldy number of documents. By narrowing the queries, as in query five and eight, we were able to reduce the return set to

Information overload, when we get too many references returned with no possibility of narrowing searches without losing important references.

No	Query	# returned
1.	information AND retrieval	80,000
2.	"information retrieval"	20,000
3.	full AND text AND information AND retrieval	10,000
4.	"information retrieval" AND "full text"	2,000
5.	"full text information retrieval"	40
6.	information AND overload	10,000
7.	"information overload"	4,000
8.	"information retrieval" AND "information overload"	40

Table 10.1 WWW queries and results

We can increase **precision**, but often have to pay with a reduced **recall**.

a manageable size (40). All of the 40 documents returned in queries five and eight are relevant, showing that it is possible to get high precision in large inhomogeneous databases by giving very precise queries. However, we paid for this high precision by lowering recall. The low recall was confirmed by the results of alternative queries describing our information need, where different sets of documents were returned. Thus, it seems that by each precise query we only receive a fraction of the relevant documents on the Web. If we repeat the same queries today, after the search engine has had time to index even more pages, we will find that the problem of information overload is even worse. Today, query one returns nearly ten times as many documents, and even the precise queries (five and eight) return an unmanageable result set, with respectively 800 and 2000 references.

While the documents returned are relevant in the sense that they cover the topics of interest, they do not necessarily fulfill our information need. Some of the information may already be known to us, some may cover aspects of information retrieval that are not of interest and some may be in an "unpublished" or unedited form that makes it difficult to rely on the information. While formalizing the information need by a set of words or a Boolean expression is complicated in any system, the inhomogeneous nature of the Web makes it difficult to use when high recall is of interest.

Search engines use different schemes in order to weight the results, giving us the most **relevant** references first.

The search engines may try to help us cope with information overload by listing the most relevant links first. For example, it can put a priority on pages that include the terms in their "keywords" tag, pages where the terms are included early in the text or perhaps more than once, or can prioritize pages that are linked by many other pages (as Google does). While these schemes cannot guarantee a reasonable order, they are important. Without relevance rankings, Web search engines would be unusable in most cases. However, if these schemes are too transparent, Web authors can use countermeasures to avoid their page getting a low priority, for example, by expanding the keyword section.

10.6   Filtering

We face the same discussion when we have the inverse problem—that of filtering out unwanted (e.g., pornographic) material, from the Web. Such filters can be based on:

1. An automatic analysis of the Web page, for example, excluding the page if it includes words such as "sex," "porn," and "tits."

2. A manual categorization of a website by a "filter" agency.

3. A manual categorization of a Web page by the page author.

A 100 percent **filter system** is impossible to achieve. At best, we can develop filters that remove some of the unwanted pages (but with the risk of removing pages of interest).

All of these methods have their drawbacks. An automatic classification may remove pages that are nonpornographic, but still includes the filter words. For example, in Swedish the number six is spelled "sex." There are also pages that discuss pornography that give sex-advice, etc., that can easily be removed by these filters. Some filters try to identify skin color in order to remove pages with nude pictures. They may pass through more than the burka-dressed Afghan women, in practice, however, such a filter can never work. The information gap between the "skin color" algorithm and the goal of removing pornographic pictures is too great, just as it is difficult to evaluate the semantics of text just by looking at individual words.

A manual categorization is simpler, but also implies some form of censorship. However, the censor element may be reduced if there are many categories and where the user at the browser herself can choose what to exclude (setting the filter on or off, or determining the filter level), based on a categorization set by the page authors. This requires that everybody follow the standards, something that may be difficult to achieve considering the global inhomogeneous nature of the Web. The censorship element becomes more troublesome if we leave categorization to a special agency and, anyway, the enormous number of websites will make such a solution impossible.

10.7 Quality

Since everyone has the option to be a writer on the Web and since there is no reviewing at all on most pages, we cannot always take what we get back for granted. On the Web we can find everything, high quality scientific documents, school papers, propaganda, correct information, incorrect information, advertisements, official sites and unofficial sites, company sites and personal sites, and more. Today, we let school kids access this repository, while we not so many years ago had a very careful screening process of textbooks and other material. But perhaps this can be seen as an advantage. On the Web we know that we cannot take what we find for granted, we have to be critical, review the source, and perhaps try to get confirmation from other sources. That is, with the Web we can train our kids in being critical, instead of letting them accept everything in the textbook at face value.

We face another problem if we want to publish information found on the Web. Most often information on the Internet and Web is presented without any copyright notice, like the joke we presented in chapter 1.2. But we have no guarantee as to where it came from in the first place. Text and images are cut from copyrighted Web pages, scanned from newspapers, magazines, and books, and put on the Web, without any reference to the source. In many ways the Web is used in the same way as oral channels, but while an oral story is never told with exactly the same words as in the original, on the Web we can get an identical copy.

With all the unedited material on the Web we have to be **our own editors** (i.e., to evaluate the correctness and quality of the information we get). This is perhaps more an advantage than a drawback?

If we cannot trust the information itself, neither can we expect that the results from the search engines be presented in any fair order. The advantage of coming on top of the list (a search on "hotel London" returns a set of 1,370,000 documents) is so great that businesses are willing to pay a premium to be prioritized. A more honest way of implementing this is to add relevant banner ads to the search results, making it easier for the user to distinguish between the commercial and non-commercial result set.

But perhaps this is what we should expect, listings in paper-based directories, like the yellow pages, are also based on what one is willing to pay. It is perhaps more important that the search engines do not filter out any (legal) sites, which gives us the possibility of finding a page even if it is put at the bottom of a large result set (or we may try a narrower search).

Exercises and Discussion

1. Use a search engine to find information on a specific car model. How many of the first ten references listed in the result set are relevant? Calculate a simplified precision based on this limited result set. Do a new search, this time you are interested in finding the number of Web pages in the world today. Try to formulate a query and calculate precision based on the first ten references returned. Discuss the differences between these two search situations.

2. You are going to stay overnight and need a hotel. Perform a search for a hotel in *New York City*. How large is the result set? Is it difficult to get an overview? Now, search for a hotel in my home town of *Molde, Norway*. How large is the result set now? Then try finding a hotel in *Thule, Greenland*. How large is the result set? Discuss the differences.

3. A simple filtering system for email removes all messages that include at least three of the terms "sex," "credit card," "free," "prescription," "discount." While this certainly will find many spam messages, there may be important personal messages that are also removed. Can you find examples of the latter? Discuss the problem of filtering out spam messages.

Notes

1. Introduced by Kent, A., Berry, M., Leuhrs, F.U. & Perry, J.W. 1955. Machine Literature Searching VIII. Operational Criteria for Designing Information Retrieval Systems, *American Documentation*, 6 (2), 93-101.

2. Yet another problem may be that the search engines produce biased results, where sites can pay to get a high ranking, where links to the competition are removed, etc.

3. There are exceptions. Adobe, for example, offers a search engine that looks into PDF files.

4. www.altavista.com.

5. Olsen, K.A., Sochats, K.M., and Williams, J.G. 1998. Full text information retrieval and Information overload, *The International Information and Library Review*, No. 30, pp 105-122.

11 Organizing the Web—Portals

Portals initially provided the organizational service of structuring the Web in a menu hierarchy.

Today, after ten years with the Web, there are so many Web servers that, as we have seen, even the 12-digit (32-bit) IP address scheme needs an expansion. Each of these servers can be filled with many thousands of pages. With all this information, organization becomes an important issue. This is what the general portals try to do, offering a "table of contents" for the Web. These are presented hierarchically, often in a tree structure[1] and using hypertext links from one level to the next. For example, on the home page, the root page, we may be offered the generic term transportation; clicking on transportation gives a new page with airlines, trains, boats, etc. Hierarchical menus are a traditional way of organizing material. They are simple and allow users to navigate a predetermined structure. The overall task is broken down in steps, with a simple choice at each step, until the user gets to the "leaf" nodes, the Web pages with the information he seeks.

Menus provide simple user interfaces when the menu is structured along our needs, and when data fall in clear menu categories.

A menu hierarchy works fine as long as it follows our needs. Restaurant menus are a good example of a logical ordering. The appetizers are of course presented first, followed by main dishes, with desserts last. Main dishes may be categorized into meat, fish, and poultry. There may even be subcategories to satisfy vegetarians. While such an organization supports the order process for most guests, it is of little help when our needs do not follow the standard approach. In a restaurant this is no big problem, as we can ask the waiter to tell us which dishes satisfy a salt-free or celiac diet. On the Web, there may not be a human being to handle these exceptions. If we are looking for a cheap airfare from Paris to Pittsburgh, we may not be satisfied with a travel $\rightarrow$ air $\rightarrow$ airlines organization, as it will be impractical to access the site of every airline. If we try to find a hotel in a large city, we may be overwhelmed by the thousands of sites that a portal may offer. Here a subdivision into locations and/or prices would be welcome.

While a hierarchical structure may have unlimited depth, navigation in large structures is often complicated. On each level we use menu terms as a link and header for the next subsection. The problem is then to find nonoverlapping terms, where each term describes a distinct subset of the information space. For example after hitting travel, this subset may be divided into new subsets such as transportation, lodging, and insurance. Transportation may be further divided into air, boat, train, etc. The disadvantage of a deep structure is that we may have problems finding sites that are covered by more than one menu item, for example, packaged tours or cruises with airfare included.

To some extent broad menus, cross-structural links, filters and search engines may address these problems. A broad menu offers more choices on each level. For example, if all travel-related links can be offered on one page, such as different forms of transportation and lodging, package tours, cruises, insurance and other travel-related services, etc., a user will get a better overview of the alternatives.

While a hierarchical structure is a simple way of organizing material it has the disadvantage that related sites might end up far apart in the structure. For example, a hotel in London may be cataloged under travel and perhaps under the subcategories lodging and hotel, while the city itself may be cataloged under a country header. Then it will be convenient to have a link from the hotel to the city site, and vice versa, from the city site to the hotel. Such cross-structural links may violate the tree-structure organization, where there is only one path from the root to the leaf nodes, but are convenient when more than one organizational strategy is to be implemented. The disadvantage is that the possibility of getting "lost in hyperspace" increases, as there may be many paths to a given node.

Filter queries provide a means of limiting information and work in formalized areas. When we have to extract meanings from word occurrences, filters may break down—as with most other natural language systems.

Filter queries offer the possibility of limiting information, for example, to show a restaurant menu with only salt-free dishes. Here computer-based menus have clear advantages over their paper-based counterparts. A list of used cars can be shown initially with all cars. Then the user can set up a filter query, for example, limiting the presentation to cars less than five years old, which have four wheel drive and cost less than $12,000. For each new filter term the list can be redisplayed, letting the user decide if more terms are needed.

Ideally, we would like a system that could organize the world according to our needs, but this requires that the computer system has a semantic understanding of both the information that it classifies and our needs. This is not the case with general Internet portals, but may be achieved for more specific portals where the underlying data have the necessary formalization level.

As with search engines, portals only index a small part of the Web. A site can be submitted to a portal, giving the URL

Portals try to make a living out of the traffic that goes through their site.

and the most logical location within the portals' hierarchical structure. General portals try to make a living out of the traffic that goes through the site. This can be achieved by selling commercials in the form of banners, very similar to billboards on a busy corner. While the initial purpose of portals was to organize the Web, the traffic generated to these sites has opened the way for other business models. Today, we see that portals try to offer all types of services to users, from traditional indexing services to online sales and auctions, of both symbolic and physical products. While this may be a valid business model for some sites it is clearly not a valid model for all sites. Traffic may disappear if a site becomes too similar to other, perhaps better, sites. Many TV stations and newspapers have tried to use their customer base to create general portals, without success.

The most successful have connected the portals to their main business (e.g., newspapers that offer classified ads online, general TV channels that offer background information on their programs or shopping-channels that sell goods online as well as through the traditional TV/telephone channel).

Exercises and Discussion

1. Create a diagram of the top level structure of Yahoo! (www.yahoo.com). Try to describe the structure for one or two menu items all the way down to the leaf nodes (the actual Web pages).

2. Choose a portal for a TV company (www.nbc.com, www.abc.com, or any other). What kind of information and services is offered? What do you think is the aim of this portal? Discuss.

Notes

1. In a tree structure each page will link to a number of "children," each child will again link to its children, and so forth. A typical tree structure is the family tree. On the Web we seldom see these true tree structures, where each node has only one "mother." Theoretically Web pages are network structures, since every node can link to every other. There may even be links from children to mothers. However, if we overlook these odd links, we will in practice find that most Web pages are ordered in a hierarchical structure.

12 Web Presence

As we have seen, one of the basic ideas of Tim Berners-Lee, the inventor of the Web, was that everybody should be an information-provider, not just a consumer of information. He foresaw a network of scientists that could access each other's papers and scientific data. Of course, the Web expanded early to other user groups on a world-wide basis, not only on geography but also for applications.

The democratic nature of the Web is in contrast to most other media, where content is created by a privileged few. Berners-Lee implemented his ideas by keeping the structure of the Web pages simple, formalizing only on the layout level. With one-way hypertext links anyone could link to anyone, no permission or central link storage was needed. This enabled anyone to create a Web page, using HTML and a text editor, a Web tool, or just saving MS Word documents as HTML.

Web users exploit the possibility of being information-providers, as seen by the **billions of pages** that exist on the Web.

It seems that many of us have an incentive to create content, to present ideas, opinions, or hobbies. We call in to radio and TV programs and write letters to the newspaper editor. However, with radio, TV, and newspapers there are practical limitations as to what and how much they can and want to publish of customer's responses. On the Web, there are no limitations. Berners-Lee's simple syntax and the lack of formal requirements have removed usability problems and we are in the process of reducing technical limitations by robust and cheap technology. A clear incentive combined with few barriers has given us billions of Web pages. We create home pages for our children and ourselves, for firms and institutions, professional organizations, nonprofit organizations.... There are no editors, no consultants. The author alone determines what is to be published. When the page is stored on the server it is automatically accessible for the whole world.

Earlier the only other media which offered inexpensive nonedited publishing was wallboards and flypapers. One can reach quite a number of readers with leaflets with a good organization and enough volunteers for distribution. Still, as with wallboards, there are practical limitations both in volume and geographical locations. In contrast, there are no geographical limitations and no upper theoretical limit to "circulation" on the Web.

Theoretically our home page can be seen by the world; in practice most of us get very few real "clicks." More than 50 percent of traffic goes to sites controlled by a few major companies.

If we want **hits** on our Web pages we must advertise the existence of the page.

People that know us can easily find a link to our Web page by using a search engine, providing name and other **formalized information**, such as address and position.

In practice, it is not so easy to get "hits" on a Web page. There are billions of pages and perhaps as many authors as readers. In fact, if you want to hide confidential information, it might be a good idea to put it on the Web. The chance that someone will access your page, and actually read the contents, is pretty remote. In principle, any Web user that has the page URL can retrieve a page posted on the Web. However, to get visitors we need to make the URL public. As we shall see, this is where we depart from the notion of the democratic Web. In practice, we are no more equal on the Web than anywhere else. Money and power have as much influence on the Web, as in any other media. In 2001 four major companies controlled more than 50 percent of the surfing time on the Web.[1]

I have a personal home page that lists my background, professional interests, publications, etc., together with a picture and address information. It is submitted to and has been indexed by some of the major search engines, and can be found by a search on my name. Alternatively, it can be found by a link from the list of employees at the institutions where I work, or from home pages to my courses. With this I get some hundred hits a year, mostly students that follow links from course pages, but also visitors to the institutions where I am affiliated or perhaps from scientists that followed up on my papers. That is, accesses to my home page are based on my "popularity" in the real world, where perhaps only a fraction of the people that are connected to me in some way or other find their way to my home page.

However, this is just what we have to expect, and perhaps what most of us want to achieve. When you find out that your old friend, Bill, from college has been hired by one of your customers, and will be in on the next meeting, it is very convenient to be able to gather some updated information from his home page. You have no problem to find his official home page at the customer's website, and from here Bill has a link to his personal page. You find that he is still married to Jane, that his small kids are in high school (oops!), that he is a representative for the local chapter of the Republican party (no longer a radical). The picture will certainly help you to recognize him (even if Bill, like most of us, does not update the home page picture—the exception to the rule that updated information is the better). Of course, Bill will access your home page to get the same information. We avoid embarrassing situations, and get information that would have been very difficult to get without the Web.

A nonprofit organization can present its URL in the letters or newsletters they send to their members. If they have been smart and lucky, they have been able to get a site name that describes their organization, for example, www.aids.org, www.cancer.org, and so forth. These are addresses where one may try to find these organizations. In the private sector firms have been willing to pay quite a lot to get such "topic" addresses, www.bank.com, www.tv.com, www.loan.com. As long as the extensions, such as dot-com and dot-org, clearly categorize the type of institution a topic name can be an advantage. The downside is that of trust. Are we willing to go to these "generic" sites, such as bank.com, or is it easier to follow the well-known brand names. All in all, the effectiveness of these names may be exaggerated. Why should we go to tv.com?

A physical world presence and a well-known brand name are important when establishing a web-site.

Some well-known companies and institutions can rely on the knowledge of their real-world name as a basis for their URL, expecting users to add the necessary extension. It is thus easy to find IBM on www.ibm.com, MIT on www.mit.edu, the engineering organization IEEE on www.ieee.org, or the White House at www.whitehouse.gov. Thus, the advantage of a well-known name extends itself to the Web, especially if it is short, and easy to spell. Foreign names, long names, and names containing special characters may cause a problem, even if the name may be well known. In most cases a wrong guess by a visitor may give an "unknown page" message, sometimes the visitor may get something different from what he expected—another institution or at worst a page that tries to mimic the intended site.[2]

In the physical world location sets a context for many names, this context is removed on the global Web and names get over-loaded.

The global URL naming scheme is not without problems. There may be many Joe's restaurants and many businesses that use an acronym such as SAS, but there is a place for only one joe.com and only one sas.com. In the physical world this is seldom a problem. We use the local directory when we want to call Joe's to reserve a table, and will not even know of the other Joe's in the world. Similarly the directories will help us distinguish between SAS the airline, the software company, and the others. But on the global Web we do not have this context. The extension may help us distinguish between company X, university X, and the nonprofit organization X, but within a domain there can only be one of each.

Other organizations and companies have to rely on existing channels to the customers to promote their website, promote the site by marketing or hope that a search engine will offer a link to their site. Marketing a URL through existing channels can be as simple as providing a URL on product packaging, buildings, cars, trucks, or airplanes and including the URL in all advertisements. On the Web, the site can be submitted to search engines for indexing, so that their link will turn up in a search for the company name, and perhaps also in a search for their products. A firm can include links to their major customers and suppliers in their Web page, and hope that everybody else will do the same for them.

For new Internet startups, heavy marketing may be needed to reach customers, if one is not as lucky as to get attention by the media.[3] Many sites have used traditional marketing channels, TV, radio, newspapers, and junk mail, in addition to marketing on the Web. For the latter banners, images with a site link can be placed on popular sites. In addition, some search engines or portals can be paid to put a priority on the site by inserting the link first in the search results, highlighting the link, etc. The need for these campaigns has been a heavy expense for start-ups and in many cases has been the cause of their downfall. There is also evidence that continuous campaigns are needed to keep the interest for a site, that users turn away as soon as the marketing stops. Here, existing brick and mortar companies have a clear advantage. They can use their well-known name as a URL, use existing channels to promote their Web address, avoiding or reducing the amount spent on additional marketing.

However, even for these it may be expensive to run a website, especially if the site only attracts a small customer base. Some companies have had success by a modest and simple approach to online sales, for example, using a system where the customer can get information and order online, but where the actual product is picked up or mailed from a nearby store. The philosophy here is to view the brick and the online channels as alternative ways of communicating with the customers, not as exclusive options, and to use the brick infrastructure as a basis for the "click" channel.

The greenhouse effect and other environmental problems have shown that we live in a world of limited size. Still, it is inhabited by more than six billion people. In the United States alone there may be as many as twenty million businesses. Thus, it is not easy to be seen, in the real world or on the Web. The Web has given us a tool for presenting ourselves or our company to the world, but we will have to compete with many others for attention. Globalization, accelerated by the Web, makes the difficulties worse. Being seen is not a big problem if we establish a store in a small town, but is likely to be a challenge when our market area extends local boundaries, perhaps also national boundaries as is often the case for many businesses today. The Web is both the solution and the problem.

Exercises and Discussion

1. You have just established a new Internet book store, www.mystore.com. Your task is now to get people to access your site. Discuss how this can be done.

2. Your bookstore (see above) has been in business for several years. Christmas is coming up and you want to tell established customers about new books and holiday offers. Discuss how this can be done.

3. How can you make your own home page more accessible to others?

4. The CIO (Chief Information Officer) of Bank of Pittsburgh has established the site bankpittsburgh.com for the bank's Internet services. In addition to this URL she has obtained bankpitsburgh.com, bankpittsburg.com and bankpitsburg.com. Why do you think that she also obtained these "unnecessary" addresses?

Notes

1. America Online, Yahoo!, Microsoft, and Napster, a report by Jupiter Media Metrix 06/04/2001. Traffic to Napster has most probably turned to other sites that can offer free music downloads.

2. It would be a good idea for any company to obtain the most common URLs that people use in order to find their site, including common spelling mistakes. Some institutions also go as far as to get control over the addresses that could be used by their critics, such as hateX, noX, etc.

3. For example, the search engine Google managed to establish itself without marketing. Their search results were so good that several newspapers, among these US Today and Le Monde in Paris, told the story. A top ranking by PZ Magazine did not hurt either. See http://www.google.com/corporate/history.html.

13 Mobile Computing

Where is the **killer application**? Can wireless technology offer any promise?

Disillusioned by the seemingly limited opportunities to make revenue based on standard Web and Internet applications, many have looked to wireless for the new killer application, basing their hopes on the success of mobile phones. To many, the lack of success of WAP (Wireless Application Protocol) technology in the European market must therefore have been a disappointment. WAP defines a protocol for accessing Internet from mobile phones, allowing the telephone to be used as a terminal, for email and Web applications. The failure of WAP may be due to the fact that it is a premature technology, with limited functionality and bandwidth, perhaps also with some security holes. Some of these problems are addressed by the next generations of wireless services, for example, the UMTS.[1] However, as we have seen many companies are making money on simple SMS messages, a technology at the opposite end of the specter. Maybe advanced Internet functionality is not what is needed on a cell phone?

First, when moving from an analog to a digital world there is always the possibility of adding extra functions at low cost. Digital watches, telephones, calculators are prime examples. While some of the add-on functions may be useful, they are as often ignored by users. The problem is partly that these functions are hidden behind invisible user interfaces, and that a manual or extensive exploration is needed to invoke the functions. Partly the problem is that many of these functions solve nobody's problem and they are added more because it is possible than because they cover a real need. Even if a function would be handy in a special situation, one needs to use it frequently in order to remember codes and button presses.

A cell phone removes a **restriction** from a well-known and much-used media, the ordinary telephone.

Second, the success of mobile phones cannot in any way be used as the criterion for forecasting the success of Internet services on these phones. For customers, a mobile phone is like any other telephone, but with the important distinction that the length of the cord does not restrict mobility. That is, the main difference is that a constraint has been removed. Thus, user acceptance of these new devices is high and the competence, the routines, and the social conventions are all in place since they are ported from the fixed phones. Of course, the mobility and freedom attained have been employed to develop new services and new usage patterns. Today, a cell phone is therefore more than a phone without a cord.

Third, as a computer or terminal, the mobile phone is very different from a PC. We should remember that the advance of the new PC technology was boosted by the ease of use of the Apple Macintosh, one of the first computers with a mouse and a graphical screen. This made it possible to implement a set of usability requirements, such as:

- *Minimizing short-term memory load* by presenting all the data the user needed for performing his task, on the display.

- *Using forms* to structure output and input, informative captions, default values, selection from lists instead of typing, menus and buttons to help the user find the right command.

- Allowing *direct manipulation*, where one for example could move a file by clicking on the icon, dragging the icon to the receiving folder and releasing the mouse button.

Usability is to a large extent coupled to a large screen, good pointing device, and keyboard—not available on all portable devices.

Due to its usability the MacIntosh introduced computers to new markets, to nontechnical users, and to the home market. Remove the mouse, reduce screen real estate to a minimum, replace the full keyboard with a set of function keys with a small numeric keyboard, and you have something very different from a usability point of view. A form or a menu shown partially on the screen is something very different from having the full form or menu available. On the WAP phone, the user must scroll up and down, relying on his memory to keep track of all options. Textual input has to be coded on a numerical display, requiring more keystrokes. The coding scheme and small keys will slow down keying and increase the possibility of typing errors.

For voice communication the compactness of the unit is an advantage. The display is more than large enough for presenting telephone numbers, names, and simple dialogs, and with some experience we do not even look at the display when we enter numbers. The keyboard has all the keys needed to type in a telephone number, and keying is only needed at the start and end of a dialog. Most important, we can really use the device when we are mobile. We can walk and talk and use the telephone while we are driving (hands-free recommended). This is not so easy for Internet applications, where output is on the display and input is needed throughout the whole communication.

Using a WAP phone must feel like picking up beans with gloves on for an experienced Internet user. In the United States and Europe we are used to accessing the Internet, email, and Web from a PC. We take into account the size and quality of the displays when designing Web pages or composing email messages. In practice, WAP technology really needs special versions of Web pages, designed for the small display and limited input capabilities. But we cannot expect Web providers to offer these alternatives before the number of WAP users reaches a critical mass.

Email messages cause another problem. These may be verbose, may include a whole sequence of messages, a signature with address information and attachments. Of course, if one knows that the receiver is going to read the message on a WAP phone one would try to limit the text to a minimum, giving all the important information up front. In practice, however, it may be difficult to determine the medium for reading the email messages, and if the email goes to more than one person the only remedy will be to create different versions of every message, clearly not practical.

In contrast, Japanese firms have had success with their wireless technology, based on a different business concept than WAP. Instead of general Internet access, a Japanese customer will access a set of information sources that generate information to be displayed on his mobile phone. Further, for the typical customer this will be his only access to the Internet. He does not have the PC alternative.

To make up for the limited display space output can be given on the audio channel instead. A website with a speech generator/synthesizer could give customized information on the local weather and driving conditions, your stock portfolio, expected delays on your flight this afternoon, email headers, etc. The specification of what we want can be given up front by accessing a Web page from a PC. When calling the site the telephone number will identify the user. The data can then be generated in a stream where the user can skip parts that are of no interest, or a simple menu system can be offered—perhaps using speech recognition software if we can get the necessary quality.[2] The advantage of this approach is that we utilize the mobile phone as a voice device, the disadvantage that it will

Are the **PC functions** on a cell phone suited for mobility?

With a **text-to-voice** generator we reduce the burden on the display, and also make it easier to use more advanced functions when we are mobile.

only offer limited Web access and that the service in all respects is slower than showing data on a display.

For the more experienced Internet user the remedy could be to use more advanced units, for example, a PDA (Personal Digital Assistant) instead of a WAP phone. For general Web access a PDA may offer the minimum of usability needed. Its larger screen makes it easier to get an overview of the data; a touch-sensitive display and a pen can simplify input. The smallest and most handy PDAs come without a keyboard, but even if a keyboard is present it may be too small for convenient typing (or too big to carry around). This limits the amount of input that can be given. We should therefore expect that the most successful applications exploit mobility and information presentation, and situations where input is limited and formalized to a high level. Data can then be entered by marking checkboxes, selecting from lists and with only limited typing. Today PDAs are used by out-of-office workers such as plumbers, electricians, and carpenters to retrieve information, to document and to add invoice data (hours, material used).

PDAs can be used in conjunction with a PC, with a facility to copy or synchronize files between the two devices. Today, the most common connection uses a docking station and a cable, but new short-range wireless technology, such as the Bluetooth technology supported by IBM, Intel, Lucent, Nokia, and others. Then synchronization of data between devices can be done automatically. For increased mobility one can either connect the PDA to a cell phone or the cell phone can be integrated in the PDA. An interesting option, as an add-on or alternative, is Wireless Local Area Networks (WLAN). These communication devices are based on radio technology, have a limited range (up to 100 feet indoors, 1000 outdoors), but offer much higher bandwidth than the cell phone networks. Thus we can get inexpensive Internet connection with high bandwidth at airports, malls, hotels, businesses, etc. Between these hubs we can use the existing cell phone networks, but have to accept a lower bandwidth.

We may soon reach the critical mass needed so that Web developers create PDA versions of their pages, if not the display is large enough to show at least the text part of Web pages, perhaps after a filter program has restructured the information automatically for the PDA.[3] PDAs will also be suited for push technology (i.e., where providers "push" customized informa-

The PDA can be **connected** to other devices or the Internet using different wireless communication technologies.

Usability is increased with a **PDA**. This is especially the case with units that can offer a large display, but the size of the unit can then be a disadvantage.

tion onto your device). We cover this technology in the next chapter.

Exercises and Discussion

1. Cell phones with an integrated camera are now on the market and pictures can be sent as multimedia messages, as enhanced SMS messages. Try to find examples of how this service can be used, for pleasure or for business. What are the limitations?

2. You are in charge of promoting a high bandwidth radio-based network. Make a list for potential investors of possible cell phone applications for this network. Discuss each application.

Notes

1. Universal Mobile Telecommunications System.

2. Speech recognition has been a hot topic for many years. With fast dictionary lookups as we speak these systems may get good enough accuracy to be useful for dictating. However, extensive training is necessary to teach the system your way of pronouncing words, and the system will easily fail for persons with an accent, a cold, or if there is a low-quality channel (mobile phone?) or background noise. Systems directed toward general users (i.e., situation without training), can today only be used in the simplest of cases, with very restricted vocabularies. Smart applications offer alternatives, for example, the option of typing a telephone number where the recognition system does not understand what you are saying.

3. XML (eXtensible Markup Language) which separates content from layout may be an answer. With XML the same content can be formatted in many different ways, for example, for high resolution screens, PDAs as well as WAP phones. We cover XML in chapter 27.

14 Automated Web (Push Technology)

Traditional Web uses *pull* techniques. The user starts the browser and gives the URL of the site that he wants to see (i.e., the user is in full control when selecting sites and "pulling down" information). An alternative is to use *push* techniques, where the site pushes information to your device. This has the disadvantage that the user loses some control, but to a large extent this can be reduced by offering customized information.

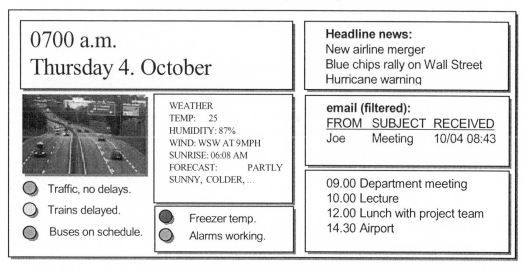

0700 a.m.
Thursday 4. October

Headline news:
New airline merger
Blue chips rally on Wall Street
Hurricane warning

WEATHER
TEMP: 25
HUMIDITY: 87%
WIND: WSW AT 9MPH
SUNRISE: 06:08 AM
FORECAST: PARTLY
SUNNY, COLDER, ...

email (filtered):
FROM   SUBJECT   RECEIVED
Joe   Meeting   10/04 08:43

Traffic, no delays.
Trains delayed.
Buses on schedule.

Freezer temp.
Alarms working.

09.00 Department meeting
10.00 Lecture
12.00 Lunch with project team
14.30 Airport

Figure 14.1 A mock-up of a personalized "wake-up" display.

Push technology can offer a **personalized** newspaper.

An example is shown in figure 14.1, a mock-up of a personalized "wake-up" display. This screen will provide all information that we need at this point of the day, information on weather, commuting, calendar, and email. The screen is personalized (i.e., while the actual information is pushed down from the server we have ourselves determined what kind of information is needed, along with the layout of the displays).

The display can be shown on a viewer that can be carried around in the house, connected to a PC or laptop using wireless technology. During breakfast the display may be changed to show the agenda for the office day. On the way to work we can get updated traffic information, connecting the display through the mobile phone or a wide-area wireless system. Now voice input and output can be used. Input will go to a voice recognition system, so that we can select the information that we need, similarly output is sent through a speech synthesizer. When we arrive at the office, the display will receive an updated version of the agenda, and other information that we need at the start of our working day—letting us scan this information while we are in the elevator. Arriving in our office, we will have the same information on the display of the office computer.

All of this technology is in place today. But at this point it is not clear which variant of the technology, or which protocols will become the accepted standards. Push technology requires broadband connection and the price of the devices will also have a large influence. As an alternative to a general unit, for example, a portable PC or a PDA with wireless communication, we may have a fixed wake-up unit next to the bed, another in the kitchen, in addition to a unit integrated in the dashboard of the car. This reduces the need for portable devices, and permits each device to be custom made for its environment.

Push technology saves us the trouble of retrieving information each time we need it, but assumes some sort of static situation where we require similar information at similar times.

The great advantage of push technology is that we can receive this information without having to give any input, except for the initial work of specifying sources and customizing screen layout. The disadvantage is the problems that may follow any type of technology, as we discussed in chapter 3. While most of us may find it convenient to get everything in one display, at the time we need it, instead of waiting for radio or TV to provide the information, it is unclear if we are willing to pay the costs of equipment, connection, subscription, etc. The new technology will also have to compete with the existing information channels, in our example even with cheap alarm clocks and thermometers. However, the expense will be much less if we use push technology on existing devices, such as our home computer, office computer, PDA, or cell phone. As with other Internet services, we may avoid subscription fees if we accept some form of marketing. This could be in the form of banner ads or, perhaps more efficiently for the marketers, as information on the display (e.g., a window with information from our local store or the gas station on the way to work). In addition, many of the interesting sources, public transportation, schools, and traffic authorities will provide useful information for free.

While the information itself is dynamic, updated perhaps several times a day, the selection is more static. This is a problem for push technology. We may have a need for information when roadwork or special events change traffic patterns or public transportation schedules, or we may need information on public transport the day the car is not working. However, this information may be of no interest on an ordinary day and may therefore not be available on the push display. Weather information may be important if it can affect driving conditions or our planned picnic, but may be ignored at other times. The problem is that the information need will be greatest in these exceptional situations. We do not need a camera to present traffic information on an ordinary day, as we know exactly how it is going to be. If the information presented by the push system becomes uninteresting it will be ignored, probably also the day that the system can show information of real interest.

Push information will work best in the situations where the type of information we need is static, but where the dynamics are in the data values. All stockbrokers have a display showing the important stock indexes and the valuation of selected stocks, the air traffic controller has a radar screen showing all planes in each sector, a security system has cameras at every important spot and Windows gives us the time and shows a bar with all open programs. In all of these cases the information presented is of interest most of the time.

Push technology works best when the **"dynamics"** are in the data itself, not in the selection of data types.

Exercises and Discussion

1. Let us assume that a push service has been established and that you have a portable viewer for displaying the information. Make a list of the information that you would be interested in. Would you be willing to pay the same for this service as for a newspaper subscription?

2. Discuss the merits and drawbacks of push technology.

15 Dynamic Web Pages

As we have seen, HTML pages contain text, images, and layout tags. We request these pages by clicking on a link, the browser will then find the URL hidden in the link, and use this identifier to issue a GET-command. This is sent to the appropriate server, identified by the IP address part of the URL. The server will use the additional folder and file information to find the HTML file, and return this page to the browser. These simple mechanisms implement the basic idea of the Web, where it is interesting to note that this functionality does not require any other input from the user than button clicks.

An important extension from the basic Web is the form-tag of HTML. HTML offers quite a selection of field types for creating forms: text fields, check and radio buttons, command buttons, and combo or list boxes for selection. This enables us to make quite sophisticated user interfaces using HTML. However, this simple set does not allow us to do any extensive error checking. An HTML form may for example offer a list box for month and another for day in month, but there is no way within HTML itself to ensure than we select a legal combination. Error checking, to catch the February 30th and other illegal dates must be performed on the server or locally, by scripts (see chapter 16).

HTML forms allow us to use a Web browser as an interface to applications, online banks, travel agency, shops, etc.

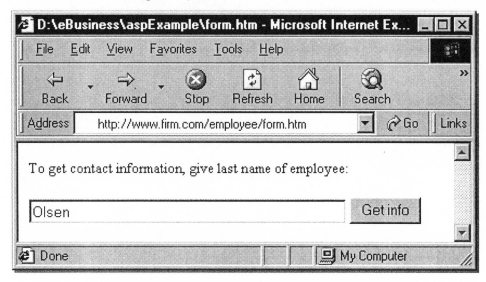

Figure 15.1 A simple HTML form (example)

In order to study the inner parts of the form concept we shall use the simple form presented in figure 15.1, a part of a directory system. Instead of providing an HTML table with name, telephone number, and email address of all employees we have instead a more dynamic system, where this information is provided by a "look-up" system based on the form shown in figure 15.1. This simple system will use the employee name provided to do a lookup in the employee database.

```
<FORM>
  ACTION="http://www.firm.com/employee.asp"
  METHOD=post id=userdata name=userdata>
  <p>To get contact information, give last
    name of employee:
  </p>
  <INPUT type=text name=lastname size=40
    maxlength=60>
  <INPUT name=info type=submit value="Get
    info">
</FORM>
```

Figure 15.2 HTML code for the form

The source for the form (in figure 15.1) is presented in figure 15.2 above. As seen, the form is identified by a <FORM> tag that gives the URL of the server page that is to receive the form data (i.e., the name of the employee). Note that the URL in this example has extension *asp*, not the customary *html*. This tells the server that this file should receive special treatment. Active Server Pages (ASP[1]) is a technology developed by Microsoft. This is only one of several different methods of creating dynamic pages, but we shall use ASP as an example here as this technology is fairly straightforward.

The form lets us provide **formalized input** (e.g., with different data separated in different fields).

Within the form-tag we have defined two input fields; the first is a text field (for the employee's name) and the second a definition of a "submit" button. When the user hits this button the browser will generate a command to the server, including the current value of the input fields. If we had used a GET-command, the values would have been appended to the command, for example, as

```
http://www.firm.com/employee.asp?
name=Olsen&Info=Get+info.
```

However, with the POST-command used here the input values are sent to the server in a separate HTTP transaction.

If the URL had indicated a file with extension *html* the server would have retrieved this file and returned it to the browser. However, since the file in question has the extension *asp*, a Microsoft Web server will expect to find a *script* in this file. A script is a simple program that can be interpreted by the server (i.e., the server reads line after line in the script and performs the operations specified).[2]

```
<%@ Language=VBScript %>
<%
set DBObj= Server.CreateObject("ADODB.Connection")
DBObj.Open "Employee"
%>
<HTML>
<HEAD>
<TITLE>Directory</TITLE>
</HEAD>
<BODY>
<H2>Contact information for <%=Request.Form("name")%> </H2>
<%
set stdset=dbObj.Execute("SELECT * FROM employeeTable
  WHERE name      = '" & Request.Form("name") & "'")
if stdset.eof then
  Response.Write("<p>No persons fulfilled search
  request</p>")
else
  Response.Write("<p>Phone:" & stdset("phone") & "</p>")
  Response.Write("<p>Email:" & stdset("email") & </p><br>")
end if
stdset.close
dbObj.close
%>
</BODY>
</HTML>
```

Figure 15.3 ASP script (example)

Server side **scripts** are simple programs that can retrieve data from forms, and generate a new Web page based on these input parameters and data from a server side database.

The contents of the *employee.asp* file are shown in figure 15.3. This script is based on Visual Basic, but we could just as well have written the script using other programming languages, such as script languages based on Java or C. As seen, the script is a mix of program statements, embedded in <% and %> brackets and HTML. While the details are of little interest here, one may identify some parts. The interpreter will execute the script from top to bottom. All code outside the brackets will be copied directly to a result file, while statements inside the brackets are instructions to the interpreter.

This script starts by identifying the script language and opening a connection to the employee database. The following HTML code defines the heading part of the result page. The *Request.Form* command is used to retrieve the value from the form data, here the value of the name field, so that this can be included in the heading. We then specify a database command using the SQL query language, a standard language for database operations. This SELECT-statement is executed on the employee database. Here we request the database system to return telephone and email address from the employee table, for an employee with a name equal to the input name parameter, the name the user provided in the HTML form.

If the database system finds this employee, we generate a simple HTML page with employee data; if not, we give a message that an employee with the given name could not be found in the database. This is achieved by the *Response.Write* statement. In the first case the headings "Phone:" and "Email:" together with the phone number and email address returned from the database is outputted along with the necessary HTML tags. In the latter case we generate the "No persons fulfilled search request" message, including the HTML tags for starting and ending a paragraph.

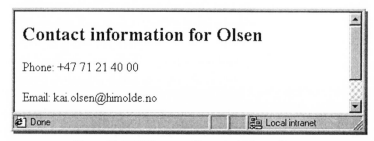

Figure 15.4 HTML page with contact information.

When this script is executed a complete HTML page has been generated. This is then returned to the browser. Note that the browser gets an HTML page back independently of what happens, either the page shown in figure 15.4 or the page giving the "not found" message. For the browser there is no difference between static or dynamic pages, in all cases it will receive an HTML page.

1. The user is on the home page of an organization and clicks on the menu item (link) for "contact info."
2. The URL of this link is sent by her browser to the server indicated by the URL.
3. The server will find the HTML file with the form description, and return this to the browser.
4. Browser displays the form, such as seen in Figure 15.1.
5. User types the name of the employee and clicks on "get info."
6. The browser contacts the server, now with the URL of the asp-script, and also submits the employee name.
7. The server identifies this as a script (due to the asp-extension) and executes the script.
8. The script generates a new Web page, partly by embedded HTML code and partly by information (on the employee) read from the database.
9. This Web page is returned to the browser, which displays the page (as seen in Figure 15.4).

Figure 15.5 Communication between user, browser, and server using dynamic pages (example)

Dynamic Web pages allow us to keep information in one place, in the database.

An overview of the communication between user, browser and server in this example is shown in figure 15.5. Note that there are many steps involved, many of which imply that HTTP messages go between browser and server.

There are several advantages in replacing static by dynamic pages. By generating the Web information directly from an underlying database we avoid storing the same information in many places. Updates are simpler and new information will be available on the Web, and everywhere else, the moment it is stored in the database. In our example, dynamic pages also have the advantage that names and email addresses may be hidden from spiders trying to collect addresses for unsolicited mail. The simple search facility that we have programmed here is scalable, as it will work independently of the number of employees.

With ASP scripts we can create **sessions**, consisting of a sequence of Web accesses.

While basic HTML is a stateless protocol, ASP allows us to declare variables that live as long as the application is running or as long as the user *session* is active. Sessions are administered by the Web server, a program that can create and terminate sessions, keep track of session variables, and keep track of all different sessions (users) that are accessing the Web site. A session may comprise of several requests, allowing us to create state-dependent systems. For example, with these techniques we can easily implement a log-on function to our directory system, where a user who has provided a correct username and password will be identified by a session variable. This log-on functionality will be handled by a script similar to the one above, which tells the Web server that a new session is established and then creates the session variable. When the user accesses subsequent scripts each script can then include code to check if the session variable for this user has a legal value. This, of course, requires that the Web server is capable of identifying each separate user. The server achieves this by using cookies, as explained in chapter 8.

Session data will be deleted when the user quits the application, for example, when he executes a log-out command. Alternatively, passive users can be thrown out of the system if they have been idle, that is, not giving any command, within a predefined time frame (ten minutes is often used as a default). In this way we avoid storing much useless information, and solve the problem of Web users that leave in the middle of a session.

The example we have shown here has been extremely simple, but it shows the principle of dynamic pages. However it is not difficult to improve our directory system, for example, to store more data on each employee (e.g., first name, position, address, fax number), to allow alternative search criteria for finding an employee (e.g., first name, abbreviated names), improve form layout (e.g., by inserting the various fields in an HTML table) or provide alphabetic lists of employees.

Web forms offer a **standard** way of accessing an application, using HTML and HTTP as the basic protocols.

The amazing thing about the Web is not that it is possible to construct form-based systems and to do database lookups; computers have performed these operations for the last fifty years. But now we have a means of accessing a database in a standard way, from everywhere. With the Internet, HTML, HTML forms, and a standard browser we have the fundamentals for universal database access. Before the Internet and the Web, access to central databases required special software and special networks. If a travel agency wanted online access to a booking system, this required leasing lines for network traffic, installing custom-made software to access the booking system, and in some cases also required special terminal equipment. With the Internet we have standard protocols for communication and with the Web standards for input and output. The airline can now offer online booking to everyone just by:

1. Designing *HTML forms* for inputting departure and destination cities, dates, times, fare types, etc.

2. *Developing scripts* that retrieve this information, access the booking database, and output HTML pages with timetables, availability information, prices, confirmations, etc.

With a browser, the form concept, and an Internet connection we can replicate the **terminal** in the bank, travel agency, or in any type of business on our computer screen.

Since all user communication is by standard HTML no installation is needed on the customer side. The customer can use her standard browser and her Internet connection to access the booking system.

This is really the second Internet revolution. With simple techniques and strong standards, customized terminals in travel agencies, banks, and in public institutions can be "moved" to our office, home, or portable computer. For many applications we no longer need an intermediary. This opens for better availability, banking 24 hours a day, 7 days a week, 52 weeks a year if we want. We do not have to call, fax, or mail forms or letters to our bank, or visit them personally in order to ask them to perform a transaction, we can do it ourselves. We get immediate response, a balance sheet that is updated to the moment and a much better overview of our account. A more detailed analysis of the applications that are opened up by these techniques is given in part 3.

When we use the browser to **access** a database application, we are not on the Web. Only the Web protocols are used. Within these applications we have a high level of formalization.

We have seen that the low level of formalization of Web pages limits the effectiveness and type of operations that we can perform. But this is not the case when we use the Web protocols as an interface tool to a database. For example, after we have given our user identifier and password by the means of a HTML form, the banking system can provide us with a set of scripts that gives us access to the banking system. Now we are in the subworld of banking. In this world we can use high-level concepts such as accounts, balance, and transfers, knowing that we will be understood. We input data, such as amount and account numbers, in forms, and the script will then execute the necessary operations toward the banking system, in much the same way as in the directory system discussed above. In this world precision and recall are 100 percent. When we ask for a list of all deposits we know that the answer will be 100 percent correct. That is, we have the same functionality as if we were operating a terminal in the bank itself.

At the same time we have lost some of the advantages of the basic Web. Information in these databases is not open to everyone, user names or passwords restrict access. When we ask the airline booking system to give us the cheapest fare, we can expect a 100 percent correct answer. However, the system has, of course, only considered fares within its own database, flights for this airline and its partners. Information is limited to booking, and we cannot expect that this database can provide us with other types of information, for example, data on air safety or accidents. The high-level concepts and operations come at a cost, they cannot be achieved without narrowing the application area.

Exercises and Discussion

1. As seen, the form concept is implemented in quite a simple manner. However, it is this feature that allows us to give structured input to a server. Discuss the various applications for forms. Could important services such as Internet banking or Internet shopping have been possible without forms?

2. Compare HTML forms to the forms used within the applications that run on a PC, for example, the print-form within your word processor. What are the limitations of HTML forms?

Notes

1. Not to be confused with Application Service Providers, service centers used for outsourcing computer functions, which use the same acronym.
2. With the Microsoft .net software, ASP scripts can be compiled, that is, translated to a more efficient form. In older versions these scripts are interpreted (i.e., the system will read a line at a time and then execute the instructions given by this line).

16 Embedded Scripts

As we have seen, the simple idea of dynamic Web pages makes it possible to use the Web as a standard interface to database systems, where HTML is used for getting input (in forms) and for presenting results and HTTP is used for data transmission. The disadvantage of such a system is that all processing has to be performed on the central server, increasing communication costs, and making the server a possible bottleneck in the system. In many ways it seems a bad resource allocation to do all the processing on the server, while the clients may be idle waiting for the next page.

On the **client side** scripts can be inserted in the HTML code to increase the functionality of the user interface.

Client side processing can be achieved by the same script technique as we discussed in the previous chapter, by embedding script commands in the HTML code. In this case the whole page, including the script commands, is transmitted to the browser that performs the commands. With client side scripts we can implement a more advanced user interface than with standard HTML. We can for example change the form layout according to input values, allow users to control a presentation by using sliders or validate the values before these are sent to the server. While we can achieve some of this functionality using basic HTML, all the error checking and processing will then have to be done on the server side, for example, using the techniques described in the previous chapter. This solution increases network traffic and introduces delays in the process that restrict the possibilities for making advanced interfaces.

For reasons of **security** client side scripts have a limited command set.

The difference between a server side script and a client side script is that the latter has only a limited command set. On the server side the software engineer will know what resources the server has, databases, program components, etc., and can utilize these to a maximum. On the client side she does not have this information. Anyway, access to local resources is restricted for reasons of security. Clients may be powerful or weak machines, may run on top of Windows, Unix, or any other operating system, and may have a diversity of peripheral equipment, but software engineers are usually interested in making scripts that can run on all of these clients. Even if we could demand a standard client configuration of machine and software resources it would have been dangerous to let a script access local disks, as this would allow a malicious or criminal page designer to embed scripts that could destroy local data, steal identities or local passwords. Therefore client side scripts are limited to performing calculations, receiving input data from mouse and keyboard, opening new windows and controlling window presentations. Even then, we have seen examples of scripts that have found loopholes in the security systems, enabling them to gather confidential information, to change system parameters, or to destroy data.

To avoid the complication of adjusting to different hardware and operating systems, scripts are executed within the browser. The browser defines a virtual standardized machine on which the scripts can be interpreted.[1] As on the server side we have a choice of many script languages for the client side, but the advantage of using Java script is that this script language is among the more popular and can be interpreted by most browsers. We shall therefore explore a Java script in more detail.

Figure 16.1 List box (example)

With scripts it is possible to give **direct feedback** to the user, without having to access the server.

Figure 16.1 shows a simple form, where the user is asked to select a discount type. If she asks for a student account we want to give her a warning, telling her that this will require a valid student ID. We can provide this functionality by a simple Java script.

```
<form name="discount" action="../redirectUser.asp"
  method="post">
  <select name="discount"
    onChange="checkDiscounts(discount);">
    <option value="">Select discount if applicable</option>
    <option value="S">Student</option>
    <option value="P">Preferred customer status</option>
    <option value="NO">No discount</option>
  </select>
</form>
<script language="Javascript">
  function checkDiscounts(discount)
  {
    if (discount.value == "S") {
      alert("Note that a valid student id will be
      required")
    }
  }
</script>
```

Figure 16.2. Form code and Java script (example)

The HTML source with the embedded script is shown in figure 16.2. While the details are uninteresting we shall take a closer look at the main parts of the script. Within the form tag we have defined an input field, a combo box (select statement) with four options. Whenever the value of the box is changed, the browser will call the script checkDiscounts, defined elsewhere in the HTML page and embedded in script-tags. It will therefore not be shown on the display, but whenever it is called (on a change of discount type) it will ask the browser to show an alert window with a message whenever a student discount is selected (figure 16.3).

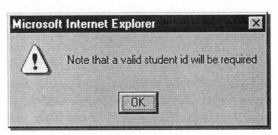

Figure 16.3 An alert window.

While Java scripts cannot read or write to the local disk in general, they have the possibility of storing, reading, and edit-

Cookies, small text files stored on your computer, aid the server in identifying who you are.

Cookies can be used to identify and track Web users.

Applets are Java programs, more advanced than scripts, that can run on a virtual computer embedded in the browser.

ing cookies (see chapter 8 for a definition). For example, after a user has provided a correct user name and a valid password for a site, a Java script can store a cookie on the client computer with a date and a user ID. The next time the user accesses the site cookie information can be retrieved, and it can be decided whether to give the user direct access, without bothering him with the login procedure. It may not be as safe as requiring a new login, but may be a good alternative when we prioritize convenience over security.

Cookies may persist for days, months, or even years. Many websites use cookies to track user profiles. At the first visit to a site or a group of sites the browser is instructed by a script to store a cookie with a unique identifier on the client's computer. This cookie is read at subsequent visits, and the site has the information necessary to connect all these visits to the same client, making it possible to draw a more complete profile that will be of value for direct marketing. A client can tell the browser not to accept cookies, to give a warning every time a cookie is stored or to delete all offline information, including cookies. However, many sites will not function if they are not allowed to store cookies on a client.

In order to get complete control over the appearance of the user interface one needs something more than simple script languages. This can be done through applets, Java programs that run within the browser. These also open the way for real client-server programming, where the applet can communicate directly with the server, perhaps using the server as a database machine for storing and retrieving records. The disadvantage of applets is that many users, due to security restrictions, do not have the capability of running applets. For example, many firewalls, hardware and software devices that control Internet access, will not accept applets.

What we have seen in the last two chapters is that HTML, created to define a common layout formats for documents, has been extended by forms and scripts. While these new constructs are rather primitive compared to the functionality of many programming languages, they allow us to use a standard browser to access computer systems. Here forms are used for input, standard HTML for output, server side scripts to access databases, and embedded scripts to improve the usability of the interface. In practice, these constructs have opened the way for all the new Web-based businesses that we see today, Internet banks, online shops, booking systems, etc.

Exercises and Discussion

1. Let us assume that one knows, by the means described in this section, the identity of each user that accesses the website for an Internet store. For what purposes can this information be used? Discuss.

2. Let us assume that you are very concerned about privacy and security. You will never let go of your credit card, never offer your social security number, and on the Internet you have chosen the maximum security level possible for your browser (no scripts, no cookies, no downloads). What will be the consequences? Will you be able to attain the same service level as anybody else?

3. With forms and scripts we enhance the functionality of Web pages. However, are there differences between a Web-based user interface and the interface you can get when you run a program locally on a PC? What will happen as the continuous improvement of Web interfaces continues?

Notes

1. A browser is a piece of software that runs on top of the operating system (e.g., Netscape running on top of Windows). If we use Unix or the Linux operating system we need a different version of the browser. This is no big problem as the browser is installed only once. However, if we design a Web page with embedded scripts it would be complicated if we needed different versions of the script for every possible operating system. To avoid this problem, and to increase security, a script runs within a virtual machine. This "machine" is really only a piece of software within the browser that can interpret and execute the script commands.

17 Peer-to-Peer Computing

The mainframes of the 1970s were huge machines, accessed from dumb terminals. These time-sharing machines had the clear disadvantage that the response time increased as more users logged on. We then got the PC with local processing power and a local disk, practically eliminating response times, at least for the simplest operations. The disadvantage was that a stand-alone PC did not offer the possibility of sharing programs and data archives with others. Client-server computing was the solution, connecting the local PC to a server. The server provided a platform for common programs and databases, while the client provided a platform for fast local computing. As we have seen, the Web has embraced this model. Locally we run a browser that displays the pages retrieved from a Web server. But in contrast to traditional client-server computing in a local area network, the Web is biased toward the server. All data are stored on the server and most processing is performed here.

To achieve a secure and standard platform, browsers only occupy a fraction of local resources. The local disk, for example, is only used as a cache for previously retrieved pages and for storing cookies. On the server side, at least for the more popular sites, scalability is a major problem (i.e., serving all accesses with a reasonable response time). Here huge investments are made in server farms (sets of servers) and database replication (copies of a database on different systems) to handle increased traffic. Thus, at the same time as we have underutilized resources locally we have strained resources centrally.

The obvious solution to this problem is to move more of the processing and the data to the client. This has been done within scientific communities to solve large computational problems. Peers access a central site and get their small part of a big problem, along with the software needed to do the computation. The process will then run on the client machine as a low priority background job, utilizing idle time on the processor. Results will be returned automatically to the central site. Using such a system a large user community was able to break an RSA[1]-coded message presented in the *New York Times* in 1996, a problem that would have taken a supercomputer many years to solve on its own. Today, distributed-computing companies are soliciting members by offering payment, prices, or the ability to support a good cause (e.g., where members offer their accumulated computer power to solve heavy algorithms within medical research, biology, economics, etc.). Clearly a cheaper solution than renting space on a supercomputer, at least for the jobs that can be run effectively in this distributed environment.

While these examples are controlled by a central server, using the local machines only as low-level assistants, we can envisage more "democratic" systems where the local machines get a more important role. This can be done by keeping just a register on the central server or by eliminating the need for central processing altogether. The latter will be named a true peer-to-peer (P2P) system, while we can call the first a P2P enabler. Napster was perhaps the most well-known P2P enabler, a system for sharing files of music. The idea is as simple as it is smart, a central site with an archive over all music files and their location along with downloadable software for the client. Music files (today often in MP3[2] format) are stored on the clients that also had a role as servers in the Napster network. After installing the client software a user would access the central registry to search for the files she wanted. From here she would get a list of clients/servers that had a copy of these files, with an indication of the type of network connection (bandwidth) for each. Probably she would then choose to download the files from a client/server with a high-speed connection. After this process the files would be stored on her local machine, and could then be made available to others.

As seen, P2P incorporates the democratic ideas of the Web, where everybody is both a consumer and a provider, at least in the technical sense. While some of the music files organized by Napster were without copyright, most were MP3 files that have been captured from copyrighted material, for example, from CDs. Since the actual copying of files was performed on a peer-to-peer level and no files were stored centrally, Napster had hoped to be on the right side of the copyright laws, but the courts did not agree.

This did not affect their users to a large extent, since there are many other alternatives. One legal bypass can be to establish the central register in an international zone or in a country with more relaxed copyright laws. This may not be necessary, however, as there exist P2P implementations that do without the central register. An example is Gnutella,[3] a site with a set of P2P programs that can be downloaded. When running, the P2P program will scan the Internet looking for hosts. In a short time thousands of hosts will be found. The metaphor used is that of

P2P applications can be controlled by a central server, or operate autonomously.

Napster, the first P2P enabler, supported a system for sharing files of digital music.

P2P incorporates the **democratic** nature of the Web, allowing free access to data.

True P2P systems can operate without any central computer.

standing at the seashore, looking toward the horizon. From each viewpoint a different set of hosts will be seen, and since these may connect and disconnect from the Internet, it is a dynamic and changing sea. When a user initiates a search to the system it will be forwarded to these hosts; if the file is not found these will pass on the request, and so forth, until a successful result is achieved or until all hosts within the horizon have been tried. When a file is found the address of the location will be passed back along the line, to the originating hosts that will download the file. With these systems the record associations have had some success in going after the users instead of the hosts offering the P2P software.

Newer P2P programs also have the ability to download from several sources simultaneously, one piece here, another there. In the end the pieces will be put together to a complete file. This makes downloading more efficient and since sharing is by parts of files, it is somewhat more difficult to use legal action against its users.

Autonomously P2P systems are **robust**, but often require more network traffic than systems organized by a central server.

On P2P networks the collective content of all machines is at the control of each individual machine. Since these true P2P systems do not have any central register they are very robust. If one part of the network falls out, the system will just pass searches on in another direction. It is also robust with regard to legal action, as there is no central organization than can be attacked. A copyright infringement action would have to be directed toward the individual users. A technical disadvantage is that the distributed network requires more bandwidth than centralized systems, robustness comes at a price.

Gnutella works for any types of files. The drawback of these highly distributed systems is that they rely on each individual user to label the files correctly. That is, all the problems with regard to differences in language, vocabulary, background, etc., that we discussed with regard to keyword searching (chapter 10) will manifest themselves here. The exception is for files that may be labeled according to de facto standards, such as music files (artist, album, song), movies (title, year, actors), books (author, title, ISBN), and software (name of program, version, producer). But even here one has to rely on the accuracy and good intentions of other peers. So, while P2P implementation is a decentralized and distributed system it relies on some common vocabulary for file requests to work properly.

A true P2P system is the **combined** product of all participants.

A P2P system requires that most users are willing to be producers (i.e., to share their disks, part of these, or individual files with the user community). They must also be willing to offer part of their bandwidth for uploads (i.e., for other users that are copying from their machine). A problem may be maliciously oriented individuals that propagate data viruses or offer their files with a false description. For example, pornographic material may be labeled as fairy tales, amateur music as Rolling Stones, and Nazi propaganda as textbooks. Still, sites such as Gnutella have attracted large user communities that seem to be willing to take the risk and to offer processing power and bandwidth for the good of the user community.

These user communities have been established without any marketing at all, just by use of the jungle telegraph. This is very interesting at a time when we often see that dot-coms fail due to the heavy marketing costs. Can commercial sites be established in the same ad hoc cost-free manner? Perhaps not! The Napsters have an aura of illegality and offer some sort of group feeling—"let us get together and make fun of the big companies." It is, of course, also important that they offer something for free that until now has been rather expensive. The album that you can get free on a P2P network may cost from $10 to $20 in a store. However there is always the chance that some creative marketing advisor can manage to hide a business model within a Gnutella- or Napster-like model.

Today, due to the copyright laws, content producers, from authors to publishers, can get paid for content. P2P has already proven to be a threat to the music business, and as more content is available in electronic formats, these systems may make it difficult to sustain copyright laws also for movies and books. While some talk about the end of the publishing business as a whole, we will certainly see big changes. Probably the answer lies in meeting the technological challenge with new systems instead of trying to maintain the old through legal actions.

As we have seen, P2P systems have several disadvantages. If we could subscribe or have a pay-per-view system, customers may choose to use an official site. Such a site could offer good quality, large repositories, site overviews, excellent search systems, powerful servers, high bandwidths, and much better security than P2P. However, since they have to compete with free systems the fees will have to be very moderate. This works well with videotapes, where low rental fees combined with tedious copying process is a barrier against pirates—at least until we can download digital videos efficiently on high-speed networks.

An autonomously P2P system—a set of computers connected on the same level—poses a threat to **copyright** laws, as the "responsibility" is spread over the whole network.

P2P technology can be used to develop new and fast **search engines** that work independently of pre-made indexes.

P2P is not only restricted to illegal copying of files. There are now efforts underway to use P2P techniques as a basic for more general search tools. Each client will then have a piece of software that performs the local part of the searching. Since a global search can be broken down in searching a set of clients, each offering its own hardware for the processing, it is possible to perform searches on the fly, in contrast to traditional search engines that use a premade index. These new search systems will be able to find new or newly updated material. They will also have the ability to look into content that is invisible on the Web, for example, files of different formats, product catalogs, and database systems. The disadvantage is that they in practice can only search a part of the net and that they require that all clients have installed the software needed. Local searches may be delayed due to higher priority local jobs, and will demand that a client be up on the net—as with all P2P systems. Of course, in a more central system we will require that the server be running at all times, but servers usually run in a more stable environment than clients, and will also have more support personnel. If the query request can be fulfilled with a found/not found status, searches can be terminated as soon as a peer reports a positive result. When the query cannot be fulfilled or in situations where high recall is needed, for example, to find the best result, the complete P2P network has to be searched. This may be time-consuming and resource intensive. Since these systems, like any P2P system, have to rely on the users, they seem to have the best possibility of succeeding in an Intranet environment.

Exercises and Discussion

1. In the not-so-far future we must expect that all audio equipment is connected to the Internet and that huge disks are a part of every system. Then it will be common to play music directly from the disk, without relying on intermediate formats such as a CD or DVD. Discuss the implications for the record industry (publishers, shops).

2. P2P networks are a treat to the music industry. Discuss the implications for other content providers, such as film companies and book publishers. Will the situation change when more and more computers are connected to the Internet through broadband systems?

Notes

1. RSA, developed by Rivest, Shamir, and Adleman, 1977, is a system that offers both encryption and authentication (through digital signatures). RSA stands for the first letter in each of its inventors' last names. The security of RSA is based on the assumption that factoring of large prime numbers is difficult.

2. MP3 (MPEG-1 Audio Layer-3) is a standard technology and format for compressing files of sound. MP3 manages a compression rate of 12 to 1 while preserving the original sound quality.

3. http://www.gnutella.com.

PART 3

Formalizing Business-to-Consumer Applications for the Web

Traditional Internet applications are categorized as either business-to-consumer (B2C) or business-to-business (B2B). With B2C we expect that in the normal situation we have a computer at one end of the communication line, a person at the other. Of course, this person will also use a computer to access the Internet, but the big issue is that in this case output from the website is presented for human beings. This simplifies applications, as the human beings can read and understand nearly any layout or format, at least when it is well organized. This implies that objects and actions may be formalized on any level, as characters or as higher-level concepts. It is no problem for us that Amazon requires an email address, USAir an account number, and the *New York Times* a user name for identification. It is no problem that some sites ask for our name in one field, while others have separated this as first, last, and initials. That is, no rigid standards need to be in place for a B2C application; the flexibility of human beings allows for nearly any type of interface. Of course, the interfaces will be easier to use if we keep to familiar terms and commands, and try to follow the look and feel of other systems and interfaces that are known to the user.

As we have seen, there may be situations where the user interface does not provide the flexibility needed, for example, for handling exceptions. Then the B2C model can usually be replaced by a person-to-person correspondence. This can be done by allowing the customer to call in, send email, use instant messaging, or fill out a Web form. That is, we can use the Web system as a means of handling a large part of the transactions in an efficient manner, but can move to a more flexible (but less efficient) medium, such as telephone or email, at any time. In this respect B2C systems give us the best of both worlds. Note that the person at the other end of the communication line may be a private citizen using the Web from his home computer to buy Christmas gifts, or an employee operating on behalf of her company. There is no fundamental difference if the items to be bought are to be paid privately or by the firm, if the websites are open to the public or only to employees. The similarity, that we have a person at one end of the communication line, is more important. Applications will be formalized to a higher-level when the person communicating is an employee, rather than an ordinary citizen. In the employee situation the items that can be ordered through the B2C site will be limited (perhaps to office stationery), and shopping will usually be performed under predefined contracts.

We shall define B2B as communication between computers (i.e., where the "end users" are computer programs). The idea here is to set up efficient processes that can be automated, without the intervention of humans. B2B applications need a common vocabulary and a common format for data in order to communicate on a semantic level, for example, to send an order form from one computer to the other. To avoid misunderstanding and errors the format of the order, for example, the number of data fields, the type of each field, field identifiers, etc., must be specified. Data has to be provided in a way that both computers can interpret. For identifiers, such as a bank account number, some sort of global identifier will be needed, for example, prefixing the account number by a country and routing code. B2B is not only a matter of transferring bits, it is also a question of elaborate standards. With B2B applications there are no human beings in the loop. This makes it more difficult to jump to a more flexible medium to handle exceptions. To keep up efficiency, the computer system should itself be able to handle all common exception situations. Thus, the systems become more elaborate and more expensive to build. We will return to B2B in part 4.

In our discussion of business models for B2C we shall start with the all-symbolic applications and present these in order of formalization level, starting at the lowest. After presenting information-providers in chapter 18 and online services in chapter 19, we move to applications that have a physical part, products that have to be distributed to other channels than the Internet, in chapter 20. As we shall see, some products that are mainly symbolic today, such as books, newspapers, and video-cassettes, can be distributed in symbolic form when the right infrastructure is in place. That is, when the technical limitations we face today are removed. We discuss these issues in chapter 21. Similarly, we shall discuss the case when traditional and cultural constraints are removed in chapter 22.

In presenting these applications we shall focus on the formalization part, showing that the formalization level of each area will define the level of efficiency for the applications. Naturally, the Internet and the Web can only handle the symbolic part of an application. The physical part, for example, the transportation of goods, will have to go on other channels. As we shall see, this will restrict the practicality of many applications. In presenting our examples we shall try to define parameters or metrics that can be used in categorizing application areas, and to help us to see where we can reap the greatest benefits of the Internet technology.

In order to offer a comprehensive discussion of these issues we shall include both fundamental and practical arguments. While the need for formalization can be called fundamental in that this is a requirement that exists independent of which technology we use, technical arguments will change as the technology develops. For example, while the results of Web searching will depend on the formalization level of a query compared to the formalization level of documents or other data, an application such as downloading of movies will be practical only with higher bandwidths than what most of us have today.

We shall end this part by showing in chapter 23 how important it is that systems handle both the open and closed parts of a task, that is, that they can cover the whole range of users' needs.

18 Symbolic Services—Information-providers

All-symbolic services can be performed exclusively via the Internet, making it possible to move from a world of physical distribution of information to an electronic, reaping all the advantages of the new technology.

With a very small investment, companies and institutions can have a presence and be an information-provider on the Web. The information can be stored in static, premade HTML pages or be retrieved from databases using dynamic pages. It can be offered to the public, or be limited to customers and employees; it can be provided free or sold based on a pay-per-page or subscription model.

> It seems to be easier to get **revenue** from providing infrastructure (equipment, communication lines, ISP-provider) than from content.

Pay models have been difficult to implement. Many view the Web as a free source, similar to broadcast TV, and are, with some exceptions, not willing to pay for content. This does not make the Web a free medium. The user has to provide the equipment, the computer hardware and software, and the connection and will have to pay the telephone company and the ISP (Internet Service Provider) for access to the net. There are many valid business models in this chain, for example, computer manufacturing, ISP services, network installation, and maintenance. In this chapter, however, we shall concentrate on content and the other services that the technology can provide, not on the technology itself.

In addition to paying for the equipment and access, as users we have to spend time, skills, and energy to find what we need on the Web. While the Web can provide information on almost everything, it may not always be easy to get what we want. In a job situation it may therefore be quite expensive to retrieve information, even if the source is "free." However, where one uses the Web for entertainment the fun may be in the process itself, in "surfing" the Web for interesting stuff.

> Internet/Web services offer customization, the user can choose what she wants to see, but requires a higher **level of activation** than other media.

Compared to other media, such as TV, radio, and newspapers the Web requires a higher activity level from the user. This is both an advantage and a disadvantage. On the Web the user is in control, she can follow the links she finds interesting, provide her own keywords for searching, and go to the sites she likes. During sessions she has her eyes fixed on the screen, hands on keyboard and mouse. This is very different from the TV viewer, where the only input required is a button click for channel selection.

18.1 Web presence

The Web can be used to present a company, an institution, or an interest group. The cost of creating and maintaining Web pages is often very small compared to other means of dissemination, such as using brochures, direct mail, or advertisements. The Web has also other advantages, such as the possibility of integrating many different media, easy updates, and nearly unlimited storage space. While small organizations may choose to develop a minimum site, perhaps creating the site as an in-house job, larger institutions will often use professionals, graphic and Web designers, to create a quality site with high functionality.

Application parameters:

Formalization level:
  Low (character)

Product form:
  Symbolic

Complexity:
  Low

For a small institution a Web presence, done in the right way, will be very inexpensive marketing. It is also a simple way to provide customers with information such as address, maps, employee directories, etc. While some of these pages will be static, other pages can be created based on information from company databases. For example, instead of maintaining a separate telephone directory on the Web, this should be created on the fly, based on information in the employee database, such as mentioned in chapter 15. Access can be public (Internet), mainly provided for users within an organization (Intranet), or only to users with a password (Extranet). Users can access the site by giving the URL, by using a preset bookmark, a link in another Web page, or by using a search tool. To simplify access institutions try to acquire simple URLs, for example, the company name with a .com suffix, and to present this URL in advertisements and on products (as we discussed in chapter 12).

While such a site will be read-only, simplifying security, there will often be some ways of sending data to the company. This can be achieved by offering an email address or by using HTML forms to provide more formalized input. If a mail address is embedded in a "mailto" tag, the browser will automatically open a mail message to this address when the user clicks on this mail link. Forms can be embedded in HTML pages, and form data can be retrieved and stored by a simple server script (as presented in chapter 16).

While a Web presence will not give any direct revenue, it has several advantages for a company and its customer:

- *New customers can be attracted*, perhaps finding the site through a search tool or a portal.

- *Reduced switchboard load* as customers may get information directly from the Web page.

- *Faster access for customers to information* over the Web than over the telephone.

- The Web can provide *more detailed information* than brochures.

- *Easy updates*, a new version is available the second it is stored.

- Since information from a website is in *electronic form*, it can be forwarded to others, stored on a computer, inserted into other programs, or printed if needed.

- *Reduced need for advertisements* in printed catalogs, such as yellow pages.

- Customers can create *hypertext links* to the site from their own Web pages.

- *Other advertisements can be simpler*, as additional data can be offered on the website, for example, by giving the URL in an advertisement.

The website is the **virtual face** of the company, and care should be taken to provide a look-and-feel and a level of service that is conformant with the company as a whole.

For many companies, telephone, fax, and letters may still be the principal means of communication. Still, the Web advantages are so clear compared to the costs that most companies and institutions have and should have a Web presence today. In fact, customers expect that there will be a Web page, just as they expect a listing in the yellow page directories.

When establishing a site it is important to note that the Web will be a face of the company, perhaps the only face for many customers. The same care as one takes to keep the brick and mortar offices clean and inviting, should be taken for the website. Each company has its own "look and feel." It may be focused on simplicity or functionality, it may be traditional or modern, but the website should convey the same impression as other interfaces to the customers, whether they are offices, brochures, advertisements, products, or services.

However, the simplicity and low cost of establishing a website may be a trap for many firms. If detailed information is provided the site will need to be updated often, and many firms have not established routines for this. That is, they order a website as they would a brochure and forget that a site should be a living thing, that it is accessed today as well as in the future. In contrast to information on paper the customer will expect that the display provides a fresh and updated copy, with valid information as of today. If price information is provided the Web page must be updated with every price change. If we list names of employees, persons that have left should be removed from the list.

This is not always easy. My college, for example, replaced the standard term-oriented schedule with a daily version, but without establishing a system to track changes in courses. Now all courses are listed using the predetermined schedule, in addition to special events marked for each day. However, the students now expect that all information is updated on a daily basis. My early email warnings of lectures cancelled or moved are then ignored, as students expect that these are overridden by the new daily itinerary, that is, they expect (reasonable enough) that the latest version is the one that counts. This was no problem when the itinerary was given for the whole term. The remedy is either to track all changes, offering a correct daily schedule, or to list course itineraries and special events separately.

The data on the page determines the necessary **update frequency**, *more general data requires less updates than if the page contains specific data.*

If what is needed is only a minimum Web presence care should be taken in designing a general and static website, where dynamic information is retrieved from company databases. If there are no routines for regular updates one should avoid the section with "news" or all other forms of dated information. Detailed data can be included where this is generated from the company's database, for example, where data on employees are retrieved from a human resources database. The second data on a new employee are entered here they will also be available over the Web. This is especially important, as new data often are accessed more often than old data (naturally, as no one knows the phone number of the new employee).

It is reasonable to offer an email address in the "contact us" part of the page, but this implies that one needs routines for handling messages. Tests have shown that the response times for email are often very long, or that some companies do not answer at all.[1] Since many use the Internet as a "yellow page" directory, it is also smart to provide information on how the company can be reached by telephone, fax, and mail and to list all physical addresses.

Internet/Web technologies are ideal for government agencies and other organizations that want to provide **information** *to citizens or a large number of members.*

In many ways the Internet and Web technology is ideal for many public organizations, from interest groups to governments. A general aim for all of these is to offer information to their members and to the public. The openness of these institutions makes the open Internet and the Web ideal tools.

Traditionally, mass-distributed mail has been the channel for outgoing information, while these institutions have received telephone calls or letters from the public. With the Internet these contacts can be made much more efficient. Updated information can be offered through Web and email. With the Web, members or the public can be offered direct access to information archives. Information that earlier was only accessible for employees and perhaps journalists, can now be offered to everyone. In this way interest organization, covering topics from arthritis to zoos can provide their members and the public with vision statements, background information, information databases, links to other organizations of interest, archives with member input, chat rooms, contact to professionals, etc. Official organizations, working under laws to make data public, can save reports, research studies, etc., "as HTML," making them available at very limited costs.

Of course, few of us are interested in reading governmental reports. It is usually much more convenient to "hire" a journalist to go through the report and prepare a summary for us in the newspaper, adding the background data needed, interviewing the right people, etc. However, in special cases (e.g., when a new road is proposed through our neighborhood, cut-downs are proposed in local schools, or when we need a building permit), we may be interested in more in-depth information. Making these data available on the Web is very convenient for the public and is at the same time, extremely cost effective for the government. Now people can do their own searching and printing, often satisfying their information need without any manual support.

> Do not expect that everyone is interested in **in-depth information,** even when this is made available over the Web.

It is easy to overstate the importance of these information sources, advocating a new area for democracy where everybody has access to everything. But we should remember that all of this information was available before the Internet and the Web, the difference is that it is easier to access. This may be important in many cases, but the real work is often more in studying the data than obtaining the data. Today, we can get a thousand page report online in minutes, while we earlier had to order it by mail. Still, the big task is to transform these data into information and that means reading and studying. Clearly not a task for everybody.

For large sites we need to organize the information. This can be simple if we have formalized identifiers for the information we provide. For example, a university can organize their

Web pages according to courses and research areas, or one can choose to organize the information according to the needs of the user. In the latter example the home page may have links for students, for potential students, researchers, visitors, etc. This and other examples are shown in table 18.1.

Business	Formalizations
University	Course codes, names, research areas
	Students, researchers, visitors, employees
	Departments
Hospital	Departments
	Patients, outpatients, visitors, employees
	Illnesses
Telephone company	Private/business customers
	Technology (cell phones, Internet, ...)
	Services (subscribe, cancellation, invoice...)

Table 18.1 Alternative formalizations for different organizations

Note that the alternatives can be combined. A telephone company may distinguish between private and business customers in the first step, use technology on the second tier, and perhaps services on the third. Often the Web pages are organized according to organizational structure. However, this division (e.g., of a university into schools and departments), may not be obvious for the outside Web user. However, a computer system allows us to organize according to several principles at the same time, so while a departmental form may be suitable for an Intranet, the Internet part should be organized according to other principles.

18.2 Product information on the Web

The next step, after presenting an institution or a company on the Web, is to present product information. In these applications we can operate with a formalization level above characters, as we can utilize different types of product identifiers. For example, such as ISBN numbers, author names, titles, and publishers for books. Table 18.2 offers an overview of this and other examples.

These formal classifiers are often preferred to the more informal, also in the real world. For example, most perfume and cosmetics shops organize products according to brand name even if one could think of organizing perfumes according to

Business	Formal variables
Car dealer	Model, year, price
Real estate	Location, size, type, price
Booking (air)	Airport codes, flights, date, time, price category
Bookstore	Author, title, ISBN numbers, category
Music store	Artist, album, category
Software store	Program name, operating system
Perfumes & Cosmetics	Brand name, product type
Hardware store	Product type, size

Table 18.2 Formal variables for different businesses

Application parameters

Formalization level:
  Low to medium

Product form:
  Symbolic

Complexity:
  Low to medium

smell. However, in the latter case we have few words to distinguish between different smells, and such a classification would be highly subjective. Bookstores may have a shelf with recommended books, sometimes what each employee has recommended to flag the choice as subjective. But most often the more objective and formal way of presenting a best-seller list is chosen.

Product attributes can be presented both in an open and a closed form. For example, while book abstracts and reviews can be presented as text it would be natural to offer product identifiers and attributes such as price, number of pages, type of book, type of binding, language, etc., in a more record-oriented notation, simplifying both product presentation and searching. For example with price tagged as this, we can search by price or sort by price (we discussed these issues in chapter 1.3).

Not all companies can rely on established formalizations as those shown in table 18.2. For example, a gift store will have problems finding useful formalizations. Here product description must to a greater degree rely on text and images, and classification may be in more creative categories such as "gifts for him/her," "Christmas gifts" and "New items." In the physical world these stores are designed for browsing, using much space to present their items. A Web presentation of these products will probably have to follow along the same lines.

If there are many products, search tools may be necessary in order to limit browsing. Here one runs into the same formalization problems as above. While it is easy to search for a book or a movie, it will not be as easy to find the right search terms for our gift store. A textual description of each item may be highly subjective, and the user may not apply the "right" keywords when formalizing a query. This is analog to searching

Product information
can be organized in product classes, by usage, technology, etc.

the open Web. Of course, most products can be identified with item numbers, but these internal product identifiers will most often not be known by the customer. There are exceptions, however. When needing service, a customer may have the type number of the item as well as the serial number. We may also have the ISBN when ordering a book. In these situations it will be efficient if the site allows us to provide such unique identifiers, shortcutting the more flexible but less efficient search options.

In its simple form product information may be displayed on static Web pages, perhaps based on information from paper brochures and fact sheets. However, with many products it may be simpler to build these pages on the basis of information in company databases, if available. The HTML pages can then either be created on the fly, based on information from the database, or one could save some processing power by creating all the pages up front. The latter solution implies that pages are regenerated whenever there is a change in the underlying data.

But the Web is more than a brochure. With creativity the Web can be used for "try me" demonstrations, at least for some types of products. While information on a book will be sufficient in certain cases, we may want to scan the pages of a textbook or dictionary, to see what kind of detail is provided. We can do this in the brick and mortar store, but not always on the Web where unsolicited copying may be a problem. A solution may be to let the user see the complete table of contents, the index, and only selected sections or pages. For the dictionary, the user should be offered an interface for providing words for translation. This may not be as good as a visit to a brick and mortar store, that allows you to see the actual copy that you will buy, but is a surrogate that reduces some of the disadvantages of buying online.

It is just as important to use creativity to utilize the new medium where this has advantages. Amazon does this by offering customers' the possibility of writing their own reviews of books. This and other features can only be provided online. The multimedia Web capabilities can be used to present music online, by offering snapshots in MP3 or other music formats. In addition, on the Web it is possible to provide extensive background information on the performer and the music, for example, by showing music videos.

A website for a do-it-yourself store cannot let the user handle the products and materials, but can reduce this drawback by

The Web has some limitations compared to **product presentation** in brick and mortar stores, but will also open for new ways of presenting products.

giving color pictures, videos, and full documentation. The Web medium can further be exploited by offering complete instructions, with checklists for what you need and perhaps also with a consultant service available over email. One could establish a chat room for customers and, similar to a bookstore, allow customers to enter their own advice in handling tools or materials. They may also offer to keep a record of all the materials that you buy, so that you have a chance of finding the right thing when you need additional materials for extensions and repairs.

To sum up, there are many advantages in presenting product information online. While a good presentation is a must for online stores, it may provide an additional marketing channel and marketing efficiency for a brick and mortar store:

- The Web allows for very *detailed product information,* in the form of text, tables, images, animations, and videos.

- The Web allows *detailed product specifications,* and may directly tell the customer the consequence of each choice, each option.

- Customers will have *easy access* to this information, and can print it out if necessary.

- Customers can *find a product,* for example, by a search for product characteristics.

- The information is *easy to maintain.* Insertion, deletion, and modification can be performed at any time.

- *Store once, use many times.* The same data source, the product database, can be used both for providing information to customers and employees, while the user interfaces—the views of the database—may be different.

- *Information needs of customers and employees* may be satisfied just by linking to other sources.

- *The load on other and more expensive channels,* such as letter or telephone, will be reduced as information on new and old products can be obtained automatically from the Web.

Today, many companies and institutions see the advantages of providing all this information online. However, it is interesting to see that several institutions, especially institutions within more traditional areas such as manufacturing, have very weak

Web pages. While most have a Web presence, they have yet to exploit the advantages of using the Web as a medium for marketing their products. Some also limit the information on the Web to data that are available in printed brochures, not seeing that the Web offers a possibility to give in-depth information.

A disadvantage of providing product information on the Web is that this information will be available also for the competition. While this is also the case for product information on paper, there is a difference of quantity, speed, and simplicity of obtaining information. Using spiders and other programs that access your sites, a competitor can get an immediate and complete notice of new prices, new items, special offers, etc. If you are open to your customers you are also open to everybody else.

18.3 Archive access—sale of text-based content

Application parameters

Formalization level:
  Low to high
Product form:
  Symbolic
Complexity:
  Low to medium

A market for sale of information, for example, credit checks on firms and private citizens, stock market trends, etc., has always existed. With the advent of fast computers and cheap, high-capacity disk storage in the 1970s (i.e., better means of storing, organizing and retrieving information), one expected a boom in this market. But, with a few exceptions, it was found that selling content was not an easy task. Then, with the advent of the Internet and the Web it became possible to offer direct access to content archives to a much larger audience without intermediaries or special software and hardware. Thus all the technological and practical barriers for disseminating data in any form were removed. Still, with a few exceptions, the market opportunities have not emerged. It seems that there is an unwillingness to pay for content outside of entertainment.

This unwillingness to pay may have several explanations:

- Since storing and disseminating of electronic data is relatively inexpensive, the Web has been used as a *free ad on source* of revenue-generating services, to newspapers, journals, nonprofit organizations,... This competition from free sources makes it difficult to establish pay-for-access sites ("Why should I pay when I can get information free?").

- Since everybody can be a *content provider* the Web is looked upon as a free medium, where everything is and should be available without restrictions.

What it sold is usually **data**, leaving to the customer to convert data into information. This is an open process, and the "information value" of data is often impossible to calculate at the offset of this process. At the same time the process of converting data into information is expensive.

- It may be difficult to get acceptance for paying just for the right to access information. Physical media, such as paper and CDs, have a form that symbolizes value. For example, software providers use unnecessary and expensive-looking packaging to make it easier for customers to accept a high price.

- The difficulty of *assessing quality*.

- For *general information* the Web competes with other sources, such as TV, radio, and newspapers.

- Access to the source is only a small part of the work needed to find, read, and organize the information. The user may be *unwilling to pay* up front just for access, when it is so difficult to put a price on the end result. On the contrary, organizations seem to be willing to pay a lot more for consultants, but then these provide more than just the data.

- The *information need* may be very specific, and may not be served by a general archive. The data may be in the wrong form, too general, important variables may be missing, it may be too old, etc.

- *The infrastructure is not yet in place for all forms of information.* For example, an online book requires an excellent display or a good and fast printer. Online music requires at least a PC with speakers, while a connection between the PC and the hi-fi equipment would be useful. Online video requires more bandwidth than most networks can provide.

- Information-providers may be afraid of *copyright infringement* if information is provided in electronic form (see the discussion on scientific journals in chapter 22.2). Thus "valuable" information may often not be available on the Web, even if we would be willing to pay.

Closed information is easier to utilize than more open information. In many cases closed information may be used as it is, for example, as input to an automated process. With open information the process of converting data to information is more complex.

- *The problem of paying.* While large amounts, such as subscriber fees, can be paid by credit card, we still lack a general system for micro payments, for example, paying a cent for a downloaded page.

The most serious problem with information as a product is that its usefulness is difficult to evaluate (i.e., it may be difficult to convert into some form of "revenue"). While this may be easier with formalized information, such as stock prices, credit ratings, weather forecasts, and directions, this problem is more acute with more open information.

For example, some newspapers offer free access to their Internet version, but ask for a very moderate fee, let us say of $1 for accessing a paper in their online archives. However, in the end this may be too high a price! Let us assume that only one out of every five articles that we access (based on title and abstract) is of interest. Let us further assume that we only use information from a small fraction of these, perhaps one in ten (the other articles are dismissed because they tell us something that we already know, because they do not provide enough information, or because the form of the information does not fulfill our need). In the worst case, we would need to read or scan at least fifty papers to find one that is useful. The question is then if we are willing to pay the $50 needed for this information. In addition, we spend time finding the article, reading or scanning all the fifty papers just to find the one of value.

This discrepancy between theoretical and practical relevance is also found in bibliographic databases of scientific papers. It may be a valid business model to sell archive access, but a good model may require so cheap access to articles that the amount is low even after we have multiplied by fifty.

It is interesting to note that sale of pornographic material is the big exception. Sex-related words are some of the most common keywords used in searching the Web and pornography is one of the largest revenue sources. Clearly, the Web offers several advantages compared to other media for this kind of business:

- *Privacy*. Family, friends, and neighbors cannot see what one downloads over an Internet channel. Downloaded material can be stored securely on the hard drive, protected by a password.[2]

- *Availability*. Pornographic material is of limited availability in the physical world; sex shops are only found in the largest cities and in many countries pornographic material is strictly regulated. The Web offers unlimited availability.

- *Diversity*. Sex is a strong drive, and takes many forms. The Web can offer something for everybody.

- *A wide range of media can be supported*, text, images, sound, video, live video, chat, etc.

- *Inexpensive* storage and disseminating.

It should therefore not come as a surprise that these businesses flourish on the Web, even if it cannot be easy to compete in this market that also provides a well of free sources. The biggest surprise, however, may be that few other businesses have managed to build a valid business model on information sale via the Internet.

18.4 Intranet

Application parameters

Formalization level:
 Low to high

Product form:
 Symbolic

Complexity:
 Low to medium

Strangely enough, one of the most useful applications for the *world wide* Web is the Intranet, *limiting* information to those that work within an organization. While business information systems have been available for decades, the Web offers a simple, generic, and inexpensive way of implementing the same functionality:

- Use of standard software, as browsers and office tools (i.e., all employees with access to a computer will have the basic software installed).
- No additional training will be needed, as standard tools are used.
- Common format for internal and external information.
- Data that was previously stored and maintained internally can in many cases be replaced by a link to an external source (e.g., a phone directory).
- The information is accessible from everywhere. For example, employees can access company data also when traveling.

An Intranet solution becomes especially important for firms and employees that are geographically dispersed. Access to information now becomes independent of location. The foreman at a distant construction site can have access to the same information sources, the same tools and administrative facilities as those working at the head office.

Intranet/Extranet application **limits access** to a group of users, but functionality can be increased by utilizing commonalties within this group.

Since Intranet applications limit access to information one can utilize "sublanguages" that exist within an institution to offer a higher formalization level. This can be everything from product numbers to special vocabulary used within the institution. In a college Intranet application, for example, course numbers, course descriptions, departmental structure, topics of interest, etc., can be used to formalize data to higher levels and to facilitate organization of information and searching. In a business environment one can utilize product names, product attributes, order numbers, names of customers, organizational structure, processes, methods etc., to increase the formalization level.

The advantage of having an information system on an Intranet platform is that it allows customers to have access to the system directly. Universities have been pioneers in offering such systems to their students, letting all course materials, syllabuses, exercises, slides, even videotaped lectures, be available online. Many universities also let this information be open to the general public, that is, anyone can (try to) follow an MIT lecture online—free. Similar, Intranet applications can offer many advantages for the university administration, offering global access to data and letting students view and update their own records.

This simple Intranet structure works as a common memory for the organizations, a common archive where everything can be stored and retrieved. Within W3C,[3] the World Wide Web consortium, the saying goes "if it is not on the Web it does not exist." Other organizations should follow up. When everybody has access to the same data there is no need to go through others to get access and there is no excuse for not having access to the latest information. Of course, access may have to be limited to confidential data, but in principle the "put it on the Web" slogan is right.

Today, we see that the Intranet not only provides employees with static handbooks, minutes of meetings, and regulations, but also with access to systems for ordering office supplies, booking systems, payroll information, etc. On the Web it also becomes feasible to create a common experience base for the employees. This can take the form of "best practice" databases, dynamic handbooks, or databases of frequently asked questions. In this way the experience of each employee can be added to a common company experience. While this was also possible in the precomputer world, using handbooks and memoranda, the Web offers much better possibilities for entering, storing, updating, and disseminating the information. The Web has given us a common interface that can be accessed from anywhere by anybody, making it more practical to enter, update, and retrieve information.

The Intranet application offers a **common memory** and common experience base for both company employees and their customers.

A formalized database of "best practice" procedures will have the advantage of structured information, and the use of high-level concepts for retrieval. For example, one could be asked to provide date, part numbers, identification of materials that are used, etc., in a form. In the cases where these data are relevant, the form will support the input process, by structuring the input and, for example, letting the user choose between predetermined alternatives instead of having to type in data. In this way we ensure a common vocabulary and get a structure that can be processed automatically.

Not all cases can be put into predetermined forms. All of us have experienced this situation when we fill out questionnaires where it can be painful to try to fit our opinions with the standard response alternatives listed (remember our discussion in chapter 1). The remedy can be to provide more forms or to add a type that fits the new class of descriptions. Still, we need a more open form, "a blank sheet of paper" for the problems that do not fit a standard case. Even in the latter case items such as date, name, department, title should be in structured fields, leaving the "best-practice" description to an open text field. Thus, all kinds of information may be given, at the same time as basic and common data are in a structured form.

The disadvantage of providing open alternatives is that these may often be chosen for convenience, even in cases where more closed forms could have been used. With a lack of organization and structure we risk having the same data entered several times. This creates unnecessary work, makes it very difficult to maintain the data collection, prevents keeping data consistent, etc. With unstructured descriptions the disadvantage is that we only have low-level concepts (strings or words) for searching the description field. However, text-based searching will function much better here than on the open Web. Within an institution we will find a sublanguage that can aid the process. This "language" will include names of customers and suppliers, product names, names and numbers of parts, identifiers for machinery, names of processes, etc. Words that may have many meanings in the open world may be more specific within an institution (e.g., the word "grade" in a college and "bug" in a software firm). This common culture of information-providers and retrievers will boost retrieval effectiveness within an institution. But as we see, there is a tradeoff between offering open and closed forms, between flexibility on the one side, organization and structure on the other.

Formalization comes **at a price**. It is tedious to fit information into predetermined forms. It is so much easier to choose the blank sheet of paper and tell the story using our own words and our own structure.

Parts of an Intranet application can be formalized to a high level exploiting company structure and special "**sublanguages**" used within the organization.

These arguments are also valid for email systems. Most of us use a "blank form" when sending messages, but there are systems that allow us to send more structured mail. For example, to cancel a meeting we could use a special cancellation form that had fields for meeting identifier (name), date, and time. This message could then go to all participants notifying them of the cancellation. However, since a structured form is employed the email system could remove the meeting automatically from each participant's calendar at the same time as it tells a booking system that the meeting room is no longer reserved for this date and time. While these systems have clear advantages they enforce a more rigid form of communication that may be impractical in many cases.

18.5 Extranet

Application parameters

Formalization level:
  Low to medium
Product form:
  Symbolic
Complexity:
  Low to medium

A limited access Internet application, often implemented by password protection, is called an Extranet. Such systems can be used to let customers follow their own orders through production and distribution as well as for other functions. That is, we provide the customer with a window into certain parts of the company database. In this way the customer can follow the status of his order, track packages through the postal system, and should be allowed to follow the process of his insurance claim or loan application. For the customer this has the advantage that he will be better informed and for the companies that they avoid having to give the same information manually. There is also the hope that when customers get the same, or nearly the same, information that is available to the company employees, they will be drawn closer to the company.

Access can be restricted to read-only, or one can also allow customers to update parts of their records. Read-only has clear security advantages. The "Web window" of an Extranet can be implemented by using scripts or programs that retrieve the data from a company database and insert these in an HTML page that is returned to the user, as explained in detail in chapter 15.

Normally, some form of transformation is needed before the data can be presented to the customer. There may be information that we do not want the customer to see, or other types of information may have to be translated to make sense for an outsider. The internal formalization may have to be mapped to a more general formalization. For example, a product may be identified internally by a number but externally by a name. In these cases, the Web interface must perform the necessary transformations. A hospital may decide to give patients access to clinical information, but may want to add information that makes the data easier to understand, for example, giving an explanation if lab results are within or outside a normal range, translate diagnose codes to more common terms, etc. While the formal parts of a medical record can be "translated" automatically the less formal parts must be presented in its original form or be handled manually.

Since the kind of information and reports that we want to give to customers may vary, a flexible system is needed. Users within the company need a simple tool to describe data and layout of customer reports, and should also be able to determine which customers have access to which reports.

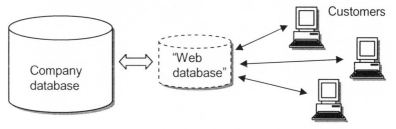

Figure 18.1 Virtual Web database.

The information provided to customers can be viewed as a virtual database that exists between the customer and the real company database (figure 18.1). In most cases, the virtual Web database will be defined by reports and access profiles that limit what each customer is allowed to see and to update, while each report is made up of data from the real database. Thus, the Web database will be a subset of the real database. It may be implemented as a physical copy, or as a virtual subset only. A physical copy has the advantage that customer traffic is kept off the main database and a security breach will not affect the original data. Such a solution works best in a read-only setting where the idea is to restrict access to information. If the customers perform updates, the changed parts have to be copied back into the original database, an action that needs additional security checking. By replicating the Web database on several servers and in many locations, one can get a system that can offer fast access to many customers. The disadvantage is that the data will only be current as of the time of the last replication.

Many institutions are offering customers such a window into their internal systems. The natural next step is to allow cus-

We can **connect customers** more closely to the company by offering access to company systems, but it may be necessary to give customers a different *view* of these data than that we offer to employees over the Intranet.

tomers to update this information directly. For example, instead of calling a newspaper or sending an email in order to change a subscription, the customer should be allowed direct access to his records, to change address, update telephone numbers, email addresses and other information, and change the method of payment. Of course, the newspaper will restrict access to some items, for example, the "amount paid" field. The advantage for the customer is that she gets 24/7/365 immediate access and does not have to provide data over the telephone or through an intermediary, while the newspaper can save on administration costs as the customers take over the maintenance of these archives.

Administering data will be simpler when everything is available online.

For the customers this also has the advantage that the data becomes available online, and it will no longer be necessary to archive all the letters received through the mail. Organizational links to all our contact points, to utility companies, banks, insurance companies, newspapers, journals, and other organizations that we support, should be available through one personal Web page. This should give us all the information we need, directly from the original sources, not from more or less well organized duplicate paper-based archives in our home.

As seen, Extranet systems have several advantages, both for the customers and the companies:

- Information is provided *automatically*, thus telephone calls to company employees are avoided.

- Customers get *updated* information.

- Data are only *archived* at the source.

- *Historical data can be provided automatically*, perhaps with tools that let you present time series of data in visual form (e.g., to show a curve of electricity usage over the recent years).

- A good information system may *tie the customers more closely to the company*. For example, from an information perspective it will now be an advantage for a customer to have as many orders as possible with the company (i.e., to get complete overviews).

- Customers can get more *detailed information* in a more flexible way than by telephone, fax or letter. For example, information on current orders can be presented in a table on the screen, printed or provided as a spreadsheet for further processing.

18.6 Handling customer input

Application parameters

Formalization level:
  Low to medium

Product form:
  Symbolic

Complexity:
  Low to medium

A disadvantage of a Web service may be that as customers go from other communication channels, such as physical contact and the telephone, to the Web the connection may become less personal. As we have discussed earlier, care should therefore be taken to strengthen these personal relationships by other means. For example, it should be easy for the customer to connect to a customer representative, through email or telephone.

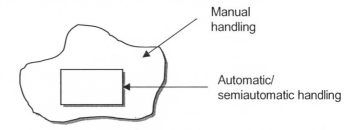

Manual handling

Automatic/semiautomatic handling

Figure 18.2 Unformalized and formalized parts.

Automatic systems can handle the closed part of customer communication. For the open parts, other channels (email, telephone) must be provided.

This is just another implementation of our basic ideas on formalization. When the formalized part of a transaction, the box part of figure 18.2, is handled automatically, it is important to provide channels for the more open parts (exceptions, etc.).

Input from customers may be a good opportunity for a sale. Since the user has initiated the dialog with his first message, and will await a reply, there is an opportunity for including additional, but relevant information. For example, when the user requests spare parts and service on her old lawnmower, we may *in addition* to giving her the information she requests provide a trade-in offer on a new model. The effect of this marketing will be dependent on how relevant the offer will be to the customer's current situation (i.e., how natural the answer will be in the context). To offer a new model when the old lawnmower has broken down could be part of a natural dialog but to offer a snow blower is not. Neither should we offer a trade-in if the customer has a new lawnmower, or if her message is a complaint on the repair that we have just performed. To some extent a smart program may be able to offer this type of response, but a program can never be expected to understand the context in the same way as a human operator. As in other situations, the ideal solution is a semiautomatic system, where the computer performs the secretarial work and a human being controls the final results.

Email offers the opportunity of having a **semiautomatic** dialog with the customer, where the computer-generated messages can be edited by a human.

Web interfaces combined with flexible product description and manufacturing processes, allow for **customization,** where products are tailored to the individual customer.

Customer input may be as unformalized as an email, but may also be in a more formal manner, for example, as exact specifications for a product. The Internet/Web provides the solution for the specification part of such products. Here we can provide interfaces that can lead a customer through a detailed specification process.

Customized products can be physical or abstract. A kitchen manufacturer can offer design programs online, where the user can specify overall measurements and functionality, and the program can calculate the need for basic modules, print list of items needed, calculate prices, etc. Such a user interface can be implemented by a downloaded script or Java Applet, or by a server side solution. The website of an insurance company cannot give you the same personal service as a brick and mortar office, but may instead offer customized insurance where the premium is based on detailed information about the insurance objects, and your utilization of these. For example, they can give you a rebate on car insurance if your company has an attended employee garage, if you drove 486 miles less than expected last year or if your son, the youngest driver, is over age twenty. This interface will allow you to choose between different options, and will immediately show how your choices affect the premium.

We have earlier discussed the advantages and disadvantages of using email message forms (i.e., to formalize email messages). The disadvantage of this approach is that it is less flexible than using open (blank) forms. However, in setting up electronic customer contact points we may at least let the customer choose a heading for the message. This can be done through a simple Web form, where the user selects from a set of alternatives. For example, when sending an email to a newspaper it would be natural to offer headings such as, subscription, advertisement, letter to the editor, news tip, etc. Incoming mail can then be sorted automatically based on this information and forwarded to the right internal email address. The advantage of this approach is that we have established a layer between the customer and internal mail addresses, which can now be changed without consequences for the outside world. The additional formalism required on the part of the customer is negligent, and if we provide an "other" alternative flexibility is maintained.

Exercises and Discussion

1. Do you maintain a letter archive at home, for example, with letters received from banks, insurance companies, public utilities? What would the advantages be if all this information were available through a personal Web page? Discuss.

2. Extranet solutions would make it possible for you, as a customer, to update your own data in employee databases, school archives, subscription files, databases of insurance companies, etc. What would the advantages be to do this job (e.g., a change of address) yourself instead of going through an intermediary? Discuss pros and cons. What requirements would you have to the user interface of the various systems?

3. In this section we discussed the advantages of letting customer select a heading for their messages to a company. However, we can go a step further and offer a set of forms for contact. For example, when the customer selects "change subscription" from a newspaper Web page we could offer a Web form for this case. What are the advantages and disadvantages of this approach compared to letting the customer just send an email message?

Notes

1. This offers many interesting legal issues. At some time we are instructed to notify organizations of changes, such as a cancellation of a subscription, a change of address, or a new mileage limit for car insurance. In some countries simple building permits (for small modifications) can be given in the form of a notice. If the organization involved offers an email address, it should be sufficient to send an email message in these cases. But what if the organization does not have routines for handling email, or if our message is removed by the spam filter? Can we distinguish a cancellation note as spam, and receive additional numbers of a journal? Or, if we see this from the organization point of view, if they provide an email address they also need good routines for handling incoming mail.

2. It is interesting to note that within this business the customers appreciate the apparent privacy of the Web, while Web privacy is a concern in all other areas. However, the privacy offered on the Web may be a wolf in sheep's clothes. With cookies the information that is provided in one situation can be linked to sites accessed in other sessions, IP and email addresses can be registered and sold to others, etc. Browsers usually store historical information, so that it is possible to review what has happened in previous sessions.

3. http://www.w3.org/.

19 Online Symbolic Services—Case Studies

Web protocols and Web browsers offer tools for creating **standardized** interfaces to databases formalized at high levels.

With the Internet the end-of-the-line for electronic information is in our office, home, or in a mobile unit. With the Web we have a standard user interface toolkit for all applications. As we have seen in chapter 15, on the server side it is quite simple to open a database system to the Internet. On the client side, no additional installation of hardware and software is necessary, since the customer uses his Internet connection and standard Web browser.

Note that this is a somewhat different application of the Web than was envisioned in the beginning. When we use the Web to connect to a banking or travel agency system, the basic ideas of the early Web:

- open to all
- everyone both readers and writers
- hypertext

are no longer important issues. The Web standards, HTML and HTTP, now have only a role for the implementation of the user interface. Beyond this point we are in the realm of the application. This has the advantage that the formalization level within each application can be much higher than on the Web. As we have seen the banking system "understands" concepts such as account, balance, and interest, allowing us to perform high-level operations using these concepts from the terminal in the customer's home.

In this chapter we shall discuss the effect of such a personal terminal with respect to services which are all-symbolic (i.e., where the complete transaction can be performed on the Internet). There is no lack of these application areas within our modern society: banking, insurance, stock market, booking tickets... to name a few.

19.1 Retail banking

The advantages of offering customers access to their own records can be enormous. A retail bank, for example, may process millions of transactions each day. Many of these transactions are originated on paper (checks, deposit notes, letters, fax, etc.), or orally, for example, when the customer provides transaction data to a cashier over the telephone or by a personal visit

Application parameters

Formalization level:
  High
Product form:
  Symbolic
Complexity:
  Low

The **Internet bank** permits the customer do the job on his own equipment, letting him pay for the connection. With the Internet the computer is the bank. Due to the high formalization level most operations can be performed automatically.

to the bank. Entering these data in the bank computer system is a major effort especially as care has to be taken to ensure correctness.

Internet banking may be offered as an alternative service to traditional banking, or by new banks that base all their contact with customers on electronic services. These banks try to offer a full suite of functions, similar to traditional banks. Personal contact with customers is through email or telephone. Paper is used only when required by law (e.g., for the initial account-setup contract). Customers access their accounts directly, using the Web as an interface to the banking system. They perform their own transactions, check balance, pay bills, print account statements, etc.

An Internet bank does not need branch offices, human tellers, cash or check handling, printing and mailing of statements, etc. In fact, the daily operating part of an Internet bank is in many ways just a computer, a server. The customers themselves have replaced the tellers, the branch offices are replaced by the home and office of the customer. Customers use their own hardware and software to access the bank system. They pay their own communication fees. Since the customers themselves handle the manual part, all other services can be performed automatically by the banking software. Thus Internet banks can (should) offer higher interest and lower fees.

But there are also additional advantages for the customers. They can access their accounts 24 hours a day, 7 days a week, 365 days a year. If all transactions are electronic, that is, no checks or other paper in the system, the account balance will always be updated. All bills entered into the system will be paid on their due date, and the system can provide an overview of upcoming payments. An additional advantage of removing paper from the system is that the customer no longer has to archive manual transaction records. Instead, all historical data are available from the Web interface, in the customary chronological presentation or, for example, presented by addressee. By a button click an Internet bank can present the customer with a list of all transactions regarding the credit card company or any other institution or account. Earlier the customer had to do this himself, by going through a large number of printed bank statements.

The disadvantage of electronic banking is that the customer needs Internet access and the skills needed to perform the functions and must do all the keying themselves. However, banking functions are formalized to a high degree, and with good user interfaces most people will be able to do this on their own. The data needed is minimal, such as amounts, account numbers, etc., so keying is limited. As these services evolve the need to key in data, such as bills, will be greatly reduced. Regular bills, for example, bills from utilities, can be entered for automatic payment, where the bill will be paid on the due date if we do not tell the system otherwise. Other requests for payment can be sent to the customer as an email message and as an electronic record to the banking system. When the customer accesses the banking system to pay the bill, all data will be available so that the bill can be paid just by a confirmation, for example, by checking off the box next to the bill.

While a pure Internet bank is just a computer, in practice some personal services are needed to handle special cases. For example, when the customer has technical problems, when he does not understand the interface, or when the interface does not provide the functionality that the user requires. The pure Internet bank tries to handle these exceptions by providing customer service over the telephone and email. But this affects costs, and the level of interest rates and fees that the bank can offer. The business model really requires that personal service be only offered for exceptions. It is therefore important that the bank monitor all personal requests, to see which of these may be handled by an improved or extended user interface. In this way similar requests may be avoided in the future.

> Internet banks need a good **infrastructure**, of internationally and nationally unique account numbers, and simple cash-free payment systems. In addition the proliferation of PCs with Internet connection needs to be high if large market shares are to be had.

This is not always possible. In principle, Internet banks use a cash-free model where all transactions are completed electronically. But, even though plastic is replacing paper money for many transactions, there are still situations where cash is convenient. Cash withdrawals are handled by cash-back services when using the plastic card in a store, or by ATM machines. However, the pure Internet banks, without physical offices, cannot easily offer the opposite service, inserting large amounts of cash into an account.[1] Thus, these banks may not be a good alternative for customers that are paid in cash, such as a newsstand agent.

An Internet bank may offer checks, but this violates the all-electronic business model and requires new channels between the bank and its customers, and between the receiver of the checks and the bank. Some countries, such as Norway, have a bank infrastructure that makes it easy to establish Internet banks. In Norway checks are the exception, all bills are paid by bank-to-bank transfers using a nationwide system. Today, the Internet is the most common way of paying bills in Norway; it has already passed paper- and telephone-based billing. Costs are an important issue here. The average transaction fee for paying a bill on the Internet is approximately 20 cents, compared to an average of 60 cents for paper-initiated transactions. With even higher transaction volumes the Internet-based solutions will be even more cost effective.

Electronic transactions have the advantage that the costs of maintaining the system can be nearly independent of the transaction volumes.

In many ways this is an identical situation to the transportation example we used in chapter 1 on formalization. As we saw, the metro system must be formalized to a higher degree before a computer could replace the driver. The Internet banks face the same situation since their business model needs a world where the formalizations are in place for all or most economic transactions to be performed electronically.

In this respect small countries may have an advantage since it is easier to agree on and establish national systems and standards, for example, for account numbers and bank-to-bank transactions. Such a formalized infrastructure, often established long before the Internet, can provide the foundation for an efficient all-electronic system, independent of cash and checks. With such a system all deposits go electronically as bank-to-bank transfers. Bills can be paid the same way, by an electronic transfer directly to the recipient's account—independent of his choice of bank. It is also of importance that it seems to be easier for the start-up online banks to establish trust in a small and homogeneous country. However, without doubt we will soon see a situation where the Internet becomes the most-used medium for bank transactions in most countries. The advantages of online banking are so great that they will remove nearly any barrier.

The impact on society of a nationwide system for electronic payments is interesting to consider. When point of sale terminals are in place and connected to the Internet the cost of yet another transaction will be minimal. Cash may then be used only for very small amounts, but even here systems are established that reduce the need for cash. For example, paper tickets for everything from a bus to a movie are today replaced by passes that can be paid by credit card. Several systems for "electronic cash" have also been proposed that can handle micro-payments with a minimum of transaction overhead. Some of these systems require a new infrastructure of "smart cards," while others are based on the Internet or on cell phones.

The Internet-based pay services are ideal for transactions that originate on the Internet, where all the data needed are already in electronic form. Mobile phone-based services can replace cash in many other situations, for example, to put a bottle of coke from a vending machine on your telephone bill by calling a number or sending a SMS message. The technology developed for electronic highway toll passes, based on radio transponders, can also be used as a basis for other payments, such as entrance to sport activities or bus tickets.

Most Internet banks try to profit by the traffic to their sites by selling other services ranging from investment offers to travel packages. This is viewed as an important business model for retail banks, as the possibilities of generating revenue on the traditional banking services decrease with increased automation. However, this business model may not be valid. Internet banks are used in a different manner than traditional banks. In an all-electronic world, it is so much simpler to set up an automatic bill payment system. For example, instead of having to pay a bill on the due date the Internet bank can be told to perform this transaction automatically, if the customer does not interfere. Customers can still check their bills by going through the data provided in an email, but in the normal situation there will be no need to access the banking portal. Already today, with the services that an Internet bank offers for automatic payments, most personal transactions can be handled automatically by the system. The day of the complete automatic banking system may not be very far off, even if there is always the odd bill that has to be entered manually.

Trust is important in all banking. While traditional banks can rely on their long standing, and can express solidity through their buildings an Internet bank must find different ways of promoting trust, for example, by providing reliable, good, and secure service. Security is an important issue in these pioneering days of the Web. In the brick and mortar world, security is implemented by ID cards, guards, surveillance cameras, and locks. On the Web users identify themselves by PIN codes, in some cases by additional codes from special paper cards or provided by password calculators. The client computer can be identified by using certificates provided by the bank and downloaded to the client, and the communication itself can go over the more secure HTTPS channel, where data is coded using advanced cryptographic techniques. In many ways, this makes Web banking more secure than traditional banking,

It may no longer be possible to create **revenue** just by providing basic retail banking services.

where it is difficult, in practice, to check signatures. But, where attacks on traditional banks may be in the form of a forged check, unauthorized access to an account or a physical attack on the cash in a branch office, a hacker may attack the whole Internet bank, perhaps gaining access to a large number of accounts. In the worst case, this may cause the downfall of the bank. However, it seems that the banks have managed to implement the necessary security level. At least, with the Internet banks we have avoided the accompanying crime that follows all other banking services, bank robbery, check forgery, credit card swindle,[2] and ATM break-in—at least until today.

Both in the physical and virtual world there exists a balance between security and convenience. Too many, too long, or too frequent changes of passwords are inconvenient, and may be counterproductive in the sense that we have to write them down to remember. Some banks therefore rely on just a four-digit PIN code for access, which gives hackers a 1/10000 probability of gaining access to the account for each attempt. Is this secure enough? For example, let us assume that this book will get 10,000 readers, and that each of you has two different PIN codes. If I say that one of these codes is 6753, at least a couple of you should cry out: How did I know that? Or, to use other words, the chances of "winning" are ever so much greater than in a state lottery.[3]

This balance between security and convenience can perhaps be determined better by each individual customer than by the bank (i.e., banks should allow for customized security in the same way as a browser allows us to set the security level). For example, we can set up the browser to disallow scripts, cookies, or Java applets. Similarly, we should be allowed to specify that our bank account should only be accessed from the office or home computer; that a certificate downloaded to a new computer should not be active before we have given an email confirmation, or that we want to provide an additional password for transfer of large amounts. Customized security recognizes that customers are different. While students may access the bank from many computers, some of us only use an office or home computer. While students often have small amounts in their account, people in regular jobs may have larger amounts available. Of course, the bank has to require a minimum-security level, but if we can reduce the risk of such an attack, and the hassle that follows, without any inconvenience at all—why

In many ways, an Internet bank is **more secure** than a brick and mortar bank. While it is still possible to break in, electronic money can more easily be traced than physical money.

If a customer is concerned about **security**, why not offer a more secure system, personalized to the customer needs?

shouldn't we have this option of customizing our own risk management?

Today, most Internet banks try to mimic the services offered by brick and mortar banks. However, as Amazon has shown for bookstores, there are many **new services** that can be provided by an Internet bank.

Banks are conservative institutions. Even Internet banks that rely on new technology for their services, have not implemented many of the new services that online information make possible. That is, to work as "information banks," providing new information-based services for their customers as a replacement of the old cash-based services. These could be as simple as organizing and printing existing information, or more dramatically, using this information to act on the customer's behalf. For example, while businesses are required to have full accounting, few consumers are willing to spend the work needed, even if most of us would be interested to see an account of last year's income and expenditures. If we agree to use the bank account and accompanying credit or debit cards for a substantial part of our expenses, allowing the bank to retrieve information on what we bought from point-of-sale terminals and bills, such a full account could be made automatically. The same data could also be used as a basis for next year's budget, perhaps provided by the bank in the form of a spreadsheet so that we could adjust the numbers ourselves.

With additional data, a good bank service, or perhaps we should call it the automatic financial advisor, should be able to give us recommendations for how we could save money next year, for example:

- Save $234/year by changing utility companies.

- Change to a different account type and get higher interest rates.

- A customer card could have given us a $56 rebate on the five overnights we had at Hilton hotels last year.

- Credit card interest amounted to $1260, with an average rate of 7 percent. Consider a second mortgage loan instead, with savings of up to $200.

- You had three visits to the Science Center, with a total of $290 in entrance fees. Consider a family membership that gives unlimited access for $110, of which $98 is tax deductible.

The bank could take an even more active role. For example, we could instruct our bank to find the best deal for utilities, let the bank automatically order preferred customer's rebates on travel, and bargain on our behalf on goods that we need. The banks will be in a good position to offer such services since they have the necessary data and the contact points both with customers and companies. It is also of importance that they are trusted.

To offer such services the bank needs information that will raise privacy issues. However, where we have earlier trusted banks with our money we now have to trust that the bank will guard this information and not let it be used to our disadvantage. Today, we expect that the bank will compute interest rates correctly. Few take the time to check these calculations. In the same way, we may trust the bank to provide the services mentioned above in the future, for example, expecting that the bank will offer us the best utility contract.

As the standard retail banking functions are replaced by a computer, making it more difficult to get high revenues on this part, banks will need these additional services to survive in the retail market. The futuristic Internet-based banks will still be in the trust business, but only parts of the bits on their disks may represent money.

19.2 Travel information and booking

Application parameters

Formalization level:
Low to high

Product form:
Symbolic

Complexity:
Low to medium

Travel agency functions such as information and booking are in many ways another ideal eBusiness application. Static information, in the form of text, images, maps, video, etc., can be presented over the open Web at low cost, using all the Web features including hypertext links. As we have seen, this can be combined with dynamic information, giving the customer updated information on availability and prices and, finally, the customer can perform the actual booking herself using the Web as a database interface.

Simplified and less expensive booking is a necessity for hotels and airlines, which are in the strange situation that the cost of selling is often inversely correlated to the price of the product. For example, a full-price airline ticket can be processed in a very short time, as the customer will usually have exact data on her plans and there will normally not be a problem of availability. For bargain tickets there are several conditions that have to be met. In addition, these are used for leisure travel, where there may be many options for dates, times, and locations. Combined with limited availability selling these tickets may involve a prolonged conversation with the customer, until the right flights are found. The Web must therefore seem to be a godsend to airlines, or perhaps it is the Web that has made cheap flights possible?

In principle, booking is an all-symbolic service. Plastic cards or reference numbers can easily replace tickets and vouchers, and the whole booking transaction can then be performed via the Internet. Removing paper tickets has, of course, other advantages. Not only will all the paper-oriented functions, such as printing, distributing, counting, storing, etc., disappear, but electronic media offer the possibility of automating check-in, both at airports and hotels. When a plastic card is used for boarding instead of a paper ticket the system will know immediately that the passenger has boarded the aircraft. This makes it possible to have updated passenger lists available at all times, also for corporate headquarters. That is, they will have updated data at any time about the actual number of passengers on their planes. Now it also becomes possible to bill the passenger for the actual boarding instead of the right to board that is expressed by a paper ticket.

Electronic media have the disadvantage that they demand a working network connection, but downloading all bookings from the central hotel or flight reservation system to the actual hotel reception or boarding-gate PC in advance can reduce the risk of failure. This will also speed up the process of validating bookings.

To limit the input needed from the customer the booking system should adjust to the customer's preferred language, capturing flight patterns of frequent flyers (if any) or letting the customer enter this information and offering the possibility of choosing among these defaults, only asking for the date for a trip. Such systems do not only offer the advantage of more efficient consumer-to-business communication, but will also connect the customer more strongly to the company, as the company that has updated and utilized the customer data in the best way will have an advantage.

It is therefore not unexpected that travel is one of the major applications of eBusiness today. From an early start with static pages with itineraries, hotel information, general tourist information, etc., we expect that all the major hotel chains and airlines offer a full electronic service today. In addition, we find the eTravel-Agencies that give us access to many different service providers. These all-automatic intermediaries have the advantage that they can send our request, for example, for a discount flight, to the online booking system of each airline, thus

---

By replacing paper-based tickets, booking can be an **all-electronic service**.

Booking is the ideal computer application: Data is formalized to a high level and there is a need for fast and continuous updates.

Travel data, available dates, flights, schedules are easier to present **visually**, for example, on a Web page, than orally, over a telephone.

saving us the time of repeatedly giving our request to each individual booking system where we try to find the best offer. Some of these intermediaries may also be in the position of giving us bargains that cannot be found within each service, for example, by their "block" bookings of hotel rooms and airline seats (similar to brick and mortar travel agencies).

The main advantage of online booking for consumers is that we eliminate or reduce the cost of an intermediary, since we perform the data entry ourselves. Of course, this is only an advantage if the savings flow down to us in the form of cheaper tickets, not if they are retained as profits in other parts of the value chain. In addition, the Internet may give us faster access than waiting in line for a telephone operator. We may also find, especially in the cases where our requests are difficult to fulfill, for example, when preferred flights or hotels are full, that the Internet may provide a better overview than we may get over a telephone from a travel agent. For example, an airline website can provide us with a calendar, marking the dates of available bargain flights, thus making it easy to find the best alternatives. Of course, if we visit a travel agency we can get the same information, but we will—in some way or other—have to pay for the agent's time. With the Internet we can review alternatives at leisure.

Will the Internet replace the brick and mortar travel agencies? To some extent, a part of their business has already been lost to eBusiness. However, travel agencies have always competed with direct consumer booking. The possibility of going to the agency or calling a hotel or airline directly, has always been an option. The question then is, to what extent does the Internet provide something different? To answer this question we shall start by looking at the brick and mortar travel agency. Simplified, this intermediary provides the following services:

1. Advice
2. Information (brochures, schedules, etc.)
3. Booking services
4. Travel insurance
5. Billing

Many of the services offered by a brick and mortar travel agency are formalized, and can easily be performed by a **customer** with access to the booking systems.

We shall consider each of these functions, in reverse order. Earlier on billing (5) was an important function for the travel agency. You confirmed your reservation by prepaying, receiving tickets and hotel vouchers. With the ubiquitous use of credit cards this service is no longer needed as hotels, rental agencies, and airlines can get a credit card number as a no-show guarantee. However, some customers may feel more protected by offering their credit card to a well-known travel agent than by providing this information via the Internet.

Many credit card companies include travel insurance (4) as a free service (when using the card to pay for travel), and year-round insurance has to a large extent replaced insurance for each trip. In addition, travel insurance can easily be offered over the Web so this is no longer an important business area for the agencies.

Before the Internet, online access to booking systems (3) used private networks. In practice, access was restricted to heavy users, travel agencies, and perhaps some large enterprises. As consumers, we could only access these systems through intermediaries, airlines, hotels, car rentals, or travel agencies. The travel agencies' advantage was that they could access many different booking systems. Today, each and every one of us gets the same functionality, without the travel agency, if we have Internet access. But do-it-yourself is not cost free. Apart from paying for the computer and the Internet service, we "pay" by using our time. On the Internet we do the keying ourselves. Novel interfaces combined with congested networks and booking systems can make this time-consuming. The large variety of interfaces is also a cause for errors, giving the wrong date, booking for one person instead of two, forgetting to rent a car.... In many cases an experienced travel agent, on a private network and with priority access, may do the job much faster and possibly better.

With the Internet and the Web, customers have access to the same data as a travel agency; the access **monopoly** to the booking systems has been broken.

The travel agency can give us nice brochures (2) printed on glossy paper. But we can get the same information, with the latest updates, over the Web. With a connection to reservation systems, we can also restrict information to availability—not showing hotels, flights etc., that are sold out, only showing discount fares, not showing outdated information, etc. Clearly more convenient than what we can get from the static brochures.

Advice (1) can be given via the Internet. For example, a good search system will help us find available flights and hotels within our price range, with the facilities we need. This will work as long as our needs can be formalized within the attributes that the search system provides, but will be more problematic where our needs are more open. For example if we want to take a trip to New York City, a website may give us the interface for hotel booking that is shown in figure 19.1.

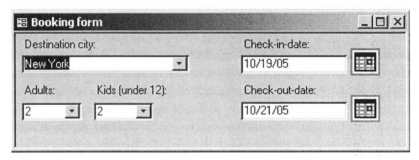

Figure 19.1 User interface for hotel booking.

Not all needs for travel can be expressed in a **formalized** language (e.g., as dates and flight numbers).

Based on this information a good system will return a list of hotels with available rooms, showing the price offered for our two-night stay. If we find what we want, a booking can be performed just by hitting a *Book Now* button next to each hotel. This is an excellent interface if our need for accommodation can be expressed by city, date, number of nights, and number of persons. But what happens when the result does not fulfill our requirements, for example, if the prices offered are much higher than we are willing to pay (often the case in New York City). Should we look for more hotels, try different dates (perhaps this is a bad weekend), see if Saturday to Monday is cheaper than Friday to Sunday or accept a lower standard? Should we try to find a hotel outside the city center and commute, but then what will this cost us or is there a bus?

We may try to look into all these alternatives by trying different dates, sorting hotels by price, looking for additional hotels, widen the range from the city center, etc., but it will be a very time-consuming job. This is especially true where additional data (e.g. on public transport), has to be collected by telephone or from different, maybe unknown, websites. One may easily spend many hours doing this job.

When customers get access to booking systems over the Internet, the travel agent needs to provide a **higher level service** if he is to be retained as a middleman. His future will therefore be in the more open areas— helping the customer to plan a holiday, offering advice, etc.

Could a human expert do a better job? Sure. An experienced travel agent could tell us right away that we will have to pay at least $400 for a two-night stay in a room with two beds in a medium-quality hotel on Manhattan, that you could save some dollars by having a smaller room, moving to a not-so-good location and that the weekend you chose was not a good one (big football game). The agent could further suggest that a family without any intention of participation in New York night life could get a much better deal by staying in New Jersey and taking the bus into Manhattan.

As we see, the problem with the Web interface is that we, at an early stage, must formalize our need for accommodation, decide on dates, etc., while the human being tries to interpret and fulfill our basic requests. There are even situations where a good travel agent would suggest a different destination for our trip, for example, "if museums are what you want to visit, why not go to Washington, D.C. instead. At this time of the year you can get very good hotel bargains over the weekends, and the museums are free...." Clearly far more than current Web interfaces can provide.

May						
Sun	Mon	Tue	Wed	Thu	Fri	Sat
		1	2	3	4	5
6	7	8	9	10	11	12
13	14	15	16	17	18	19
20	21	22	23	24	25	26
27	28	29	30			

Figure 19.2 Dates with available bargain tickets are marked.

Do we need an experienced human being to give this type of advice, or can we provide it automatically over a website? To some extent we already see efforts to move in this direction. Instead of requiring fixed dates, some sites allow us to set flexible dates, and will give an overview of discount fares available on different dates, such as seen in figure 19.2.

With more **flexible** user interfaces the automatic services can be extended far beyond simple booking routines.

By allowing different approaches to reservation systems, users could be allowed to specify their requirements to any level, for example, operating with open dates as above, limit the search to weekend trips, weekends through March, or specifying exact dates. As we have seen, flexibility could be extended to include destinations as well (e.g., any destination in the Caribbean, Puerto Rico or Aruba, any island except Aruba, etc.)— or, instead of destinations telling the system what you want to do, skiing, fishing, and visiting museums or going to the opera. While formalized interfaces can never compete with the openness and flexibility of an experienced human operator, they can certainly offer better functionality than we see today. Even if we may meet some of the same formalization problems here as we had with keyword searches, we have the advantage that the system does not make the final decision. The job of the system is only to present the most interesting alternatives to the customer, allowing the customer to select among many alternatives.

Profiles and other customer data may be used in situations where it is the eTravel agency or airline that starts a dialog with the customer. For example, many travel sites give us the possibility to sign up for bargain offers, so that they can notify us by email whenever they have an offer for a Caribbean weekend, a bargain trip to Los Angeles, or whatever product that we have expressed an interest for. To some extent, a brick and mortar agency can provide the same service, but this is so much simpler to implement using Web forms (to specify interests) and email for the actual notification, where the email message includes a direct link to the Web page with further details. These emails will be generated automatically, based on the category of the offer and a database with customers' email addresses and interests. Most current systems are rather primitive, perhaps with only an option for stating the location of interest. However, based on profile data or by more detailed information about our interests we may turn traditional marketing upside down. For example, as Pittsburgh residents we may be apprehensive of the coming winter season, and should be able to specify that we are interested in a four-day trip to a place in the sun for two adults and two children, at a budget hotel on the beach, that is—if the price is low enough. This information may then be used by the companies to find the segment that could be interested in a special offer or, perhaps more interesting, to construct special packages for these segments.

Web travel sites, especially with more flexible and customized user interfaces, should have the potential to take a large part of the travel market. For airlines, hotel and rental agencies their own Web-based booking systems will act as an extension of previous telephone booking systems. However, the applicability of the Internet for these applications, notably the ease of searching and retrieving information, will attract new and larger groups of customers. For companies such a development will have several advantages. Online booking is cost effective, as the customer herself does all the manual work. With direct booking, the company will avoid paying a percentage to an intermediary, and the increased availability of updated information may make it easier to fill up hotels and flights. Through email the companies have a fast channel for a last-minute sale,

A world-wide **centralized** booking system will be efficient, but may have disruptive effects on service providers.

Customer's **preferences** can be used to find the best offer, or to create the products that the customers call for.

for example, such as the bargain weekend offers from many airlines. Collecting data on customer profiles or preferences can enhance these sale efforts to the theoretical limit where all customers that receive an offer also accept the offer. While this is not possible in practice, the profiles may be used to identify the groups where the probability of acceptance is highest.

However, as customers, we will still have to contact each airline and each hotel/chain to get information. This is very time-consuming and cumbersome and many may prefer leaving this work to a travel agency. We have seen that even today this agency may be an automatic Web-based system. In theory such a system will be able to find the best deals if they have access to all available information, in the same way as a traditional brick and mortar agency. In practice, the situation may be very different.

Imagine yourself as a marketing director of an airline. Today, brick and mortar travel agencies have direct access to your booking system. Should you allow the Web-based agency the same service, is this just a matter of another agency or may these electronic intermediaries have a greater impact on your business? The difference between a brick and mortar and eTravel agency is not fundamental; both offer the same type of services to customers. However, there is a difference of size. While a traditional agency may have a customer base of perhaps ten thousand people, in practice limited by the population of their neighborhood, there will be no upper limit to the customer base of a Web-based agency. If a traditional agency favors another airline, this will not have any great influence on your sales, since there will probably be other agencies that favor your company. However, if the successful website agency is biased, this may have a major impact.

Control over the **formalized part**, the booking system, may be more important than control over the physical part, the planes, etc.

Thus a requirement will be that the Web system does not present your flights in any unfavorable way, for example, presenting competitors' flights before your own. But, even if fairness can be guaranteed, is this what you want? A Web-based agency with access to all booking systems will be able to present the customer with the best deal. For many of us this implies the cheapest fare. In principle, customers will be able to obtain "best fare" price through traditional systems, either using the telephone or a traditional travel agency. If the telephone is used, all airlines must be called in order to fulfill the information need. In such a situation many accept the first "reasonable" offer, knowing that further calling will take time and that the first offer may not be available later. Similarly, a human travel agent may not be willing to do much work in order to find a ticket that gives the customer a low price. So here, as in other sectors of life, the first "reasonable" deal is accepted. The computer, however, can in practice do an extensive search and find the lowest price. This creates a very different marketplace from what we have in the physical world. For example, if the Web travel sites become successful and a large percentage of all flight bookings is channeled through these systems, this will open for new low-cost airlines, as their bargain offers will come up first in any fair price-based rankings. Such a system will remove a major hindrance for these start-up companies (i.e., to be seen in the market and have customers evaluating their offers).

Established airlines can meet this potential competition by offering better service, frequent flyer programs and other offers that complicate the search for the best deal —and, they can try to ensure that the websites cannot find the best offer. This can be done by not offering access to their own booking systems to the Web-based travel agencies, by only offering limited access, by limiting the best deals to their own systems, and so forth. In this way, they may force the market and the customers to use their own systems, and to a situation where we get back to accepting the first "reasonable" deal.

While the functionality of individual airline booking systems may be as good as what we can get from the online travel agencies (apart from the price competition) when the trip can be confined to one airline only, these systems will be too limited if the trip involves flights on different airlines. For convenience and price as well as for getting help if we do not make a connection, we usually want through-tickets, naming all the different legs. Therefore, what is needed is a system that includes several airlines. Is this a market opening for the online travel agencies? Possibly, but the airlines are meeting this challenge by mergers and alliances. By interconnecting the different booking systems, or offering a centralized system for the whole alliance, the group can offer the same functionality as a travel agency, while keeping competition under control. Consumers are offered frequent flyer mileage on all the flights of the participating airlines, in order to ensure customer loyalty to the alliance (or their booking system). That is, these companies will try to capture the customer at the earliest possible moment. Getting the customers to use their website and booking system will be as important as getting them on the plane.

General, all inclusive, booking systems can be a threat to the core part of an airline, as it becomes easier to compare prices.

Price competition can be handled by making offers more **open**, less closed and formalized, for example, by frequent flier programs, different service levels, etc.

Exercises and Discussion

1. When even the pizza delivery comes with a mobile card reader that can capture your payment electronically, the possibility of removing cash altogether becomes a possibility. Discuss this situation with regard to crime, black market economy, and tax. What are the advantages and the disadvantages? Is some form of cash needed?

2. Think of the traveling you have performed in the last years, and try to make a formal description of your need for flights, hotels, etc. Is this possible in all cases?

3. For a new bargain airline, will there be any disadvantages by *only* offering booking and sale of tickets over the Web?

4. An incumbent airline has a price and discount structure that was developed for a world where most tickets were booked through an experienced travel agent. An example may be the discount that is offered to couples, if one pays full price the other is offered a 50 percent discount. Discuss the problems of developing Web-based, B2C booking systems that incorporate these structures. What is the best solution?

Notes

1. Some modern ATM machines can also accept cash, using the same technology as gas stations and others have used to scan paper bills and detect coins.

2. Here criminals have been able to use new technology to copy cards and to get PIN codes, the latter often by the use of a hidden camera. This has forced credit card companies and banks to replace the simple magnet stripe cards of today with smarter cards. The latter has a small computer on board.

3. Many banks use special password calculators that generate 6- or 8-digit access codes. These reduce the risk of unauthorized access, but require that the user has access to the calculator when she wants to use the online system.

20 Online Retail Shopping, Physical Items

Online shopping is one of the most profiled applications on the Web. The idea of shopping from home is not new, of course, catalog sales have a long history. Web advocates may not like a comparison with the very profane catalog market, but the basics are similar:

- shopping from a "catalog"
- submitting an order
- waiting for the goods to arrive

The difference is not in the principles but in the implementation. Here the Web has several advantages. The Web allows for a more comprehensive product description than a paper catalog. A Web page is highly *updateable*, in contrast to a catalog printed in huge numbers. This not only allows the store to introduce new items and remove sold-out items, but the customer can get detailed information on availability if the Web system has a direct link to the underlying inventory systems. The dynamic nature of the media also allows the supplier to introduce dynamic pricing, for example, giving a discount where sales are lower than expected, when there is additional packing capacity, etc., all the way up the value chain.

The Web makes it possible to create **virtual industries** that at the extreme may consist of a computer program only. This program can maintain a Web portal, and communicate with other virtual and physical industries. The latter is of course needed when physical products are involved.

The possibility of having an updated catalog at all times simplifies both marketing and logistics. While a catalog company has to keep large numbers of items in stock and must keep a steady supply of items, on the Web demand and supply can be better adjusted. By providing customers with a date of availability, the numbers in stock can be reduced to a minimum. Sales may go down if the customer has to wait for a shipment, but complaints will be avoided as long as the products are delivered within the promised date.

Many Web companies do not have their own warehouses. Customer orders can be directed electronically to suppliers that produce on demand or have their own warehouses. That is, the highly dynamic Web medium and the fact that customer orders are in an electronic form allow for very flexible supply policies.

While the advantages of using the Web are strong there are a few disadvantages compared to catalog sales. The customers need Internet access, and where product information is presented as pictures, video clips, etc., they need a reasonable bandwidth to be able to browse the site. Customers also need the skill to find products of interest, and to do their own ordering. This will not be a problem with younger customers, but many elderly people often find traditional catalog sites convenient and may have problems using the Web.

From a marketing point of view, the Web has the disadvantage that the *activation* is up to the user. While a traditional catalog company can generate interest by mailing a catalog, the website will have to wait until the customer accesses the site or will have to try to generate interest in other ways. This can be done by sending email messages to the customer, by banner ads on other sites, etc. Some websites even present part of their product spectrum in paper catalogs, illustrating these disadvantages of the Web.

The most interesting question is not how websites will compete with traditional catalog sales, as most catalog companies also offer Web access, but to what extent the Web will compete with brick and mortar stores. While some of the initial enthusiasm for the Web has rubbed off and many have learned the hard way that it is not so easy to change customer habits, the Web has the possibility of being an alternative sales channel to physical stores. As we have experienced, there is no magic to the Web. Yes, the interface to the customers may be somewhat different from a brick and mortar store, but many of the other functions, such as making good deals with manufacturers and maintaining a good logistics system are identical. The online store will even need better logistics systems than brick and mortar stores.

While both stores need to keep track of inventory, the brick and mortar store can have an out-of-stock problem, but cannot sell an item that is not on the shelves. An online store without a close connection between their stock and the catalogs may continue selling long after the last item disappears. Even if the catalogs show number in stock for each item, a discrepancy may have the consequence that a customer buys what the store does not have.

While the brick and mortar store leaves the problem of transporting the products on the "last mile" to the customer, letting her negotiate rush-hour traffic on her way home, distribution will be the headache of the online store. Many have learned that a promise of delivery before Christmas is not so easy to fulfill for an order taken on the 10th of December. These problems have to be solved to keep customers satisfied.

If shopping can be **formalized** as:

- Select product
- Find best price
- Order
- Pay

the online stores will have a great future.

When **shopping** is something more than just buying a product, that is, if there are open parts ("shopping as an experience"), the online store may not be a good alternative.

In addition, the online store, like any other store, has to stream-line its processes and reduce costs. The bottom line is to maxi-mize profit (i.e., to generate revenues through efficient sales and minimizing the cost of order fulfillment).

In the physical world there are some practical limits as to how far the customer will travel for his shopping; on the Web we have a global marketplace where the competitor is only "a click away." To some extent this is a new situation, but compa-nies have earlier learned to live under very similar conditions. In the physical world, the competition may be next door on the street or in the mall, or may be reached just by a different tele-phone number. Before personal transportation we had every va-riety of shop in the neighborhood. Cars made it practical to shop in a larger area. Did this increase competition? Initially, yes, but now the car has transformed the cities. There are no longer an abundance of similar shops within easy driving dis-tance, and in many areas there may only be one store or mall within a convenient distance. That is, we may still use the one grocer in the neighborhood. Not a small shop on the corner, but a supermarket that serves a much larger area. As before, if this grocer does not serve us well we may go to the competition, even if they may be further away.

We may see a similar development on the Web, where businesses have to adjust to a virtual world where communica-tion goes at the speed of light. For all-symbolic applications, where input and output is in the form of bits, the marketplace can be the world, but regulations, currencies, taxation, etc., may impose restrictions for some applications, such as banking. For businesses that have a physical part, for example, product de-livery, there may be practical limitations as to how far off we can go. Still, the Internet widens the size of the practical mar-ket. Where we previously had a choice of a few local book-stores, we can now choose between an abundance of stores of-fering Internet service. In the long run, we should expect a similar development as we had with local shops, that some will disappear and that others will expand. This may even go faster on the Internet where expansion is so much easier, in many ways independent of physical factors.

While most businesses accept some form of competition, too much competition may affect profitability. To avoid such a situation businesses have a variety of devices that diminish a too-direct competitive situation:

---

*Personal cars have had a profound impact on the retail market-place, even to the extent of changing cities, replacing active downtown areas with out-of-city malls. With the Internet the mar-ketplace has ex-panded to a **global** level. Will this have a similar impact?*

*In theory, the Internet and Web provides a global **marketplace**. In practice it may be more local, especially when physical goods are involved.*

- *Differentiation.* Concentrating on a narrower market segment, for example, parts for veteran cars.

- Different *product specter*, but also variations on models and packaging. A product found in one store may not exactly match a product in another.

- Different *service level*, from personal service to do-it-yourself.

- Different *store layout* so that shopping will be easier for the customer in a store she knows. On the Internet the user will operate faster with a well-known interface.

- Proprietary *charge cards*, so that returning to this store may represent a saving.

- Retaining *customer data*, making it more convenient to shop from a store that has all details of names, addresses, etc.

- The use of *sales, coupons, charge card rebates*, and time-dependent pricing to make direct price comparisons difficult.

- *Mailing of coupons* and special offers to customers.

In theory, the Internet opens for more **competition**. In practice, businesses have a large set of countermeasures that can be used to reduce competition.

These measures are used by brick and mortar stores as well as on the Internet, but to a different degree. On the Web it may be more difficult to have a distinctive product specter than in a physical store, as the customer has less possibility of examining and trying the product. Thus, many of the successful Web stores rely on brand names or more generic items such as books, CDs, or DVDs. But methods such as dynamic pricing, customized offers, special (and customized) store layout, are often easier to implement on the Web than in the physical world.

With such methods the competition can be kept more than a click away. For example, I shop books online at Amazon, which has an excellent user interface. I go directly to their site using a bookmark. I know the site and it takes me only seconds to find what I need. They have information on me as a customer from previous sales, so that we are close to "shopping with a click" (i.e., I can get the book with a minimum of input). From previous experience I know that they will deliver on time and that there will not be any problems with the credit card payment. Amazon has been a pioneer in offering simple-to-use interfaces, but others are following.

It is important that existing customers find it simpler to return, than to go to a competitor. One way of achieving this is to retain all data on the **customer**.

Is the competition only a click away? Perhaps this is not so. Then we would have to find a different site, learn a new interface, provide all credit data, and hope that we can trust this site to perform our business in an orderly fashion. In fact, in some ways it is perhaps easier to change physical bookstores where trust is much less of an issue. Here you can examine the actual copy, pay directly and take it with you there and then. We do not have to trust the brick and mortar store to the same degree as an online store. If Amazon does not have the books I need, I do not go to the open Web to search for other online bookstores. Instead, I go to the Internet site of a well-known brick and mortar store, transferring trust from the physical to the virtual world.

So there are already a couple of good bookstores in the virtual mall, which makes it very difficult for any form of competition to enter. According to Porter's generic competitive strategies[1] one should go for cost leadership (lower costs, broad targets) or differentiation (narrower targets). The problem on the Web is that the incumbents try to go for both of these strategies at the same time; they offer lower prices for bestsellers at the same time as they are open for high diversity. Thus we find "departments" for foreign books, textbooks, bargain books, used books, etc. While this would be a difficult strategy in the real world, it may be possible on the Web where automation makes it easier to handle diverse customer groups.

At present, there is a physical component to online sale of books, which may give advantages to the store with many distribution centers and high volume sales, an advantage that may disappear if more books are sold in electronic formats. Then the "mall" will be the world.

Will we get **malls** on the Web?

We may get a similar organization online as in the physical world. Larger stores will have their own locations, using a well-known name (URL). Smaller stores may be organized in "malls" (i.e., found within portals and marketplaces). Since trust is a strong issue on the Internet these marketplaces should be somewhat more than just a collection of businesses. For example, the portal should be able to give some guarantee as to the solidity of each individual store and payments should be processed through the portal.

20.1 Web advantages

The main advantage for the customer of the Web over traditional shopping is, of course, that the Web offers shopping independent of time and to some degree, independent of distance. A website can be accessed from any place in the world, 24 hours a day, every day in the year. For companies the advantages are that they do not have to maintain expensive stores and that the degree of automation can be higher on the Web than in the physical world.

An online store provides product information that is *searchable*. This becomes useful when the collections are large, and when there exist formalized product identifiers. Books are an ideal example. Collections may be huge, but can easily be searched (as we mentioned in chapter 18.2) using title, name of author, publisher, year of publication, or category, or accessed directly through a unique identifier such as an ISBN number. A catalog can be organized by categories and offer indexes based on title and author name, but can never provide the full features of an online search tool. For other types of products searching may be more difficult. Clothes may be described by general keywords, for example, by function (pants), material (cotton), users (men, women, children), type (jeans), producer (Levi), etc., but such searches cannot be used to pinpoint a certain product. Toys are in the same category, but here we may have an even greater discrepancy between the "need" and a formalized description of keywords. A fun birthday present for John's fifth anniversary is not easy to form into search terms.

When searching breaks down *browsing* is an option. The Web supports browsing by hyperlinks, menus, and navigation buttons. Since the whole idea of browsing is to retrieve, scan, and move on to other pages a reasonably fast Internet connection is needed. If not, the whole process will be disrupted by waiting for page downloads.

We have seen that several sites use *customer input* as a part of the information provided. Amazon and other sites give you ratings and reviews provided by other customers. You can email a friend ("Thought you'd be interested in this item.") and see which groups bought a book, or browse the "Customers who bought this book also bought" list. There is also the possibility of publishing a wish list, suggesting the kind of presents that would be welcome for the upcoming event. Some stores even allow a customer to roam their physical store with a scan-

An important task for an online store is to **formalize products** (i.e., through exact descriptions). This may be easier for some products than others.

The **store layout** is as important in the virtual as in the physical world.

ner, registering product codes. These are then stored on the Web as a gift list for the upcoming birthday, marriage, or other event.

Web ordering is more convenient both for the customer and the supplier than telephone, ordinary mail, or fax. On the customer side errors are avoided by directly moving items into a "shopping cart." This provides the customer with a readable list of items, prices and totals. On the supplier side the main advantage is that the customer provides his order list in electronic format, with the correct item identifiers, and so forth. Thus the order can be passed along on the supply chain without human interference, to credit card checking, packing, etc. The items ordered can immediately be withdrawn from numbers in stock, so that the next customer will get updated information on availability.

20.2 Web disadvantages

On the Web, the customer has to rely on a description of a physical product, there is no possibility of holding, feeling, trying and testing. While the physical store allows the user to buy the item that she has picked up, the website will send her a copy of the product described. While Web stores are restricted by the screen size the physical store has a 3D world in which to display products. This may be a simple storage space, a warehouse where goods are stacked on the floor, trying to satisfy the customer's needs with as low overheads as possible. A quite different philosophy is to sell *shopping as an experience*. A mall may try to capture customers by luxurious surroundings, not only displaying products to their full advantage but also adding atmosphere by gardens, fountains, and perhaps someone playing the piano.

There are clear differences between a **physical and virtual world**. These differences are significant in some cases, insignificant in others.

The online store may compete with the "warehouse" model, where they have the advantage that space does not have to be taken up by huge piles of physical products. An online bookstore may try to create a literate environment by offering reviews, interviews with authors, etc., but are severely restricted by the medium compared to the physical stores. Shopping as an experience is much more difficult to implement on the Web than in the physical world, where so many more channels to the customer are available.

There exists, of course, a possibility that the customer may use the physical store to find a product and then buy it on the

Web to save money. This is perhaps more a theoretical than a practical possibility in the long run. The convenience of buying the product right there in the physical store will be overwhelming. The customer will have no guarantee that she will find the same product on the Web. In addition, if this becomes a problem we will certainly get different product spectra in the physical and virtual world, since brick and mortar stores cannot survive as display spaces for Web stores.

Physical products must be **distributed** to customers. This can be a severe problem for online stores.

For many products it is also unclear if the Web has a price advantage. Even with savings in employees and rental space, the distribution phase of online shopping is very expensive. Instead of mailing twenty-five books to a bookstore the distributor has to mail one book to twenty-five customers. The transportation phase is not supported to any great extent by the Internet. A computer system can print labels, do some sorting, give information on the location of the package, and generate an email when the package has arrived, but the most expensive parts are in physical transportation. Online stores are learning the hard way that not all sales generate profits. Unwieldy, bulky, or fragile items are expensive to stock, pack, and send, so expensive that the loss on each sale may be significant. Other products may be so difficult to assemble that they put a heavy demand on customer service. When the call of the day is profit instead of market share, online stores will remove these items from their catalogs.

While a physical location in a mall or at a busy street corner may be expensive, it is also a way of marketing the store. Online stores have to take some of these expenses by additional marketing, buying ads on TV, radio and in newspapers, by banners on portals, etc.

Clearly, these advantages and disadvantages of Web stores will be dependent on the type of product. In the following chapter we shall try to make a comparison based on different product classes.

20.3   Brick and Mortar or online, a comparison

Attributes	Brick and mortar store (BM)	Online store (OS)	Comments
Physical location	Very important, a way of marketing the store.	Anywhere	In principle, an online store does not need any physical space at all, but may have warehouses to have more control over delivery.
Finding the store	Location, marketing of store	Marketing of site (URL)	Heavy marketing will be needed to introduce and to maintain interest.
Availability	On location, within opening hours	From everywhere, 24/7/365	The main advantage of online shopping, customer transportation is not needed.
Inventory	Sell what you have	Sell what can be delivered	Products can be delivered directly from their suppliers, no inventory needed in principle.
Stocking	Products must be transported to store	Not necessary (in principle).	Transportation cost per product for the BM store can be kept low by large volumes.
Product presentation	Through actual products	Description in text and images	The BM store allows the customer to see, hold, try on, test the product; the online store will have to present the product indirectly.
Search for product	Browsing through store, store organization	Organization, search tools	Both stores try to organize products into well-known categories, allowing the customer to browse within each category.
Product information	Through product itself, staff	On page or by hypertext links	The BM store needs more staff to handle customer requests, many of which can be handled automatically in the OS.
Payment	Cash, check, credit card, store card. Manual.	Credit card. Automatic.	BM needs cashiers, but can handle cash and checks as well as credit cards. Most OS rely on credit cards.
Delivery	Usually performed by customer	Mail services, special delivery	The main disadvantage of online stores. Delivery is expensive and time-consuming.
Delay	None	Days, even weeks	Online shopping is not for the impatient.
Customer gets	The product she chose	A copy of the product described.	Copy variation may pose problems for the online store.
Customer profile	For customers with store cards, limited for others	For all customers	This represents an advantage for the OS, a disadvantage for customers that are concerned about privacy issues.
Customer relations	Store cards, coupons, marketing	Online contact	In this area both types of stores can use the same media, but a BM store will need to collect email addresses manually from the customers.
Customer loyalty	Location, service, and pricing	Price, service, known URL	Location may be a mean of retaining customers for the BM store, on the Web the competition is just a click away.

Table 20.1 A comparison between Brick & Mortar and Online stores.

Table 20.1 above gives a comparison of brick and mortar (BM) and online stores (OS). As we have seen online stores sell efficiency and convenience, while the brick and mortar stores often work to give you a shopping experience. The two different models are very apparent in the business of selling books. Online stores offer large collections and discounts, and 24/7/365 availability from your office or home. Brick and mortar stores let you browse the actual books in a pleasant environment, let you take a cappuccino in their café, meet authors, listen to lectures, discuss books with their staff, meet friends.... If you know the book you want it may be easier to find in an online store. If you are just browsing you can get much information online, but the brick and mortar store may offer you the same information at a terminal in the store in addition to providing help through a customer representative. The online stores can offer discounts due to larger sales, more automation, no need for expensive physical locations, and reduced inventory or no inventory at all. However, a large marketing effort will be needed to set up an online store—to give the URL to customers, while the location itself may attract customers to a brick and mortar store.

The online store allows you to shop from home, but introduces an extra transportation phase to shopping. The customer will have to wait for the product, pay the cost of delivering individual orders, and may have to organize the acceptance of the goods, for example, by being at home to receive and sign for the package.

The brick and mortar stores allow the customer to view, hold, try on, and test the actual product. If you decide to buy, you can take this item with you now. Using an online store the customer must rely on a product description, and will usually only get a copy of the product described. Table 20.2 presents these attributes for selected classes of products. Note that the values given here are with regard to consumer sale (procurement in a business-to-business environment is discussed later). *Copy variation* tells whether there are differences between copies of a product. This factor will usually be zero or low for high-quality industrial products. A high *physical factor* expresses the advantage of being able to hold, feel, try, and test a product. The *delivery factor* expresses delivery costs compared to total costs.

Copy variation tells whether there are differences between copies of a product.

The **physical factor** shows the advantage of holding, trying, and testing a product.

The **delivery factor** expresses the cost of delivery relative to the price of the product.

Product	Copy variation	Physical factor	Delivery factor
Music (CD)	0	Low	0 or low
Software	0	0	0 or low
Computers	0	Low	Low
Cameras	0	Low	Low
Daily disposable contact lenses	0	High/low	Low
Books	Low	Low/med.	Medium
Office supplies	Low	Zero or low	Medium
Wine	0	Low	Medium
Toys	0 or low	Medium	Medium
Car parts	0 or low	Low	Medium
Paint	0 or low	High	High
Clothes and shoes	Possible	High	Medium
Flowers	High	High	Medium
Furniture	Possible	High	High
Bikes	Low	High	High
Cars	Low	High	High
Paintings, art, antiques	High	High	Medium
Groceries, industrial products	0	0	High
Groceries, natural products	High	High	High

Table 20.2. Attributes of selected product classes (consumer sale)

On the Web the customer has to rely on the product **description**, as the physical product is not available. The discrepancy between the product and its description will vary over product categories.

There are situations where customers cannot examine the actual products even when using brick and mortar stores. Then the **playing field** is more closed, and in many cases the online store will be the best alternative.

The advantage for the online stores will be in the areas where all or most of these factors have a zero or low score, the high scores will work favorably for brick and mortar stores. In addition, there are market opportunities in areas where the competition faces similar problems as on the Internet. For example, flowers have a high copy variation and physical factor which make it difficult for an Internet store to compete with a brick and mortar store—when the customer has the chance of visiting the store. However, flowers are often used as gifts for distant relatives, friends, and business partners. In this case the Internet has clear advantages over telephone ordering. The online flower shop can present pictures and can use text-based ordering to avoid errors, and so forth. It may even be possible to show an image of the actual flowers, perhaps let the user pick these on the screen, using the factors above as an Internet advantage (over telephone) instead of a disadvantage.

In the general case, we will have to rely on product descriptions online, using text, images, etc., instead of presenting the actual product. For many products this description may be as good as the real product, even better! When we buy a computer, the specifications are more important than seeing the actual cabinet. Most books can be fairly well described by title, author, and additional textual information. To give a good description of furniture and clothes may be more difficult. You want to sit in a chair, see if shoes fit, try on pants, or feel the texture of a skirt. Color cannot be reproduced very well on a computer display, and size, weight, quality, and other attributes must be described indirectly. In these cases we operate with a high physical factor. While these items can be sold online, one would expect that the number of dissatisfied customers will be higher here than where the Web description can be made more accurate. In practice, this implies that the number of returns will be higher in these areas than in others. Returns are very expensive in every way and may be the downfall of an online store. They represent lost sales, unnecessary expenses, and dissatisfied customers and need a reverse logistics system, that of receiving goods from customers, that may be difficult to implement in an efficient way.

Brand names and standardized products may be used as an alternative to evaluating the actual product. A customer could order a pair of blue Levi 501 jeans, size 32x34 knowing that they would fit. Similarly, we would know what we would get when ordering a bottle of Heinz ketchup, a Playstation II or a Jeep, Grand Cherokee. This is not the case for many natural products. An apple is not an apple. Since the variability of natural products is so great, most customers would want to select the product themselves. Even if you trust the store not to give you outdated products, you may want your bananas softer and the tomatoes harder. This is a case where copy variation is high.

The disadvantage of transportation costs for online stores can be reduced where products are small and light (e.g., CDs or contact lenses), where the cost of transportation is only a fraction of total costs (computers) or where a transportation phase is needed anyway (building materials, household machines such as refrigerators and washers, furniture). In the latter case, an online store will need local distribution centers, and this model may perhaps best be used for the online part of brick and mortar stores.

For many products the brick and mortar stores have the advantage that we can get what we want immediately, without having to **wait** for a parcel.

We could also have included a *wait* factor to table 20.2, trying to stress the areas where there is the disadvantage of having to wait for delivery of the product. This will however be very dependent on the customer. For a business, where procurement is planned, lead times of days or weeks between ordering and receiving are usually accepted. With a JIT (Just-in-time philosophy) there may even be extra expenses incurred if the product is delivered ahead of time. In contrast, ordinary consumers will usually want the product as soon as possible. But we may accept to wait for a product if the online store offers compensating advantages, such as discounts. For example, we do not buy a computer very often since it involves a large expense, and we may be willing to wait some days, perhaps even some weeks, in order to get the right model or a good bargain. While we may want to read the novel tonight, we can accept to wait some days for the list of textbooks needed for the fall term courses. In other situations, for example, when buying a car or a house, the expense is so great that we usually have a prolonged buying process. Here the Web can be an important tool in the initial "information gathering" phase, even if the final deal will be performed in a brick and mortar office.

Based on these arguments CDs and books seem to be better products for online stores than groceries. However, even within the more "ideal" areas, we see that some online stores have had problems getting the sales volume they need to keep prices low. What an online store saves on automation, small inventories, and rent may easily be lost in cost of delivery, returns, and marketing needed to get and keep customers.

A **formalization** of the business environment (e.g., by standardization of products, or clear specifications), may remove the disadvantage of the online store as there will be no need for examining the products.

There are exceptions to these factors. In rural areas there may be few brick and mortar alternatives and the Web may be the most convenient alternative. Online stores also have the possibility of offering a larger product range than brick and mortar stores and due to their world-wide customer base, may offer special products or collections. For example, to get clothes in certain sizes a customer may find that the Web provides the only practical alternative. The Web also offers a form of privacy that may be important to some customers. Generally, however, our table should provide an idea as to where the Web will have an advantage for retail sales to ordinary consumers.

Procurement within a business-to-business environment follows different procedures than consumer sale. Here specifications may be more important than handling the actual product. When a company needs a 1/4-20 aluminum NC hex nut it does not need to examine the actual item. Procurement will be based on specifications and standards, trusting that the supplier will deliver according to these. Where it is important to examine products, there will be a chance to do this through models, prototypes, or sample items. Clothes manufacturers will present their collection well in advance of the season. Actual procurement can then be performed based on product identifiers, sizes, colors, and other specifications. Even where copy variation is high, such as with natural products, there will be ways of formalizing product requirements. This can be done by specifications for a minimum quality, or using arbiters in cases where quality is in dispute. For example, the grocer getting a shipment of produce from his distributor each day will have routines to handle cases where the tomatoes are too soft. This is usually not so simple for the customer that finds bad tomatoes in the package from the online store.

While online stores introduce what is considered an additional distribution phase, getting the goods from the store to the consumer, this is a necessary part of any procurement operation within a business environment. Further, the delay imposed by this phase has less impact in a business environment where procurement is planned ahead of time, not as an impulse action as in many consumer situations.

20.4 Auctions

Online **auctions** over the Web make it easier for consumers to take the opposite role, that of *seller*.

In the established retail markets there exists a clear distinction between sellers and consumers. The sellers create the stores, choose the products, and set prices. However, in some situations we, as consumers, need to take on the role of the seller, to get rid of the old car, the bike that our daughter has grown out of, and all other goods that we no longer need. In these situations we can choose a direct marketplace like arranging a garage sale or going to a dealer or a flea market. These have the advantage that customers may examine the articles, especially important for used and old items. The disadvantage is that these forms of sale are time-consuming and that the market is limited to the customers that are physically present, with temporary markets, also at the right point in time.

Indirect channels may be more efficient and may offer the potential of larger markets. Here we can stick up a notice on a convenient bulletin board or put a classified in a local newspaper, hoping that a potential buyer will call. For indirect sales, the Internet and the Web have several advantages:

- *Location independent*. A for-sale notice on the Web is not location-specific in the same way as on a bulletin board on some wall or a local newspaper.
- *Full product description*. A "classified" on the Web is not limited by a few lines of text.

- *Hypermedia description.* On the Web it is practically feasible to describe the item for sale using pictures, even sound and video.

- *Electronic submittal.* Sellers can submit all product information, minimum price, addresses, etc., electronically.

- *Searchable ads.* On the Web potential buyers can find the "ad" by keyword searching in addition to browsing.

- *Multiple organizational strategies.* While a newspaper uses only one organizational category (e.g., based on product class), a Web portal can use multiple strategies, for example, by price or location in addition to product class.

- *Updateable.* In contrast to a classified in a newspaper, the seller can remove the ad the second the item is sold.

- *Automatic auctions.* The website can automatically handle bids, using any type of auction policy. Auctions are an ideal form for selling used items, as price will be determined by the market.

- *Simple communication.* Contact between buyers and sellers can be established using email.

While the Web often removes **intermediates**, the business model of online auctions is to introduce an intermediate.

Auction sites, such as eBay, utilize all these Web advantages even if they run counter to the idea of using the new technology to remove intermediaries, auction sites are really re-intermediation compared to direct sales between sellers and buyers.

With close to zero cost for entering, storing, and disseminating information, we can give grandmother's lamp a full description on the Web, including a picture and hypertext links to the manufacturer's site. Buyers can search and browse the site, and can sign up for automatic email notifications whenever an interesting product comes up. The site can administer the bidding process automatically. But online bidding with a deadline is somewhat different from bidding over slower channels. Smart bidders use "sniper programs" that can help them give a bid for the last seconds before the deadline, ensuring a sale without the need for raising the price significantly. False bidding does also seem to be a larger problem on the Web than

The **Web auction site** can offer the possibility of submitting complete item descriptions instead of the three-line classified ad, and the geographically wider market makes it possible to offer more items for sale than garage sales and flea markets.

Newspapers can offer **classified** ads both in the paper and online versions, giving customers the best of both worlds.

elsewhere (i.e., situations where the seller or his associates can artificially increase the prices).

The geographical independence of these sites is an advantage from the point of view that ads are offered to everyone, all over the world. However, there are often practical limitations to the distance between seller and buyer. Some items may be difficult to send across national borders, others may be too expensive to transport, being too bulky or too heavy compared to their overall value. The websites try to overcome this drawback by offering local trading (i.e., to limit presentations to within a city or region). While this works technically, one may find very few items for sale after such a severe filtering, limiting the usefulness of local trading. Here, it seems that the local newspapers still have an advantage. Many of these also present their classifieds online, offering the customer the advantage of both the paper and electronic medium.

In contrast to online shops, the pioneer auction sites have an advantage over newcomers in their customer base. While an Amazon customer may find the same books at barnesandnoble.com, the eBay customer may find that only a few items may be listed on other sites. That is, eBay's advantage today is not its software or hardware, this is available for all, but its huge database of ads that attracts a large number of potential buyers, and because of that more sellers, more ads, and so forth. Of course, this is nothing new. Start-up newspapers find it very difficult to compete with the incumbents that already have a large number of classified ads.

The heaviest competition for an auction site such as eBay must therefore come from established newspapers that offer a website in addition to their paper ads, using their basis of ads to establish a platform in the electronic market. They also get some competition from the larger portals, such as Yahoo! and Amazon that use their large customer groups to offer auction services. In addition, we see the establishment of more niche-oriented auction markets, often created on the basis of established "meeting places" such as websites of professional and amateur organizations. There is also the danger that organizations, such as universities and colleges, establish auction/for-sale sites as a free service to their students.

Exercises and Discussion

1. While a brick and mortar store can rely on a good location, a good atmosphere, good service competition in the online world is often focused on more formalized parameters such as price and availability. Discuss the implications of having a more formal playing ground.

2. As we have seen Internet bookstores can organize their site according to formalized terms such as names of authors, titles, publishers, etc. Name other businesses that have the same advantages.

3. We have earlier used gift shops as an example of a business at the low end of the "formalization" spectrum. Can you find other examples of businesses that have few formal terms to apply when they organize their shops or websites?

Notes

1. Porter, Michael E. 1985. *Competitive Advantage*. The Free Press. New York.

21 Technical Constraints—Case Studies

We discussed technological constraints in chapter 3. Here we shall discuss a set of applications that are affected by these constraints—electronic newspapers, eBooks, and scientific journals, as well as the distribution of software, music, and video. All of these applications seem well suited for the Web, as they are both formalized and symbolic, but as we shall see some of these applications may need improved technology before they will have an impact in the marketplace.

21.1 Electronic newspapers

If the idea of a newspaper is to provide the reader with the latest **news**, the Web offers the ideal distribution media.

General information can be sold in the form of newspapers, journals, books, pay-per-view TV, encyclopedias, etc. With the advent of the Web another channel for sale of information has been opened. The advantages of this new channel for providing general information are:

- 24/7/365 service.

- Continuous updates.

- Customized information, at least in the respect that the customer can choose what he or she wants to see.

- Fast and inexpensive dissemination.

- Multimedia formats, text, pictures, audio, animation, and video.

- Background information from archives.

- Unlimited storage.

Since we still maintain the paper versions, there must be other sides to a **newspaper**. Perhaps ease of reading is more important than the frequency of updates?

Today's electronic newspapers try to exploit all of these technological advantages. They use all the multimedia capabilities, offer hypertext links between related articles, and offer search tools for retrieval. They give continuous coverage of news events, with many "editions" a day and use video cameras and weather stations to give an update on local conditions. The interactive capabilities are exploited in full, accepting input from readers both in the forms of reviews, scorings, and comments and they offer online discussion groups. A problem here is that journalists often are used to working in the present, their abilities to store and organize information are not always the best. The storage, organization, and retrieval features of electronic media are therefore not always applied successfully.

However, in spite of the utilization of the technology it seems that it is extremely difficult to create a revenue base for electronic newspapers. Even if many of us access Internet sources for news, paper-based newspapers are still flourishing. We accept *paying* for the paper version that was printed last evening, that had to be distributed by cars and paperboys during the early hours of the morning, that have all these pages that we never read and all this paper that we have to recycle. At the same time we expect that the updated Web version that we can retrieve whenever we want, should be *free*.

One of the reasons for this situation is that we are conservative. It takes time to get used to a newspaper. Each has its own style, its own organization, and its own selection of topics. Today's articles are read in the context of what we read earlier (i.e., in many cases we get the whole picture in daily increments). Switching to another paper is therefore not easy. But still, with all the advantages of the electronic newspapers, including free subscriptions, we would expect that they would have posed a greater threat to traditional newspapers. However, there may be readers, especially among the younger generations, that are willing to replace the paper version with the free online version.

*Will online newspapers **replace** the paper versions, or will they create a new market?*

Another explanation for the fact that the paper versions still are in reasonable good health may be that the online papers are not viewed as real newspapers. Perhaps the new medium has created a new market in between TV and the traditional newspapers instead of competing with these. The online newspaper's advantage over TV is that we can select what we want to see—their advantage over traditional newspapers is more updated information. Their disadvantage is that they require more input from the users than the other media. When accessing an online paper we sit in front of a PC with hands on keyboard and mouse, clicking our way through the paper. With TV we only have to choose the channel, and with traditional newspapers "administrative" overhead is restricted to scanning and turning pages. The traditional newspaper can be read everywhere; it does not require an expensive and heavy viewer; neither batteries nor a power outlet.

*How important is the online advantage of offering **updated** information at any time?*

The disadvantage of not being updated to the last minute is to a large extent solved by the paper-based newspaper's "symbiosis" with TV. Due to TV we do not require newspapers to bring us the last on the latest. Instead, we use these to provide in-depth and more developed information. The traditional

The day the online newspaper is as easy to **read** as the paper version, the latter will disappear. That is, traditional newspaper will then be distributed online.

newspaper may not offer the possibility of online chat channels, but it is a cost effective way of getting information. So, instead of a takeover, we see that electronic newspapers exist along with the paper versions. The electronic versions are mostly offered as an add-on source, perhaps to generate interest for the paper version or to try to get revenue through advertisements. The electronic version also has the advantage that it is possible to get data on which articles the readers actually access, by counting "clicks," by surveying search terms and, of course, by studying readers' response in the form of reviews or email. Newspapers that have only an online version, struggle to survive regardless of whether they use subscriptions or advertisements as a basis for their revenue. They have as yet not managed to compete with the traditional newspapers. Further, the market niche between these and TV may be too small to generate the necessary income.

However, the balance between electronic and paper versions may change. Radically new display techniques, combined with high bandwidth connection and wireless technology, may alter this balance of pros and cons. If the electronic newspaper can be automatically downloaded over high bandwidth Internet connections to one or more cordless viewers with large displays with readability similar to that of ordinary paper, all papers will become "online." Most of the functionality of the paper version will be retained, and the electronic advantages will come as a bonus. Of course, the expense of bandwidth and equipment needed to receive and display the information will be an important part of the cost-benefit equation.

The newspaper as we know it will still **prevail**, even if it becomes online. That is, online technology will be a part of the evolution that started with Gutenberg's printing press.

With this technology, paper-based and electronic newspapers will merge. For the traditional newspapers, it will just be another technology breakthrough, following offset printing, electronic communication of text and photos, word processing, etc. Clearly, it will have a large impact on the printing and distributing processes, but the effect on journalists and editors may be less. However, an online paper has a somewhat different style from the traditional "deadline-"based papers. Not only will online media offer the opportunity of running the same story from different viewpoints during the day, with continuous updates, but the reader can now be given the option of getting in-depth information. This may be provided by links to background data, historical information, or to other articles. But again, care must be taken to provide these services in a way that does not require a higher activation level from the user than she is willing to accept. The role of the newspaper is to provide a general overview in the form of well-prepared articles that only require limited energy or activation from the user. In special cases, we may be willing to spend more time in retrieving information of importance, but it may not be the role of newspapers to provide this information.

Therefore, technology breakthroughs may not be a threat to traditional newspapers, only to their printers and distributors. However, literary skills may change in an online society, where information is more likely to be presented as headlines, pictures, and videos. We may find fewer and fewer *readers*, people that are willing to spend time and energy to read long articles. Online media may therefore increase the trend that we already see in some on-paper versions, toward giving information in ways that require less effort on the part of the "reader."

21.2 Electronic publishing—eBooks

Today it is a disadvantage to read from a **display**, and the eBook must therefore offer clear advantages in other areas.

The help system that comes with software products today is always online. Here one can exploit context-dependent help, offering the user information relevant to the problem at hand. A search system is invaluable in finding information in these formalized settings, and hypertext is used to link related articles. The most advanced systems offer automatic demos, animations, and dynamic examples. The help system can be updated with every new version of the software, or offered in an always updated version on the Web. Since we are already online when using the software, the disadvantages of an online system are removed. The online help system is now easier to access than any paper counterpart.

This online functionality will also be important for many other forms of manuals, especially when the manuals are so large that they are difficult to access in printed form. So, the online version may be preferred even if one needs a viewer, a PC, or a customized device, to access the manual.

Information overload, when we get too many references returned with no possibility of narrowing searches without losing important references.

We shall use the help manual of a word processing system as an example. Table 21.1 shows some of the "formalizations" that can be used in organizing such a manual. As seen, the formal concepts come from many different areas, but they all come together within a common context in the word processing system. This makes it quite easy to organize both the structure and the search facilities in such a system. Some systems even offer the user the option to state her question in natural lan-

Formalization	Examples
Typographical terms	Font, paragraph, header, margin
Commands	Print, Cut, Paste
Drawings	Line, rectangle, arrow
Graphical effects	Shadow, rotation, display order
Language	Spelling, grammar, thesaurus
User-interface terms	Window, menu, toolbar, button
Computing terms	File, auto recovery, database
Equipment	Printer, keyboard, mouse
Standards	ASIII, HTML, XML

Table 21.1. Formalized terms in a word processing system

guage, relying on the fact that the restricted context will limit the scope of questions. For example, such a help system will give a reasonable answer to the question "how do I print?" but probably not to "What should I write to my girlfriend?"

For other types of publications the online advantages may not be so clear. For example, an eBook novel seems to have more disadvantages than advantages. A novel is read from start to end. The degree of formalization is low. The reader is not requested to jump back and forth in the text. We do not really need a dynamic link from page 215 to page 18 to find out if James was the cook or the butler. If such a link was needed, it would be simpler if the author added the title when he reintroduced James on page 215. That is, it is the responsibility of the author to organize the text so that it can be read sequentially. Similarly, updates and electronic searches are not usually needed in a novel. The only online advantage for a novel may be the low cost of disseminating and the large electronic storage capacity. But this may not be enough to counter the disadvantage of having to use a special viewer, a laptop, or a PDA to read the book. Take it out in the sun and the text disappears; it is not recommended to take it to the beach and it is a catastrophe if it is lost. The advantage with the paper version of a book is that it comes with its own high quality and low priced "viewer" that can be adjusted to the type of book: paperback, art book, atlas.

However, with the high costs of storing paper books, only the most popular books may find a place in the bookstores and in the storage rooms of the publishing houses. In electronic format there will never be an "out-of-print" situation and with the low dissemination cost it may be profitable to keep all books that have a minimum of interest in the system. Just as movies are first released in theaters, then on videos, we may see that books are first released on paper, then in electronic versions.

Textbooks and scientific journals fall between manuals and novels. Today, most of these are still disseminated on paper. However, if we look ten to twenty years into the future we should expect to have lightweight viewers that combine print-on-paper quality with screen flexibility ("electronic paper").[1] The very last update of journal papers and textbooks can then be downloaded to the viewer via the Internet, footnotes and references can be in hypertext format, the author can include further readings, and we can use search tools to find what we are looking for. There will be no need to keep errata, as errors can be corrected at once, and new updated editions can be created as needed.

> The online **advantages** are directly connected to the formalization level of the publication, the more formalized the greater the advantage of indexing, search, and hypertext systems.

Formalization	Examples
Organization	Parts, chapters, headers, exercises
References	Author, title, publisher, URL
Terminology	Formalization, symbol
Equipment	Computers, displays, printers
IT applications	Web, email, Word processing
Directions	B2C, B2B, P2P
Concepts	eMusic, eBook
Standards	ASCII, HTML, XML

Table 21.2 Formalized terms in this book

Table 21.2 shows a list of some of the formal terms discussed in this book, terms that can be used for organizing and searching an electronic version. In a more traditional textbook we would find more of these formal terms and definitions, which could support an electronic version to a greater degree. If we go all the way to handbooks, we are close to the manuals described above, and at this stage the advantages of having an electronic version become apparent.

> The **eTextbook** of the future will be so dynamic that the distinction between a book and a piece of software will disappear.

Disseminating books in electronic form also opens the way for new business models. Instead of buying expensive textbooks from publishers, states, counties, or businesses can organize textbook development themselves such as using the "competition model" often found in other creative activities, such as within architecture and art. The winners can then be paid to develop their textbook concept in full, and the books can be put on the Web available for all students for free. While this model could be used also with paper-based books, the simplicity and savings of disseminating via the Web will be a powerful incitement.

With an "evolving" book metaphor, the writer may incorporate comments and make modifications suggested by readers or reviewers. Thus, if you download the book tomorrow, you may get a different version than you would get today. This will change our concept of editions and make referencing somewhat more difficult (the part referenced may no longer exist), but may give us better books.

The next generation of textbooks can be *dynamic* far beyond hypertext. A book on physics can include virtual experiments where students perform simulations within the textbook such as driving cars around narrow curves, letting objects slide down ramps, swing on strings, etc. In college mathematics the textbook will have an interface to mathematical program packages that can simplify, execute, or visualize formulas. Teaching material, such as slides, comments, and references given by the lecturer, can be connected to "hooks" provided in the book. Similarly students can add their own comments and examples. In this way, a dynamic book may be customized to the particular educational institution, lecturer, and student.

The technologies for online dynamic books are here already. What we need now are **standards** and improved viewers.

Most of the technology to do this is available today, and it will just be a matter of time before the standards and the equipment needed are more readily available. Then, the question will not be if we *want* to read a textbook on the screen or on paper, we will *have* to use the online version in order to take full advantage of the dynamics. As we have seen earlier, writing has already moved online, and it is just a matter of time before reading will follow, at least for some type of books.

As long as it is easier to read on paper than on the screen, electronic versions will only be used where the online **advantages** are most prominent.

Transferring scientific journals, textbooks and other documents from paper to electronic media will have a great impact on publishers, bookstores, and libraries. The tasks of printing, handling, storing, and transporting the physical copy will disappear. As with software the cost of making an additional copy will be close to zero. Thus pricing schemes of dynamic books will most probably follow those of software, where individuals or an educational institution pay a license for the right to download books. In all respects it may be better to view a dynamic book as a piece of software. As with software, the cost of creating a dynamic book will be high. In addition to the more traditional services, such as editorial tasks, graphical design, and marketing, dynamic books will need expertise in creating animations, video, and sound clips. It will thus be a major effort to produce and maintain a dynamic book. As with software, the high cost of development can be spread over a large number of users.

Document type	Easy update.	Hypertext	Search tools	Dynamics
Manuals	High	Very high	Very high	High
Textbooks	Medium	High	Medium	High
Other books	Low	Low	Low	Low
Scientific journals	High	High	High	Medium
Other journals	Low	Low	Low	Low
Newspapers	Medium	Medium	Medium	Low

Table 21.3 Advantages of electronic representation, degree of importance.

Until the day that we can make viewers as large, flexible, and with as good a quality as paper, we will need additional arguments to find the electronic document representation most useful. Table 21.3 shows how important the added online functionality will be for different types of documents. For example, the online functionality of easy updating, hypertext and extensive search tools will be more important for a textbook than for a novel. So, while we find the electronic form convenient for manuals, even with the limited quality displays we have today, an electronic version may be useful for textbooks in the near future, but we may find it advantageous to read a novel in paper form for many years to come.

21.3 Video on demand

Today, we can buy or rent movies in VHS or DVD representation. The large rental market and channel TV show that the customer accepts a pay-per-view model, and that the lack of a symbolic value of ownership will not be a barrier for online video. However, generally we do not have the infrastructure in place for downloading and playing high quality videos interactively today since such a service will demand high bandwidth

Video on demand is a formalized and symbolic service. It is here already for some users, but needs new technological break-throughs either in compressing or in network technology to be available to all in full quality.

networks from the source to the consumer and viewers in homes to play the videos.[2] Today, the only viable solution (i.e., if we want quality video and a high level of functionality), will be to lay optical fiber into each home, clearly a very expensive enterprise. Thus, while it is easy to say that video on demand may be an important Web application, with very much of the same advantages as downloading music, it will take time to get the infrastructure in place or to develop new technology that bypasses the need for high capacity networks.

With such technology in place, we may get a larger "underground" market for movies as we have for music today. The industry will try to protect copyright by putting movies on formats with built-in encryption (i.e., they will try to bind the business models of today with the technology of tomorrow). The problem is, of course, that there are numerous intelligent and often well-educated hackers that will see it as a challenge to break these formats.

An intermediate model that has been tried is to provide the video on a cheap storage medium, such as a digital videodisk, only using the Web to implement a pay-per-view policy. This has not been a success, but new, high capacity storage devices can make this a valid way to overcome network limitations. The advantage over rental is that we can view the movies when we like and we avoid the return process. The disadvantage is that we have to get the videodisks in advance.

21.4 What can we learn?

The future lies in the **boundary** between possibilities and con-straints.

When discussing new technology it is easy to focus on the pos-sibilities, trusting the scientists and engineers to filter out the weaknesses and limitations. But history tells us that while we can achieve enormous breakthroughs in some areas, the devel-opment may be very slow in others. We also see that prophe-cies often are too optimistic in the short-term view, and perhaps too pessimistic in the long term.

While the constraints of formalism are fundamental, tech-nological constraints may be removed by long-term scientific and engineering efforts. However, sometimes development may take a great leap forward, surprising all of us. The devel-opment of VLSI techniques and the microcomputer suddenly offered much smaller and much cheaper equipment, removing many of the barriers that limited the use of computers. HTTP and HTML offered a similar leap forward, enabling us to use the emerging Internet for many new services. Less spectacular, but as important are the surprisingly high bandwidths that we can get today on the ordinary twisted pair telephone line that goes into our home. The boxes that we put on either end of the existing cable enables us to use the infrastructure for telephone, built over many years, for totally new applications. Perhaps the next surprise will be a print quality display, or an everlasting battery?

Exercises and Discussion

1. It is harder to read large texts on the computer display than on paper. A way of overcoming this problem is to increase the use of headers, pictures, diagrams, and dynamic references, reducing the amount of text. In the long run, do you think that electronic newspapers (and TV) have an influence on reading habits, for example, so that people get less used to reading books?

2. Which of the following books will you prefer to have on paper and which will you prefer to have in an electronic format, to be viewed on an ordinary desktop PC:

   - Cookbook
   - Travel guide
   - Crime novel
   - Dictionary
   - Medical handbook

3. Revise the question given above, but expect this time that you have a lightweight, battery-operated portable viewer for the electronic version.

Notes

1. The early versions are here already. Sony has a product out based on technology developed by Phillips.
2. The more patient Web users download movies as a background task over today's "broadband" connections, but this operation may take many hours, even days to complete. These movies, often pirate copies, are usually viewed on a PC.

22 Cultural Constraints—Case Studies

In chapter 4 we discussed a set of cultural issues that could limit the acceptance of new technology or new services in the marketplace. Here, we shall present a set of case studies. These applications seem promising based on our knowledge of the technology and they are well within technical and the more fundamental constraints. However, the success of these applications may be influenced by cultural and social issues.

22.1 eMusic

Downloading **digital music** is an ideal Web application, it is formalized, symbolic, and the technical infrastructure is in place. The question is not if this will be the future, but if it is possible to find viable business models for this service.

The web is clearly a **disruptive** technology for the entertainment industry. In the long run it will be difficult to maintain existing business models when users can get music or movies from the net.

Software and music are in many ways ideal for Web distribution. These all-symbolic, digital products can easily be transmitted via the Internet using current compression techniques and connections. Downloading of music files via the Internet has flourished in later years as more consumers have the possibility of retrieving, storing, and playing these files. With CDs music is already represented as bits, and modern PCs have both the ability to store large amounts of music (in compressed form), and to play this music, for example, through a hi-fi system. Several Internet sites exploit this symbolic nature of music, to allow customers to exchange music files, often music that has been captured from CDs and other sources.

It is understandable that the record industry has looked upon Napster and its followers as a threat to their business. There are other ventures that are less centralized than Napster and thus much more difficult to fight legally, and if this is not enough—a service may be set up in a country with weaker copyright laws. Without a central site the record industry goes after the users instead, suing students, parents, and grandmothers. To some extent they have succeeded, putting a scare into many.

The problem is that the Internet is just the natural dissemination vehicle for this type of data. With digitalization the music has been separated from its representation. The industry may wrap the CD in nice packaging, including a booklet. However, in the long run the physical formats will disappear as online formats have more to offer. While the music itself is formalized on a low level (as technical binary codes), it is clearly indexed with the names of songs, albums, and artists. It is therefore easy to find a piece of music on the Web or in a customized database integrated into the hi-fi system. Online, one can also take advantage of the possibility of fast dissemination of new songs, and of providing multimedia additional information, such as music videos, along with the audio. In an all-symbolic form a new copy costs practically nothing to make, it can be compacted to a size that makes downloading practical and can be stored in high-capacity well-organized disk storage. Alternatively, with reliable and high capacity networks the audio (or video) can be *streamed* to the users. Then the bits are sent more or less directly to the booster, so that only a small cache is needed locally for storing (to adjust for small discrepancies in bandwidth).

Digitalized music can easily be moved from one device to the other (e.g., from a PC to a portable MP3 player or to the audio equipment in the car). Today computer-based music has the disadvantage that it requires more "administration" to select and play compared to a CD or DVD. However, customized hi-fi systems that integrate large hard disks and boosters with simple-to-use interfaces may soon be common. With this the "package" advantage of a CD may be partly overcome. An exception will be music as a gift. Here the physical formats have a clear advantage.

The record companies can meet this threat by offering pay-per-use or subscription sites, realizing that the Web needs different forms of packaging and distribution than traditional channels. They try to take control over the new technology by using cryptography and access codes to limit copying, to deny conversion to other formats and, in some cases, to ensure that only their own equipment is used to play the music. The drawback of such a scheme is that their customers cannot take full advantage of the new media. This implies that they create a market for the pirates that not only can offer a free service but also a more flexible product.

Today pricing of these services is comparable to that of buying a CD in the record store. It is doubtful if customers are willing to pay this much in the long run. If they do a large part of the job oneself, they certainly want a discount. There is also the question of symbolic value. Users are not accustomed to pay as much for just a right.

"One cannot compete with free" says representatives for the music industry, but most users would welcome a pay site, avoiding the problems of downloading from dubious sites. Such sites would be an instant success if files where offered in standard formats, without codes, and at a reasonable price. We see that customers are willing to pay quite substantial amounts for their newspaper, cable, or Internet subscription, so why not offer unlimited access at a similar price? Unlimited access in a world where a copy can be produced at zero cost is not difficult to offer. Total revenues may be as high as what one has today, especially as many parts of the current value chain would be unnecessary. We also see that new models are emerging based on the new technology. There has been an "open source" for software in many years, and "open music" sites are now emerging. These offer a contact point between musicians and the audience.

22.2 Electronic scientific journals

From our previous discussion, scientific papers should be a prime candidate for electronic publishing: a speedy publishing process, hypertext links to references, possibility of including background material, electronic searching, and an inexpensive world-wide dissemination. Today, a large part of the university library budget is used to pay for journal subscriptions, and increasing expenses make it difficult to maintain a wide coverage of journals. Access to information is severely restricted as the poorer universities, especially in underdeveloped countries, cannot afford the $10,000 to $20,000 subscription fees that some of the most well-known journals demand. The paradox is that all the basic costs of preparing these papers are paid by the very same universities that have to provide the subscription fees. Most scientific papers are written, reviewed, and edited by university employees and researchers funded by scientific foundations.

eJournals are an interesting Web application. All arguments, on a practical, economical, or professional level, are in favor of the electronic version. Still, less than 10 percent of all journals are available in electronic form today.

Historically, scientific papers were offered very cheap or for free through the research community, first by personal communication then through membership in professional associations. The professional publishing houses came into the process later, to take care of administration, publishing, and dissemination. Today, the Internet and the Web may help us to return to the former "ideal" situation.

With new technology, the author can create the paper in a publishable format. The review process can be handled on the Web using software that aids the editor in finding available reviewers, that notifies them and collects evaluations. The reviewers can add detailed comments directly in the manuscript.

All correspondence between editors, reviewers, and authors can go through email or Web. When the editor accepts the final version it can be posted on the website for the "journal," and the system can send an automatic email notification to all subscribers that have shown interest in this type of paper. The site may also offer readers the possibility of adding comment or reviews, to vote on interesting papers, or to create a chat group for a paper where needed. That is, through new technology we may reinstate the personal correspondence and in-person discussion groups from the early days where the number of researchers was low. This system will be inexpensive, and offers the opportunity of opening free access to scientific information.

As seen, the advantages of going to the new medium for these types of publications are paramount, not unexpectedly, since Berners-Lee created the Web on the basis of the needs for such an application. However, with a few exceptions, most journals are still disseminated in paper form. Some organizations may offer an alternative online version, for members or subscribers. But there exist only a few true electronic journals that do not piggyback on a traditional paper version. In total, less than 10 percent of all journals are in electronic form today.

From the discussion above, one would think that the advantages of an electronic version would surpass any difficulty while reading from the screen. If not, these limited-size papers can easily be printed for easy of reading. Universities may be conservative, but one would expect that the need for cutting expenses should demand a more rational solution. We should therefore expect that the sum of functional and economic arguments would be a driving force for electronic publication. So why are most journals still also offered in paper form, and why have so many journals high subscription fees?

The publishing house will, of course fight a transition to a new medium. With paper journals, the publishing houses are needed to handle printing, distribution, and subscription. With an electronic medium these parts can be automated, and the publishing houses will no longer be a necessary part of the value chain. With electronic journals it will be difficult to retain the high subscription rates and "illegal" copying may be more difficult to control. We see a similar development as with record companies, also to the extent that publishers are trying to bind the new technology to existing business models.

While the publishing houses own the copyrights for previous publications and for journal names, their most important

> The traditional **publishing houses** are no longer needed in the process of creating and distributing the journal, but they own the most valuable asset: the journal name.

The Web has removed the constraint on the **size of a volume**—for scientific journals this can be a disadvantage!

staff works for the universities. Therefore, it should not be impossible for the research community to establish new, electronic journals. However, perhaps the scientific community is also skeptical; perhaps there are arguments beyond the rational? While a paper journal is a means of disseminating scientific articles, it is also a symbol. A paper in the right journal can be an important step toward tenure, funding, or a better faculty position. Since a paper journal, for practical reasons, has to limit the number of pages per number, only the best articles are published. Over the years a number of high-ranking journals have emerged in every field. These journals are well known in the entire scientific community, and it may take years to build up a similar recognition for a new electronic journal. It may not be so easy to retain the quality level in electronic journals, where there is no practical limit as to the number of papers that can be accepted. So, while the subscribers in the form of the readers and the paying institutions may see the advantages of an electronic medium, both authors and publishing houses may want to retain the paper versions. The persistence of the scientific paper journal shows us that it can be difficult to get acceptance for new media when this implies a cultural change. Institutions and people that master the playing field will be reluctant to abandon their positions, and accept a new area where the rules of the game are different.

While most recognized journals are still in paper form, alternatives have been established. Most interesting is archives of electronic papers, where everyone can "publish." These sites are especially important for third-world countries that cannot afford the subscription fees of the paper journals and that may also be hampered by inadequate postal systems. These sites offer a possibility of publishing as well as gaining insight into the research results of others. Access to these sites, including publishing, is free. Here we have the interesting situation that third-world countries are forced to use a service that in many ways works better than that we find in the more developed countries.

Nevertheless, in the long run, the practical advantages of online media are so great within this area that the paper versions will disappear. An important weapon for the eJournals will be their availability. Papers in eJournals may therefore be read and referenced more often than papers published in the traditional journals, and references are as important for an academic as the name of the journal. Without the symbolic value of the paper version it is also doubtful if current subscription fees and business models can survive.

22.3 Distance education

Distance education offers flexibility both in place and time. It has been an option to students that were willing to study on their own, at home or at work, following their own schedule. These distance education programs have worked with traditional textbooks and other forms of text-based support material and have often followed a plan with a sequence of "letters," where each letter described a problem to be solved. Answers to these exercises have been returned to teachers using ordinary mail.

With every new technological breakthrough, tape recorders, video players, computers, and CDs, it has been predicted that this would boost distance education. However, these hopes have not been fulfilled. Distance education has, until now, only been a niche market. Today, the hopes are based on the Internet and the Web. Both universities and private companies are investing huge amounts in this area, in what they believe will become an important market.

The Web can handle many of the **closed aspects** of education, such as presenting lectures and material. But what about the open, more social parts?

In order to understand the possible impact of the Internet and the Web in this area we need to have an idea of which processes and functions are involved in teaching. A traditional college course, for example, will have three major stakeholders that are directly involved: students, professors, and their assistants (often Ph.D. or graduate students). The course will be based on a predetermined curriculum, syllabus, and schedule, but the professor is usually given great freedom as to how the course should be structured and to the material to present. Course topics are covered by textbooks and other written material, such as scientific papers and descriptions of projects and exercises. Lectures are given in classrooms or auditoriums that may seat from a few to several hundred students. Most professors will present lectures using a blackboard or overhead projector or will use the PC with a video projector along with slide presentation software (e.g., PowerPoint).

Class-based teaching opens a dialog between teachers and students, where students can ask or answer questions, give comments, participate in the lecture or teaching, or have class discussions. The degree of interaction will be very dependent on the size of the class, and the culture. Not all students dare to talk in public, and in some cultures the respect and authority of the teacher will be a hindrance for a good dialog. In addition to participating in classes students are expected to study on their own, read background material, and do exercises and projects. In many courses the "learning-by-doing" paradigm is seen as important, and students will be expected to write and present papers, to solve problems, to develop systems, or to do practical laboratory work—depending on the type of course. This independent work may be supported, supervised, and graded by the professor and her assistants.

At face value the Internet and the Web may support all of these activities. As we have discussed the Web can support any type of written material, with the additional advantage of integrating text, animations, sound, and video. With reasonable bandwidth students can follow the slide presentation on the Web, including the teacher's narrative. With a broadband connection it becomes possible to get a video presentation as well.

For many courses, the Web can be used to create a virtual laboratory, for example, with the software development tools that are needed for courses in computing science. We should also expect that many of the experiments in areas such as physics, chemistry, and electrical engineering that today are performed in physical laboratories might be performed in a virtual setting. In other areas, such as social science and economics, computer simulation may become an attractive tool. Professor-student and student-student communication can be handled by email, chat rooms, newsgroups, or bulletin boards, as we discussed in the chapter on email. Simple tests can be performed directly on the Web; and possibly examinations if one can get a guarantee that it is the right person that performs the test.

In analyzing the effects of a new technology, try to see what it offers compared to **existing technologies**. This gives us some real data in making a prognosis.

Thus, it seems that we should expect an exploding market for online education. But, before we invest our money and our time in this area let us try to play the devil's advocate. We will then notice that many of the advantages offered by the Web were also available in pre-Web time. For example, in the mid-1980s and later, with the advent of the CD-ROM, it was possible to offer courses that used text, video presentations, and virtual laboratories on a computer. What the Web has offered with regard to presentation is a simpler way of updating and distributing this material, nothing more. This may be important for some types of courses such as courses offered to very large user groups at such a low price that the cost of distribution has an impact. However, if the student base is large enough, satellite

When the computers handle the formalized functions, **humans** must take care of the more open tasks. This "work sharing" must also be reflected in education, where it will be more important to give students an understanding and an overview of a field, than to concentrate on the lower level details. Using these principles it becomes difficult to implement all-automatic teaching systems, where the computer also tests the students.

TV broadcasts are an alternative (i.e., where the full broadband capabilities of TV can be utilized). While such a system simplifies distribution and the equipment needed on the receiving end, it has the disadvantage that input from students has to go over a different channel, for example, a telephone line. Here the Internet offers the advantage of two-way communication. For the higher-priced courses the distribution advantage of Web should have a more moderate impact. Offline media, such as video cassettes, CDs, and DVDs, will be advantageous when technical constraints, such as low bandwidth connection and slow response times from Web servers, limit the functionality of a Web application.

One may intrude and argue that the Web offers unlimited access to information. While this is true, students at the lower levels do not often go outside the required and suggested readings to get information. For most, the textbook and other required material will be more than enough. Another pro-Web argument is that it allows for online tests, with the possibility of saving test results directly on the server. This takes us back to the early efforts to develop an "electronic teacher" that could give students immediate feedback and grade tests automatically. Such a system will work where the formalization level is high, but not when questions are more open.[1] However, it is a paradox for education that the computer works best for testing types of knowledge that are no longer needed, because of the computer. While a student needs a good understanding of language, spelling can be checked by the computer. While it is important to have an understanding of the basic principles of mathematics, detailed calculations can be performed by the computer. However, higher-level concepts and basic principles cannot easily be checked by formalized tests.

Exceptions may be found in more training-oriented courses, where the idea is to teach students to react correctly to different situations. Here simulations and scenario-oriented systems may be used to check that the student has the correct response in the right situation, for example, when training operators to handle complicated machinery. Not unexpectedly, the more formalized tests will work best for these formalized applications.

All in all, the Web alone may not be enough to boost distance education. But the Web combined with email offers a simple system for two-way communication. With email, teachers and students have a technology that may replace some of the interaction that they have in class and through personal ad-

Combining Web and email, we get two-way communication that can support the open parts. The question is then if the student can manage without the social learning environment that is provided by a physical school, or if this environment can be offered in other ways.

vice. As we have seen (chapter 7), email offers one-to-one, one-to-many, and many-to-many interaction. A teacher can reach all students with one mail message and students can return questions and answers to exercises with email. In principle, this is just a replacement of the old fax or letter channel, but is far more efficient. Further, students can reach each other and participate in discussion groups. Thus, chat and email can to some extent replace informal and formal group work at a school or university. Perhaps the most important feature of email in this setting is its asynchronous nature, allowing both students and teachers to retain the time-based flexibility of distance learning.

Will these new methods replace traditional teaching? The answer is no. Being a student, keeping up motivation and organizing one's work are difficult in the best of circumstances. In the physical world, one can hope to get inspiration and support from professors and fellow students in a good learning environment. Motivation is much more difficult with distance education, where all or a large part of the work has to be done in isolation. The motivation or influence that a professor can give to a student will be much stronger in a physical environment than over virtual channels. Email and chat groups may give some support, but it is easier to drop out of these than in a physical environment, where someone may come and look for you if you do not turn up.

An understanding of the technological possibilities and constraints can help us find the best applications for **eLearning** systems.

For this reason alone, it is unrealistic to expect that online or distance education will replace a physical presence of both professors and students at a school or university. Many will also advocate that schooling has important social functions as well as the formal teaching part. In a good educational environment, students learn to organize their work and to interact with their peers, in addition to the more formal aspects. In looking for good applications for online education, we should try to find areas where the motivation may be strong enough to overcome the lack of a physical educational environment, and where the drawbacks of not having such an environment can be minimized.

Adult education and training are especially suited for **eLearning**.

We may find such areas within adult education, especially where the intent is to give additional or upgraded information. Here students will have the experience and background needed to get a personal feeling of the topic and to participate in discussions. In addition, many are in work situations where it may be difficult to follow scheduled classes, so that we can maximize the advantages of distance learning. Ideally, such courses should be taken at work, where it is easier to establish a good educational environment, for example, by establishing groups of employees that follow the online course. These groups can then provide the necessary social support. Another application may be for schools that want to offer a large range of courses for their students such as offering basic courses the traditional way and more specialized courses online, hoping that the students selecting a specialized course will have the background and motivation to work online.

Distance education, in spite of all the technology, is often an expensive product. Traditional education, especially at lower levels, can be offered in huge classrooms with streamlined setups and students that are physically present use each other as information sources and will often have a similar background. Being together in the same environment also forms the students into groups, so they to some extent can be advised and treated as a group more than as individuals. In contrast, distance education students remain more isolated; they may have very varied backgrounds and will need more personal advice. This limits the number of students that can be advised by each professor. In addition, the cost of preparing online courses may also be high. Some companies spend as much as $1,000,000 to prepare a three-credit course, including all the material needed. Distance education is therefore not a means to make teaching more efficient or to reduce the cost of education. It is, as we have stated earlier, more a way of accommodating students that cannot be physically present in a classroom at a given time. This was the case before the Web and seems to be the case also with the Web.

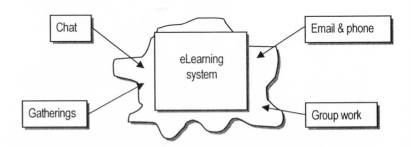

Figure 22.1 Distance education over the Web –supporting open tasks.

To sum up we may return to a figure used previously (figure 22.1), here in a more specific setting. Let the rectangle represent what a distance learning system may provide of services, and let the more diffuse boundary represent traditional education. While the electronic system can offer a large set of services there are parts, social environment, physical presence, etc., that are left out. We may cover some of these areas by expanding the electronic service. For example, if we offer good email contact to teachers that can give personal advice, we have a door toward more open services within the electronic system. Or, we may let distance students meet physically at certain times during the term, to provide motivation and a set of community feeling. Efficiency, however, will be highest when we are able to perform all services within the system, for example, presenting material, performing quizzes and exams, etc. As we have seen, this will be simplest to achieve in the more formalized training applications (i.e., where the discrepancy between the rectangle and the irregular figure is at a minimum).

22.4   Marketing on the Web

On the Web, many sites try to survive using the TV model, offering free programs and generating income from commercials. Until now, the idea has been to get as many "clicks" as possible, using these data as the Web equivalent of numbers of viewers, listeners, or readers. But, the Web is a very different medium from TV, and experience with ads on TV may not be directly transferred to this new medium. Therefore, let us start this chapter by comparing these different forms of marketing channels.

The user initiates a Web session at a time she chooses herself. From a "cold start" point she has to turn on the PC, wait for the operating system to load, open the browser, and wait until the connection to the ISP provider has been established. On Local Area Networks (LANs) with direct Internet access the connection will be set up immediately, but may take a minute or two using a dial-up connection.

The Web has the advantage that the user has the possibility of selecting what she wants to see. The disadvantage is that it requires a higher **activation level**.

When the home page is displayed, the user needs to be actively involved, both cognitively and physically. As we have seen she will be sitting in front of the PC through the whole session, hands are on the keyboard; eyes on the screen. Each screen involves choices of where to go next, what to read, and what to type. A new screen may be obtained by a simple click on a link, or by entering URLs or search terms from the keyboard. The user will use all senses, brain, eyes, and motor operators (right and left hand), possibly also ears and voice. She needs the training and experience to master the medium, in order to satisfy her needs. Even then, the sequence of pages downloaded may include repeats and many pages with little or no value for the user. In addition, there is the overhead needed to create this sequence of keystrokes and mouse movement. Response times may be substantial, depending on network traffic, server speed, and to a large extent, the bandwidth of her Internet connection. Thus, through parts of the session she will be waiting for a page to appear, a passive phase in an otherwise active session.

In contrast, a medium such as TV may be activated with a single button click. Professional content creators have created or selected the stream of sound and video that is received. Today a viewer has no way of influencing this data stream, but has the option of selecting a different channel. To watch a particular program the viewer will have to synchronize her schedule with that of the broadcast, or program a recorder to capture the program at the right time. TV viewing, after channel selection has been performed, does not require any active participation from the viewer. She can choose the degree of involvement, follow a program with all senses open or let the TV be just a background activity. She can watch TV sitting down on the couch or she can walk around. Hands are free, allowing her to do other things while watching.

Due to the different "activation" levels, it seems improbable that the Web will replace a large part of TV viewing. More probably, the Web will compete with media and activities that require similar activation levels, such as shopping, getting information from paper documents, using the telephone, and so forth. And, of course, we may use the Web to download movies and programs that we can watch at a time we chose ourselves.

With the higher activation level care must be taken that the **ads** do not come between the user and her goal.

Superficially, one would expect that ads would have a greater effect on the higher activation Web than the low activation TV where users are more passive. However, with the higher activation level and clearer focus of the user the ads may come between the user and her goal, with the risk of providing negative feelings toward the advertisers. The pop-up ads may be especially annoying for the user who is on the Web to satisfy an information need or to perform a service, less annoying for the user that is only "surfing." Today we see that many users install programs that remove pop-ups,[2] proving that these are considered annoying and also showing the possibilities we have using digital media. It is not so easy to remove the ads from a TV.

On TV, due to the more passive viewer participation, advertisers are allowed to capture the whole channel for an extensive duration. This allows for a stronger marketing influence, but with the drawback that viewers may not accept to spend three hours to see a two-hour movie or to get an abbreviated version. They may switch to other channels during the break, use the fast-forward on the video player or leave for pay-per-view or subscription channels.[3]

On the Web the most effective **marketing** may be the ads that help the user to accomplish her goal.

Since the activation level of the Web is higher than for TV, users will generally not accept the fact that the full channel is used for advertisements. Less intrusive than the pop-ups are the banner ads. We have earlier compared these to highway billboards. Billboards are put up on sites with heavy traffic, hoping to grasp our attention using images, colors, and animation. They try to do this without interfering too directly with our driving. Billboards have the advantage that they can use "spare capacity," since the driving, especially in simple conditions, does not need all our attention. On the Web we may have some spare capacity when waiting for a download, otherwise all our capacity is used for scanning and reading pages and in making decisions as to where to go next. While advertisers do everything that is possible to attract attention toward their banners, there is a tendency for users to be focused on the task, finding a link, entering data in a field, using the browser commands, and ignoring the banners.

Perhaps the banners and pop-up windows should only be present in a "while you wait" context (i.e., popping up in the seconds after we have clicked on a link and until the page is displayed). Even then they may be too intrusive for an active user. Another alternative is to integrate the marketing in the material that is returned to the user. Banners try to do this by adjusting to the context. To some extent this was possible with the billboards (e.g., by marketing hotels and casinos on the road to Las Vegas), but banners may be set up for the needs of a single user. The question is then, how do one know what the user needs?

This question is quite simple to answer in query situations. When we search for a hotel the banners display hotel advertisements. For example, when a user gives keywords such as *London*, *hotel*, and *discount* a smart ad would direct him to a London hotel site, showing bargain hotels only. That is, both the banner and the site that the banner points to should be customized according to user needs.

The ads will have an even more direct impact if they appear in the result set from the search engine. This will be especially effective if they can aid the user in satisfying her information need. While traditional media companies try to separate ads from the journalistic contents, we have seen that this separation is not so clear on the Web where search engines and portals can give their sponsors a favorable presentation in the result set. From a marketing point of view, this is, of course, an ideal solution. Some search returns result in two different data sets, first a set of paid entries (advertisements), then the results from the open Web, a more ethical alternative.

Ads in newspapers and journals have some of the same advantages as on TV. The activation needed from the user (i.e., to pick up the periodical), is very limited. Paper ads have a further advantage over TV in that they have a low intrusion factor ("I am here, read me if you want"). Catalogs and (junk) mail advertisements offer some of the same advantages, but do not piggyback on other incentives for reading as in a newspaper. There is, therefore, the high risk that the user will disregard the ads, not even opening the catalog. However, this risk may be even greater on the Web, where the user has to go through several steps in order to access a site. It is interesting to note that even dot-com's send out paper catalogs, clearly showing the need to attract non-Web users, or to get the attention of passive Web users. For marketers, it is a clear disadvantage that on the Web the user has to perform the initial steps of accessing a site, while activation is in the hand of the marketers on TV, radio, and to some extent also newspapers and junk mail. It is therefore necessary to have some sort of initiation, a banner ad on another site or an ad in other media.

Email offers another channel for direct mail, but with the risk that it will be treated in the same manner as a direct mail letter (i.e., discarded without opening). As we discussed in chapter 7 junk mail has become a huge problem, especially for users with email addresses that are presented in public where they can be retrieved automatically by spiders. As we have seen, the cost of marketing through email is marginal. In the same way as pop-up windows these ad messages often come between the user and her goal. While they may be removed easily, junk mail messages have the disadvantage that they clut-

While newspapers try to make a clear distinction between editorial material and advertisements, not all websites and search engines have followed the same **ethics**.

Email marketing is so inexpensive that even a marginal response rate can make it cost effective.

ter up email systems and also impose the danger that we delete an important message by mistake.

But there are also advantages to email for marketing. It is less intrusive than a telephone call and cheaper to send than surface mail. Computer-generated email offers new possibilities of a high degree of customization. The most effective email offers will be based on a previous customer history, and will give the user an offer that is relevant. If it comes from a source with established relations with the user, it may pass the danger of immediate deletion. While too many messages may be annoying, most users will allow a "conversational exchange" of messages. For example, when we have initiated a contact by subscribing to the local paper, we may accept to get an email offer of a Sunday paper extension, if we have bought a book written in Spanish from Amazon we may find a note about their new Spanish collection interesting, and so forth. That is, for every message we send we may accept a relevant message in return, as we discussed in chapter 18.6.

Many sites allow us to subscribe to news, for example, about new books by specified authors, to bargain flights, technical issues, etc. The advantage is that the activation part is moved from the user to the information-provider (from a pull to a push system), the disadvantage is that we may get overloaded with information. Good systems include an unsubscribe reference in each mail (one that works), making it easy to delete or alter the subscription.[4] That is, these systems acknowledge the problem of information overload, and see that there is little point in pushing information on an unwilling user. They may also get more subscribers, when the information to unsubscribe is so readily available.

To sum up we see that general Web marketing has several drawbacks compared to other media, the higher activation level of users being the most serious problem. But as we have seen, the Web also allows for more customized marketing (i.e., marketing directed toward the needs or interests of the specific customer). In order to do this the sites need to be able to retrieve user needs, and, if efficiency is to be maintained, to do this in a formalized manner. This is quite similar to other problems of formalization. With regard to Web searching we have seen that a user must formalize his information needs through a query. With regard to marketing the site has to formalize the user's needs or interest. While the precision does not have to be very great, the success of the marketing will be directly related to

> Push sites do not require activation on part of the user, but can **overload** the user with information if they are not used carefully.

> The Web allows for a form of "inverse" marketing, where the customer describes needs or interest. It is then up to the system to find or create offers.

how close we are to users' needs. We may capture this information directly by asking the user to describe his needs in a formalized manner. We presented an example in our discussion of the electronic travel agency, where users could express an interest in certain vacations, formalized by places, dates, prices, etc., letting it be up to the system to establish relevant offers. Alternatively, the necessary information can be captured indirectly by studying queries, the Web pages that the user visits, his history with the site, etc. We shall study these possibilities below.

22.5 The electronic customer

Are customers on the Web less loyal than what we expect in the physical world, or is perhaps the word "loyal" not relevant for customer relations? We may be loyal to persons or a higher cause, but are we really "loyal" to a business? Are we loyal to the only airline that services our hometown, or to the bank that gives us the best service, the lowest fees, and the highest interest rate? Are we loyal to the neighborhood service station, perhaps paying somewhat more for an oil change than a larger chain would charge, but knowing that they will be there the day we cannot get the car started or is this just an overall strategy from our side? We may be loyal to the local grocer that we know well, but this may be more of a personal than a business relationship. The same may be the case of the deeper relationship between buyers and sellers that may be bound together by personal relationships and mutual trust, sometimes intertwined to the extent that the future of both rely on the well-being of the partnership. However, the word loyal may give the impression that the customer, or the company, will be there whatever happens. This is a dangerous belief to have in any form of dynamic world, physical or virtual. On the Web, the competition can only be a click away.

Technology changes the **relationship** between companies and customers, by removing old channels and establishing new. Until now this development has gone from open to more closed relationships.

With increased competition from all sides, contacts are of a less personal form than before and thus less "loyal." This is clearly seen in the retail business. Not so long ago we would find neighborhoods and towns where most shopping was performed on a very personal basis. Then the business could be carried out with a long-term view and not always on a transactional basis. Customers kept to the same local store, paid the standard price, and got personal service. The grocer would bring the groceries to your house for free and give you credit the day you could not pay. The shop owner knew your preferences ("we got in some really nice cheese today"), the family ("you know the cake that is your husband's favorite, today it's offered at half-price") and had a fairly good knowledge of your economy.

Then we got malls and superstores that could attract customers from far away with lower prices and huge inventories. Without the personal relationship, business had to be performed on a formalized and transactional basis. There was less possibility of using personal customer information or I-owe-you-one type of business. Everybody paid the same price and got the same service, formalized by store regulations.

However, in the same way as a new technology (cars as a commodity, malls, and large stores) removes the possibility of having a personal relationship with retail customers, today a different technology (computers) offers possibilities of building a new type of relationship. Some of the information that the local grocer got from informal channels and had in his head can now be obtained from more formal channels such as point of sale terminals and credit cards. We will get data on name, address, telephone number, and on the items that were bought. The same information can be retrieved over the Web, with the addition that we also get information on what the customers did not buy. That is, as we have seen we may retrieve information on what the customer did from the moment he "entered" the online store. We collect information such as what pages he visited, items that were placed in the shopping cart, carts that were left abandoned, and so forth. And, if the customer has a personal Web page, we can collect information about family, birthdays, etc.

> While the Web offers a formal channel of **communication**, it also allows a company to collect more data on its customers, data that may be used to build a sort of "personal" relationship.

On the Web we have a possibility of really getting to know the customer. This information can then be used to offer products and services that should be of interest. The more accurate the information is the more direct the offer. For example, most of us would appreciate this email from our bank "Last year you have had a minimum of $10,000 on your checking account. This amount would have generated an additional interest of more than $200 on our preferred customer savings account. Please let us know, by a reply to this message, if you would like to open such an account." We may also accept the following note from our insurance company as useful: "We have been informed that you have signed up for a climbing trip to the Himalayas. Please note that your standard travel insurance does not cover such trips. Would you be interested in extending this policy?" but may wonder where they got the information. But most of us would be very concerned about our privacy if email marketing from pharmacy companies were customized, offering remedies for all our illnesses.

Personalized marketing may raise privacy issues.

While there are unlimited possibilities of gathering personal information in an online world, there are rules and regulations that protect our most private data. For other types of data, privacy policy may vary from company to company. But there are also practical limitations. When buying a new car you may be interested in information on all cars that fulfill your needs. A Web portal may capture your information needs, and offer this information to dealers. But from the day you accept the best offer, you will no longer be interested in this type of information. In many ways, it may be irritating to get (good) offers too late. Similarly, there may be a good reason why you want a large amount readily available on your checking account, and you may have gotten your special climbing insurance from another source than your regular insurance company.

Creating and maintaining a **customer profile** by formal means is a very difficult task. The system will not have all data available, may not grasp the context, etc.

The problem is, as we have discussed earlier, that the formalized sources may only get part of the picture. The local grocer will not offer a cake for the husband if he knows that he was taken to the hospital in an ambulance yesterday with an open ulcer. Can a computer (i.e., the formalization) manage these important details? We see that any type of profile information has to be used with care, especially when we do not have the whole picture. In their simplest form, profiles can be used to customize online ads, to select the most appropriate ads, increasing the chance that they will be notified. In a more advanced form it can be used to augment both Web searches and websites. If the profile shows that a customer is primarily interested in bibliographies and art, an online bookstore can rearrange its display so that these sections are the first she sees, and where the new and bargain book displays offer bibliographies and art books at the top. This should be done with care, so that the site looks familiar when the customer comes back, not rearranged completely because she bought two art books. A smart customization policy should ensure a positive effect if the profile is correct, but no negative effects if it is wrong. This can for example be achieved by only customizing the special displays for bargain or new items, but keeping the main store structure intact. That is, we have to acknowledge that our formalizations only capture a part of the picture.

22.6 The electronic employee

Many of us perform our work in front of a computer screen, using software and hardware on the office PC, local server, or the Internet. With a PC and Internet at home, there seems to be no apparent need for many workers to commute to the office. The work can just as well be performed from a distance. This was a situation that was already envisaged with the emergence of the first data communication networks. However, most of us still go in to the office every day. Office space is as expensive as ever, the roads and public transportation are as packed in the rush hours as they ever have been. If some of us stay at home to work it seems to be very few.

A job has both **open and closed parts**. The computer can perform some of the closed parts, and can support some of the open parts, but perhaps not all?

Will the Internet and the Web change this situation? While it does not offer anything fundamentally new, the Internet allows for easy and inexpensive network access and the Web provides us with a homogeneous interface tool. Thus, some practical limitations have been removed. But there are other more important limitations to working at home. While access to computer files is a part of nearly all office work, there are other parts that are as important. For many of us the day is filled with formal and informal meetings with coworkers. While some of the formal meetings may be carried out using electronic communication, from a simple telephone or chat meeting to a more advanced videoconference, this may not be the case for the informal meetings. We meet in the hallway, around the water cooler, and at lunch. Even formal meetings have informal parts, when we whisper to the person next to us or continue the discussions during breaks. These people-to-people meeting places are an important part of lubricating the ongoing formal processes. Here we can advocate our view off the record, receive information, discuss policies, solve problems, make decisions, practice diplomacy and generate ideas. Contact with coworkers is also essential in building a community feeling, the idea of working together for a common goal.

Virtual channels will make it more difficult to build and maintain strong bonds between employees and companies. This may turn out to be a drawback for both parties.

Working at home, alone with the computer, will not provide the same attachments. We may communicate with coworkers using telephone, email, or videoconference equipment, but this is a far weaker form of contact than face-to-face meetings. In the more formal setting people play roles, and over the net we will mainly see our coworkers in their role as manager, engineer, consultant—perhaps not so much as full persons. This has social disadvantages for employees, but may also be dangerous for an employer. Employees without any strong personal attachments to the company or their coworkers may be susceptible to quit whenever they get a better offer. And they may get one! If the only connection to their place of work is through the Internet, these people can work for any company in the world. They will not be limited by commuting or by social bonds, such as for "physical" workers.

Computer and network technology offer a new way of **organizing work**, especially for the more formalized jobs. But these are also the jobs that the computer can remove.

But a high turnaround rate may not be the only problem with people working at home via the Internet. All firms get into situations where they may have to demand an extra effort from their employees, for example, to finish a big contract within deadline, to overcome production problems, to overcome temporary financial difficulties, etc. Then, they have to rely on existing bonds between the firm and its personnel. These may be positive; employees may have a good relationship with the company and a belief in its future; or more negative in that they do not have any good alternatives for employment in the area. Nevertheless, these bonds may provide what is needed in order to weather the crisis. These bonds may not exist or not be as strong between a company and its eEmployees.

This model does not tell us that work at home is not an option, but we have to know the consequences independent of being employees or employers. The negative effects can be reduced if work is divided between home and office, and if the company creates additional meeting places and contact points for their employees. There are also situations where work at home is ideal, and where a company can accept that there are not any strong bonds between employees and the company. This is especially the case for employees that do work on a commission or a transactional basis, for example, telephone operators that provide information, book tickets, and register orders. This type of work can be done with a telephone and a computer terminal; perhaps in another country. It does not require a high degree of training and can be ideal for part-time work. The formalized nature of the task makes it easy to check both quality and efficiency, but, of course, also makes it easier to develop computer systems that do the work. We again see the paradox, jobs that are made possible by the computer can often be replaced by the computer.

22.7 Collaborative work

Collaborative work has been a buzzword for the last decade, and many looked at the Internet as the medium to leverage applications where we join forces to write a document or to perform a project. Clearly, there are many applications where the Internet has proven to be an important tool for administering projects with many geographically dispersed participants. The Linux project, an international collaboration to develop a free Unix-type operating system is a well-known example.[5] Wikipedia[6] is another. Here the idea is to develop an international open-content encyclopedia in many languages. The Internet has simplified efforts to organize international research projects and made it easier to administer large projects with many different participants. Some companies manage to put 24 hours a day into projects, by having employees in different time zones cooperate.

However, in spite of these examples we have not seen large increases in collaborative efforts that many envisaged with the Internet. It seems that there are personal, cultural, and other barriers against participation. There are many open questions: who does the work, when do we work, who gets the praise, the criticism, and so forth, that are not so easy to answer. The interpersonal relations that we have with coworkers help to overcome difficulties in ordinary projects and in cooperative work. This common ground between participants is usually a prerequisite for successful collaboration in a virtual environment.

22.8 Games

Games let us create visual worlds that are formalized to high levels with well-defined objects, rules, and goals.

Humans are a game-playing race. Part of our leisure time may be used for physical games as diversified as soccer, golf, sailing, and basketball; for more intellectual games such as chess, bridge, or Monopoly; or the more personal, such as role-playing games. Games create a world of their own, formalized to higher levels than in the real world. The goal is clearly defined for both soccer and chess, as are the rules of the game. However, soccer and most other physical games operate in a physical world where there is room for interpretation, so we need a referee to tell us if a move is in violation of the rules or not. This is in contrast to intellectual games where the operations often are formalized. Playing a card, for example, or making a move in chess may be performed with full precision. The card is played when it is on the table. We select a chess piece by picking it up and confirming the move when we let it go. In principle, no referee is needed to interpret the rules.[7]

We should therefore not be surprised to see that games are a major application area for the home computer today. A computer is just the place to create virtual worlds, to keep track of rules, and to compute scores. Using the power of a modern PC these worlds can be visualized using multimedia techniques, with animations, sound, and dynamic input. With simple local area networks more than one person can participate in the same world, and we may for example have car races where each person steers his own car. Today, we see a tendency for these applications to be moved to more specialized equipment, to game machines that are designed for just this job.

The Internet offers new opportunities for the game enthusiast. This is an area where collaborative "work" is flourishing. While games often are modeled on real-life situations, the higher formalization level (stricter rules, simpler goals) makes it easier to collaborate. Participants from different cultures may have very different values and ways of working, but all have accepted the "rules of the game." This higher formalization level removes the need for personal relations that is so necessary in real life.

With the Internet we can **play** with and against other people—geographically independent. This is one of the most successful examples of computer-supported collaborative work.

On the Internet, more persons can join the game than what is possible in the real world. Organizing a game is much simpler when participants do not need to be physically present. We may play chess with an opponent anywhere in the world or persons from different continents may "take a seat" for a set of bridge. Thousands of people may come virtually together to play against each other. Some games are played synchronously while others are asynchronous. There also exist ongoing games where we may join at leisure, but where we have to find partners that can protect our interests when we are off the game, preferably partners in different time zones, so that we are not all asleep when the enemy forces attack. Games on the Internet may move into a realistic setting, when we receive telephone calls, emails or SMS messages from the game system during the day.

The disadvantage of game playing on the Internet is that many games require high bandwidth to produce all the "necessary" effects. However, by running parts of the software locally the communication lines can be used for compact data only. For example, the central system keeps track of position, course, and speed of all forces while the local machine performs the actual visualization of the spacecraft.

Chat programs, based on text, sound, and/or video, fall in the same group. The factors that may hinder a good group relationship are present, but since there is no pressure to participate and achieve they have little or no negative effect. However, even here cultural barriers such as language may have an influence. When I saw that my niece was on a chat program I thought it was so interesting that she was able to make friends from other parts of the world, until I noticed that she was chatting with a group in the neighborhood. On the other hand, pen pals on the Internet can have more frequent contact than with snail mail and there are many examples of people making good friends, or finding partners, on the net.

Perhaps the Internet, as developed by a scientist, may have gotten off to a false start. Maybe this is not primarily the medium for serious business or for in-depth data. Instead, it may end up as a media directed toward entertainment, following the home computer as a game-playing machine.

> Global participation in **collaborative work** requires more than communication technology.

Exercises and Discussion

1. We have discussed the problems that face the record industry, when digitalized music becomes available for free over the Internet. Will the film industry and book publishers face similar problems? Discuss this question with regard to copyright, digitalization, and new technologies.

2. We have seen that the advantages of going to electronic media are high for scientific journals. Will there be similar advantages for journals and magazines that are directed toward the public (e.g., magazines on boating, hunting, cooking, etc.).

3. Make a study of the tasks you do as a student or in your job. Which of these could be performed from home (provided that all the technical parts were in place)? Let us assume that all these tasks were performed from your home, what would the long-term effects be?

4. A travel agency services a large part of its customers over the phone. It is now discussing two different models to save money: (1) Letting call center employees

serve customers from their home; (2) Outsourcing the call functions to India, to take advantage of low labor costs. In both cases employees will have access to the same booking systems as they have in the agency today. Discuss these options. What problems may occur?

Notes

1. There are numerous hilarious examples of how some of the early systems performed, for example, the father that saw that his daughter got a "Wrong answer" from a simple math program—"The answer to 3 + 4 is 7, not SEVEN."

2. An example may be the Google Toolbar, that can be downloaded from the Google website (www.google.com).

3. With a digital format it becomes possible to skip commercials automatically. This may force the advertisers into a different model, integrating ads and programs in a seamless manner (e.g., by placing products in movies, shows etc.)—just as in the early days of TV.

4. Note that spam seldom is stopped by using an unsubscribe, as this often may be taken only as a signal that this is a working email address.

5. See www.linux.org.

6. See www.wikipedia.org.

7. In practice, we should perhaps have a referee to stop fights about the creative words that are created in a game like Scrabble and to interpret the not-so-clear answers in Trivial Pursuit.

23 A Better Model?

The Internet and the Web have opened the way for a new method of doing business, even if calling it "a new economy" may be going too far. With the exception of a few services, such as search engines and portals, not many *new* applications have been a success. While the Web offers astonishing numbers with regard to the number of pages and users, it has as a rule not been very good *economically*. The few successful business models in the consumer market have been in automating existing services, such as retail banking, booking, auctions, and to some extent shopping. Even here "success" is often measured more in number of users and sales than in profits.

As we have seen, banking is a prime target for Internet technology and online banks are starting to get solid market shares where they have the most advantage, for example, for bill payment. But will online banks with a full range of services be able to put an end to brick and mortar banking? As we have seen, the advantage of Internet banks is that all services are formalized to a degree where they can be performed by a computer, based on customer's specifications. However, although banking is a formalized application area there will be services and situations that fall outside the programmed functions. We may need help when we are buying a house, exchanging foreign currency, performing cash transfers, and getting a new credit card the day someone stole our wallet. In these situations the Internet bank may not be able to provide the service we need. They based their model on preprogrammed functions, and there may not be a function for the more ad hoc services. In addition, it may not be cost effective to offer functions online that are seldom used. Not only do these make the systems more expensive to develop and maintain, but an abundance of functions may also result in complex user interfaces that are difficult to understand for the ordinary user.

Internet banks will try to handle exceptions by offering a telephone or email connection, in addition to the Web interface. But this will be an impersonal form of contact (we call the company number or use a generic email address), and the range of services that can be provided will most probably be limited, often set by the constraints of the system that is used by the call center. That is, constrained by another formalized system. In exception situations we will probably be much better off with a

Services have both open and closed parts. We need providers that can offer both.

We need a model with automatic services at one end and **human support** at the other. In between there is a place for computer-supported services (i.e., where the user performs the task with the help of the computer).

local brick and mortar bank, where we may have a long customer relationship. Based on these relations, the bank can offer a very flexible service level.

While most traditional banks offer online services as well as the traditional one, they have problems competing with the low fees and good interest rates of the pure Internet bank. But why should we have to choose? Why can we not get the best of both worlds? That is, low fees for the online services, and flexible personal service when we choose to use the brick and mortar part of the business, probably at a higher fee. These combined services will be simplest to implement for a traditional bank that already has the local offices and personnel. While there will still be customers that do not have an Internet connection or that are willing to pay the cost for a personal service, one should expect a transition to more complex services in the brick and mortar part of the business. This part will handle the exceptions that cannot be performed via the Internet. Over time the nature of the physical bank will change. Most of the services that are performed today at the counter will go online. Most customers may arrive with an appointment, and use the brick and mortar bank for the more complex cases where personal handling is needed. Fees will follow the service level, from low cost or free services online to the more expensive manual services.

Customers will expect a personal level of service from such a bank. This is easy to provide to customers that use the brick and mortar bank frequently, as they will be known by face at the bank (provided that the turnaround of bank personnel is not too high). The challenge will be to offer the same level of service to the online customer that is seldom seen in the bank offices, until the day he calls from Rome, Italy explaining that his wallet has been stolen and that he needs a cash transfer immediately. Can the bank provide this service to a stranger? With the right systems this should be no problem. Within seconds the operator should have all data on the customer available, for example:

The open and flexible services offered by human operators can be enhanced and made more efficient by **computer support**.

- Predetermined questions and answers that can be used to verify identification.
- A list of the customer's accounts.
- A short automated history of relations between bank and customer.

As we have seen, we have a similar situation to the one we discussed with regard to airline flight booking, where a good computer system can help an arbitrary call center operator to provide personalized service (chapter 19.2).

Humans will always be more flexible than computer programs. It is expensive, difficult, or sometimes impossible to develop systems that can handle all our wishes and peculiarities, while a professional human agent often can handle this in her stride. While we may find the Internet very useful for performing a simple airline booking, we may need personal advice to find a good hotel at the destination. An interesting model for a travel agency would be to offer both the formalized and unformalized service, combining the advantages of the computer and the human being as in our "idealized" bank above. On the Internet, the customer can provide the formalized data on airports and dates, do some preliminary study of destinations, and perhaps use the online booking system to choose a set of alternatives. To this formalized booking the customer can add a request for a hotel, for example, "suitable for kids and near the old part of the city." The agency could then use the formalized data directly in the processing, acknowledging flights, etc., and use the additional data to find the most suitable hotel. Profiles could be kept of each customer, from credit cards to travel patterns and requirements that could be used as background information. The agent could then use her experience and knowledge of the family's preferences (other profile data, non-formal data from the booking) to select a set of suitable offers that should be returned to the customer (email or presented over Web).

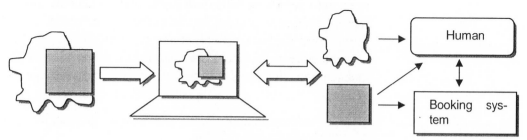

Figure 23.1 Formalized and unformalized parts.

This human/computer model is based on our ideas about formal and informal parts, as illustrated in figure 23.1. The initial need, for example, for a booking, has closed and open parts,

Many services have both **open and closed parts**. While the closed parts can be handled by a computer, a human is often needed to take care of the open parts.

illustrated by a rectangle and the uneven shape, respectively. The user interface should capture both parts and transmit these to the booking system. The formal part can be implemented by check boxes, listing of alternatives, and data provided in separate fields, such as dates, name, address, and credit card number. Informal parts can be provided as annotations in text form. Both parts can be augmented with profile data that also have their closed and open parts.

The booking service will get both types of data. Some services may fall entirely within the formalized range (e.g., booking of a simple ticket) others may be a combination of the two (as explained above) and there may be requests that fall in the informal range (e.g., "an inexpensive place in the Caribbean for a family with two kids ages eight and twelve, for a week during April"). A booking that is completely described by the formal data may be handled by the computer system without human intervention, while the travel agent will take care of requests that include open data. Of course, the computer will be an important tool for the agent when performing these parts even to the extent that the computer system may retrieve keywords automatically from the open part in order to get the data that the agent needs. For example, based on the keywords "inexpensive," "week," "April," and "Caribbean," the travel agent may be provided with a list of alternatives at the moment she gets the request.

The incentive for the customer to describe his wishes in a formalized manner is that the booking may then be performed fully automated, fast, and at low cost. The manual service will be slower and more expensive, but here the customer can draw on the experience of the human agent, to find the right place for a vacation, a good hotel, etc. These are the services that a brick and mortar office provide today, but in this combined model these services may be provided more efficiently.

There will be no clear distinction between the formalized and unformalized tasks, between the closed and open applications. For example, with extensive hotel descriptions the Internet application may directly suggest "suitable for kids and near the old part of the city" or suggest alternatives in the Caribbean. An important task for the developers of the online part of the system will be to monitor all services that are provided by the human agents. This information may be used to find functions that can be formalized, offered as a support tool for the human agent or as an online function that can be used by the customer directly. In practice, this may imply adding additional data and more flexible search functions, as we discussed in chapter 19.2. In this way an online agency can handle more orders without having to increase its staff.

In the age before computers all these services were handled manually. Then, the manual services were made more efficient by adding computer support. With the Internet the customer can operate the system directly, but this does not imply that it is cost effective for the customer to do all the services herself. Professionals, in banks, travel agencies, insurance offices, etc., have always provided value outside of just operating the computer system. The ideal model should then be to retain the experience and know-how offered by these professionals, but use the Internet as another means of providing more efficient services.

This combined model may be efficient in other areas as well. As we have said, the expense of getting the product to the customer is a severe limitation for online shopping. But some of the advantages of shopping online can be retained when the online store works together with a brick and mortar store, for example, when the online store uses the logistics facilities that are already in place. In practice, this may imply that the more bulky goods are transported to the customer from the brick and mortar store, or that the customer picks up the items there, while smaller items can be sent through the mail. This model does not offer shopping independent of location, but many of the other online advantages are retained.

Even if the Internet makes it possible, it is not always **cost-effective** for the customer to perform all services herself.

Exercises and Discussion

1. In this chapter we have discussed a combined formalized/unformalized model for Internet banks and travel agencies, with both closed (automated) and open (manual) functions. Another application for such a model could be the office of a general practitioner. Discuss such an application based on your (probably limited) knowledge of what a doctor does. Try to categorize possible services on a closed—open, automated—manual scale.

2. Are there other areas where this combined model may be applied? Try to name a few.

PART 4

Formalizing Business-to-Business Applications

In **B2B** environments we have a computer at either end of the communication line. This opens the way for automatic transaction handling—if the necessary standards are in place.

The advantage of having a person at one end of the communication line is that we can utilize the flexibility of human beings to adapt to nearly any type of user interface. While a common look and feel of the Web forms may simplify input, it is by no means required. Humans adapt intelligently to the purpose of a given interface, as long as it is flexible and well organized. Neither is it a problem that information is presented in different ways or that some use the shopping cart metaphor and others do not. This flexibility has allowed for a fast growth of services for consumers.

In principle, all types of business-to-business applications can be organized the same way, by asking customers to fill out online forms. While this has the advantage of being flexible, it will often be inefficient, as the data needed may already be stored in an electronic format. Also, where a private citizen or an employee ordering office supplies may send a few orders a year, we may have thousands of orders a day in a B2B (business-to-business) environment. Here a manufacturer, for example, will have full and detailed descriptions of all the components that go into a product. These will be stored within his ERP (Enterprise Resource Planning) system, a system that can handle all types of business functions. A production order, or a plan to produce this product, will generate a set of procurement orders, many of which will go to external suppliers. Today, these may be printed on paper, sent by mail, or faxed to the suppliers. The manufacturer will certainly not see it as an improvement if he has to reenter all the data in the supplier's Web forms.

As an alternative the manufacturer could send procurement orders as email messages that could be generated automatically by his system. However, this would just move the problem to the receiving end, asking the supplier to transfer the order data from email into their own order system. Without a well-defined format for these messages this would have to be performed manually, similarly to the retrieval of data from orders that have arrived by surface mail or fax.

The solution is obvious. We must let the two computer systems, the ERP systems for both the manufacturer and the supplier communicate on a high formalization level. That is, on a level where both computers "understand" the format and the meaning of every data field.

Data exchange is discussed in general in chapter 24, while formalized data exchange and standardization are discussed in chapter 25. The traditional EDI-standard is presented in chapter 26, and the newer markup language, XML, in chapter 27. Interesting new applications of these B2B technologies, Web services, automated value chain, electronic marketplaces, and outsourcing are presented in the last four chapters of this part.

24　Data Exchange

A formalization within a company will often be valid just for this context. B2B applications require **standardization** of these formalizations over groups of companies.

B2B would be simpler if all companies followed strict **standards** in the type of data they stored and in storage formats. But since this is rather utopian, one tries the simpler way of introducing standards for data transmission.

B2B solutions are not simple to realize. First, we cannot expect that manufacturers and suppliers use the same ERP[1] or database systems and even if they do, data values within one system may not be understood by the other. For example, the part identifiers and customer numbers may be proprietary to each company. A length of ten may be in millimeters in the one system and in inches in another; an amount of a hundred may be in dollars or any other currency; etc. That is, even if each system is formalized, the formalization is only valid in a given context. When data is transferred from one company to another, they are taken out of context. We must therefore establish a common area for both the manufacturer and the supplier, ideally a context that will work for all manufacturers and all suppliers.

Technically, we will have the simplest case if we define a standard high-level formalization that could be used by all companies. Then B2B communication would be just a matter of transmitting bits. However, this is a utopian situation. Not only must we expect that companies use different systems, but also that they store different data and use different formats. The idea is then to define standards for *transmitting* data. That is, each company has the freedom to do whatever they want internally, but when they want to communicate with others in a high-level form, data must be converted to the overall standard.

We implement this concept by establishing a "transfer format" where each field of the data set is clearly identified. In addition, we need to describe which fields need to be included in a valid data set, and perhaps also allow optional fields. This has to be done for every document that we want to pass electronically between manufacturers and suppliers, for purchase orders, transport documents, invoices, etc. For each field, we have to determine the range of allowed values, and the measuring units that are to be used. For example, we can determine that all lengths shall be given as millimeters; that both the manufacturers' and suppliers' part numbers shall be included; that references to another entity (e.g. a customer number), should be replaced by detailed data on this entity; that amounts shall be given in dollars or, where foreign currency is involved, given by the currency code and perhaps also an exchange rate.

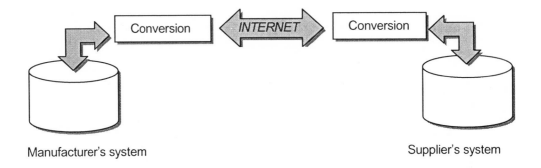

Figure 24.1 Formalized data exchange based on a common format.

The idea is illustrated in figure 24.1. Data is retrieved from the manufacturer's database and converted to a common electronic format that both systems can understand before transmission. The data package is then transferred electronically to the supplier using the Internet, where a similar conversion process will retrieve the various data items and store these in the supplier's database, for example, in an order file. Such a system will be fast, reliable, and very efficient, but it requires that the parties involved can agree on and develop the necessary formalization.

Of course, when firms start to use B2B applications we will also see a tendency to follow more global standardization within each company. Until now, the task of database administrators has been to define standard formats for each company, to avoid unnecessary formats and duplication of data. With more communication to outside partners the conversion process will be simpler if data already follow more global standards. This is quite similar to the development of railways and other communication systems. As long as these are developed on a local scale, each developer can use the gauge that is most suited for his application. But as these expand one will see that the value of the local network increases if it can be connected to other networks, and the need for standards emerges.

B2B communication formalized to high levels can do away with most of the paper that is used in communication between businesses. Instead of printing an order, sending it by mail or fax, and requiring the receiving party to key in the necessary data in their own system, the order can now be stored accurately in the supplier's ERP system a split second after it has been sent from the manufacturer.

In the first phase B2B allows us to go from paper to all **electronic communication**, where orders, invoices etc., can be handled automatically or semi-automatically.

While the first phase of B2B will be to make existing processes more efficient, the main advantages may lie in the second phase, where we utilize the technology to build new and closer relations between businesses. We will then see that many of the messages that are sent today, such as purchase orders and invoices, may be quite unnecessary in this new model. A car manufacturer, for example, may generate purchase orders to a tire supplier based on an overall production plan. However, if the supplier has direct access to the plan (i.e., to the manufacturer's ERP system), no purchase order will be needed. The plan will provide the supplier with all the data needed for accurate deliveries. With these data the supplier can be connected virtually to the assembly line, so that there will be no need for the car manufacturer to stock tires, except for the tires needed until the next delivery. Since the supplier has all the data needed, and will know immediately if there is a change in the plan, it is possible to reduce batches to a minimum, for example, to a situation where tires are supplied every day. Furthermore, we see that there will be no need for the supplier to send an invoice to the manufacturer. Since we can assume that all cars have tires, the supplier can be paid based on the number and type of cars that leave the assembly line.

The process that we see here is typical of the way we use computers. At first, technology is used to speed up manual processes, for example, by replacing surface mail by electronic communication. In the next phase, we see that many of the processes from the old, paper-based world may no longer be needed and that we can remodel the world based on the new technology.

The foundation of this evolution is a formalized system. This enables the computer to perform high-level operations automatically. However, as we have seen, many of the operations within the business world are already formalized, especially within larger businesses. Here high transaction volumes, the need for efficient and secure handling combined with regulations (tax, industrial, others) have made strict formalizations necessary. Parts of the infrastructure needed for B2B applications are therefore already in place.

From the 1960s, banks, insurance companies, airlines, and other large businesses established proprietary networks for internal electronic communication. Today, these organizations have a long history of transferring money, database records, documents, orders, invoices, etc., using proprietary formats or

In the next phase we can organize **partnerships** in such ways that we can do without these messages (i.e., where the information can be retrieved directly from the underlying information).

B2B requires a high **formalization level**, but in many businesses, especially the larger companies, part of this formalization is already in place.

formats that have been established through national and international standards, such as EDI (Electronic Data Interchange). We should have this in mind when we discuss new possibilities. In contrast to B2C applications that were enabled by the Internet, computer-supported B2B applications have been here for nearly fifty years. We must assume that many companies, especially the larger, have already realized a large part of the B2B advantages. It is therefore incorrect to see B2B as something new. This is an ongoing process that started many years ago, long before the advent of computers.

What Internet technology provides is a general network that is so inexpensive that all firms will be connected. In addition, there is a promise of new standards that may simplify B2B applications, for example, XML (eXtensible Markup Language) as a common format for the transmissions. This development offers a possibility also for the medium and smaller companies to participate, to get involved with B2B.

> B2B requires a high level of **IT maturity** within each business. The job for B2B is to connect these IT systems.

B2B applications assume a high level of computerization within each company. If the order processing of the supplier were manual, there would be no advantage to receiving an electronic order since a fax or email would have been just as good, perhaps even more convenient. However, when the receiver has the logistics systems in place, an electronic order can be inserted directly into his ERP system. The data can then be used to refine production plans, purchases, etc. That is, in a world of many automated and formalized islands, B2B offers the possibility of automating the communication between these.

Exercises and Discussion

1. Discuss the differences of realizing B2C and B2B applications.

2. A solution for the exchange of data between organizations is to define a standard global format. We have such formats for character coding (e.g., ASCII codes) and the format of a Web page (HTML). Would it be possible to also define standards for orders, invoices, or technical product specifications?

3. An inch is 2.54 cm. Does this imply that we automatically can convert all inches into centimeters just by multiplying by 2.54? (Hint: Think of the way we use measurements in everyday life).

Notes

1. ERP systems handle product descriptions in the form of Bill-of-Materials. Based on these data structures and a production plan, the ERP system can automatically generate procurement orders to suppliers and job orders to the production and assembly facilities. The ERP system keeps track of inventory, generates invoices and payment orders, etc. In short, an ERP system is one huge software package that can handle all administrative information services in a company. Some well-known vendors of ERP systems are SAP, Baan, Oracle, and PeopleSoft.

25 Formalized Data Exchange

As long as we have humans in the loop we have **flexibility**. The penalty may be an inefficient system. All-automatic systems are alluring, but we need to formalize the response in most of the situations that can occur, leaving only the most complex cases for human intervention.

Business-to-business communication is traditionally performed using telephone, fax, letter, or email. The data itself may be entered in free form, for example, given orally over the telephone or in an open email message, or may be more structured, for example, as an order form. Flexibility is maintained by having human beings at both ends of the communication line. This allows us to handle nearly any type of exception. We can send an order for a hundred units, and ask for delivery by truck, but can add a comment that five units should be sent immediately by air. The supplier may call us and say that he can deliver seventy within the deadline, but needs two more weeks to produce the last thirty, alternatively we can get these in a compatible model. We can argue and bargain and persuade him to work overtime in order to give us at least eighty within the deadline. In everyday communication these "exceptions" are frequent, but cause few problems since both the form of the data and the processes are flexible.

The drawback is that manual handling is time-consuming and efficient. Routine orders can be handled much more efficiently with business-to-business communication, keeping the human beings out of the loop. That is, if we view the human being as an intelligent and flexible, but slow "machine," it is inefficient to use this expensive "machine" for routine cases that can be handled by the less flexible but very efficient computer. However, the computer requires formalized data and processes. Not only do we need to agree on low-level exchange formats, such as using HTTP protocols and the syntax of the communication, such as using XML, but we also need formalization on a semantic level. For a purchase order, for example, we must agree on which data should be included, in what format, and how the data is to be interpreted.

The process of **formalization** is a complicated, technical, social, and diplomatic task that has to be performed by humans.

This task is very similar to what a database administrator performs. Before a company can set up its internal systems for storing data, someone must determine the format of the different record types. This is not an easy task, especially in firms that have exploited the freedom of using manual routines. For example, what kind of data should describe a customer, a supplier, or a product? One will usually find that different departments have very different opinions of what is needed. The job of the database administrator is to find the structures that fulfill the requirements from all parts of the organization, and that can be used to describe all the customers, suppliers, or products. Clearly, this formalization process is not an easy task. It will require several meetings with the involved parties, and good diplomatic skills to find the right balance where there are conflicting interests.

While difficult, this formalization has the advantage that data may be stored once within the legacy system of the company, and can then be used for all applications. The idea is "store once use many times." The value of the data increases as it can be made available for the whole organization and used for many different purposes. Not only do we get more in return for taking the effort of storing the data in the first place, but data quality will also improve as data is used in more applications. With the Internet and the Web, these data can be made available also outside of the business premises, for example, by Intranet and Extranet implementations.

Note that this standardization is not without costs. Many enterprises that have installed ERP systems have found out that while the company as a whole may benefit from standard data formats and having one system, each department or production line may be unsatisfied with what the general system can provide. Often the ERP system replaced proprietary systems that were developed just for the need of a department. Replacing a good solution with a mediocre is not easy. These problems will be most severe in diverse enterprises, which may incorporate very different business units, each with their own culture and business models. Here the idea of one overall system (one overall formalization) may not work.

We need **translations** when moving from one formalized system (context) to the other.

Standardization is also necessary in data communication between organizations. But here we have the additional complication that we have stakeholders from several institutions that may have different ways of doing business. In trying to connect these different worlds we may find different vocabularies, processes, formats, ways of encoding data, etc. We see the same type of problem when we go from one country to another. We may find a different currency, keyboards, and standards for cell phones, voltages, videotape, and TV formats—even different ways of presenting date, time, numbers, and zip codes.

What we see is that formalization is context dependent. What is clear and unambiguous within a department, company, or country, within a given context, may not be as clear in another context. For example, the supplier identifier in an order record will reference a local supplier file. If this record is to be transferred to another company or context, the supplier file has to be sent along with the order or the identifier has to be replaced by the contents of the supplier record. If we look at the record itself we may find that the one company registers different data than the first, that addresses and telephone numbers are given locally, that one firm offers two address fields, another only one, and so forth.

While the post office may force some standards for addresses, at least within a country, businesses have often complete freedom in representing more internal data. For example, when doing some consulting work for a foundry that produces ship propellers, we found that a number of different coordinate systems were used by their customers (ship yards and manufacturers of propeller systems). While all had an axis parallel to the propeller shaft, it could be called x, y, or z, the positive direction could be forward or backward, and the origin could be on the axis or having an offset from this. Some customers even used several coordinate systems within their organization, an inheritance from engineering firms that had been acquired or merged with the company.

What we find is that these firms have enjoyed and utilized the freedom to make a choice. This choice was unproblematic as long as the drawings were used only within the company, but creates problems whenever the specifications go to the outside. In the foundry this lack of standards was addressed by identifying the coordinate system used, and mapping these into a common in-house system—yet another coordinate system. An alternative would have been to try to work out standards, perhaps involving manufacturer organizations or international standards committees. But standardization work is a long and tedious process. Even if such standards were accepted it would have taken years before these were used in every engineering drawing and in every specification.

While computer technology has increased the reward of success, offering efficient and error-free communication between businesses, it is of little help in the standardization process itself. This is a social process where the participants have to define a common ground that everyone can adjust to. The process is somewhat simplified in the cases where a large manufacturer or service provider can set the requirements, forcing its major suppliers to follow its standards. While this is

On isolated "islands" people enjoy the freedom to design their **own systems**. This can become troublesome when the islands are connected to other parts of the world.

Computer technology, especially the Internet, offers great rewards when the formalization process has been performed, but may not offer **significant help** in this process.

an efficient way of establishing the data formats, it has the drawback that suppliers may have to conform to different formats for different customers. The manufacturer may also find that the "take it or leave it" policy may not work for all suppliers. Suppliers where this manufacturer is not a major customer may just "leave it," not finding it worth the effort to conform to the new formats.

In some cases, de facto standards emerge. For example, many businesses exchange data electronically using Adobe's PDF format,[1] Microsoft Word documents, Excel spreadsheets, or Access databases as "attachments" to email. The data can be read manually, or imported into other programs. In the latter case, Excel and Access define what we can call a medium-level formalization, providing a name, a format, and a value for each data element. On a higher level the trading partners must agree on which data elements should be included and the overall record structure. Still, spreadsheet and database formats provide a useful way of formatting data, and may offer a convenient method for simple B2B transactions until higher-level standards are accepted.

Control over "de facto" standards is a very important competitive advantage.

The value of a company such as Microsoft is not in its products alone. We can get as good word processing, spreadsheet, and database systems from other vendors.[2] Microsoft's advantage is the fact that many of their products have become de facto standards. This is true not only for the data formats, but also for the "look and feel" and functionality of the user interface. If we change to a new word processor we may have to retrain personnel, not the computer experts that have learned the basics and can easily accommodate to a new system, but the people who have learned word processing through MS Word. Their knowledge will be connected to the details of this system, command names, menu organization, icons, etc., and even if another system is based on the same principles, retraining may be an effort. And, of course, whenever a document is to be sent outside the organization, conversion to the "standard" Microsoft format may be required (the conversion job usually falls on the organization using the less common formats). While this may be implemented as a "save as Word format" instruction, automatic conversion never manages to cover 100 percent. There will always be effects that are not reproduced identically in the two systems.[3]

But we cannot expect to get these de facto standards in every area. Then standards have to be developed, approved, and—the most difficult part—used. As we shall see in the next chapter, the work to establish B2B standards started more than thirty years ago, and has been an ongoing process since then.

Exercises and Discussion

1. Go to the Web and access company Web pages in different countries. Write down the postal addresses given. Study the discrepancies in the formats. Are these discrepancies causing any major problems for international postage today? Will these cause any problems for B2B applications?

2. In some countries lengths are given in yards, feet, and inches, others use the metric system. Clearly it is possible, in B2B applications, to convert from the one system to the other by a simple formula. Is this entirely unproblematic?

3. *Group exercise (for two or more persons)*:

   Let us assume that each of you represent a company, a manufacturer of a type of equipment. Choose what type of equipment they produce, *independently* of other group members.

   a) Working independently, make a sketch of a formalized order form that customers (retail shops) can use to order items. Describe the different data fields that will be included in such a form.

   b) Compare forms with other group members. Are there any discrepancies?

   c) Try to work out a common form for all companies. Discuss the difficulties you encounter.

Notes

1. Adobe Portable Document Format (PDF) is a de facto standard for electronic document distribution, preserving fonts, layout, graphics, etc.

2. An example is OpenOffice.org. This office package is provided for free, we can even download the source code.

3. Earlier, simple ASCII text files were used as a basic medium for transmitting documents between all types of programs. Today, HTML and other standards that retain layout information are offering better alternatives, allowing for a somewhat higher formalization level than ASCII. In the coming years XML may provide a higher-level document form, but even with XML we cannot expect that 100 percent of a document will be preserved from one system to the next. Microsoft will thus most probably retain their "standard-advantages" for a system such as Word and Excel.

26 Electronic Data Interchange (EDI)

The work to formalize
and standardize **EDI**
started in the early
seventies.

From the moment computers were used to store data within businesses, the inefficiency of making a printout, sending the printout by mail, and letting the receiver key the data into his computer system was recognized. The first networks for electronic transmissions were therefore established very early in the history of computing. These used proprietary formats, for communication within one enterprise or between business partners. The actual communication took place using private networks, for example, by dial-up communication over ordinary telephone lines.

Formats were established within an enterprise, or between an enterprise and its major suppliers. This had the disadvantage that many different formats were in use. A supplier could find that each of its major customers had its own data interchange format. Efforts to work out standards started as early as in the 1970s when the Transportation Data Coordinating Committee (TDCC) developed the initial electronic data interchange (EDI) formats for data transportation. Today, there are two widely accepted EDI standards—X.12 developed by the American National Standards Institute (ANSI) and EDIFACT, a standard developed by the United Nations. EDIFACT has been used mainly in Europe and the Pacific Rim.[1]

The standards are based on a transaction set that equates to a paper form, for example, an invoice or a purchase order. Each transaction set specifies the actual data items that are included, the fields in the paper form, and a computer-readable format to allow the business-to-business interchange of the transaction.

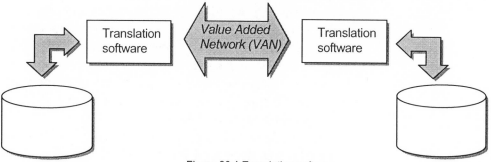

Figure 26.1 Translation software.

The EDI standard requires complicated **coding**, is only readable for machines, and is most often implemented using proprietary networks.

While these standards set strict requirements for the interchange, each business may still use its own database systems and in-house formats. The mapping to and from the EDI standard is performed by translation software, such as illustrated in figure 26.1. The communication software itself will be quite similar to that of an email system, and can be implemented as an extension to such a system.

EDI transactions can be transmitted over any type of network. Until now, expensive Value Added Networks (VANs) have been used. While VANs provide a high level of security the expense of establishing and maintaining these networks has been a limitation to the use of EDI, especially for small- and medium-sized businesses. Further, EDI requires a unique solution for each pair of trading partners, where the implementation of the standard may be complicated by the use of different versions, even by different interpretations of rather complex guidelines.

EDI with its fixed commands and rigid structure is not an open tool. To make the implementation and running of an EDI system cost effective, large transaction volumes are needed. These volumes are found in the bigger businesses that may also have the advantage that they can force their trading partners to use EDI. Still, on a world basis, EDI is used only by a fraction of the businesses that are potential users of business-to-business systems.

Since the EDI standards were developed at a time when bandwidth was an expensive commodity, care was taken to make the EDI records as compact as possible. This compressed form has the disadvantage that it is quite complicated to develop the translation software and to perform the complex coding into the EDI standards. An even larger problem is that this coding makes EDI records unreadable by human beings. That is, EDI records are designed for business-to-business communication, and can only be used in this context. In practice, this is clearly a limitation to the wide acceptance of EDI usage. A firm may have to create two different types of record formats, EDI records for the suppliers or customers that support B2B and manual (paper) records for the others.

Today, we have a different communication infrastructure to the one EDI was developed for. Instead of expensive private networks we have the Internet. This does not imply that EDI must be abolished, but that we need EDI on the new Internet platform. This can be done by using EDI on top of the new

Internet standards, getting the advantage of the Internet at the same time as we hold on to the results from the development of the EDI standards.

Exercises and Discussion

1. Try to find, from the Web, information on the early history of Electronic Data Interchange. When did the first B2B applications emerge (i.e., when did companies start to interchange data between computers)?

2. Clearly, the usage of the EDI standard has been limited by its complicated coding scheme, and by its reliance on VAN-networks. Discuss what will happen if EDI is offered on the Internet. Will we see a rush of new companies using EDI as a platform for B2B, or are there other constraints?

Notes

1. Efforts are under way to harmonize the two standards, not an easy task due to fundamental differences in both syntax and semantics.

27   XML

With the Internet, its global addressing scheme, and the relatively inexpensive connection and usage fees, we have an important part of the infrastructure for business-to-business applications. However, while HTTP gives us the underlying communication protocol, we need new standards for a formalized description of data on a *semantic* level. HTML, as a layout-oriented language, cannot provide the functionality needed.

XML is a tool for describing structured documents and data records, a tool that can be used to define new languages for storing and transmitting data on a high formalization level.

XML[1] seems to be a promising effort in this direction. XML is a vehicle for describing markup languages. That is, while HTML is a specific markup language, XML is used to construct such languages. In XML, tags (such as <title>) are introduced by the users, they are not specified in XML itself. Further, XML has constructs that make it possible to define the *structure* of a document.

XML is a subset of SGML (Standard Generalized Markup Language), an ISO[2] standard. In principle, SGML will provide the functionality we need to describe semantic documents, but SGML is a fairly complex language with a large number of constructs both for creating and presenting documents. Due to its complexity SGML has never been a success, therefore the scaled-down XML version has been developed, trying to retain much of the functionality with limited complexity.

```
<?xml version="1.0"?>
<!doctype address SYSTEM "address.dtd">
<address>
      <street>2000 Fifth Avenue</street>
      <city>Pittsburgh</city>
      <zipcode>PA 15260</zipcode>
</address>
```

Figure 27.1 XML document (example)

With XML the individual data elements are marked (tagged) according to a DTD (Document Type Definition). A simple example is shown in figure 27.1 above, an XML document with address information.

```
<!element address (street, city, zip-
code)>
       <!element street (#pcdata)>
       <!element city (#pcdata)>
       <!element zipcode (#pcdata)>
```

Figure 27.2. XML Document Type Definition

This document refers to the DTD shown in figure 27.2. This is the type definition or form that tells which fields are included in the address. From the DTD we see that the address type, as we have defined it, consists of three elements, each of which is of the basic type *pcdata* (basically text, however with the possibility that there may be markup references included). If we compare our example to traditional paper forms, figure 27.2 will be the blank form and figure 27.1 the filled-out form. The difference is that in XML the field descriptions are given as named fields, not as boxes and lines. XML also allows us to describe more complex "forms" than what is possible on paper.

Note the generic nature of the language. Tag names are not static as in HTML. Instead, these are introduced in the DTD part, which also determines the structure of the form or document, for example, that an address consists of the three elements: *street*, *city*, and *zipcode*. XML is a language for *defining markup languages*, such as the simple "address language" described here.

In newer versions of the XML standard the basic DTD is replaced by a *schema*. A schema offers a set of basic data types (string, decimal, date, etc.) that lets the user restrict the values of elements and also to build new types based on the basic types. We can specify the cardinality, the number of occurrences of elements and can include choice statements, for example, stating that a name can be given in one field or as separate entities for first name, last name, and initials. The idea behind the schema concept is to extend XML so that it can be as useful for handling data records as it will be for structured documents. With schemas, XML has taken a great step in the direction of programming languages and database systems.

In the above example we have introduced names, such as address, city, and street, directly in the DTD or schema. This works fine for simple cases, but what happens when enterprises start to create their own vocabularies. For example, we may then get many different definitions of "street." Just as what could happen if different companies create their own paper

XML started out as a system for describing **documents**, but has in newer versions moved toward also encompassing data records.

forms. For example, they could use various lengths for the field, some would have name and street number in the same field, others would have separate fields for each entity, and so forth. What we need is a system for creating unique vocabularies. In XML this is done through the concept of a *namespace*. A namespace has an identifier that is unique on a global basis. A name in XML will then consist of a local name, for example, *address*, from a given namespace.

```
<item
    xmlns:invoice=http://www.acmeinc.com/inv
    xmlns:delivery=http://www.acmeinc.com/deliv>
    <invoice:street>
        P.O.Box 5440
    </invoice:street >
    <delivery:street >
        45 Main St
    </delivery:street >
</item>
```

Figure 27.3 A XML document using namespaces

Since XML will be used across boundaries, whether of enterprises or countries, it is important to ensure the uniqueness of **namespaces**—the vocabularies.

An example is shown in figure 27.3. Here we have identified two namespaces, *invoice* and *delivery*, using an URL-like syntax to define unique identifiers. Note that there may not be any files at the given URL locations, as we only apply this syntax to ensure that invoice and delivery have globally unique identifiers.[3]

In XML it is assumed that the browser will know the location of a schema (this will be the case for standard vocabularies), if not, the location can be offered in a special *schemalocation* element. Within the document we then prefix each name with the name of the namespace, here *invoice* or *delivery*. Thus *invoice:street* will be a reference to the name street within the namespace invoice.[4]

Note that namespaces also help us to clear up the problem we discussed in chapter 12 with regard to an overload of acronyms and names in the real world. While the acronym SAS is overloaded in a global context, SAS as a value to the element *airline:name* (*name* within the namespace *airline*) should be unique. That is, namespaces help us define a formalized context, an area delimited from other parts of the world.

With a schema it is possible to check the *validity* of the document. That is, we can require that every element used within an XML document be declared in a DTD. Alternatively

XML documents will be read by a computer and must therefore abide to strict **syntactical requirements**. That is, we define a high-level formalization and try to ensure that the formalization rules are followed.

the document description can be defined through the document itself, without any explicit DTD. Thus, a DTD/schema is not a required part of an XML document. However, without the type definition it is only possible to check if the XML description is *well-formed*, that tags have an end tag, and so forth. The requirement for a well-formed, possibly also validated document, distinguishes XML from HTML. While HTML browsers ignore unknown tags and accept documents that do not follow the syntax, for example, where end tags are missing, XML will give an error message in these cases. Flexibility is an advantage for a presentation language, where the output is for human beings, but when the documents are to be read by "dumb" computers, a higher level of formalization is needed. If not, we cannot ensure a correct interpretation.

A supporting specification called the Document Object Model (DOM) offers a platform- and language-independent interface to XML documents. The DOM provides an API (Application Program Interface) to the XML documents that can be used by, for example, a Java program or a Visual Basic script to update a document's structure and content, or to retrieve the various data elements. In many ways the DOM works both as a query and a programming language, enabling programs to work on the underlying data using high-level concepts. This is especially important for XML, since most XML documents will be created and read by programs, in business-to-business communication environments.

The tools provided for implementing the DOM model are Xpath and XSL/XSLT. Xpath is a query language that allows us to navigate the document structure, for example, to select all headers from a document, all zip codes that start with the number 15 or all courses that student "John Doe" is enrolled in. That is, if we are writing programs that work on XML documents, this tool will aid us in retrieving all elements of the document or just the document parts that we need.

When a document is defined at a high level, as in XML, it can be **converted** to many other forms automatically (e.g., to HTML).

XML does not contain layout information. However, in those cases where XML documents are to be presented to human beings, an accompanying description will explain how the document is to be formatted. This description can be provided by the XSL (eXtensible Stylesheet Language). XSL consists of two parts in addition to Xpath, a *transformer* (XSLT) and a *formatting language* that describes how the document is to be rendered in a browser, a PDA or for example on a high-quality printout. In this process it may be necessary to remove information, for example, if the document is to be rendered on a PDA, or to add information, for example, by creating a table of contents or an index when the documents is to be rendered in printed form. XSLT will aid us in these processes. Another important function for XSLT will be to transform XML documents into HTML, PDF, or other formats that may be of convenience for a special situation or application.

These transformations are made possible by the fact that data are stored in a high-level, structured form. The XML version contains more information than the lower-level forms of HTML or PDF. With XSLT it becomes possible to differentiate documents for internal use in an organization, in much the same way as a database system lets different applications access or view different parts of a record. Documents and other types of data formalized as XML may therefore be used for many different purposes.

With XML we have a tool for **defining standards** and with the Internet the vehicle for implementing the XML applications. However, the standards themselves need to be developed, and require general acceptance to be useful.

One should note that while XML provides a formalized syntax and a framework for defining semantics, it does not provide the higher-level standards that we need for making the applications. As we discussed in the introduction to this chapter formalization within one area may not be valid in another, whether it is another country or another company. An important task for the standardization committees in the years to come will therefore be to define both the syntax and the semantics of standard vocabularies. That is, for each type of document one will have to provide a schema, define the namespaces, and describe what type of data is to go into each element. Ideally, these descriptions—at least the syntactic parts—can be stored in *repositories*. These are global databases where both senders and receivers can find the schema descriptions. Repositories will also guarantee that the parties use the same version of a DTD.

With an integration of **EDI and XML**, we can bring along thirty years of standardization effort.

The standardization work needed on top of XML will be as tedious and complex as standardization always has been. But, this work does not have to start from scratch. There are efforts underway to create an XML/EDI, utilizing the thirty-year effort that has gone into developing EDI. A clear advantage to this work is that both XML and EDI have recognized the need for sublanguages (i.e., vocabularies defined for groups of organizations). Just as EDI has standards for the transportation business, for airplane maintenance, and for customs handling, work is under way to establish standard XML vocabularies for a large number of areas, for chemical data, mathematics, data on mining, geographical data, etc. The EDI sub-languages, or transaction sets as they are called within EDI, can therefore be accommodated within the XML philosophy.

In order to move EDI to XML one has to define schemas and namespaces for all the EDI transaction types. While the schema development will be a technical translation from EDI to XML structure, the namespace definitions will be more of a social process where political issues such as language independence will be a major factor. If successful, this effort will make EDI more readily available for small and medium-sized businesses. Translation software, from internal formats to XML/EDI, will be very much simpler than the old encoding programs, since the DOM will offer a convenient interface. Transactions can be sent via the Internet, reducing the need for special Value Added Networks or, where the greater VAN security is needed, the competition from the Internet will reduce the cost of using these networks.

The XSL formatting will also be an important part of an XML/EDI standard. A large manufacturer can now format all its business transactions using XML/EDI. The larger suppliers can then process these transactions automatically on a business-to-business basis, while smaller suppliers may choose to have the data presented as a form in their browser or printed on paper for manual in-house processing. As we have seen, this can be done by using different transformation and formatting descriptions.

There are two types of **standards**, those defined by national and international standard committees, or those that come from a dominant market position.

While the development of official standards is a long and complex process, it is not the only way toward standardization. As we have seen, in areas where we have a winning product, this may define a de facto standard. There are disadvantages in monopolies, but it is perhaps the only way that we could have established "standards" in many areas. The process of determining a format and the scope of one system is always simpler than defining a standard for all systems. The disadvantage of a monopoly is that we do not get fair competition for licensing fees and functionality, but the advantage of being able to attach MS Word and PDF documents to email messages, knowing that these documents will be received without any conversion errors, is tremendous.

Word processors will soon have the possibility of saving the document as XML. In this way XML can piggyback on the de facto document standards. The advantage of publishing documents as XML instead of HTML on the Web is that this will allow for somewhat higher-level searches, for example, for attributes such as date, author, headings, language, and number of pages. With an advanced "save as XML" function the user should be able to choose a document template, for example, a template for a scientific paper, and the word processor could then extract titles, authors, affiliations, keywords, references, etc., from the document under the supervision of the user. These data could then be formatted using a "scientific paper" vocabulary, offering the possibility of using higher-level searches, at least within the vocabulary covered by this type of document. Similarly, XML documents can be created based on the standards used for database systems. New versions of these systems offer converters from their own internal formats to XML. An enterprise can then export data as XML. The receiver will need to have the same database system to do the opposite conversion, or will have to build a program that processes the XML record directly.

As we see XML is a flexible tool that can be used to capture existing standards, both official and de facto. It will encourage and simplify the work of defining new high-level standards in many areas. But the real problem is not to define XML nor to define suggestions for standards, but to have these standards accepted by the user communities. Acceptance of standards implies a change of routines and software; legacy data may become outdated or must be converted to new standards. This may be an expensive process.

Not everybody benefits from the acceptance of standards. Standards imply a leveling of the playing field, and may provide leverage for some companies and disadvantages for others. We discussed this in chapter 19.2 with regard to airline reservation. With a standard for describing available airplane seats (destinations, dates, prices, and restrictions) it will be easy to find the cheapest fare. This is a clear advantage for a new bargain airline and a clear disadvantage for the established companies. As we have seen, the latter may therefore find it more convenient to keep their own reservation systems, using their proprietary formats, restricting access from other computer systems and perhaps also having pricing policies, restrictions, and frequent flyer programs that make direct comparison complicated. So while standardization may be a means to run society more efficiently, it may also impose a threat to many. Since the standardization work itself is so complicated, there are also many possibilities for major companies to impair standardiza-

The **acceptance** of standards may be a threat to established companies, even to the society as a whole in the cases where standards are a barrier against innovation.

tion efforts wherever these may entail a threat to the existing power structure. In the tough market that we have today, it is of vital importance to control the channels to the customer. If these are lost, the company may end up as a subcontractor, in fierce price competition with others that can perform the same service.

Even for society as a whole the standards may pose a threat in that these may have a tendency to freeze progress and technology, and to be a barrier against competition. While each of us may benefit from the de facto standards of Adobe and Microsoft products, these established formats make it nearly impossible for others to enter the market. A competing product will have to be dramatically better, perhaps based on a new disruptive technology,[5] to persuade customers to leave the convenient position that the standards provide. This power that follows ownership of a standard follows countries as well as individual businesses. While the American GPS (Global Positioning System) today defines a standard for navigation, we see that the European Union is creating its own system,[6] to avoid the American dominance within GPS.

Large enterprises may use a monopoly position to force everybody to accept a standard. This was the case when AT&T, the parent company of the Bell System, reshaped the American telephone network around 1920. But this monopoly also served as a lid on new business models and creativity within the communication area for voice and data. Today, we have many businesses in this area but have lost many of the standards. We experience this problem, for example, with cell phone systems that are not universal. However, with active involvement both from governmental and international standards organizations, it should be possible to merge the advantages of standards with the advantages of free competition. Without this involvement we will get incompatible systems, and be back to a situation where effectiveness can only be achieved by having a dominant player in the market.

Exercises and Discussion

1. XML can be used to describe forms as well as documents. Let us assume that the book you are reading is to be represented as an XML document. On the lowest level we could have a tag for a paragraph (e.g., <paragraph> *contents of paragraph here* </paragraph>). Try to make a list of other tags that would be useful for representing a book structure.

2. Let us assume that a standardized XML format is established for documents and that all word processing systems can open and save documents in this standard. Discuss the benefits of having such a standard. What will the implications be for companies such as Microsoft, which control the current DOC format, and Adobe, which control the PDF format?

Notes

1. The development of XML can be followed on www.xml.org and on the www.w3.org websites. There are also several good textbooks out on XML, but be certain to get a new edition.

2. International Standardization Organization.

3. This is a really smart idea, with the drawback of confusing users as we normally view an URL as a pointer to a file.

4. To avoid too many prefixes (really not a problem in most cases since XML normally will be produced by a computer program) XML allows us to have a default namespace.

5. A technology that creates new markets and as such is better suited for start-ups than for the incumbents. We cover disruptive technologies in chapter 32.

6. Galileo, a European navigation satellite system costing more than 3 billion euros.

28 Web Services

With XML we have the tool for creating standardized data exchange and storing formats. When a vocabulary and a document format have been established for an application, we can create a document on one computer and send it to another. We are then ready for the next step (i.e., to define *services* on a computer system that can be accessed from the outside). For example:

- We can offer an automated weather forecast system. Based on a location (name or coordinates) from the calling computer, we return a forecast for this area.

- A point-of-sale system can call a Web service of a credit card company, providing the card number, the date, and the amount, and can get a verification code back.

- With an article number as input, a Web service can return the number of items in stock.

With a Web **service** we may access services from one computer on another, independent of location, programming language, or operating system.

But isn't this just what we have talked about in the previous parts of this book, services that have been established using Web browsers and HTML? No, this time we are within B2B applications, with a computer at both ends of the communication line. That is, instead of just presenting the returned data on a Web page, the calling computer can use these data for further processing. Take the forecast, for example. When the forecast is received the calling computer can reformat this and present it to the user in any conceivable way; it may even translate the forecast to another language (perhaps using yet another Web service), send out a warning to drivers if certain parameters in the forecast are present, store it for statistical reference, and so forth.

A set of protocols and standards s are established to handle these Web services. The SOAP[1] protocol, for example, defines an envelope that contains the data that is transferred between the two computer systems. WSDL[2] is used to define the details of the services, and the idea behind UDDI[3] is to provide a "yellow pages" system where services are described. We also have a new version of development tools that help developers to implement these services. A well known example is Microsoft's dot-net architecture.

Web services can be used to model the information interface between various parts of an enterprise. Thus it offers an alternative to the "total" system approach.

In principle Web services are nothing new. From the very start we had the ability to call subroutines (services) within a computer program. However, then the administration of the call, sending the data to the routine, transferring control, returning the results were handled within one programming system. We later got the ability to call "services" within other programs on the same computer system, for example, using Microsoft's OLE[4] feature or standards such as CORBA.[5] However, with Web services we have gone all the way. Now it is possible to call services on other computer systems, independent of the program language used to implement these systems, independent of the operating system they run under and independent of location. In practice, this makes it much simpler to use computer resources and data at different locations. We can concentrate on the services, independently of how these are implemented. Note that this is yet another implementation of the encapsulation principle that we discussed in chapter 2.1.

There are those that feel that Web services will revolutionize the way we do business.[6] But as with XML, the tools only offer a way of creating these services; the job of establishing the standards are as hard as ever. In addition, companies may feel that they lose control over their information resources by opening their computer services to anyone. There are also other problems that arise when we try to formalize connections between businesses. We shall return to these matters in part 5.

Independent of this discussion, Web services may have a great impact on how we organize the computer systems within a company. From an early beginning with a large number of independent programs, many companies have tried to get control over their data and computer services by installing one total system (i.e., an ERP system that takes care of everything). The idea has been to store data in one place only, and to let these data be available to the whole organization through this one system. This is not easy to achieve. There have been many failures on the ERP path, and those that have succeeded have used very large resources to accommodate the system to the enterprise. Since the ERP system is a general system, one often finds that each division within the company was happier with their old proprietary systems that had been tuned to their needs.

Web services offer a way out of this situation. Instead of forcing one system on the whole enterprise, each part can implement the system they want. That is, each division can choose their own system. In result, they must offer a set of Web services to the rest of the organization. Instead of standardizing on an ERP system we define "interfaces" between the various parts. For example, the CEO will need financial data from each division, and a Web service that retrieves these data from the divisional systems must then be implemented. A transport division will need information on which goods that arrive, container types and weight, and all other divisions must provide these data through a Web service. Of course, defining what services are needed, the data they are to provide and the data formats will be a major task. But within a company one will usually have the mechanisms, from a management, social, and technical view, that are needed.

Web services may also have a great future for government agencies. Today, for example, my college has to use a student administrative system selected by the government, so that the Department of Education may get the data they need. It would be much more flexible if the Department, instead of deciding on a system, defined a set of Web services that each institution had to offer, for example, services that could return number of students, credits, grades, etc., and all other information that is needed. Behind such a standard interface, each institution could implement these services as they saw fit. Most often such a service would retrieve the data from the institution administrative database, but there would be nothing to hinder an institution for typing in these data whenever the Web service was called, as long as they conformed to the required data format.

While Web services clearly are a part of our discussion on formalization (i.e., of "closing" the world), we see that they also open the possibilities for greater "computing freedom." Within an organization, we can maintain basic ideas of storing data only once, for making data available to all, for defining standard processes, etc., and at the same time let each division chose the computer system that best fulfills their needs.

Exercises and Discussion

1. As an alternative to installing an ERP system for the whole organization, you want to propose a system based on Web services. How would you go about to organize this work, to define the services that each part of the organization would have to implement?

Notes

1. SOAP (earlier Simple Object Access Protocol) is a protocol intended for exchanging formalized and structured information in a decentralized environment (i.e., between indepentent computer systems). The message within a SOAP envelope is described using XML. The protocol contains all information needed to transmit, receive, and process messages.

2. WDSL (Web Services Description Language) describes how to access a web service and what operations it will perform.

3. UDDI (Universal Description, Discovery and Integration protocol), acts as a directory model for Web services.

4. OLE (Object Linking and Embedding) is Microsoft's proprietary mechanism for allowing documents and applications to access data and subroutines in applications.

5. CORBA (Common Object Request Broker Architecture) is an ISO standard for managing distributed program objects in a network. It allows programs at different locations and developed by different vendors to communicate.

6. John Hagel III. 2002. *Out of the Box: Strategies for Achieving Profits Today & Growth Tomorrow Through Web Services*. Harvard Business School Press.

29 Automated Value Chain

The real advantage of B2B is that the whole **value chain** can be automated, based on the availability of data records with a high formalization level.

Seconds after the customer has hit the submit button the order is received by the online store and entered in their database system. The Web interface has ensured that this is a complete order, formalized by including unique product identifiers and specifications, such as size and color. Probably the website has also checked to see if the products are available. The online store's computer system verifies credit card information. This is done by sending transaction records with credit card number, expiration date, and the amount electronically to the credit card company. The result, an approved/not approved status, is returned to the online store with an electronic signature, a code that the store uses to verify its claim if there is any dispute at a later date.

The online store may have its own warehouses or may just pass the order on to the manufacturer or distribution center. The order will be directed to the most convenient warehouse, depending on product availability, distance to the customer, and load factor. The products will then be collected, packed, and sent to the customer using the postal system or any other delivery service. The date and time of the sending will be noted in the online store's system, which will initiate another electronic transaction toward the credit card company, this time to get credit for the full amount. The status of the order can be made available to the customer over the Web interface, so that he can follow the order through the system, until the delivery truck arrives. All order data will be retained in the database system of the online store. These data are needed if there is a dispute or if the customer uses his rights to return the products, it will provide important background data for overall statistics. It can also be used to create a customer profile, as we discussed in part 3.

With high-level, B2B communication, the front-end company can be **all symbolic**, for example, handling customer contact only and relying on sub-contractors for all other operations.

The store's ERP system will at all times keep track of what is in stock. The system will be preset with different replenishment procedures for different products. For some items, the system may generate a replenishment order when stock levels go beyond a preset safety point, for others it may need confirmation before a reorder is sent or it may be instructed to remove the product from the website when there are no more items. The decision as to which procedure to use will depend on type of product, its popularity, availability, demand variation, time to replenish inventory, and so forth. The ERP system may use historical data to aid the procurer (purchaser) in determining a replenishment scheme and to set reorder points, and so forth, but this is not a closed process. Historical data may be an indicator for future demand, but new models, new technology, or a shift in trends may cause abrupt changes. There are no formalized methods to determine these events, and a human procurer has to use all his skill to predict future demand.

A replenishment order may, for example, be coded as an EDI transaction and transmitted to the supplier on a VAN network, as an XML-coded transaction on the Internet, or perhaps printed out and faxed to the manufacturer. While many online stores have impressive websites the technology behind the scene is not always as modern. Some suppliers still rely on manual systems, only a few may have implemented EDI and the promise of new standards is still just that. That is, the infrastructure of a fully automated value chain is still not in place for most firms.

The idea is to **capture** the data in a formalized form as soon as possible (i.e., directly from the customer), then utilizing these data through the whole value chain.

However, let us assume that suppliers have XML/EDI, and that the replenishment order is sent automatically at the moment the numbers in stock fall below the replenishment point (reorder level). We will now have a similar situation to the one above, but now the customer is the online store. The routines of payment, pricing, etc., will be different in this case, probably regulated by agreements set up in advance. These agreements will be a part of the ERP systems of both the store and the supplier, and will be used to determine discounts, forms of shipment, etc. Based on these agreements it is quite possible for both systems to handle all transactions automatically, without any intervention of human beings. However, for control purposes, many companies put a person in the loop, to verify the transactions.

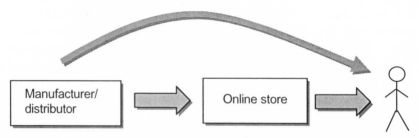

Figure 29.1. Product delivery to customer, through store or directly from supplier.

The supplier can fulfill the replenishment order by taking products out of stock and sending these to the online store, or by creating orders for having the products produced, similar to the situation we have just described for the online store.

Now we have the possibility of simplifying the value chain as shown in figure 29.1, letting the manufacturer or distributor send the product directly to the customer instead of through the online store. This has the advantage that we avoid a shipment (from the supplier to the store) and handling of products at the store.

In this case the online store will be nearly virtual, without any products, warehouses, etc. Its business model must therefore be to make money on its website and its customer base alone. This can be a valid model, if the store manages to maintain its customer base and does not give too much control to the suppliers. But, the model also has some logistical problems, especially for exceptions. The customer order may include products from different suppliers. Without a central warehouse or packaging center the order will then have to be sent as several packages to the customer. This may be inconvenient for the customer, especially when the package must be collected at a post office or a distribution center.

Returns will pose another problem in these cases, handling what we can call "inverse logistics." To where should the items be returned? This situation may be handled by offering the customer preprinted return labels, but requires that the customer keep the labels and that she connects the right label to the right product, not an easy task.

Information technology may be used to **streamline processes**, keeping stock levels to a minimum.

The need for keeping products in stock may be reduced by JIT (Just-In-Time) techniques, where the idea is to use the flexibility of modern manufacturing plants to avoid large production batches, reduce work-in-process inventories, and maintain direct ties to vendors that offer a "streaming" supply line. With smaller set-up costs, it is possible to reduce lot sizes to a minimum, perhaps making it possible to produce on demand. The book that we order from the online store could be printed and bound based on our order, making it unnecessary to print large editions or to keep volumes in stock and avoiding the need for bargain sales to get rid of large inventories. For many products, however, the economics of scale are valid. While produce-to-order may be an excellent production philosophy for some products it is not accepted for others. In most cases ordinary consumers, at the end of the value chain, expect to get what they buy immediately.

Henry Ford's "any color as long as it is black" worked at a time when consumers bought their very first car. Today, we emphasize diversity, and are open to new features, designs, and products. Most of us have satisfied the need for transportation and look for more when we buy a new car. Since people come in all types and shapes, it is difficult to fulfill the needs of customers with one product, or even a range of products. The answer is *customization* where the individual customer can specify what he wants. While some engineer-to-order manufacturers may allow the customer a high degree of control, for example, to determine the capacity and design of pump, a crane, or a ship, others offer the customer the choice between predetermined variants. This is the production model for many car manufacturers, where customers can specify color, engine type, size, air conditioning and hi-fi system, configuration of seats, etc.

With modularization of products or efficient manufacturing processes it becomes possible to produce or assemble based on **specifications** from the customer. With IT technology, these individualized products can be produced as effective as serial products.

This *assemble-to-order* production philosophy is ideal for PC manufacturers. Here the actual assembly process may be performed in a short time, since it is based on high-level components such as boards and devices that may be inserted in a rack, and the time of delivery can be kept within an acceptable range. Instead of just placing an order for a premade configuration the website gives the user the option of customizing her own PC, for example, by specifying processor, the size and type of memory, accessories such as sound and video boards, operating system, application programs, etc. The store will have a manufacturing plant that assembles these PCs based on customer's specifications. The great advantage is that these components may be used to produce a large variety of products, in some cases the variety may be so large that the average number produced may be less than one for each possible product. For example, if there is a choice of five cabinets, five processors, ten memory configurations, five operating systems, ten displays, five keyboards, and twenty different software configurations we have a set of 1,250,000 possible configurations. Such a product range is often needed to accommodate the needs of demanding customers, and can only be implemented on the basis of an assemble-to-order philosophy.[1]

Customization has two parts. First we create a **virtual product** in collaboration with the customer, and then this product description is "copied" into a physical product.

The Web offers excellent support for customer specifications, whether the product is a PC, a car, or an insurance policy. We can view the specification process as a virtual assembly line,[2] where the idea is to create a virtual product (description). For a PC specification the virtual process will precede the physical, for others the virtual and physical assembly processes may to some extent go side by side. This will be the case when constructing a ship or a building. Here the detailed design and specification process can be performed at the same time as the physical processes, of course, with the specification process ahead of the physical.

In many cases the virtual parts are becoming more important than the physical. The creativity, complexity, and greatest rewards are in the virtual process. In many cases we may view the physical process as copying, from the virtual original to the physical "copy." While the Web can support the specification phase of customization, this production philosophy may require very flexible production and logistics systems. It will also be product dependent. While a computer manufacturer can insert almost any board in a rack, a printer company may delay putting a power supply in a printer until the destination is known, and a manufacturer of paint may postpone putting in the dye to the last possible moment (often in the shop) these methods cannot as easily be used where variations are more deeply integrated in a product. An air-conditioning unit in a car, for example, cannot easily be offered as an add-on item, but has to be integrated in the car through the production phase. Car manufacturers handle these cases by using advanced logistics systems that control production according to customer specifications. That is, cars are often not produced before the order is in. The production facilities and suppliers are then controlled directly by the order sequence. While this may be known days in advance, exceptions may occur. In some cases both inside and outside suppliers have to be able to deliver components with a lead time of a few hours.

An alternative is to accommodate customers' need for personification of products by offering superficial variation (i.e., hiding a standard product in "packaging" with high variation). The snap-on "individualized" covers for cell phones are a typical example. However, while it is easy to get a cell phone in the color we want, we may have more problems finding a telephone that allows customized functionality, for example, a telephone with large keys, higher speaker volume, and simple functions for the elderly. That is, we are offered the McDonald's variant of customization (meal number, type of drink, sizes) instead of the more expensive restaurant model that allows for more custom control.

When the computer systems are in place the possibilities of handling customized orders as efficiently as mass production becomes a reality for many industries. The customer's click on the submit button may then create an all-automated chain reaction through a large value chain, where each system uses the data for its own purpose, accepting messages at one end and creating new messages at the other.

The requirement is that all processes and all data are formalized. Then the complete value chain can be controlled automatically without the intervention of humans. With flexible, computer-controlled machinery, we may even set up the machines and control the production part based on the data that originally was sent by the customer.

Exercises and Discussion

1. For each of the examples given below, draw a diagram of the value chain. In addition to the customer include the parts of the chains indicated in each example (e.g., online store, warehouse, packaging facilities). Payment in all cases is by credit card. Based on the diagram discuss how data is transmitted in the system and indicate, in the diagram, examples of data that are transmitted between the parts of the chain.

    a. An online music store that offers digitalized music. Customer select albums or tracks from an extensive online archive, pay-per-track using their credit card and are then allowed to download the music.

    b. An online music store that sells CDs. CDs are stored in an automatic warehouse. Items are picked by robots and are packed by an automatic facility. Whenever the number of items goes below 50 a replenishment order is sent to a central production facility.

    c. An online sports store. Through the website the store offers a wide range of sport products. The store is completely virtual—it does not have any physical facilities. Instead they have agreements with a number of manufacturers. When a customer order is received each manufacturer involved will get his part of the order.

The manufacturer will then mail the products directly to the customer.

2. For each of the examples above discuss the possibilities of formalizing all processes (i.e., the possibility of automating the whole value chain).

3. For each of the examples above discuss how out-of-stock and return situations can be handled. Is it possible to formalize these events (i.e., to handle these automatically)?

Notes

1. It is interesting to note that many PC manufacturers do not utilize fully the advantages of customer specifications. Since both my office and home computer run the next-to-last version of the operating system, I want this also on my new laptop. However, only one manufacturer out of the five I considered offered me this choice. Yes, I may be in a minority group, but the sum of all minorities over all options may be quite a large group.

2. These ideas are discussed in more detail in Olsen, K.A. & Sætre, P. 1998. Describing products as programs, *International Journal of Production Economics,* vol. 56, no 1.

30 Electronic Marketplaces

Instead of taking the products to the marketplace, we offer the symbolic **descriptions** of the products. In this virtual setting it becomes possible to inverse the process, letting the customers specify their needs as well as letting the producers specify what they have for sale.

In their simplest form, electronic marketplaces may be based on the same technology as retail shopping, database access through an HTML-based interface, using forms to provide input data. These marketplaces may be "sell-side" organized by groups of vendors, "buy-side" where a number of purchasers go together to define joint requests for quotes or it can be organized as an automated brokerage service that tries to match buyers and sellers on common ground. The advantage of using the Web is as for other forms of electronic shopping, global access, larger markets, and simplified transactions.

In these early stages of Internet and Web technology many firms have used electronic marketplaces with great success for the procurement of non-production goods (i.e., material needed to keep the administrative parts going, such as office equipment, supplies and computers). While having an unimportant percentage of accounts payable, these items may take up a large part of the total transaction volume. Often the cost of handling an order will be higher than the cost of the products. The savings by automatic procurement in this area may therefore be high, at the same time as we are talking about simple products that are easy to specify. Through the Intranet an employee may request the articles needed by browsing through catalogs from the firm's approved list of vendors, adding items to her shopping cart. This request can then be forwarded to her boss for approval, and is then handled automatically by the procurement system. When the employee receives the goods she will be asked to verify quantity and quality. With verification, of course given online, the system can automatically transfer the right amount to the vendor, based on predetermined contracts. No invoices or manual handling are necessary. Since all transactions are electronic, this automatic system may in many ways give a more comprehensive view of all costs than a manual system. Since most transactions go automatically the procurement department can use their resources on a higher level, to search for vendors, negotiate contracts, and handle exceptions.

This model can, of course, be used also for production-related goods. By establishing company-wide portals one achieves a centralization of the buying power that can be used to leverage the purchase process, to lower prices, to automate transactions, and to get faster cycle times. Companies within

The Internet and Web are ideal for implementing these virtual, all-symbolic **marketplaces**, organized as sell-side, buy-side, close partnerships, or as auctions.

the same field may establish common portals to create greater buying force, but at the same time having to acknowledge that procurement will no longer be an area of competition, at least for the goods covered by the portal. Similarly, sellers may present themselves through a common portal, to offer a larger variety of materials and, perhaps also, to reduce internal competition.

Online auctions have the advantage that sellers and buyers do not have to be physically present at the same time or in the same location. These are in many ways an ideal application for the Web, utilizing the inexpensive ways to describe items and global access in a system that can organize the bidding process automatically. On a sell-side auction, the vendor gives a description of what he has and buyers will then bid for the products in a forward auction, where prices move upward. In a reverse auction, a buyer will specify his needs, and sellers will bid to fulfill these needs, with prices moving downward. Each auction goes until a preset deadline.

In practice, the sell- and buy-side partnerships could not have been established on a broad basis without modern communication technology. While input via forms works for retail shopping or auctions it is not practical for general B2B transactions. The next step for these marketplaces is therefore to accommodate business-to-business transactions, making it possible to perform procurement processes automatically.

We shall use a bike manufacturer as an example. This manufacturer sells bikes via the Internet. His business idea is to allow customers to "design" their own bike, based on the principles that we explored in the previous chapter. This is achieved by an advanced generic (general) product structure that describes all the possible variants of a bike. On the Web interface the customer will be led through the design process, getting a choice of components and add-ons for each part of the bike. When the process is completed the manufacturer will have a description of the virtual bike with all its components. A due date for delivery can be promised based on the availability of these articles, but let us assume for simplicity that the manufacturer guarantees a one-month deadline for all bikes.

The job of the MPC (Manufacturing Planning and Control) or ERP system will now be to get these items within the deadline, taking into account the time needed for assembly and transport to the customer. Some components may be in stock; if not they must be produced in-house or ordered from a supplier.

To be efficient, electronic marketplaces will demand a high degree of **formalization**, both in the communication between organizations and within organizations.

In-house production will require the need for complete production plans, and will trigger a need for lower-level components, perhaps in several layers. With the necessary data, the MPC system may perform these tasks automatically. The materials will be ordered from individual suppliers based on predefined procurement contracts that specify delivery times and prices, while others may be obtained on the open market. In the latter case, it is possible to let the manufacturer's computer send out a request for quotes, or to perform the bidding in an auction-based market. Bids, purchase orders, and other data may be transmitted as XML documents, using a standard vocabulary so that the computers at the other end can understand the data on a semantic level. The supplier's computer can now perform an identical process, setting up in-house production orders and generating orders to its suppliers.

Ideally, we can see a streamlined value chain from the customer down to the producers of raw materials, where all communication is electronic. In practice, it will take time to get the necessary infrastructure, the computer systems, and the standards needed in place. But the firms that succeed will have a clear advantage over the others. Not only can they allow the customer to specify her individual variant and not only will they have great savings by automatic electronic transactions, but they will be able to utilize data updated to the last moment. When the customer hits the submit button her order can be known through the whole system. The whole value chain can base forecasts on data updated to the last second. The standards and connectivity offered by the Internet and Web technologies may have a tremendous impact in this area. But it requires a high degree of formalization. The standards must be in place before the different computer systems can understand each other, as we have seen not only the underlying communication protocols, but also the syntax (e.g., XML) and the semantics (vocabularies and more).

Formalization offers a more streamlined world. However, as we have seen something may be lost when we try to mold an open world into a closed system. This problem can be reduced by having two systems, a formalized and automatic system for routine transactions and a manual system for exceptions. The efficiency of such a system will then be determined by the part of the transactions that can be set up automatically and by how easy it is to perform the manual tasks. In a B2B environment one would expect that a larger part of all transactions would be

We formalize to **automate**, but at the same time we reduce flexibility in the handling of exceptions. These often have to be taken care of by manual channels, but for reasons of efficiency we would like to use these as infrequently as possible.

formalized than in more consumer-oriented applications. In B2B it may be possible to formalize even the exceptions, for example, setting up formal procedures for quality control and for returns of products that do not conform to these requirements. In a B2C setting, the only practical solution may be to let quality be determined by the consumer (e.g., by a liberal return policy).

There may also be limitations as to what is possible to formalize. Auctions or price negations are like a game of poker. Information may be incomplete, it may be interpreted in different ways and psychology is an important part of the decision process. While formalized methods have a part, the non-determinism of human nature plays an important role. In fact, one may argue that negotiations of this kind and bidding can only be performed in an open world. Even if it is possible to implement some unpredictability in an automatic bidding system, it seems that the more natural direction for an automatic system will be to use all the available information to calculate rather than negotiate a price, or to use this information to support a human negotiator.

The formalization itself will have a deep impact on how we do business. In a more open world competition may be based on special products and features, add-on services, high quality, low prices, reliable deliveries, good service and customer support, personal relations, etc. A formalized world will allow for fewer competitive parameters. For example, if the bike manufacturer's computer requests a quote for one hundred battery-powered bike headlights, a formalized handling of the quotes may be as simple as accepting the lowest bid. In the real world, however, functionality, technical solutions, and quality play an important part in addition to personal connections and, not least, trust. Of course, some of these attributes may be incorporated in the request for quotes and in the quotes, but this makes automatic procurement so much more complicated. For example, how is quality expressed in formalized terms and how do we define a formalized function to balance functionality and price? How do we determine trust, and can we ascertain a cost for the possibility of a delayed order? As we have discussed earlier for B2C applications, we may not get the best price from the nearby garage, but we know that he will be willing to help us out the day the car breaks down. Similar considerations apply to B2B worlds.

Are we willing to formalize and automate all parts of a business process, or do we also require **informal** knowledge, experience and intuition (i.e., manual handling as a part of the processes)?

We conquer the world by using **both** manual and automatic processes, using the human being in the more open parts (e.g., negotiation), the automatic processing on the closed parts (e.g., transaction processing).

We may get the benefits of both open and closed systems by defining the computer as an assistant to the human being. In this scenario the human procurer will negotiate the contracts with the suppliers, do the bidding, or select the best offers, while the computer takes care of the "paperwork," doing the secretarial work automatically. This may imply creating and transmitting purchase orders based on the predefined contracts, or sending out requests for quotes based on the specifications set up by the procurer. In the latter case, the computer will receive and present the quotes, allowing the human operator to make the decisions. This provides a balance between flexibility and automation, a possibility of taking advantage of both the open and closed world.

Within limited domains it may be possible to achieve full automation in a painless manner. This may be in domains where there exist rigid standards, or for example where products may be described completely by specifications. Some raw materials and simpler products fall in this category. However, even then there may be distinctions between products, eighty gram, white, A4, laser printer paper does not tell the whole story, but we may choose to ignore the differences to get the efficiency of an all-automated procurement process.

> For many applications the computer should be viewed as an **assistant**, where the human makes the decisions and the computer takes care of the "paperwork."

Exercises and Discussion

1. When accepting an offer we may go for the lowest price. However, in most cases it is important that we can establish trust. We will need to know if the supplier can deliver on time, and that all products are delivered according to specifications. In a manual world trust is often established on a personal level. This becomes difficult to maintain in a virtual world. Discuss the possibilities of how we can establish trust here, that is, if it is possible to formalize trust.

2. Using manual methods a procurer usually sends an RFQ (request for quote) to his two major suppliers, to get information on availability and price for a component. In order to increase competition our procurer now decides to submit the RFQ to a global virtual marketplace. Discuss what kind of formalizations that are needed to make this possible.

31 Outsourcing

B2B applications make it easier to **specialize**, to fulfill the demands of a more complicated business environment, where each part only covers a very narrow area. The whole, a large organization or a project, can then be created out of these specialized parts, from groups, departments, or individual companies, using B2B techniques.

The emerging companies in the early part of the twentieth century had to do everything themselves. The car manufacturers had rubber plantations, produced tires, and owned the ships that transported goods and materials. While this was a necessity due to the lack of a working business infrastructure and to reduce uncertainty, it was also a way of making another buck, implementing their business model in the whole value chain. Today, the need for more specialization makes it difficult to master all activities along the value chain. Businesses try to concentrate on core functions, outsourcing everything else to suppliers and service providers. The man at the door may no longer be a company employee, but is hired from a security company that can offer the necessary training, keeping updated with laws and regulations, and so forth. The call center functions can be outsourced, perhaps to quite another part of the world where one can draw benefits from low wages. A business no longer needs to run its own computers or software, but may let an ASP (Application Service Provider[1]) handle these functions. Shipyards in the industrial countries may concentrate on design, planning, and perhaps refitting of ships, leaving the more simple welding part to underdeveloped countries where wages are lower. Similarly, software companies may have programming groups in India. Manufacturers, of everything from computers to bikes, may leave the actual production of parts to others, concentrating on core functions such as design, marketing, sales, and assembly.

Outsourcing requires that the services can be formalized (e.g., as a **contract**). The advantage is that specialists can perform the services; the disadvantage that more open functions may no longer be fulfilled.

Fundamental to the possibility of outsourcing is the way the process can be described in a formalized way. This may be easy when setting up a contract with the security company. We want them to have a guard at the door at all times during office hours. The call center functions may be as simple as to take telephone orders and enter these in the computer system. Manufacturing of parts that are clearly specified may be moved from an in-house facility to an outside supplier. However, even with such simple functions there may be informal parts that may be lost when a process is outsourced. The firm's own doormen were able to provide directions, they knew employees and major customers by name and face, and could let them in without having to ask for a pass, they could say if someone was in or not, they were an extra resource that could be used in special events, etc. While many of these functions can only be performed by personnel that know the company well and not by an outside agency, we could try to incorporate some of these functions in the outsourcing contract. However, we may run into the same problems that we have discussed earlier, the complexity of foreseeing every possible situation.

We find a similar situation in the call center. When giving the next order, customers may comment on the service given on previous orders thereby providing valuable information that may be lost if the collection of this additional information is not a part of the contract. Even outsourcing part manufacturing may cause problems. When this was performed in-house we had opportunities to modify plans and handling emergencies than what a contract to an outside supplier usually will allow.

Trust is also an important factor in outsourcing. A firm may find it cost effective to outsource the operation of servers and databases to an ASP. But this is like choosing a bank. The firm must rely on the ASP to offer the necessary service level and keep all the company data secure, just as they must trust the bank to guard their money. But while banks are working under strong regulations and guaranties offered by the government, there is no such thing for the ASP. The ASP may not be able to maintain the service level, may fail to protect the data or may go belly up. Either way, our firm may be in a critical situation.

Some of these outsourcing activities are only possible with electronic communication, while others are facilitated by better communication. The outsourcing of call-center functions or computer operations cannot be done without computer networks. Manufacturers rely on these networks to have efficient communication with suppliers, for sending purchase orders, specifications, drawings, etc. The faster and cheaper we can perform these transactions the easier it may be to outsource activities. Some predict that Internet and Web technologies may lay the fundament for completely new business models. We shall return to this discussion in part 5.

With **global access** to information more and more processes and services can be performed in any location, by any type of organization.

Not all functions are good candidates for outsourcing. Core competencies should be kept in-house. If we lose track of these parts, we also lose track of the business. Core competencies should be the value that we add to the chain, it being management, marketing, a patented design, or production techniques. In these dot-com days we see that hired project teams create Internet banks and online stores. While this may be an efficient way of using resources too much control may be given to outside consultants. If we are in the banking business we should get involved in the design of the user interface and the functionality that the Internet bank is to provide. This will be similar to a brick and mortar bank or store manager, who will clearly have ideas on store layout and levels of service.

Exercises and Discussion

1. A company plan to close down its in-house information system department and to outsource all IT functions, from operating computer systems to defining overall information systems strategies. The idea is to save money and the argument is that an outside supplier may do the job as well as the in-house department. Discuss this situation with regard to:

   a) The company being an airline.

   b) The company being a local supermarket.

Notes

1. Not to be confused with Active Server Pages, Microsoft's technology for implementing dynamic Web pages, which we covered in chapter 15.

PART 5

Interfacing with the Web of the Future

The predecessor to Internet, the Arpanet, was demonstrated as early as in 1968. TCP/IP came a few years later. In its more than thirty years' history the Internet has passed its years of infancy and become a mature technology. We have had HTTP and HTML for nearly half of this time, long enough to see that some of the first enthusiastic visions have been dampened. In this part, we shall try to take a look into the future. We shall base this effort on our basic understanding of the technology, knowing that there are clear limitations as well as interesting possibilities.

The killer **application** may be found more easily in what we have, than in what we will get. The future is here, today!

Many of the most interesting applications for these technologies are here already. In this category we find email and online symbolic services. As with other technologies diffusion takes time, even where the advantages are very clear. We can call this horizontal dissemination; the same services get more users. While not very interesting from a technological viewpoint, this dissemination of technology may have an impact on both businesses and society. It makes a great difference when 90 percent of the population uses a service rather than 10 percent.

Prophecies of vertical dissemination, toward new services, require more creativity. Here we shall try to avoid falling in the "if we get more" trap (i.e., to present killer applications that are based on more computing power, more bandwidth, or new computer technologies). While we can expect Moore's law to continue being applicable at least for the near future, we already have more than enough computing power for most applications. As we have seen earlier in this book, the acceptance of new applications has a social side as well as a technological, and we shall concentrate on the social side in our futuristic discussions.

We start this part by introducing the concept of a disruptive technology in chapter 32. We call a technology disruptive when it removes the foundations from industries based on existing technologies. An interesting question here is whether the Internet and the Web are disruptive. With the Internet and the Web it becomes easier to establish what we call virtual businesses (i.e., businesses that may exist without their own offices or plants). In chapter 33 we discuss the possibilities and the limitations.

While HTML formalizes on a layout level, XML and newer standards offer the possibility of higher formalization levels. This is the topic for chapter 34, where we discuss the possibility of establishing a semantic Web (i.e., where data are organized as meaningful items, not just as formatted characters).

32 A Disruptive Technology?

Disruptive technology is characterized by:

1. Smaller, lighter, more flexible, simpler....
2. Initially less capacity.
3. Cheaper per unit, but often not with regard to capacity.

(1) opens the way for new markets. (2) and (3) make it difficult for the incumbents to use the technology—it is not suitable for their customer base, nor their cost structure.

The Internet and the Web have been called *disruptive* technologies, the term Clayton Christensen uses for a technological innovation that changes the rules of the marketplace. In his book *The Innovator's Dilemma*,[1] Professor Christensen uses the disk drive industry as his main example, showing how firms that based their products on new technology (smaller drives) drove the well-established competitors out of business. The problem for the incumbents was that the new technology did not serve their markets, which demanded high storage capacity at a low price per byte. They used, and had to use, their expertise to improve the technology that was needed by their customer base. However, with the new smaller disks the startups were able to capture specialized markets where the small size of their units was an advantage, the PC market and later on, with even smaller units, the market for portable computers. In the next phase, improvement of the new technology made it possible to compete with the lower end of the high-capacity market, and later on, to dominate the whole market.

Christensen finds the same trend in the excavator industry, where the established technology was cable-actuated machines. Just after the war, a different technology based on hydraulics emerged, for example, backhoes that could be mounted on a tractor. These low-capacity devices with limited reach were no real competition to the cable-actuated market, mining, and general excavation. Instead, the firms with this new technology had to find new markets, concentrating on farmers, residential contractors, and other areas where digging was performed by hand. However, as with the disk drive industry, gradual improvements of the new technology soon made it possible to go into the lower end of the mainstream market for traditional technology, in the end putting existing companies out of business.

In many cases the incumbents had the same knowledge of the new technology as the startups. But they had a customer base and markets that initially could not have been served by the new technology. As important, these firms had developed an organizational structure that matched these markets. The fate of Digital Equipment provides an excellent example. Digital used new technological advances to develop a minicomputer in the sixties, a smaller, more robust, and less expensive machine than the existing mainframes. At first new markets had to be created for these less powerful computers, but with gradual improvement of the technology minicomputers started to take market share from the mainframe manufacturers. When the next disruptive technology wave arrived in the mid-seventies, with Very Large Scale Integration (VLSI) and the microprocessor, Digital tried to compete in this new market for personal computers. However, selling PCs with a price tag of a few thousand dollars is very different from selling minicomputers for some hundred thousand. Such a disruptive change of products and markets affected the whole organization, product development, marketing, technical support, and training. Digital would probably have been much better off creating a new firm for the PC line of products, instead of trying to sell such a cheap and simple product through an "expensive" organization. As Professor Christensen shows, very few organizations have managed to survive these technological breakthroughs. Digital did not; a few years ago it was bought by Compaq, one of the new PC startups.

The Internet and the Web are clearly disruptive technologies for some firms. For many years the encyclopedia business was an interesting and profitable market for publishing houses, especially so for the Encyclopædia Britannica that has been in business since 1768. These collections of articles, mostly written by professionals, were offered in multiple-volume collections, arranged alphabetically with cross references between articles. While paper has disadvantages as a storage medium, especially with updates, many encyclopedias tried to compensate by using all the advantages of this medium, high-quality paper, illustrations and pictures, leather-bound volumes that looked impressive in any bookshelf. However, with home computers, CD-ROM and later on the Web it became impossible to keep to paper only, as the computer had so many advantages with regard to multimedia, searching, hypertext cross references, updates, and storage capacity. The result was major changes in the encyclopedia market. First the CD-ROM created a market for simple encyclopedias that offered superficial articles on just a few issues, but which explored the multimedia capabilities of the new technology—hypertext, video, sound, and animations. Then the Web, with its nearly unlimited information sources, undermined other parts of the market for the more in-depth encyclopedias.[2] And if we want a more traditional organization, the Web-based Wikipedia project, mentioned earlier, offers a free multi-language encyclopedia with more than 30,000 articles.

In retrospect, it is interesting to note that many of the advantages of the Web over paper media for encyclopedias should also be valid for newspapers. But, as we have seen in chapter 21.1, the Web has still not offered any serious competition to the paper versions of newspapers. The difference may perhaps be that the full encyclopedia in many ways was an illusion. Few private homes were really in need of in-depth articles over such a range of topics, and many encyclopedias with their gold letters and leather cover were perhaps more a part of the furniture than an active information source. When the Web seemed to take over the more formalized aspects such as that of providing information, it became impossible to maintain high sale volumes on the "furniture" aspects. While the large set of volumes earlier could give an image of an academic or at least an information-seeking individual, today they may present the image of someone that is out of touch with modern technology.

The Internet and Web technologies will be "most disruptive" in the **formalized all-symbolic area**, where full services may be performed over the Web (e.g., booking, banking) or when products may be delivered in symbolic form (e.g., software, books, music).

Of course, an Encyclopedia offers a guarantee for quality that you cannot get from open searches on the Web. However, the need for information that may arise in a private home covers a very large range of topics, and will often be very informal in nature. The Web is the ideal source for serving this information need. It offers updated information, information over an extremely broad range of topics, but also in-depth information. For example, if you are considering Egypt for your next vacation, the Web can offer data on history, places to see, prices, hotels, accommodation, flights, etc., down to letting us perform the actual booking. Hyperlinks are clearly advantageous for this type of informal browsing, and the disadvantages of having to start up the computer, find the sites, and read from a screen are not very apparent for these ad hoc information needs. Thus the Web offers more advantages and less disadvantages for the encyclopedia type of information needs than, for example, for the daily newspaper.

Are the Internet and the Web **disruptive** technologies? In many areas they offer simpler, more flexible, and cheaper services, but the "capacity" or possibilities are not very far from existing channels. That is, the Internet and Web services are often an add-on option to the more traditional services.

With encyclopedias and a few other exceptions the Web has not had the effect of a disruptive technology. The limitations posed by the Internet and the Web, which we have explored in the previous parts of this book, are certainly one reason. But a major difference between the Web and disk drives or backhoes is that the incumbents are not locked into a specific technology. The Internet and the Web are available for all, and may be used in addition to other channels. Brick and mortar banks, travel agencies, stores, and others may use the Internet and the Web as alternative channels. It does not matter if just a small part of their customer base is attracted to the new medium, as long as this can be offered as an alternative. As we have seen, there may also be clear advantages in giving the customer a choice of which channel to use in each case. Then simple transactions can be performed online and the more complex by using the telephone or visiting the brick and mortar agency in person.

The incumbents may also have a brand name that can be used to promote the website and an Internet address can be included in their advertising at no cost. Companies that distribute physical goods can base the Web sales on an existing system for procurement, warehousing, and distribution. If it becomes difficult to make money on the online part these stores have greater freedom in adjusting the online offers, for example, using the site to market their whole range of products but limiting online sales to products that are simple to pack and send. In a time when many "dot-coms" have filed for bankruptcy, a well-known chain of brick and mortar stores will express security and solidity, also online.

Even when there are few technological limitations for firms that want to establish alternative market channels on the Web, some may find that their existing channels do not accept such competition. When other PC manufacturers tried to imitate Dell's success in selling computers via the Internet, offering the customer the possibility of specifying her individual PC, they were faced with serious opposition from their dealers, finding it difficult to maintain both channels. However, the technology is still no more disruptive than that these firms face a choice, or that they have to find some sort of compromise to handle channel conflict.

The technologies themselves are **open to all**. With modern tools it may be quite a simple task of setting up a Web channel for an existing business, especially if the IT infrastructure is in place.

For some technologies, being the first one out gives an important advantage—they own the land, the resources, the plants, the know-how, or the technology and it may take years for anyone else to follow suit. This is not always the case for software development. There are no resource limitations; there are bits enough for everyone. The exception may be expert personnel, but these can be persuaded into changing jobs. In software development the pioneers have to make all the mistakes themselves, and have to take the risk of learning how to utilize a new medium. The software needed to run an Internet site is available to everyone, and while other industries try to keep their technology behind closed doors, on the Web the important part, the user interface, can be seen by all.

While many of the old companies may regret that they were late in applying new technology, it is, as we have seen, never too late to establish an alternative marketing and sales channel based on the Web. As with other new technologies the newcomers take all the risks, but where the manufacturers of new disk drives, computers, or backhoes are guaranteed success (at least until the next disruptive technology) when their technology takes off, the Web offers no such reward.

The exceptions are start-ups that have found niches that have emerged based on the Internet and the Web. Auction firms, such as eBay, are a good example. Their large customer base is good protection against competition on the Internet. It is not so easy for another start-up to get a similar base. But, as we have seen, sites such as Yahoo! and Amazon also offer auction services, and newspapers join in larger alliances to create websites, using existing classified ads as a base. Nobody has a monopoly on Internet technology, it is available to all.

Yahoo! is another example of an Internet niche, a portal that organizes and provides access to other websites. Yahoo! had the advantage of being one of the first portals and today the sheer number of sites that they have cataloged gives them a clear advantage, perhaps strong enough to keep the competition away a few more years.

New technologies may be disruptive for producers, but seldom for **users**.

If we return to Christensen and his examples within the disk drive and computer industries we see that these technologies were disruptive for the manufacturers, not for the users. Users moved from the mainframe, via the minicomputer to the PC without problems, replacing the machines as they became outdated, changing suppliers along the line without any major problems. To study disruptive effects of Internet and Web technology we should perhaps look more toward the production part, as the banks, travel agencies, and online stores will be mere users of the technology. But even here we do not find many disruptive effects. The Internet is not a new network; it is just a new protocol, the data is transported on existing networks. While the possibility of getting large revenues on voice traffic is diminishing as the monopoly effects of owing the network are reduced, the increased traffic and new technologies are an opportunity for telephone companies and other network owners. Customers may replace the traditional phone by a cell phone, or may use the Internet for their calls,[3] but an agile telephone company can cope with these changes. So even if there are many new competitors in the telecom area, we will not find any disruptive effects (i.e., if we keep close to Christensen's definition).

This does not imply that it is "business-as-usual." The Internet and the Web have, and will, transform many businesses. Travel agencies, bookstores, automobile salesmen, local shop owners, banks, and many others are having a tougher time due to the Internet and the Web. But, at the same time the new technologies are offering opportunities for these businesses. That is, we should distinguish between disruptive effects were there are none or few possibilities of survival, and hard competition that allows the most responsive to survive.

In the examples of disruptive effects above, we see that this was not just a matter of one technology or the other, but that the technology and the markets formed businesses. This allows for an efficient organization—until the day we have a major change. It has been said that the U.S. railway companies would have been better off today if they had a vision of being in the transportation business, rather than in the railway business. But can one company manage to run trains, buses, and aircraft efficiently, with each part competing with the others? Perhaps the only valid model is to form a company for each technology. But this is just what the modern capitalistic markets allow, that an investor may go into the transportation business, setting up different companies. However, each company needs a technological and market base to become efficient. A mainframe company cannot sell PCs.

Just as a company selling million-dollar computers may have a problem adjusting to selling thousand-dollar computers, a bank that has been making money on traditional banking services may have a hard time adjusting to a situation where most of the transactions are performed online, at very little cost and minimum revenue. But this is an ongoing process that runs over many years and that also includes other technologies than the Internet, such as credit cards, ATM machines, and electronic payment in stores. In the end banks may look quite different from today, we may see new banking constellations, but few banks will be locked in a dying technology. Already most banks offer online services as well as offline, assimilating the new technology into their organizations. We see a similar development in other areas as well.

While there are few exceptions of organizations forced out of business due to the Internet and the Web, these technologies are often "disruptive" for many of the services performed, often requiring painful **reengineering**.

Exercises and Discussion

1. For each of the technologies described below, discuss possible disruptive effects for the businesses indicated:

    a) Laser technology used in vision correction procedures, possible effects for sellers of eyeglasses and contact lenses.

    b) Digital cameras, possible effects for photo shops and laboratories.

    c) Digital music, possible effects for record companies and music stores.

    d) Email, possible effects for postal organizations.

    e) Ubiquitous broadband service for video and DVD rental.

2. Let us assume that most homes at some time in the future will have the necessary bandwidth to stream or download TV programs. What effects do you think that this will have on TV viewing? For example, will we see the eleven o'clock news at eleven, or at a time that we decide ourselves?

Notes

1. Christensen, C. M. 2000. *The Innovator's Dilemma*, HarperBusiness. See also Christensen, C.M. and Raynor, M.E. (2003) *The Innovator's Solution: Creating and Sustaining Successful Growth*, Harvard Business School Publishing Corporation.

2. Encyclopædia Britannica is still in business, offering CD-ROM or DVD versions for a reasonable price, and a much more expensive print set — along with a free Web service (see www.britannica.com). That is, offers for every wallet. Even then, they are struggling.

3. This is called voIP, voice over the Internet. It is available for anybody that has a broadband connection, and exists as a free service (open software) or as a subscription service. The first imply that both parties need to have installed the voIP software, and the PC (with a microphone and speakers) is used for the communication. The usability, quality, and reliability of this service is low, but it is free! In the latter version you are connected to the ordinary phone network. You need a special connector (modem), but can use an ordinary phone for dialing. The difference is that while the ordinary phone network is line switched (i.e., you get a line between yourself and the person you are calling), the IP solution sends the voice as packets over the Internet. Today, line switching offers more reliable and higher quality than packet switching. In practice, there is nothing that hinders the incumbent phone companies to offer packet switching. Therefore the competition from new IP-based phone companies cannot be called disruptive, but it will certainly offer heavy competition to the incumbents and reduce prices, especially for long distance and international calls.

33 Virtual Businesses

The whole, the collection of all the services that is to be performed, can be a **virtual company** (i.e., a company that only exists as a network of other companies). Such companies may be formed for a contract, a project, and may not have a life span of more than a few years.

New standards such as XML make it easier to create *virtual businesses*. These may for example take the form of several smaller companies establishing a permanent partnership in order to bid on larger contracts, an ad hoc creation for a special project or a limited partnership to coordinate procurement. With the standards in place the partners can have joint access to information, specifications, engineering drawings, inventories, product structures, reports, etc., as if they were one company. This access can be on a B2B or B2C basis. Email will also have an important role in facilitating communication between partners. Ventures like these are, of course, nothing new. Movies have been made on a similar basis for years, and large buildings are set up in close cooperation between many partners. However, there are reasons to believe that better communication and better access to common information may make these forms of partnerships more common.

There are also those who expect that these new technologies will have a profound effect on how we organize a firm. With simpler, automated ways of performing transactions, it becomes possible to organize companies around a free agent model. For example, if you ask your colleague Jane to help you out, your project may be billed for the ten minutes of her time. The technology may be used to create smaller work teams within bigger organizations, operating as firms within firms. While Napoleon and his generals controlled the battle from a position where they could get a full overview, modern communications offer the possibility of letting the soldiers work in smaller patrols with a high degree of autonomy—sharing a common goal and a common information infrastructure.

The **formalized parts** of a virtual organization may be handled using B2B services on top of modern communication technology.

The basis for such a utilization of communication technology is, as we have seen, that the processes, tasks, and responsibilities can be formalized to a high degree. This will be easier to achieve in some organizations than others. The clearer the goals, the more hierarchical the organization, the more quantitative data that are used the easier it will be to manage virtual companies or work teams within an organization. When the goals are unclear and not easily formalized, when organizations are flat and where data is qualitative, the traditional company model may be the better. If Jane's help is sold in minutes, it is quite easy to set up an automated billing process, but if she uses her experience and knowledge to help your project out of a difficult situation her value should perhaps be measured in other terms. Then a more traditional company model where everybody works toward a common goal will work better than an entity consisting of separate molecules, with formalized communication channels only.

The reputation of a company is, to a large extent based on its personnel. A virtual company will have the problem of being trusted. Are we willing to offer the contract to a company that was created with the sole purpose of serving this contract? We may if we trust the expertise of the individual partners, but if these consist of a very large group of very small businesses we may have a problem. The project organizer may be a trusted firm, but will this firm risk its reputation on a conglomerate of microfirms? What will happen if there are problems underway, will each partner only look at its contract, or will it be willing to put in the extra effort that is needed to achieve the overall or common goal? But these partners may not see a common goal. They have been hired to do just this small part of the project. Exceptions and problems that arise during a project may place a severe strain on a traditional company, but here the feeling of being in the same boat will be much stronger. Employees may be willing to put in an extra effort in order to save the reputation of the company or their jobs.

Can we accept to work for a **virtual organization**? The closed parts of our needs may be satisfied, but what about the open parts?

There is also the problem of recruiting the right people. Long-term benefits such as financial security, health insurance and educational opportunities that many workers have come to expect from their jobs may not easily be converted into monetary terms. In addition, a job provides social contacts and a professional identity that may be difficult to offer within virtual organizations. Some of the missing parts may be provided by professional organizations, such as the now historic guilds. Still the work hours are a large part of our life and most of us may want a more solid base than a virtual company (see the discussion in chapter 22.6).

As we can see, the effects of technology on organizations are not just a matter of how fast we can create, transmit, and handle transactions. While many firms have enjoyed positive effects from creating small autonomous workgroups in production, often a very formalized area, it may not be as easy to do the same within the less formalized part of the organization. In this symbolic world we also run into the additional problem that formalized processes can be automated by a computer, thus the remaining tasks may be the open ones that have to be handled by human beings. However, even if the individual tasks may be open it may be possible to draw a formalized boundary around a set of functions. This is what we do when we split a firm into departments. But this kind of formalization will have limitations, and may be very restrictive if we take it too far.

Exercises and Discussion

1. A group of investors have established a virtual university that has as its primary aim to provide educational services using the Web for offering distance education. This university will have no employees except from the university president and a few secretaries. All other services, administrative, teaching, or research will be contracted out to other parties. For example, as a teacher you may be contracted to offer a course, using the material that the university has bought, communicating with students using the email and Web systems set up by the university's IT contractor. Discuss this model. Will it work? Can you see any potential problems?

2. Let us assume that the model above will be used by many universities (i.e., that the virtual organizational model becomes the norm). Discuss this situation.

34 Semantic Web

Today we have:

- "Open" Web (mostly HTML)

- Formalized systems (Web only as an interface)

The **semantic** Web, the effort to create an open Web with higher formalization levels than what HTML and existing formats can provide.

Today, we operate either in the open, but low-formalized Web based on HTML or use the Web as an interface to formalized databases. The idea of a *semantic* Web is to formalize the open Web, letting us operate on a high formalization level also outside the proprietary databases.

An example may clarify the difference. When we are within an airline booking system we can use formalized terms such as date, flight, and destination. There will be no ambiguity. For example, "San Francisco" identifies an airport and not a monastery, US740 a flight and not a part number, and so forth. That is, we have all the advantages of being in a closed and formalized system. In opposition, when we operate on the open Web we have all the ambiguity of natural language to cope with. Here "US740" may have many meanings. This makes high-level operations on the data, such as searching, more difficult. A solution is to formalize the data also on the open Web. That is, instead of describing only the layout of Web pages (using HTML) we can try to describe also the structure and content of the data. With all data formalized to a high degree we have the foundations for a semantic Web, a place where the machines can "understand" the data. In this chapter we shall explore some of the advantages by such a system.

We started this book by introducing the concept of formalization, showing that the kind of processes that can be automated can be directly derived from the formalization level of the data. With XML and similar languages we have the means to describe these formalizations for data on the Web. Some of the higher-level standards are already in place through the work that has been performed for EDI. This may be the start toward a semantic Web, where data is described on a meaningful level, not only as fonts and characters.

The difficulty of establishing the standards that are needed has been explored in previous chapters, and we have seen that this will be a long and tedious task. However, let us assume that one day we will have these standards in place, that we have really attained a semantic and functional Web, with necessary bandwidth and robustness. Let us further assume that the Web transactions have a large part of the market, within the areas where they are competitive (symbolic products or B2B). Using this as a point of departure, we shall try to explore what kind of functionality we can achieve, returning to some of the examples that we have discussed earlier.

We shall first present a set of services, which may be offered through a semantic Web. Then we shall discuss the possibility of realizing these services, first from an optimistic view, at least from the point of the technocrats, then from a more critical standpoint.

34.1 Scenario: With a semantic Web

A semantic Web will open the way for high-level **automated services**.

With a semantic Web we will have agents that can help us with our daily activities. The agent is a computer program that has a complete profile on the customer. This may look like "big-brother" but may be implemented in a very simple way. When initiating the agent we will provide it with all necessary data, addresses, names, link to profiles of family members, credit card information, account numbers, identifiers, preferences, etc. This information will be protected by lock and key, through cryptography, passwords, key cards, etc. The agent may be a separate program, or a distributed set of functions, some of which may run on our personal computers, others which may be implemented by a service provider, everything from a bookstore to our bank.

Below we explore some of the functions that this agent *theoretically* can provide.

Utility contracts

Software **agents** can negotiate and "sign" contracts for products and services.

Based on data on usage of telephone, Internet connection, electricity, and gas the agent may be instructed to negotiate contracts with utility providers. This can be done by going to the semantic Web to retrieve price information, or by accessing a brokerage service to get a bid on these services. The agent can present the different bids to the customer to let her take the final decision, but may also be instructed to go for the best offer using quantitative data only in evaluating the offers. For utility services, where we may assume (hope?) that the service level may be similar between all participants, an automatic decision process may be a good alternative. When the contract has been negotiated the agent will automatically pay the suppliers based on contract prices and usage, and apply current and historical data to verify the accuracy of the bills. Since transactions go automatically at low cost, payment may be on per unit or per day basis, making it easier to change supplier or to incorporate changes in prices, etc.

Booking

If our requirements and the Web itself are formalized, the **software agent** can browse the Web, looking for bargains, for services, or products that we need.

Based on preferences the agent may be instructed to notify the customer of upcoming events, football games, movies, plays, etc. If the user shows an interest, the agent may suggest possible dates, based on the user's calendar and ticket availability. When confirming a choice the agent will book the tickets, pay for them, and offer the booking system the identification number of the user's personal radio transponder that will be used to let her through the gates at the event.

Booking for travel can be performed in a similar manner. The agent can browse the Web for good offers based on general preferences, or we can give it the specifics on our next holiday, dates, locations, participants, etc. To find suitable flights the agent will go into all airlines' (semantic) Web pages, finding schedules and prices and calculating the best offer. This calculation may include price minus rebates such as frequent flyer mileage, travel time (perhaps calculated as a cost), service level, probability of delays (based on airline statistics), cost of delays, and so forth. It may then show us the best alternatives, or just choose the best offer.

For locations and hotels the choice will include qualitative factors that can be mapped into dollars by a standardized "star" categorization. The agent will then provide the user with all the necessary information, organized and presented according to the required quality level and other preferences, many of which can be retrieved from a general profile (requirement for a non-smoking room, swimming pool, downtown location, etc.).

When traveling abroad the agent can verify that our passport is still valid (the information needed can be stored locally or fetched from a government site) and that our standard travel insurance covers the trip. If not, the agent will go to the Web to negotiate coverage for this journey.

Shopping

We will perform online shopping through the agent that will help us to collect product information. When we find what we need the agent will search the whole market for products that fulfill our specifications, find the best price, or perform bidding on our part, transferring the data needed, perform the financial transaction, and give us notification when the goods arrive.

The agent will organize all relevant information on the product, such as a user manual, service instructions, and warranties. It will also monitor news sites and the home page of the manufacturer, and retrieve relevant product information: updates, errors found, recalls, etc.

Shopping for services

Services can be presented in a formal way, as for other types of products. We may want to choose our hairdresser, dentist, and doctor ourselves, but the agent can at least provide us with a list of candidates—based on our preferences. In other cases, when we need an electrician or a simple service such as buying foreign currency, the agent can negotiate a deal, to a large part dependent on data already available.

Banking

While the **agent** can perform the simplest functions automatically, it can be used to gather background information on more complicated matters, supporting the user in making a decision.

The agent, running on our PC or as a part of the banking systems, will pay bills automatically based on the information that it has on contracts, shopping, etc., but will ask for confirmation before paying irregular bills. It can at any time provide us with a complete financial overview, and can—on our behalf—negotiate interest rates, and so forth. For most customers, banking will be an automatic background activity that needs very little supervision.

Health information

The agent can retrieve information of interest and perform all necessary archiving and linking operations, in many ways functioning as an automated and personalized **database administrator**.

The agent will protect all private information. It will keep track of all health records, and collect updates from hospitals and general practitioners. The agent will store information on all drugs that we take, and may offer extensive background data on any of these. It can notify us of side effects of combinations of drugs, or that we should take special care using drug X because of the high blood pressure, pregnancy, or any other condition that the agent can find in our health records. It may even be programmed to follow up on the doctor's recommendation, giving us a warning every time we buy cigarettes, liquor, or chocolate.

Persons and institutions that offer the right credentials can access our health register to get data. The doctors that treat us will therefore have all necessary information available, independently of when and where we have been treated.

Specific information

The agent will monitor a set of information channels, such as online newspapers, official sites, etc., for information that may be of specific interest for us. Based on its knowledge of where we live, where we work, commuting, what stocks we own, the institutions where we are customers, which schools our kids attend, our hobbies, our favorite actors and performers, etc., the agent will prepare a list with links to actual information. This may be everything from a change in local train schedules to news that our insurance company may have financial problems. Such a system may not exclude the need to read newspapers or watch broadcast news, but it can be used as a more direct source of finding specific information that should be of special interest.

Accounting

The agent will have access to all our financial data, and can at any time give us an overview. This can be a complete financial overview, a visualization of utility costs over many years, what kind of items we have bought, and detailed information on all of these. The agent can perform simple data mining tasks to find trends in the overall data collections, for example, communication patterns, who we contact by telephone and email, number of outgoing and incoming calls to each party, and so forth (preferably password-protected for each family member).

Job seeking

Based on the CV and our preferences the agent can monitor the job market, and notify us whenever an interesting position comes up. It may even do some initial negotiating with the computerized agent of the employer (e.g., salary, work location, requirements) to see if it is worth notifying the user.

Schedule

The agent will have all the information necessary to set up a complete schedule for each day and week. It knows that we have a club meeting every Friday at 6 p.m., and will automatically reschedule if a meeting is moved or cancelled. The agent can do this based on monitoring incoming, structured email, or better—by communicating with the (computerized) agent that is in charge of the club meetings.

At work

We will have agents for all of our **roles**, both at home and at work.

We will have a similar functionality at work, where agents will help and support us in performing our role in the company. Just as our role today can be that of managing a number of assistants, our future task may be to manage a set of agents that perform a transaction. Each agent will have a scope of responsibility. It may operate with autonomy within this scope, but must report its actions, perhaps in the form of summary reports. Outside the scope it should gather all relevant information on the problem at hand, present this information to the user, and affect the decision made by the user. It may be a learning system, so that it may take the decision itself the next time it encounters the same problem.

The agent will monitor the company's Intranet, notifying the user of all relevant information. However, more often it will communicate with the company agents. That is, the human employees may be protected from the underlying databases, email, and other information channels. Instead, this information will be provided to the agent that makes the decision if this is to be presented to the user, in what form. The agent may also include additional background data if this is needed.

34.2 The optimistic view

Formalizing services will be advantageous both for customers and companies. The latter will now get access to important data, not only on what customers do but also on what they want to do, their preferences, and future plans.

Services, such as described above, will clearly be advantageous to most of us. If an agent can perform the tasks as securely and as well as we can do it ourselves, most of us would welcome an automatic system that could spare us the hassle of performing these administrative tasks.

On the supplier side, the companies can use such a highly formalized system to sell available capacity in telephone networks, to fill planes, movie theaters, and hotels. The data gathered can immediately be applied in the whole value chain, to adjust capacity to demand, for planning and forecasting, etc. Predefined resource availability, for everything from concerts to flights, can be filled to capacity by dynamic pricing policies. With Internet connection to customer's agents the bidding can be performed quickly and efficiently.

Companies may use more than transactional data. The information in a customer's profiles may be even more helpful.

The **future** will bring a system with dynamic, not static, prices. A price for a product or service will be the meeting point between what you are willing to pay and what the provider is willing to accept. Prices may be determined by bargaining, as in auctions, or by dynamic functions, such as with airline tickets today.

When we update our profile telling the agent that we in the future will be most interested in first-class hotel accommodation, this can be used by providers as an "early warning" of customers' preferences. With accumulated profile data for many customers new trends can be spotted early and travel offers or packages may be created to accommodate these needs. Businesses can compete on price or, for example, try to accommodate a market segment that values service and regularity. These segments can be found based on preference data collected from customers' agents and from data on what the competition offers. The task will be simplified by the fact that all information is available on a semantic level.

In a stable environment we may then get an ideal balance of supply and demand, few empty seats on airplanes and few products in stock. Information will go to the people who need it. The boom and bust cycle of production and the economy will be replaced by a situation where access to updated and valuable information helps industries to produce the right products. If the market turns from product A to B, the signals may be captured so early that the industries will have a chance to alter their production plans. With shorter set-up times, assemble-to-order policies and just-in-time supplies these changes may be implemented fast and accurately.

With all underlying transactions in an electronic format, formalized to a high level, most of the higher-level functions can be formalized as well, such as accounting, statistics, and customer management. Since these functions can be performed automatically, they can be run continuously, offering updated data at all times.

The **semantic Web** will just be an extension of what we have today within the proprietary databases than can be reached through the Web.

There is no magic to these services. They are all clearly within the range of what we can achieve with the systems and standards that we have today. This is exemplified by the functionality of Web services offered (e.g., by banks and airline companies). The semantic Web is just taking these systems another step, where all data are organized at similar formalization levels. Many organizations already have these functions implemented, not on a global basis, but within the boundary of their own systems, using proprietary standards, data, and computer systems. The only thing that is needed is to let the formalization cross the boundaries of the institutions, to merge these into common standards and formats.

34.3 The more critical view

Formalization often implies that processes and data become more rigid, more **static**. To maintain the flexible and dynamic nature of our society, unformalized processes are required.

From a strictly technical viewpoint these formalized systems are attainable, but they may be a utopia if we use a more open view. Within organizations we will find that only parts of data and processes have been formalized, and, as we have seen, different organizations have applied different formalizations. We live in a highly dynamic society that does not adjust to fixed rules. Yesterday's data may be uninteresting tomorrow. There may be rules, regulations, and fixed processes, but exceptions are frequent. These "unformalized" parts have been recognized as an important side of our society. Laws and regulations, for example, are presented in a general manner, without being too specific. They can therefore be applied to situations that were not foreseen by the lawmakers, still retaining the original interpretation of the law. This would have been impossible with very specific and formalized laws. The whole system of judges, lawyers, and other "law interpreters" is a product of a dynamic and unformalized society.

While we in previous chapters have discussed the problems of *attaining* the necessary standards for achieving a semantic Web, let us here explore the difficulties of maintaining a formalized society. The communistic experiments through many years and in many different countries have clearly proved that central planning is not a viable solution. Clearly the distributed system of capitalistic countries, where the market is served by many independent firms, is more robust. But what will happen in this market if information is available to all? Not only information that needs to be interpreted, but exact data formalized to a high level. This will be the case when our agent goes to the market to buy tickets, set up utility contracts, insurance, etc. In such a system consumer needs are expressed in a formalized manner. There will be no place for personal service or qualitative factors, at least not if they cannot be formalized in a quantitative manner by the agents. The computer systems of the service providers will bid to fulfill these needs, as specified in the request for quotes (RFQ). When RFQs for all customers are in the same format we will have a situation identical to that of all customers going together to get a bid on their accumulated needs, that is, a global implementation of the idea of joining to obtain greater market power. But this will not be like the contract meetings that large manufacturers have with their suppliers, an open process performed through negotiations. This will be a formalized bidding process between computers that in the end may be based on price only.

In the short run this will give consumers lower prices, as agents go for the best contracts. In the long run, however, the service providers will have to adjust to this "centralized" market force, and there will be a danger that the needs of an accumulated market force can only be fulfilled by a few large suppliers, perhaps only one. The efficient but narrow formalized channel to consumers will limit the parameters for diversity. That is, a centralization of buying power may be mirrored in a centralization of providers.

We have previously used the airline industry as an example. Today, bargain airlines have to use heavy marketing to get into the market, to tell the customers that they are there and offer telephone numbers and Web addresses. Still, it will be a difficult task to have all customers consider their offers. If we get a semantic Web where available flights and needs are expressed formally, all price-sensitive agents will automatically choose the startup bargain airline. The major airlines will have to follow suit, and we will get a repetition of the situation we had when air transport was deregulated. This time, however, competition will be even more severe as all parties have access to all passengers and all the information. Companies may try to build consumer loyalty through frequent flyer and similar programs, but this will have little effect if the agents are able to convert these systems into a discount value. They may try to offer additional advantages, but these may go unnoticed if agents are not programmed to take these into account. In the long run we would expect that one or a few large companies or partnerships would come out as the winners, as these may compete with startups on an even basis on each flight, but have the additional advantage of providing connections to further destinations.

For industrial products a high formalization level will, as we have seen, simplify transactions in B2B environments. When needs are expressed formally, with completely unambiguous specifications, any supplier can bid on any RFQ. That is, if we can assume that the fulfillment of contracts is also performed in a formalized way, that we can guarantee delivery according to specifications at the right time. In such a system, since all transactions are performed automatically, no personal contact is required between buyer and seller. While this opens the way for an efficient procurement system, it requires that

---

Initially a formalized market, with a formalization of both consumers' needs and the availability of product and services, may lead to greater **competition**. However, greater competition within fewer dimensions, perhaps on price only, may result in buy-outs and mergers (i.e., to monopolies).

A more formalized market, where up-to-date information is available for all, makes it possible to perform meticulous **synchronization** of supply and demand. However, disturbances may then have large effects, as everybody tries to adjust to market changes simultaneously.

other parameters, such as trust and the guarantees for contract fulfillment are also formalized. This will be the case in a situation where there are only a few major suppliers, or where there is some form of supplier certificate that can be rewarded to firms that have good operating procedures and that can show a history of order fulfillment. However, as we have seen, a more likely scenario is close partnerships along the value chain, where transactions are formalized within the chain. Achieving a formalization on this level, where the different industries are committed to a partnership, is much easier than any form of a more global standardization.

When all needs are expressed in a formalized manner it becomes possible, as stated above, to balance supply and demand. This may be advantageous when customers' preferences go from model A to B, but what happens when demand for all models goes down? Customers may have been scared by signals of a slowing economy, a bear market, higher interest rates, etc. Without a semantic Web such changes in consumers' preferences may have gone unnoticed, production may have proceeded as usual and if the reduction in demand were temporary, nothing would have happened. In a formalized world the demand reduction will be recognized immediately, production would be reduced by laying off workers or by working shorter weeks. This will make the situation worse, reducing demand even further. We get a system with positive feedback, a spiral where consequences get more and more severe. We got an example of this situation in the stock market crisis of 1987, where the downturn of the stock market triggered computerized agents to sell, making a bad situation worse.

In many markets this is avoided by arbitrariness in the system, often sustained by the informal nature of data and decision processes. Products and services come in all forms, formalized and standardized specifications or prices are often not available. Customer needs may be poorly expressed and are often open for alteration or persuasion. Add the constraints within the physical world, such as the location of stores or the time spent to evaluate the market by manual methods, and the result will be an unformalized marketplace that works along many dimensions. This marketplace is both dynamic and flexible, niches may appear or disappear, and opportunities may come or go. Human brokers act on intuition, scraps of data, and personal contacts (i.e., on open information along with the more closed). Then there will often be a buyer to match every seller.

A formalization within companies or in alliances of companies will, in most markets, leave open parts and **niches**, opportunities for other businesses, preserving the dynamic and robust nature of the system.

Enterprises and individual businesses may formalize parts of the market, by streamlining value chains, products, and services. We see examples in chains of everything from banks, to fast food restaurants, coffee shops, supermarkets, and video rentals, with common business ideas, marketing, procurement, product and services. We see examples in alliances, mergers, and buy-outs when individual companies offer common interfaces to their information systems or install company-wide ERP systems. However, while these "formalizations" may force some of the competition out of business, due to the effects of larger market power and more efficient systems, they will also create new business opportunities, for example, filling out the bits and parts that are not covered by the more formalized organizations. The organizations that perform these niche functions are the oil that keeps the (capitalistic) machinery running. They are always there to ensure the dynamics of the system, looking for any opportunity to open new markets, to increase their market share. The opportunity may come as change of consumers' preferences, by deregulation (such as in the telecommunication industry) or regulation (new environmental laws), by the failure of other companies or from new technology and new processes. That is, the open parts, the unformalized parts, offer the diversity that is needed to ensure the robustness of the whole system.

We may use an analogy to a situation from the animal world. When egg-laying grouse in the Norwegian mountains are hit by a summer snowstorm the hens react very differently. Some stay in the nest independently of the duration of the storm, while others leave after a short time. If the storm is short the patient mother will have saved her eggs, but if the bad weather prevails she will have exhausted all her resources and will not survive. However, in this case the not-so-good mother has survived, and may get another chance of raising new generations, perhaps in the same season. That is, diversity provides robustness.

However, it may be unnecessary to argue for the dangers of a completely formalized market. Most companies will not have it! If we return to the airline industry, we see that the companies use the same technology, even down to identical aircraft, and operate under the same rules and regulations. Today, the competition is based on the network of flights that they provide and on sales and marketing. With a standard for flight booking they may try to accommodate different market segments, or be stung

Many businesses will try to avoid a semantic Web as they may **lose control** over data, and because competition may be too great.

in fierce price competition where consumer's agents always select the lowest fare, at least when the itineraries are comparable. It will be like two gas stations next to each other on the same side of the road, with only price as a way of attracting customers.

Today most businesses try every trick to avoid direct price competition. Car insurance has a price, but also offers such different coverage rules that they are difficult to compare. In a formalized world the agents will require similar rules or a means of converting coverage into price, so that the best offer can be selected in an automated manner. The advantage of providing this information for the insurance companies will be that they can now bid on the RFQs from the agents automatically; the disadvantage is that they miss an opportunity for diversity. If today's policies are any indication of what will happen in the future, we should see companies use any means to avoid direct price competition. This may be as easy as keeping full control of their own databases, with products, specifications, prices, etc., only offering access through proprietary systems, such as most companies have chosen to do today, at least for the formalized parts of the data.

The acceptance of **low-level standards** will be beneficial to most organizations. Higher-level standards, however, may be viewed as a threat.

"Store once, use many times" may be a goal for most industries, that is, to enter data in a format so that it can be used by many applications, for many purposes. This is difficult enough to achieve within one company, but may be impossible on a global basis. Again we have to return to the ambiguousness of natural language. If an agent is to have any hope of finding information that is of interest, based on profile data, both the information and the profile must have a high formalization level. If not, the agent will operate with lower precision and recall levels, returning uninteresting information and missing items of interest. To achieve a higher formalization level the information producers must agree on common vocabularies, and so forth. This is, as we have seen, not an easy task, and perhaps impossible on a global level, where different languages and cultures will complicate the issues even further.

While low-level standards, such as ASCII, HTML, and SMTP are of benefit to all, the acceptance of higher-level standards is much more intricate, as these have a higher impact on the way we perform functions. Through the history of computing the most open systems have had greatest acceptance: the blank page of the word processing system, the open message part of the email system, the empty spreadsheet matrix or

HTML that formalizes layout only. These systems do not press a rigid methodology or format on users. Users are free to use these systems as they wish—to implement their own "standards" or lack of standards on top of these open systems. Global standards for describing information may therefore be very far away.

The success of the "blank page" systems may also tell us that a semantic Web is a utopia. We want systems that can help us perform everyday functions with as little pain as possible. For some processes we accept a higher formalization level, but will often have to strengthen or establish new open channels parallel to these, to handle exceptions that cannot be forced into the formalized parts. These alternative channels, often on a personal basis, can more easily be established within a business or between close partners than in a more global system. That is, even within a company the informal parts may be needed to "oil" the machinery.

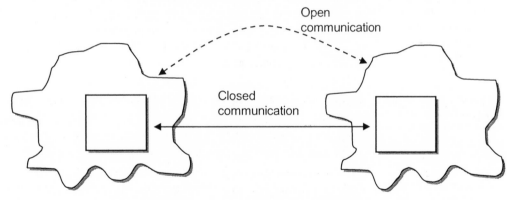

Figure 34.1 A semantic Web supports communication between formalized parts, not between the open parts.

In many processes one has to take care of both the **open and closed parts**. A high-level formalization of a process may therefore require that alternative, unformalized, channels be opened.

The problem we face is illustrated in figure 34.1. To get a complete system we need communication channels between both closed and open parts, but a semantic Web only supports the formalized transactions. While the formalized systems allow for contact on a global basis, for example, finding the supplier with the best offer, the informal channels will set strict limits to how wide we can go. The open channel is needed to support the formalized part, for example, a knowledge that the supplier will do his best to fulfill the contract, that he may be willing to help out in an emergency, that he may accept changes even after the contract has been signed. That is, we need a (personal) relationship that is strong enough to support all the situations and exceptions that occur in a real world.

34.4 Discussion

We have shown that society moves:

- *From atoms to bits*, *from physical to symbolic*, from physical workers to information workers, from a focus on manufacturing of physical goods to a focus on marketing, management, and organization.

- *From unformalized to formalized functions*, moving from lower- to higher-formalization levels, the acceptance of global standards, or standards within closed partnerships.

- Toward *automating* symbolic and formalized functions through the use of information technology.

- *Store-once-use-many-times*, using the data that is initiated by the customer through the whole value chain.

The **reward** for formalizing functions and services is automation. During the industrial revolution automation was achieved by the use of machinery, today information technology is the automation enabler.

The automation is the reward for formalizing functions. Today this formalization process goes on mostly within organizations, or within close partnerships and alliances of organizations. As we have seen, by automating the value chain the reward will be greater than what is possible to achieve within only one organization. While these organizational changes lead to greater efficiency, something may be lost on the way. The local supermarket, now a part of an international chain, may use a company-wide product register, which makes it cumbersome to offer local products. The flights offered by a local carrier may not be shown as alternatives when we book flights through the Web system of a large alliance. As we have seen, something is always lost when we perform a formalization process. However, in an open society we have seen that these "lost" parts may offer a market and an opportunity for smaller organizations. For example, a farmers market in addition to what the supermarket offers.

Naturally companies wish to retain control over their processes and data. They understand that the value is more in the bits than the atoms, more in the symbolic than physical parts. An industrial manufacturer in a developed country can no longer compete on the ability to perform the necessary physical processes, such as cutting, bending, and welding steel plates. These processes can be performed much cheaper in countries

In waiting for the new breakthrough technology, we learn to use what we **already have**. Equipment becomes cheaper, standards become more accepted, usability and functionality increase, and we get proficient in the use of these services.

where wages are lower. To survive, they have to manage the more complex part of production, that of organizing the process. They are moving from atoms to bits, it is the data and the processes that are the important part.

As for other companies they may create alliances or merge with others in order to control larger parts of the market, and may go into close partnerships with their suppliers to streamline the value chain, but they will not be willing to put their data on an open Web, not more than airlines and others that see that control of data is of primary importance.

Thus, the semantic Web of the future may already be here, in the form of Intranets, EDI, and other standards, local standards used within organizations, partnerships, and alliances, and the proprietary databases that are offered to the consumers. They all want you as their customer, but to access their data you will have to enter into their world, where they at least have some control over your actions and your choices.

Exercises and Discussion

1. Select one of the scenario services discussed in chapter 34.1 above and try to make a sketch of the formalizations involved for an electronic agent that has as its primary task to offer *information.*

2. Select one of the scenario services discussed in chapter 34.1 above and try to make a sketch of the formalizations involved for an automatic agent that has the power to negotiate and (digitally) *sign a deal.*

3. Find a set of exceptions that may occur in everyday life, such as moving to a new house, a new of job, a change of family situation, new preferences, etc. Discuss the formalizations above with regard to these exceptions. Which of the two solutions (to exercise 1 or 2) are most robust?

PART 6
Summary

35 Lessons Learned

This chapter offers a short summary of the main topics covered in this book: formalization, the Internet, and the Web, and the effect these technologies have on jobs, businesses, and society.

35.1 Formalization and automation

Faster, cheaper, smaller, mobile—important factors in the advance of computer applications, but as we have seen everything is constrained by formalization. A formalized description of procedures is necessary before we can use the computer to perform a task. Quite naturally really, since we know that this machine in the end executes fairly simple numeric statements, load, store, add, subtract, multiply, compare, etc.

In our world many tasks fall into the formalized category. Some are simple, such as an alarm clock. Here the program (the formalization) may be expressed with a program that checks every minute to see if it has reached the time setting for the alarm and performs the necessary steps to sound the alarm when this is the case. Such a program can be expressed by a few lines of code. Other programs may be complex financial transaction systems that consist of many millions of code lines.

As we have seen formalization was an issue long before the advent of computers. Formalized procedures offered the possibility of streamlining processes, to handle large volumes of data and to enforce control procedures. This has been a necessity for the first large warehouses and banks. But the need for formalization is not limited to data and administrative processes. Already in 1764 James Hargreaves managed to build a spinning machine that spun a tread from eight spindles. That is, he managed to formalize the process of spinning. Later on these hand-operated machines were powered, first by steam, later by petrol and electrical engines. This opened for automation, a tremendous advantage that was gained whenever a mechanical process was formalized and implemented in the form of a machine.

Similarly, computers allow us to automate data-based processes as long as they are formalized. Banking has been used as a primary example in this book. In a very short time, less than fifty years, most banking operations have been automated, taken over by the computer. In theory, it is possible to handle all common banking operations today by a computer (i.e., a bank is a computer). In theory, no manual operations are needed. In practice, however, we may need some manual handling to set up accounts, to handle special functions and exceptions.

While it is as difficult as ever to formalize processes, the computer has increased the incentives (i.e., the rewards are higher). The possibility of establishing practical computer-based solutions has also been increased with the advent of the Internet and the Web, for example, by allowing the customer herself to do the job.

Operations must be formalized to a high level if we want to automate. This is, for example, possible in most banking transactions. For more open tasks that cannot be fully formalized we use the computer as an assistant. Word processing is a typical example. Here the human performs the high-level task of composing the letter, while the computer (the word processing system) handles low level tasks such as formatting, storing, printing.... Then the only requirement is that the text is formalized on a lexical level, or perhaps also on a semi-syntactical level to offer assistance on spelling and grammar.

Note that the computer's way of performing a task may be quite different from that of a human. We have used navigation as one example in this book. Instead of navigating by use of light emitted from stars, we send up artificial "stars" that transmit electronic information that makes it possible for quite simple devices to calculate a position anywhere on the surface of the earth.

35.2 Internet and the Web

While formalization of applications is a requirement, the Internet and the Web have made it much more practical to let the consumer do the job herself, without involving intermediates. First, this enabled all of us to go to the Web to get information and to provide information on home pages, and so forth. The Web is quite unique in this respect, as it allows one and all to be writers/publishers, without any external sensor or editor.

The formalization level of HTML is on a lexical and layout level (i.e., represented as characters, formatting commands, and images). Thus, all types of textual and graphical information may be represented on a Web page. This has been the groundwork for the rapid increase of the use of the Web. No special skills are needed to create a Web page,[1] no additional standards are needed and the costs of using the medium are low.

We have explored the use of the Internet and the Web as an interface to special databases, banking systems, booking systems, etc. With these technologies special software, networks and protocols are no longer needed. Instead we use the common browser as our interface tool, format pages as HTML, and send data using the HTTP protocol. At the server end data can be retrieved from HTML forms and used to access proprietary databases. Results can then be formatted as HTML and returned to the user as an ordinary Web page. The intermediates, which earlier were in control of the terminals to these database systems, may no longer be needed.

With higher formalization levels (e.g., using XML to describe data records and documents), traffic on the net can go directly from one computer system to the other, excluding humans from the loop. This offers a promise of developing effective value chains, passing data along the chain automatically, but requires high-level standards. This standardization effort has, and will be, a long-term effort.

35.3 Constraints

As explored earlier, ideas and applications may be constrained by technical, legal, or social factors. However, while these may slow the introduction of new technology and new business models they will seldom act as long-term barriers.

With regard to computer-related technology we see that the advances that started fifty years ago are continuing at a rapid phase. Technological constraints are removed every day. New technology has made it possible to increase the bandwidth on ordinary (twisted pair) telephone cables significantly, offering broadband service to homes and businesses without having to lay new cables. Similarly, technological advances in very large scale integration have given us light-weight computers that have opened for new mobile applications. Radio frequency identification systems may soon replace bar codes, avoiding the necessity of scanning and opening for better identification of goods and a range of new services. A step further on we have a promise of lightweight, paper quality displays. Perhaps this is the product that can give us the paperless society? While we recognize that there are technical constraints, the new technical solutions based on improvement on existing technology, smart inventions, or radical new solutions often come as a surprise. In many cases we see that technical limitations are circumvented, using smart solutions to offer new services even within the existing constraints. The text- and picture-based message service on cell phones is a good example.

Companies may use copyright laws to slow the introduction of new electronic services, for example, by still providing scientific journals in paper form. But, as we see, the advance of the new technology cannot be stopped. When customers, in this case students and researchers, prefer the electronic form publishing houses are forced to follow suit. A record producer may love the LP format, but must move on when all customers expect to get the music on CD or DVDs. For copyright reasons one may wish to retain these representations, but when customers want music in the form of downloadable and flexible files, record companies are forced to offer such a product.

The customer and user may also act as a barrier for new technology. However, today we see a new generation that is used to and willing to, often eager to, adopt new gadgets and services. With improved user interfaces the underlying technology, it being a computer system or a cell phone, is hidden from the user, making it easier to adapt to new devices. We also see that knowledge and experience from one system can be taken along to the next, often without the need of additional instructions or manuals.

This ease of applying new technology is hampered by spam, viruses, and unreliable programs. Some misuse the open and democratic form of the Internet, Web, and email protocols to send viruses that at the worst result in the loss of data, but which always are an irritating part of using a computer system today: unwanted pop-ups, the slowing down of communication lines, programs that no longer work, set-ups that are changed, etc. Mass distribution of spam is still legal in many states, but may have as negative effects as a virus. It clogs down networks and computers, makes if difficult to utilize low bandwidth devices, and increases the chance that important messages are deleted or overlooked. While the virus problem can be reduced by more secure operating systems, browsers, and email programs, spam may probably only be stopped by new laws and regulations. In addition more secure standards will be important in solving both of these problems. For example, a mail protocol where the sender's ID cannot be changed or removed would be welcome.

35.4 Effect on jobs

Computers, the Internet, and the Web will have and has had an effect on all jobs. Some are radically changed, even removed, by the direct effect of these technologies. Others are indirectly affected, for example, by the possibilities the new technologies give of outsourcing tasks.

Job	Job description	In danger of disappearing?
Airplane pilot	Works in a formalized environment.	Technically possible, but for psychological reasons, not probable.
Air traffic controller	Formalized environment.	Yes, there may still be humans to handle exceptions and to supervise the systems, but most routine cases will be handled by a computer system.
Metro driver	Formalized tasks in a formalized environment.	Yes, already in progress.
Mail and message services	Retrieving, transporting, etc., of messages are formalized operations.	Yes, by the introduction of electronic messaging services such as email.
Toll plaza employees, ticket collectors	Payment of toll, selling, and retrieving tickets.	Yes, with new technology (radio transponders, etc.) and payment systems (over Internet, credit card) these tasks can be performed automatically.
Switchboard operator	Mostly formalized tasks.	Yes, many jobs have already been removed with automatic switchboards and later, by digital systems.
Warehouse worker	Mostly formalized tasks.	Picking and storing items can be performed automatically by robots if the environment is formalized.
Industrial worker	Mostly formalized tasks.	Many jobs have been removed over the last forty years due to computer-controlled machinery.

Table 35.1 Jobs with many closed (formalized) parts (i.e., jobs that can be automated).

If you can give an exact, detailed description of your job, you are in the danger zone. Your job can then be formalized, and automated with the help of a computer. This may happen for jobs as different as metro train drivers, cash register operators, or personnel working at toll plazas. That is, the automation we have seen in industry is now continuing outside of the plants. An overview is offered in table 35.1.

Job	Job description	In danger of disappearing?
Bank employees	Most tasks are formalized.	Yes, have already had huge impact. More jobs will disappear as more customers get Internet access and Internet literacy.
Insurance salesmen	Many tasks are formalized.	Yes, the customers may specify their insurance needs directly over a Web interface.
Music store employee	Open (advice, help, personal service) and closed (retrieving, payment) parts.	Probable, record stores lose market shares as customers download music directly from the net.
Travel agency employee	Open (advice, recommendation) and closed parts (booking).	Yes, for the simplest tasks the customer can do the job with a Web-based booking system.
Photo laboratory employee	Develop and print pictures.	Yes, with digital cameras the customers can do the job: select, cut, annotate, and print if necessary.
Booking services	Many tasks, such as booking a ticket in a movie theater, are formalized.	Yes, the customer can perform most of these tasks on the Web.
Typists	Formalized.	With word processing we perform the typing ourselves. Unnecessary intermediates are removed at the same time as we get direct access to useful tools (dictionaries, spelling checker, drawing tools).
Gas station attendant	Formalized.	With charge cards and computer-controlled pumps the customer can do the whole job.
Information services	Large parts may be formalized.	Yes, as customers access the information systems directly.

Table 35.2 Intermediates that may no longer be necessary.

In this book we have given many examples of jobs that are affected by the fact that the customer herself gets access to the "internal" systems using Internet and Web services. While the threat of automation has been here for many years, this is a new way of removing "unnecessary" jobs. With direct access to company systems, many intermediates are no longer needed, as seen from table 35.2. With improved user interfaces one should expect that customers may perform more tasks themselves as the complexity of the tasks are reduced. Better back-office systems, the internal systems of businesses, may also open for new applications where customers may do the job themselves.

Job	Job description	In danger of disappearing?
Industrial worker	Mostly formalized tasks.	The Internet and the Web makes it easier to outsource many of the remaining industrial jobs to low-wage areas, keeping design and marketing where it is.
Repairing industrial products	Mostly open tasks (exceptions).	Yes, many industrial products are so cheap to manufacture that repairs are no longer cost effective. That is the open job of repairing is replaced by the closed job of producing a new item.
Computer programmer	Mostly open tasks, formalizing the real world as a computer program.	Parts of this symbolic activity can be outsourced to countries with lower wages.
Engineering	Mostly open tasks.	Yes, with modern communication networks parts of engineering work can be outsourced to a country with lower wages.
Call center	A personal level of service often wanted.	Yes, with global communication networks the call can be taken anywhere.

Table 35.3 Jobs where a global economy supports outsourcing to low-wage counties.

Table 35.3 above gives some examples of jobs that are indirectly affected by the Internet and the Web and a more global economy. For example, with better communication (symbolic on the Internet, over telephone) and physically (by transport networks, in air, on road, or by sea) it becomes much easier to outsource parts of the administrative and production jobs to low-wage countries. In principle many types of jobs can be affected, but in practice outsourcing is easiest for the simplest and most formalized tasks. For example, a programming task that is clearly specified may be performed anywhere in the world. For other more open tasks, continuous discussions with users may be necessary and the programmer or systems developer must then be able to participate in meetings with the customers. This requires command of the language spoken, and it will be useful if the programmer participates in the same culture as the users. These factors will also influence other types of tasks. Even simple call center tasks can involve situations where a thorough understanding of the customer's problem is needed. In practice, this may be difficult to obtain for a person living in a different country and culture.

Note that some jobs, such as call center operators, are also affected by other mechanisms. With the Internet and the Web the customer may retrieve some information directly (directory services, user manuals, FAQ, etc.), avoiding a telephone call.

The relatively formalized call center functions that serve customers that don't have Internet access or the ability to find the information they need themselves, can often be outsourced to another country. However, with improved user interfaces and a more Internet-experienced population these jobs will be of a temporary nature.

Outsourcing may also affect quite different jobs. For example, homes for the elderly may be established in countries with low wages, a healthy climate, and an abundance of skilled workers, instead of importing these workers to high-wage industrial countries. With better communication, both electronically and physically, one may still keep in touch with relatives back in the "old country," even to the point of reading the local paper on the Internet. The elderly of today may not welcome such a solution, but this may be a natural option in the future for a more globally oriented population.

Job	Open/closed	Computer takeover?
Bus driver	Works in an unformalized environment (roads and traffic).	By formalizing the environment (e.g., building a metro line).
Law enforcement officers	Works with exceptions (i.e., when citizens are not following the laws and regulations).	Only for a few areas that can be formalized (e.g., speed control and some other forms of surveillance).
Lawyers, judges	Many open parts, work in the interface between laws and the real world.	No, even if parts of their job (information gathering) are made more efficient with the computer.
Health care workers	Works with people, very few formalized parts.	Only in a few areas, such as cardiac monitoring.
Plumbers	Works in the real world, few formalized parts.	No, but new technology may increase efficiency.
Executive positions	Few closed parts. Take decisions based on overall strategies, often with incomplete data.	Only indirectly (e.g., if the technologies remove the foundation for the company).
Entertainment	Most jobs are open and will be performed by humans.	Indirectly, if computer games and animation take larger market shares.
Teachers	Most tasks are open, individual handling of students important.	Parts of training-oriented programs may be offered by the computer.
Waiter	Both open (recommendation, serving) and closed (taking an order, billing) tasks.	Not likely, customers are most often willing to pay for a high level of (human) service.
Sales personnel	Closed (taking an order, billing) and open tasks (e.g., advising/persuading the customer).	In cases where the personal contact is limited (over phone, email) a computer may do the job.

Table 35.4 Jobs with many open parts (i.e., jobs that cannot easily be taken over by a computer).

To survive we need to be good in areas where the computer does not perform well (i.e., we need to concentrate on the open, unformalized tasks). This can be everything from driving a bus, teaching, working in health care, law enforcement, and entertainment or to offer help with complex banking or travel services. While both physical and administrative routine tasks in business may be in danger of being taken over by the computer, executive positions are not. Here the strong ability of humans to make decisions based on overall strategy and with incomplete data is important. Some examples are offered in table 35.4.

35.5 Effect on businesses

In a much-debated paper, "IT Doesn't Matter," Nicholas G. Carr[2] advocates that as information technology has become a commodity, its strategic importance is lost. While this may be true in the general sense, businesses will have to adjust their business models to the new technologies. As with any other technology or market trend it is important to get things right from the very start. There may be many implementations of Web presence or of B2C systems, but as we have seen it is important to offer flexible and simple to use systems. Looking to the competition in the air we see that new emerging airlines are employing the Internet better than the incumbents. Early birds in other areas, such as Amazon, eBay, and Yahoo! that have offered well-designed applications have got a strong foothold. In some cases a new methodologies may give a latecomer a chance. Google came later than most of the other search engines, but has become the most used through a smart implementation of relevance rankings.

An Intranet solution may offer huge benefits. It may be used to streamline business processes, to reduce administrative costs, and to build a community feeling. Contact with customers can be improved through Extranet and B2C solutions, and B2B offers a promise of effective interchange of data. This is especially the case were one company or group is in control of the complete value chain, then the difficult questions of standardization are somewhat easier to solve.

Clearly, businesses are affected by the same factors as jobs. The Internet and the Web have, and will have, disruptive effects in many markets. We have used airlines, banks, travel agencies, record companies, publishing houses, and software firms as examples. But we could have found as good examples in many other areas.

Returning to airlines we see that a first effect of Internet booking is that the customers do the job themselves. This requires a reengineering of the company. First, a major group of employees are no longer needed; at least there will be much fewer jobs than before. Second, in order to facilitate Internet booking, the airline needs a simple price and discount policy. Complicated discounts, for example, to couples where one gets a discount if the other pays full price, is not easy to implement over the Web, as it requires a link between the two tickets. Third, with Internet booking the customers get very price conscious. We normally ask to get the cheapest offers up front. Then other factors, such as service, meals, seat space may be ignored. That is, today the Internet and bargain airlines are determining the rules of the game, and the incumbents have to adjust their business models to this situation (but this may change!). Finally, we have seen that the Internet and Web offers new possibility for marketing. We can notify customers whenever we have something to offer that may be of interest (based on profile data, etc.) or may design new offers in accordance with customer's wishes.

The incumbents will be forced to play along, like it or not, they may see existing business models threatened by new technology, they may try to hold back the advent of new business models but will in the end be forced to follow suit. If they are reluctant to offer new services there will always be a startup that sees a market niche.

35.6 Effect on society

We have seen that computer technology along with the Internet and Web standards have had effects on both jobs and businesses, sometimes only resulting in minor changes, sometimes causing disruptive effects. We may use some of the same categorization as above in discussing effects on society (i.e., formalization, changes in job market and outsourcing to low-wage countries).

We have seen that the change from a cash-based to an electronic economy offers new possibilities. While cash is anonymous, money represented electronically is not. If cash were removed altogether, perhaps with the exception of coins and small bills the internal revenue services would get full control with the economy. Crime would of course still be possible, but without cash it would be much more complicated for criminals to take part in the efficient money-based economy. They would have to swap goods and services, setting them a thousand years back. It may be a few years before the infrastructure is in place to make it possible to remove cash altogether, but governments may want to explore the possibilities that are offered by an all electronic economy. There are, of course, possible infringements on privacy, but this is also the case for a cash-based economy. For example, all persons that have cash or handle cash today face the risk of being robbed, a risk that will be significantly reduced in a cash-free society.

Today we see that the U.S. government is leading an effort from paper-based to electronic passports. We have the same arguments as in the discussion above. An electronic passport is difficult to forge, and offers the possibility of automatically retrieving background information and travel patterns. As with electronic money, the new passports raise privacy issues; they can be used both to support the rights of individuals and to threaten these.

Just as businesses develop systems where the customer does part of the job herself, state agencies are also offering B2C systems. In many cases the government organizations have been ahead of the private sector here. They have opened internal databases and offer all types of information to citizens over the Web. In many countries we may email politicians and administrators, and may fill out many types of applications over a Web interface.

Electronic voting systems are discussed today. While this may make voting more reliable and more efficient, there are important questions on security, privacy, and accessibility that need to be discussed before this becomes an option. This is absolutely one area where we should be extremely cautious. Also note that telephone-based voting has never been an issue, even if such systems could have offered a more effective process.

Today we see that the Internet and the Web is accelerating the process of establishing a global economy, the process that was started by the dramatic changes that we have seen in the world in the last decades: establishing of the European Union, opening of China, breakdown of the Soviet Union, and new trade agreements. This rapid transition has made the huge wage differences between countries very apparent. Thus, the indirect effects of Internet and Web, facilitating the outsourcing of jobs to low-wage countries, may have stronger effects on the work-force than the direct effects (i.e., the loss of jobs due to automation and B2C systems).

No problem, says many economists. Outsourcing will give cheaper products and services that will open new markets and create incentives for making new businesses. There may be short-term disruptive effects, but in the long run the boost in productivity growth will counter the negative effects. We should not be that sure. Within every country we find areas that have high unemployment rates, areas that have been left behind due to a change in the economy, transport networks, or technology. In a more global economy industries and businesses can move freely across national borders. Today they may move where labor is inexpensive, tomorrow they may move to areas that have the highest growth, thus accelerating the processes. We may then see similar effects on countries that we have today in special areas within a country.

In the end, however, more global communication and cooperation should result in lower entropy (i.e., we should expect that the differences between countries will be reduced). In the meantime we will have to live with these differences, for example, accepting that some jobs can no longer be performed in areas with high wages and a high standard of living. We need systems in place that can handle these effects of a dynamic and global economy. Remedies may be educational systems, for basic education and for retraining to new jobs. A good education normally leads to an unformalized job, where the danger of being removed or outsourced is less than for simpler tasks. Retraining may be necessary when jobs have a short life span, so short than one job will not last a lifetime.

Notes

1. The simplest way may be to use the "Save as Web page" command in our word processing system.
2. Carr, N.G. 2003. IT Doesn't Matter, *Harvard Business Review*, May, pp. 41-49. See also his book, "Does IT Matter? Information Technology and the Corrosion of Competitive Advantage," Harvard Business School Press (April 2004).

36 Advances in Technology

When new technologies emerge the focus is, of course, on the possibilities. Prophesies go for helicopters as common as cars, drugs that can let us live much longer, interplanetary travel, home robots, cars that steer themselves, lightweight roll-up displays, thinking computers. However, when these technologies face the real world the limitations and drawbacks become apparent. The new technology is often adapted, but technical, practical, and social factors limit the application. It can be a success in some areas, but not in all. Technological revolutions are not common.

It is many years ago since the first men walked on the moon, even then it is a sensation when an ordinary (but very wealthy) citizen gets a week in outer space. Interplanetary travel is still science fiction. We have some of the technology in place, but the challenges ahead are enormous. We use helicopters today for many functions. But they are expensive; the technology is complex and needs expert maintenance and expert pilots. The idea of a people's helicopter is perhaps farther away today than when the technology was invented. We still use motor cars for personal transportation, more than a hundred years after they first hit the roads.

With all the technological advances of the last century we feel that everything is possible, that it is just a matter of having enough resources. To some extent this is true. We can move the technology ahead by concentrating our resources, but there are limits to what we can achieve. A powerful and lightweight battery could define the market base for a range of new products, from functional long-range electric cars to clothes with built-in heaters. But advances in battery technology seem to go slowly, although the economic incentives are enormous. Similarly, a display screen with the same quality and flexibility as paper could revolutionize the presentation of printed material, but most displays are still based on CRT (Cathode Ray Tube) technology that was invented before World War II. CRT displays are now being replaced by LCD (Liquid Crystal Diode) displays that are thinner, lighter, and use less power, but still cannot compete with paper in quality. The first versions of "electronic paper," with paper-like letter quality, offer a promise of radically new displays somewhere into the future.

A more fundamental problem is the open nature of our world—it has so many different facets. Scientists and engineers have developed ground vehicles that run on Mars, but imagine the difficulties of developing such vehicles for the Earth, for negotiating any type of terrain: high mountains, rivers, jungles, the open sea, glaciers, and deserts. The diversity is even greater when we look at social functions and the way we perform work. Developing technology that can be used by all types of people of all cultures is a great challenge. The contrasts are so great that most technologies will only have a chance of being used by a fraction of the population (i.e., where the interface of the technology can adjust to the "interface" of an application area).

We see this in our homes. While housework is simplified by the use of many gadgets, to help us cook and do the cleaning, we have as yet not seen the home robot that automates these functions. We can cook a meal in three minutes with a microwave, but this does not imply that the process of making a meal is automated. The microwave only helps us out with parts of some functions, and may be a disappointment compared to the early predictions of the automatic kitchen. A vacuum cleaner may be more efficient than a broom, but we still have to operate it ourselves. Most of us would have given a fortune for a machine that could clean the whole house while the family was off at school or work. Why can we not get this product with all the advances in sensor and computer technology? In fact, the technology is here, also the very first products.[1] The problem, if we can see it this way, is in our homes. They come in too many forms and shapes and are furnished in so many ways that it is still impossible to make a gadget that serves them all. A modern warehouse with automatic robot trucks is impressive, but here the environment is customized for the robots: plane surfaces, infrared or wire controls for direction, standardized shelves, standardized loads, everything in its right place, etc.

– These atoms are supposed to make everything superfluous...
– Sure enough, but give me a glass of beer anyhow!

(Storm P.)

The greatest technological breakthroughs have often come in areas where there is a formalized environment already in place. A new technology for computer memory does not have to conform to all facets of an open world, but only has to adjust to the pin and address standards that are already in place. A new printer technology will, in principle, only have to conform to standard formats of paper and printer cables. Mobile phones can rely on the technical and social standards of telephony established over more than a hundred years.

The Internet and the Web were introduced to a world where most of the physical environment needed was already in place, a proliferation of computers, a very large group of "computer literates" and the means of electronic communication (data and telephone networks). The Internet and the Web offered the standards needed (e.g., SMTP, HTTP, HTML) for the utilization of this net for new applications.

We have explored these applications in this book, and tried to discuss their merits and disadvantages. As we have seen, in many areas these standards define the necessary base to establish new services. With SMTP and MIME on top of the technological infrastructure we have what is needed for global electronic mail, perhaps the most important application for these new technologies. With HTTP and HTML we have what is needed for universal distribution of documents, based on text, pictures, sound, and video. The low formalization level of these applications, the open email message form and the layout format of the Web, sets no restrictions to what we want to send, to what we want to present on the Web page. In this respect these applications interface to a large part of the world. They require that the basic technology be in place, the PCs and the networks, that users can read and write and that they have a minimum of computer experience especially in the case of Internet/Web devices. Thus these applications "interface" to very many users, and can be used for very many different tasks.

The most important contribution from Internet/Web technology is its offer of two-way communication within a global system. These advantages are utilized fully for email, which without doubt will emerge as the winning service of the new technologies. It is just a matter of years before all, or nearly all, business correspondence will go as email both between businesses and between businesses and consumers. The asynchronous and text-based message system makes it more convenient than telephone for most communication transactions and it is faster, more flexible, and cheaper to process than ordinary letters.

Web technology opens the way for many different applications. Some of these can be implemented using HTML only, like home pages of private citizens and institutions. Others can rely on existing formalization, such as online banking, travel services, and some B2B applications. For others, society will have to adapt, for example, by establishing new standards, before the new applications can be put to use. As we have seen, this can be a difficult process.

As an information-provider the Web has to compete with existing media channels, such as TV and newspapers. The Web provides the possibility of interaction. While this allows the user a possibility of selection (e.g., by clicking on links or providing search terms) it requires that the information requested is available and demands more active involvement by the user. Broadcast channels such as TV and newspapers can put more effort into creating the information as only one or a few streams have to be offered, and the users limit their involvement to that of selecting channels. We solve this as Winnie the Pooh does, by saying yes to all offers. The Web will be used where two-way communication is important, where we can specify our needs. In other cases the traditional channels will prevail.

When the Web first emerged the initial hope was for a democratic system where everybody was both an information-provider and a consumer. These opportunities in the technology have been taken to the point where everybody has a home page—but to what effect? Today we find that most of the Web traffic goes to a few major portals. Only a small fraction of Web traffic goes to other URLs than the professional sites. As we have seen, the large institutions are as powerful on the net as elsewhere. However, in addition to the traffic to sites offered by professional providers, there is an "underground" activity. Users join globally in providing and accessing information on their hobbies, illnesses, interests, and political views.

As with other technologies, guns, drugs, cars… we find both advantages and disadvantages for society. Social interaction across real and virtual borders is clearly an advantage, and the Internet/Web technologies provide the necessary infrastructure to let this *open* communication happen. At the same time, these technologies offer people the opportunity to limit information and conversation to within a group. This *closed* form of communication can lead to polarization and fragmentation, perhaps the opposite of what we need when we share the same small world.

The applications on the Web that we have today are limited by low bandwidth on the last mile (to the consumer), by not enough router and server capacity, errors, hacking, viruses, spam, and by bad user interfaces. These limitations set restrictions on the efficiency of many Web services. We can expect improvement here as we go along and get more experience in running these services and if we look into the future we may see robust broadband networks all the way into our homes. However, there is no guarantee that these services will be offered within the Internet/Web area, they may just as well be offered on proprietary and closed networks, like cable TV.

It is difficult to predict what the future will offer in the form of new technologies. The encompassing nature of Internet and the Web is something that few could have foreseen, even if most of the underlying technology has been in place for a long time. In other areas technological breakthroughs have given us broadband networks and extremely powerful and affordable computers. What we know is that, independently of the technology, the applications must "interface" with users and their society.

In this book we have focused on the part of the interface that has to do with formalization. Formalization is a requirement for all-automated processes, but formalization may be performed on different levels. The lowest levels offer great flexibility and user freedom, and are thus easily accepted. Higher levels offer greater advantages with regard to efficiency and automation, but will often require changes in the application environment. The need for these changes in the technological interface may slow the acceptance rate and in some cases be a barrier against technology adoption.

Notes

1. The first self-operated vacuum cleaners are already here, such as the Electrolux Trilobite. This has ultrasound sensors to avoid hitting walls and furniture, and can charge itself. However, the cleaner requires a "formalized" environment, everything on one floor, space to go under furniture (at least 16 cm), easy access from one room to the other, etc.

Index

About the Author

Kai A. Olsen is a professor of Informatics (Computing Science) both at Molde College and University of Bergen, Norway. He is an adjunct professor at School of Information Sciences, University of Pittsburgh. Olsen's main research interests are user interfaces, man-machine communication, and logistic systems. He has been a pioneer in developing software systems for PCs, information systems for primary health care, and systems for visualization. He acts as a consultant for Norwegian and U.S. organizations.